NIGHT+DAY PARIS

Alison Culliford

PULSE GUIDES

Pulse Guides' *Night+Day Paris* is an independent guide. We do not accept payment of any kind from events or establishments for inclusion in this book. We welcome your views on our selections. Please email us: **feedback@pulseguides.com**.

The information contained in this book was checked as rigorously as possible before going to press. The publisher accepts no responsibility for any changes that may have occurred since, or for any other variance of fact from that recorded here in good faith.

No part of this book may be reproduced in any form without permission in writing from the publisher, except by a reviewer who wishes to quote brief passages for a published review. This publication is a creative work fully protected by all applicable copyright laws, as well as by misappropriation, trade secrets, unfair competition, and all other applicable laws. The authors and editors of this work have added value to the underlying factual material herein through one or more of the following: unique and original selection, coordination, expression, arrangement, and classification (including the itineraries) of the information.

Distributed in the United States and Canada by National Book Network (NBN).
First Edition. Printed in the United States. 30% postconsumer content.
Copyright © 2006 ASDavis Media Group, Inc. All rights reserved.
ISBN-10:0-9766013-8-9; ISBN-13:978-0-9766013-8-8

Credits

Executive Editor	Alan S. Davis
Editor	Christina Henry de Tessan
Author	Alison Culliford
Copy Editors	Gail Nelson-Bonebrake, Elizabeth Stroud
Maps	Chris Gillis
Production	Jo Farrell, Samia Afra
Cover Design	Wil Klass, Clara Teufel

Photo Credits: (Front: l to r) Les Byerley, Hôtel du Petit Moulin, Martt Lawrence; (Back: l to r) Bar Fontainebleau-Hôtel Meurice, Les Ambassadeurs-Hôtel de Crillon, Kong, The Louvre-Mary Lou D'Auray; (Inside cover top to bottom) Kong; Palais de Tokyo, Peter Spiro; (p.4) Mary Lou D'Auray; (p.8) Corine Thulier.

Special Sales

For information about bulk purchases of Pulse Guides (ten copies or more), email us at bookorders@pulseguides.com. Special bulk rates are available for charities, corporations, institutions, and online and mail-order catalogs, and our books can be customized to suit your company's needs.

NIGHT+DAY
The *Cool Cities* Series from **PULSE**GUIDES

P.O. Box 590780, San Francisco, CA 94159
pulseguides.com

Pulse Guides is an imprint of ASDavis Media Group, Inc.

The Night+Day Difference

Pulse of the City

Our job is to point you to all of the city's peak experiences: amazing museums, unique spas, and spectacular views. But the complete *urbanista* experience is more than just impressions—it is grown-up fun, the kind that thrives by night as well as by day. Urban fun is a hip nightclub or a trendy restaurant. It is people-watching and people-meeting. Lonely planet? We don't think so. Night+Day celebrates our lively planet.

The Right Place. The Right Time. It Matters.

A Night+Day city must have exemplary restaurants, a vibrant nightlife scene, and enough attractions to keep a visitor busy for six days without having to do the same thing twice. In selecting restaurants, food is important, but so is the scene. Our hotels, most of which are four- and five-star properties, are rated for the quality of the concierge staff (can they get you into a hot restaurant?) as well as the rooms. You won't find kids with fake IDs at our nightlife choices. And the attractions must be truly worthy of your time. But experienced travelers know that timing is almost everything. Going to a restaurant at 7pm can be a very different experience (and probably less fun) than at 9pm; a Champagne boat cruise might be ordinary in the morning but spectacular at sunset. We believe providing the reader with this level of detail makes the difference between a good experience and a great one.

The Bottom Line

Your time is precious. Our guide must be easy to use and dead-on accurate. That is why our executive editor, editors, and writers (locals who are in touch with what is great—and what is not) spend hundreds of hours researching, writing, and debating selections for each guide. The results are presented in four unique ways: The *99 Best* with our top three choices in 33 categories that highlight what is great about the city; the *Experience* chapters, in which our selections are organized by distinct themes or personalities (Hot & Cool, Classic, Bobo, and Romantic); a *Perfect Plan* (3 Days and Nights) for each theme, showing how to get the most out of the city in a short period of time; and the *Paris Black Book*, listing all the hotels, restaurants, nightlife, and attractions, with key details, contact information, and page references.

Our bottom line is this: if you find our guide easy to use and enjoyable to read, and with our help you have an extraordinary time, we have succeeded. We review and value all feedback from our readers, so please contact us at **feedback@pulseguides.com**.

Coffee at Les Deux Magots

From the Publisher:

I've had the travel bug ever since my first summer job during college—escorting tour groups around Europe to evaluate them for my parents' travel company. When I retired from the paper business ten years ago, I set out on a journey to find the 100 most fun places to be in the world at the right time. The challenge of unearthing the world's greatest events—from the Opera Ball in Vienna to the Calgary Stampede—led me to write a guidebook.

The success of *The Fun Also Rises*, named after Ernest Hemingway's *The Sun Also Rises*, which helped popularize what has become perhaps the most thrilling party on earth (Pamplona's Fiesta de San Fermín, also known as the Running of the Bulls), persuaded me that there were others who shared my interest in a different approach to travel. Guidebooks were neither informative nor exciting enough to capture peak experiences—whether for world-class events or just a night on the town.

My goal is to publish *extraordinary guides for extraordinary travelers.* **Night+Day**, the first series from Pulse Guides, is for Gen-Xers to Zoomers (Boomers with a zest for life), who know that if one wants to truly experience a city, the night is as important as the day. **Night+Day** guides present the best that a city has to offer—hotels, restaurants, nightlife, and attractions that are exciting, never stuffy—in a totally new format.

Pulse Guides abides by one guiding principle: *Never settle for the ordinary.* We hope that a willingness to explore new approaches to guidebooks, combined with meticulous research, provides you with unique and significant experiences.

By the time I did the "grand tour" of Europe with my parents, I had a reading familiarity with the icons of the major cities—London Bridge, the Coliseum, the Parthenon, and, of course, the Eiffel Tower. In Paris we stayed at a hotel from which we could catch a glimpse, over rooftops, of that magnificent structure. Expectations of disappointment were immediately replaced by the thrill of that moment. I hope that we can, with this guide, provide you with many such experiences in this awesome city.

Wishing you extraordinary times,

Alan S. Davis, Publisher and Executive Editor
Pulse Guides

P.S. To contact me, or for updated information on all of our **Night+Day** guides, please visit our website at **pulseguides.com**.

TOC

INTRODUCTION 9
Night+Day's Paris Urbie 12

THE 99 BEST OF PARIS 15
- Always-Trendy Tables 16
- Bistros 17
- Brunches 18
- Café Terraces 19
- Celebrity Spotting 20
- Chic Museums 21
- Classic Hotel Bars 22
- Cocktails with a View 23
- Concept Stores 24
- Contemporary Art 25
- Dance Clubs 26
- Eiffel Tower Views 27
- Fine Dining 28
- Gay Bars 29
- Guided Tours 30
- Hipster Hangouts 31
- Jazz Clubs 32
- Late-Night Eats 33
- Literary Bars 34
- Live Music 35
- Lounge Bars 36
- Markets 37
- Meet Markets 38
- North African Dining 39
- Of-the-Moment Dining 40
- Outdoor Dining 41
- Parks 42
- Power Lunches 43
- Seafood Feasts 44
- See-and-Be-Seen Clubs 45
- Spas 46
- Statuary 47
- Vodka Cocktails 48

THE PARIS EXPERIENCE ...49
Hot & Cool Paris ...50
- The Perfect Plan (3 Days and Nights) ...51
- The Key Neighborhoods ...55
- The Shopping Blocks ...56
- The Hotels ...57
- The Restaurants ...61
- The Nightlife ...73
- The Attractions ...79

Classic Paris ...84
- The Perfect Plan (3 Days and Nights) ...85
- The Key Neighborhoods ...89
- The Shopping Blocks ...90
- The Hotels ...91
- The Restaurants ...93
- The Nightlife ...102
- The Attractions ...107

Bobo Paris ...116
- The Perfect Plan (3 Days and Nights) ...117
- The Key Neighborhoods ...121
- The Shopping Blocks ...122
- The Hotels ...123
- The Restaurants ...126
- The Nightlife ...134
- The Attractions ...143

Romantic Paris ...148
- The Perfect Plan (3 Days and Nights) ...149
- The Key Neighborhoods ...153
- The Shopping Blocks ...154
- The Hotels ...155
- The Restaurants ...158
- The Nightlife ...166
- The Attractions ...171

PRIME TIME PARIS ...177
Prime Time Basics ...178
- Eating, Drinking, and Clubbing ...178
- Weather and Tourism ...178
- National Holidays ...179

The Best Events Calendar ...180
The Best Events ...181

HIT THE GROUND RUNNING 187
City Essentials 188
Getting to Paris: By Air 188
Getting to Paris: By Land 191
Paris: Lay of the Land 191
Getting Around Paris 191
Other Practical Information (Money Matters; Tax Refunds; Phone Calls; Safety; Gay and Lesbian Travel; Traveling with Disabilities; Print Media; Radio Stations; Shopping Hours; Attire; Size Conversion; Clubbing; Drinking, Smoking, and Drugs; Time Zone; Additional Resources for Visitors) 194
Useful Vocabulary 200
The Cheat Sheet (The Very Least You Ought to Know About Paris) (Neighborhoods, Churches, Performing Arts Venues, Parks, Shopping Districts, World-Class Museums, Flea Markets, Cemeteries, Riverbanks, Singular Sensation) 203
Party Conversation—A Few Surprising Facts 209
Just for Business and Conventions 210
Paris Region Map 212

LEAVING PARIS 213
Overnight Trips
Champagne 214
Châteaux of the Loire 216
Deauville 218
Day Trips
Auvers-sur-Oise 220
Chantilly 221
Chartres 222
Fontainebleau and Vaux-le-Vicomte 223
Giverny 224
St-Germain-en-Laye 225
Versailles 226

PARIS BLACK BOOK 227
Paris Black Book by Neighborhood 228
Paris Black Book 233
Paris Unique Shopping Index 252

Paris Action Central Map 254
Paris Neighborhoods Map 255
Paris Métro Map .... Inside Back Cover

About the Author

Alison Culliford left a jet-setting lifestyle as travel writer for British Airways' in-flight magazines to settle in Paris in 2001, and has hardly been airborne since. She worked for three years in Time Out's Paris bureau, freelances for *The Daily Telegraph, Time Out, The Times,* and *Vive La France,* and is the restaurant critic for the English-language Paris magazine *Gogo.* She lives in a forgotten corner of the 19th arrondissement and travels everywhere by bike, having perfected the act of seeming to have stepped out of a taxi.

Acknowledgments

Thanks to the many friends and acquaintances whose tips and morale-boosting helped make this book possible, in particular Marie-Noëlle Bauer, Kate van den Boogert, Anna Brooke, Gaby Brookes, Bill Burroughs, Simon Cropper, Natasha Edwards, Nigel Garnett, Helen Harding, Rosa Jackson, Colm Pierce, Katherine Spenley, Kari Stunell, and Rupert Wates. Thanks especially to Corine Thuilier for perfecting my French vocabulary, and to Christina Henry for her constant support and patient editing. Thanks to Eleanor Culliford for spending whole days at the Louvre while I finished the final chapter. Lastly, thanks to Derick and Eleanor Culliford for being there.

Alison Culliford

Introduction

Welcome to Paris, the fun capital of the world. Or at least it was in the 1890s, its naughty heyday of brothels, boozers, and extravagant cabarets. Can Paris still make the grade? You bet your bottom euro it can, but it's not necessarily the high-kicking Doris's girls that are the main attraction. Camp and glitzy it can be, but then so can so many other places. What Paris has got, and knows it's got, is class. Even when it's down at the heel, Paris is still chic. Reach into your pockets a bit and you're talking the pinnacle of perfection, the icing on the mille-feuille. They call it "jusquauboutism," no half-measures. From the eight courses of your menu dégustation to the chandeliers in the palace hotels to the sheer scale and scope of the culture, Paris is premier. It does what other cities can only copy and looks down on them with an aristocratic smile.

Paris: What It Was

The lip-smackingly seductive name of Paris came from a mud-dwelling Celtic tribe called the Parisii, the first settlers on the right bank of the Seine. After the Parisii burned down their citadel rather than surrender in 52 BC, the Romans rebuilt the city on the left bank with a forum, amphi-theatre, and baths—the latter can still be seen today at the Musée de Cluny—and two arenas, located in the Latin Quarter and in Montmartre, remain.

Thereafter everyone wanted a bit of Paris. In 486 AD northern France fell to Clovis the Frank, who made Paris his capital in 508. His dynasty of the Merovingians was followed by the Carolingians and Charlemagne. The city became a center of Christianity with churches and monasteries established in the Latin Quarter. Sacked by Vikings in the 800s, Parisians retreated to Ile de la Cité.

Key Dates

52 BC	Romans conquer the Parisii and name the city Lutetia.
508	Clovis makes Paris his capital.
1163	Building of Notre-Dame begins.
1682	Louis XIV moves the royal court from the Louvre to Versailles.
1789	The French Revolution breaks out.
1804	Napoléon crowns himself Emperor.
1853	Baron Haussmann starts changing the face of Paris.
1871	The Communards seize power and are massacred in the streets.
1944	Liberation of Paris from the Nazis.
1968	Student riots and workers' strikes bring the country to a halt.
1980–95	Mitterrand's architectural *grands projets* change the face of Paris.

The French kings built up their stronghold and established trade guilds, which were the origin of the still highly regulated trade laws and taxation system. Under Philip II (1180–1223) Notre-Dame went up and the Louvre was begun as a royal stronghold and dungeon. With its monastic centre on the Left Bank, administration on the Ile de la Cité, and trade on the Right Bank, Paris was a magnet for pilgrims, scholars, merchants, and charlatans who flocked from across Europe. In the 14th century, its population was devastated by the Black Death; thousands more died in the 100 Years' War with England. The English ruled in the first half of the 15th century, despite Joan of Arc's efforts to expel them. Charles VII accomplished this in 1453.

The 16th century brought printing and the Italianate court of François 1er, who patronized Leonardo da Vinci and filled the Louvre with works of art. Religious fervor was at its height, with the massacre of 3,000 Huguenots on St. Bartholomew's Day, 1572. In 1594 the pragmatist king Henri IV decided "Paris is well worth a mass" and converted to Catholicism so that he could rule in peace. Henri was just about the only king who liked Paris enough to live there, improving the Louvre and building the Tuileries palace (later burned down in the Commune), Hôtel de Ville, Pont Neuf, and Place des Vosges. The latter was the center of aristocratic life in the Marais, with jousts, duels, and romantic trysts taking place in full view of the courtiers who lived in its mansions. Henri met a sorry end when he was murdered in a traffic jam by a Catholic fanatic.

By Louis XIV's time, the city had a population of 400,000, most of them crowded into unsanitary tenements. The Sun King took refuge in his palace at Versailles and left the day-to-day running of the city to powerful finance minister Colbert. At the same time, the arts were flourishing, with playwrights Molière and Racine the celebrities of the day and Voltaire drumming up support for Enlightenment philosophy. Growing discontent at the harsh taxes imposed on the poor eventually exploded in the Revolution of 1789, whose focus has gone down in history as the storming of the Bastille even though this event was one of the least bloody of the Revolution, and the handful of prisoners inside were mainly writers or wayward aristocrats who had been put there by their families. Louis XVI was imprisoned in the Temple (now a park in the Marais) and eventually guillotined in 1793. Thereafter, the Terror ensued, with the fanatical

> **Paris is still a city that loves to party and protest. It is a mixture of glamour and grunge, tradition and innovation. Paris is a visitor-friendly city, increasingly so every year.**

guillotining of 20,000 Parisians, many of whom were far from enemies of the Revolution.

Before long Paris had another autocratic ruler, Napoléon, who came to power in a coup d'état and crowned himself emperor in the cathedral of Notre-Dame. Napoléon beautified the city, building the Arc de Triomphe, the Madeleine cathedral, and the rue de Rivoli, and brought it into order with his innovations of the arrondissement system, street numbering, the metric system, and sewers. Meanwhile, his looting armies filled the Louvre with countless foreign works of art.

> **Camp and glitzy it can be, but then so can so many other places. What Paris has got, and knows it's got, is class. Even when it's down at the heel, Paris is still chic.**

Nineteenth-century Paris experienced a massive population boom, causing a further highly combustible combination of overcrowding and squalor. In 1830 the "trois glorieuses" days of street fighting ended the reign of Charles X (yes, France did have a monarchy after the Revolution), who was replaced by "constitutional monarch" Louis-Philippe. This was the age of the English dandy, and foreign aristocrats and nouveaux riches flocked to Paris to shop in its covered arcades. In the "nouvelle Athènes" below Pigalle, Delacroix, George Sand, and Chopin were the decadent in-crowd; meanwhile Balzac and Victor Hugo attempted to sensationalize the plight of the poor. The 1832 cholera outbreak reveals how unsanitary the city must have been. In 1837 gas lighting and public transport in horse-drawn omnibuses was established, but this wasn't enough to stem the discontent. Revolution broke out again in 1848, felling the gentleman-king.

The second half of the 19th century saw Paris transformed by the building program of Napoléon III and Baron Haussmann. The six- and seven-story apartment blocks and wide boulevards, grand railway stations, and parks are all the work of Haussmann, who ruthlessly tore down medieval Paris and created the biggest building site the city has ever known. The point was not only to improve sanitation but to control the population—boulevards were thought to be more difficult to barricade.

It didn't work. Napoléon III's foreign policy was a disaster and ended in the Prussian siege of Paris in 1870, when the poor starved and the rich ate elephants from the zoo. The city surrendered in 1871 and a provisional Revolutionary government called the Commune was set up. Some 20,000 insurrectionists died, barricades went up, and many landmarks were burned down.

Night+Day's Paris Urbie

Night+Day cities are chosen because they have a vibrant nightlife scene, standard-setting and innovative restaurants, cutting-edge hotels, and enough attractions to keep one busy for six days without doing the same thing twice. In short, they are fun. They represent the quintessential *urbanista* experience. This wouldn't exist but for the creativity and talents of many people and organizations. In honor of all who have played a role in making Paris one of the world's coolest cities, Pulse Guides is pleased to give special recognition, and our Urbie Award, to a pair of individuals whose contribution is exemplary.

THE URBIE AWARD: Gilbert and Jean-Louis Costes
Lipp, the Deux Magots, and the Café de Flore were all started by entrepreneurs from the inhospitable Aveyron region. But all this is nothing compared to the empire created by the Costes family. Brothers Gilbert and Jean-Louis moved up to Paris and worked as a waiter and bartender respectively in their twenties. Now, with seven prestigious addresses and part ownership of around 20 others, they've created a name that's synonymous with Parisian chic and glamour. The Costes brothers can be credited for changing the very face of Paris restauration and hotelery.

The firstborn was the Philippe Starck–designed Café Costes in 1984. It closed in 1993, but Paris was hooked. Soon after, Hôtel Costes, Café Beaubourg, Café de la Musique, Café Marly, Café de l'Esplanade, and Georges restaurant on top of the Centre Pompidou proved the Costes had conquered the capital. Their winning formula was all-day dining on light, international-flavored cuisine; staff who all look like models; and spectacular design. Models, fashion designers, and film stars flocked to drape themselves on the tasseled velvet banquettes. The Costes also secured some fabulous locations: few of the world's museums can boast people-watching like that of Café Marly or Georges. To top it all, Hôtel Costes started bringing out its own musical compilations, which traveled worldwide as ambassadors of Parisian lounge culture. Now there's also the high-fashion *Costes* magazine.

From morning coffee at the new Le Village café to late-night cocktails around the Hôtel Costes bar, the in-crowd loves Costes just as much as it did ten years ago. To join the club, just swish through those dark glass doors and order a dry martini.

Under the new Republican government, the city was quickly rebuilt and Haussmann's plans completed. Clean, sumptuous, and filled with bourgeois attractions such as the opera and new department stores, Paris became a major tourist attraction. Socialites came for the races and haute-couture collections, and a series of Great Exhibitions showed off Paris' splendors, including the Eiffel Tower and its new Métro system. Paris entered the period of its greatest elegance and vitality, which continued until World War I.

The relaxed morals and joie de vivre of the Belle Epoque, with its flamboyant decorating style, morphed into Art Deco and the jazz era, which the French called the *Années Folles* (the crazy years). American jazz musicians such as Josephine Baker and Sidney Bechet were fêted, and foreign writers and artists such as Hemingway, Man Ray, Chagall, and Picasso found refuge and inspiration. The bohemian center moved from the northern edge of the city in Montmartre to Montparnasse.

The Depression hit Paris hard, and Revolutionary politics flared up again in a city where unemployed workers had few means of survival. In 1940 the Germans invaded. Hitler made a tour of its major sights, deciding that Paris was too beautiful to destroy. After four years of hardship and an appalling toll on the Jewish community, the city was liberated in 1944.

Paris: What It Is

After the war, and with the influx of Algerians after its war of independence, Paris needed cheap housing, but a decision was made to protect the inner historic area. While Paris proper, the 20 arrondissements within the Périphérique ring road, houses only 2.2 million people in an area of 41 square miles, greater Paris, known as Ile de France, has a population of 11 million. These are two different worlds. The Paris within is a city of beauty and late-night urban buzz. The *banlieue* (suburb) surrounding it covers huge housing projects, banal suburbs, and some smart commuter villages. The exception is La Défense, the high-rise business district out on a limb. A change is afoot, however, detected in the eastern suburb of Montreuil, which, though still grungy, has spawned a host of loft conversions and a spillover from the arty 20th arrondissement.

The Centre Pompidou, opened in 1977, was a great success, and President François Mitterrand, elected in 1981, added a series of other grand public works including the I.M. Pei pyramid in the Louvre, the Bastille Opera, and the Très Grande Bibliothèque. Recent attractions have included the conversion of the Palais de Tokyo into a fantastic contemporary art space and the old wine warehouses of Bercy into a shopping village. Areas to watch are the 13th, where a host of architects have been drafted in to build a utopian quarter of university, business, housing, and recreation, and the Quai Branly, where a new Jean Nouvel museum worthy of the amazing collection of primitive and tribal art is scheduled to open in the fall of 2006.

Socially, Paris is still a city that loves to party and protest—head to Place de la République on a Saturday if you want to relive, albeit in muted form, the spirit of '68. It is a frustrating, elating mixture of glamour and grunge, tradition and innovation. Despite the legendary rudeness of waiters and the impatience of drivers, Paris is a visitor-friendly city, increasingly so every year. The fun-loving mayor, Bertrand Delanoë, has brought in a host of free activities from ice-skating to rollerblade zones, Paris Plage (an artificial beach created on the banks of the Seine in the summer) and a cultural Nuit Blanche that make Paris a year-round party. The top-end hotels, bars, and restaurants are still the crème de la crème. Most of all, Paris is still Paris, embracing modern trends but refusing to give in to globalization. Taste it, smell it, live it, and chances are good you'll want to come back for more.

Welcome to fabulous Paris ...

THE 99 BEST of PARIS

Who needs another "Best" list? You do—if it comes with details and insider tips that make the difference between a good experience and a great one. We've pinpointed the 33 categories that make Paris exciting, magnetic, and unforgettable, and picked the absolute three best places to go for each. With a little help from Night+Day, the City of Lights is yours for the taking. Make the most of it.

Always-Trendy Tables

#1-3: In a city where restaurant fashion changes almost as fast as the models at the prêt-à-porter collections, it takes a special recipe to stay in vogue. These three have got it and are still pulling the A-list years down the line.

Costes*
239 rue St-Honoré, 1st, 01.42.44.50.25 • Hot & Cool

The Draw: A-listers galore throng here to cocktail and dine to a world-famous soundtrack in a sumptuous setting.

The Scene: Decorated like an Italian palazzo by the inimitable Jacques Garcia, the Costes has many rooms with different moods, arranged around the see-and-be-seen courtyard and always filled with a choice international clientele from the worlds of fashion and film. *Daily 7am-2am.* €€

Hot Tip: Be in the right place at the right time: the lounge lobby to see models arriving during Fashion Week; the terrace for lunch; and the black bar for sultry nighttime cocktails with the in-crowd.

Georges
Centre Pompidou, 6th floor, 4th, 01.44.78.47.99 • Hot & Cool

The Draw: The 360-degree view of the Paris skyline from the top of the Centre Pompidou is matched by the beautiful people who dine here.

The Scene: Jacob and MacFarlane's décor is like installation art in itself. The room buzzes with a fashionable crowd dining on fusion cuisine served by staff who look like models. *Wed-Mon noon-3pm and 7:30pm-1am.* €€

Hot Tip: Come at night for the view, and in summer book a table on the stunning rooftop terrace.

Maison Blanche
15 av. Montaigne, 8th, 01.47.23.55.99 • Hot & Cool

The Draw: The exclusive ambiance, gorgeous rooftop location, and a steady stream of fashion and film faces.

The Scene: Imaad Rahmouni's crisp and modern décor is the perfect setting for the inventive, contemporary cuisine, which keeps the movers and shakers coming. The view inside and out—with eight-meter-high windows overlooking the Seine and the Paris rooftops—is spectacular. *Mon-Fri noon-1:45pm and 8-10:45pm, Sat-Sun 8-10:45pm.* €€€€

Hot Tip: The silk alcoves and the window seats fill up fast—reserve well in advance.

Best

Bistros

#4–6: Bistros started in Paris, when Russian soldiers yelled "bistro, bistro" (quickly, quickly) to get fed before returning to their barracks. Now they range from nostalgic checked-tablecloth establishments to contemporary, trendy eateries, the defining factor being great comfort food that won't break the bank.

Au Bon Accueil
14 rue Monttessuy, 7th, 01.47.05.46.11 • Classic

The Draw: Highlights include an Eiffel Tower view from its streetside tables and a friendly ambiance.

The Scene: Seated on the terrace, or on wicker-backed seats in the stylishly updated interior, prepare for some fabulous food, bistro style. Despite its location near one of the world's premier tourist attractions, this place puts the emphasis squarely on what's on your plate. *Mon-Fri noon-2:30pm, 7:30-10:30pm. €*

Hot Tip: If you're here in the hunting season, don't miss out on the lièvre à la royale (hare in a creamy broth).

Le Pré Verre
8 rue Thenard, 5th, 01.43.54.59.47 • Classic

The Draw: A buzzy Left Bank atmosphere and great modern bistro food with a Mediterranean slant.

The Scene: Local publishers, academics, and shop owners gather for noisy lunches at this tightly packed modern bistro with a great jazz theme. *Tue-Sat noon-2pm and 7:30-10:30pm. €*

Hot Tip: Get here early, and insist on a table upstairs, which has a far more inviting atmosphere.

Le Square Trousseau
1 rue Antoine-Vollon, 12th, 01.43.43.06.00 • Bobo

The Draw: This is a dream bistro with an Art Nouveau interior dating back to 1900, delicious, filling food, a jocular staff, and outdoor tables on the edge of a picturesque square.

The Scene: Bobo locals and film people carouse over bottles of red wine in this superb setting. If you go to no other bistro, come here. *Tue-Sat noon-2:30pm and 8-11:30pm. €€*

Hot Tip: The specials of the day, which you'll find chalked on a blackboard, are often a good pick.

Brunches

#7–9: Paris was slow to recognize the joys of brunch, but now cafés and restaurants all over town are offering this Sunday afternoon option, mainly from noon onward. Here are three of the most opulent environments in which to indulge in this new pastime.

Les Ambassadeurs
Hôtel de Crillon, 10 pl. de la Concorde, 8th, 01.44.71.16.16 • Classic

The Draw: Crystal and marble surroundings and a sumptuous feast drawn from four countries.

The Scene: The Crillon restaurant's World Brunch pulls in celebrities and those who love to be pampered as suited waiters glide around pulling silver domes off Italian risotto with black truffles, Parisian grilled chicken, Norwegian smoked salmon, or American seafood. Béatrice Ardisson's lounge music adds a discreetly hip vibe. *Mon 7-10:30am and 7:30-10pm, Tue-Sat 7-10:30am, 12:30-2pm, and 7:30-10pm, Sun noon-3pm.* €€€€

Hot Tip: Snag a window-side table for the view over Place de la Concorde.

Café Jacquemart-André
158 bd. Haussmann, 8th, 01.45.62.11.59 • Romantic

The Draw: Dreamy brunch under a Tiepolo ceiling.

The Scene: Romantic couples and art connoisseurs look skyward at the fluffy clouds of an Italian masterpiece while enjoying the earthly pleasures of croissants, smoked salmon, and eggs. *Daily 11:45am-5:45pm.* €

Hot Tip: Leave time to visit the museum, which has a romantic story all its own and some beautiful artwork.

Les Orchidées
Park Hyatt Paris Vendôme, 3-5 rue de la Paix, 2nd, 01.58.71.12.34 • Hot & Cool

The Draw: Cool contemporary setting and delicious food.

The Scene: Upscale professionals and publicity-shy celebs love this sophisticated brunch in a smooth hotel setting. Jazzy music sets the ambiance and the food is top notch, with a variety of light and luxurious main dishes following the salmon, eggs, and croissant buffet and a choice of Champagnes. *Daily 6:30am-7pm.* €€

Hot Tip: No matter how much you've already indulged, don't leave without tasting one of Jean-François Foucher's fabulous desserts.

Best

Café Terraces

#10–12: Sitting on a café terrace is one of the number one reasons to be in Paris. Who cares if it's not sunny year-round when there's this much atmosphere? Being on the terrace means being on view, and it's quite all right to stare—everyone does.

Café Marly
Cour Napoléon du Louvre, 93 rue de Rivoli, 1st, 01.49.26.06.60 • Classic

The Draw: A terrace in the cloisters overlooking the glass pyramid of the Louvre gives this Costes café a practically unbeatable location.

The Scene: For breakfast, lunch, dinner, or drinks, Café Marly is always full, with a mixture of scenesters and discerning tourists. You can't help but feel superior lunching on antipasti here as you look down on the queues that snake around the pyramid to see priceless works of art. Inside, glass windows look down onto the Cour Marly sculpture gallery. *Daily 8am-2am.* €

Hot Tip: The café is open late at night when the pyramid is illuminated and the tourists have gone home.

Les Deux Magots
6 pl. St-Germain-des-Prés, 6th, 01.45.48.55.25 • Hot & Cool

The Draw: Extending around two sides of Paris' most famous café, this is the terrace par excellence, and a prime people-watching spot.

The Scene: A fixture on the St-Germain beat, Les Deux Magots draws a truly eclectic crowd. Jet-setters seem to prefer the garden terrace on the square, boxed in with shrubbery, tourists the view over Boulevard St-Germain, and eccentric old ladies the glassed-in terrace on Square St-Germain. *Daily 7:30am-1am.* €€

Hot Tip: The hot chocolate is still the best in Paris.

Pause Café
41 rue de Charonne, 11th, 01.48.06.08.33 • Bobo

The Draw: This is a mecca for hipster scenesters, who congregate here the minute the first rays of sun appear.

The Scene: The Pause is not pronounced "pose" for nothing. Its neighbors are film and recording studios and a fashion school, hence the clientele. Copious fish and meat dishes are served at lunch, and it's black coffee all the way at other times. *Mon-Sat 7:30am-2am, Sun 9am-8pm.* €

Hot Tip: Best seen during the day through a pair of designer sun specs.

Best Celebrity Spotting

#13-15: This being Paris, there are two types of celebrity—the French ones who are megastars here but might not even clock a two on the international scale, and the world-class ones. Here's where to find the latter, particularly during Fashion Week.

Davé
12 rue de Richelieu, 2nd, 01.42.61.49.48 • Hot & Cool

The Draw: Everyone who's anyone has eaten here at one point or another; few who aren't ever do.

The Scene: Davé Cheung numbers hundreds of top models, designers, photographers, and film stars among his personal friends. There is little room for mere mortals in this Chinese restaurant whose raison d'être is celebrity, but you can always try. *Mon-Fri noon-2:15pm and 7-11:15pm, Sat 7-11:15pm.* €€

Hot Tip: Be a top model, or know one. And don't even bother trying during Fashion Week.

Emporio Armani Caffé
149 bd. St-Germain, 6th, 01.45.48.62.15 • Hot & Cool

The Draw: In the heart of the St-Germain designer district; fashion and film stars are regulars here.

The Scene: One of the few places where the people featured in the pages on the magazine rack are actually present in the café. As well as for seeing the A-list patrons, it's worth visiting for top-quality Italian produce, whose provenance is cited in the menu. *Mon-Sat noon-midnight.* €€

Hot Tip: Weekday lunchtimes are the hottest scene.

Le VIP Room
78 av. des Champs-Elysées, 8th, 01.56.69.16.66 • Hot & Cool

The Draw: Owner Jean Roch has made a career out of having VIP friends, and his club hosts celebs of all types, from Bono and Grace Jones to Gwen Stefani and Paris Hilton.

The Scene: With sports cars massing on the pavement, a line out the door, and a select clubbing experience inside, Andrée Putman's spectacular new décor and exclusive ambiance is pulling in even more celebs than before. *Tue-Sun midnight-5am.*

Hot Tip: Dress to kill, but don't expect many celebs in August, when they all decamp to St-Tropez.

Best

Chic Museums

#16–18: Paris is the city of museums, but not all of them are full of dusty old antiquities and Impressionist paintings. For the fashion factor, check out the following addresses.

Fondation Pierre Bergé Yves Saint Laurent
3 rue Léonce-Reynaud, 16th, 01.44.31.64.00 • Hot & Cool

The Draw: Just to be in the former couturier's former HQ is enough for some; others will delight in the chance to see his creations up close along with selected artworks from his private collection.

The Scene: After Yves Saint Laurent retired from the couture scene, his long-term partner Pierre Bergé created this small museum to exhibit pieces from the carefully preserved archive, alternating with exhibitions linked to YSL's muse and creative entourage. Former clients of the couturier are often seen here. *Wed-Sun 11am-6pm. Closed Aug and between exhibitions. €–*

Hot tip: The collector's edition of the Love postcards in the shop make chic "Wish you were here" send-outs.

Musée Baccarat
11 pl. des Etats-Unis, 16th, 01.40.22.11.00 • Hot & Cool

The Draw: More for the Philippe Starck décor than for the crystal itself, this museum has become a premier fashion draw since it relocated to the posh 16th arrondissement and opened a fabulous restaurant.

The Scene: Baccarat's historical and modern crystal collections provide the starting point for a wonderland of refracted glass, mirrors, and Murano chandeliers. *Mon-Sat 10am-6:30pm. €–*

Hot Tip: Combine a visit with lunch in the restaurant, but reserve well in advance as it's incredibly hot.

Musée de la Mode et du Textile
107 rue de Rivoli, 1st, 01.44.55.57.50 • Hot & Cool

The Draw: Top-class fashion exhibitions cover modern masters and thematic displays drawn from one of the world's most precious archives.

The Scene: A well-clad crowd of designers, journalists, and fashion students always patronizes the shows at this premier fashion museum. Well-created exhibitions make use of dramatic lighting and video footage to explore the creator's art. *Tue-Fri 11am-6pm, Sat-Sun 10am-6pm. €–*

Hot Tip: Don't miss the Galerie des Bijoux jewelry gallery, which is included in the ticket.

Classic Hotel Bars

#19–21: Paris' hotel bars have lately woken from their slumber as trendsters wised up to the fact that one perfectly mixed martini is worth ten jugged margaritas. Happily, these bars haven't budged an inch on the cosseting cocktail experience they have always offered.

Bar César
Hôtel de Crillon, 10 pl. de la Concorde or 6 rue Boissy d'Anglas, 8th, 01.44.71.15.39 • Classic

The Draw: The very definition of a classic hotel piano bar, whose location makes it one of the prime Fashion Week rendezvous.

The Scene: Buzzing during the collections, quiet and classy at other times, the César benefits from two talented bartenders who'll make you feel like you belong. It's named after the crazy glass mosaics by the artist César around the bar. A pianist adds *Casablanca* atmosphere. *Daily 11am-2am.*

Hot Tip: The Baccarat cocktail: rosé Champagne, cranberry juice, Grand Marnier, and lime served in a Baccarat crystal glass.

Bar Fontainebleau
Hôtel Meurice, 228 rue de Rivoli, 1st, 01.44.58.10.10 • Romantic

The Draw: The dark, high-ceilinged room with 19th-century frescoes of the Forest of Fontainebleau is prime seduction territory.

The Scene: Smooth-talking young men in velvet jackets with their dates and the occasional low-key celebrity staying in the hotel look at home in the classy atmosphere. *Daily noon-2am.*

Hot Tip: Best for an apéritif, enjoyed to the sound of tinkling piano music from the Winter Garden.

Bar Hemingway
Hôtel Ritz, 15 pl. Vendôme or 28 rue Cambon, 1st, 01.43.16.33.65 • Classic

The Draw: Colin Peter Field is the draw here—officially the best bartender in the world, he seems to have stepped right out of the pages of P.G. Wodehouse.

The Scene: Kate Moss and her friends are regulars, among other distinguished clients, who nestle in the low, comfy seats in a fug of cigar smoke. Colin Peter Field regales them with his repertoire of witty anecdotes and occasionally puts a record on the wind-up gramophone. *Mon-Sat 6:30pm-2am.*

Hot Tip: Order the Lemon Charlie, a homemade limoncello created especially for Kate Moss.

Cocktails with a View

#22–24: Nothing adds to the cocktail experience like a sublime view. These addresses will take you to seventh heaven as you sip a martini while watching the sunset over Paris monuments.

Bar Panoramique
Hôtel Concorde Lafayette, 3 pl. du Général Koenig, 17th, 01.40.68.50.68

The Draw: On the 33rd floor, baby, you can't get much higher in this town. The fantastic nighttime panorama encompasses the Eiffel Tower, Arc de Triomphe, and La Défense.

The Scene: Business travelers and couples settle into the luxurious leather seating for the spectacle of the Paris skyline. The mirrored, '70s bar is in the center, and blue banquettes have been arranged in tiers as in a theater, facing out toward the windows. *Daily 5pm-3am.*

Hot Tip: Come before 9:30pm; after that the piano bar incurs a minimum charge of €20.50.

Jardin Plein Ciel
Hôtel Raphael, 17 av. Kléber, 16th, 01.53.64.32.00 • Hot & Cool

The Draw: Set in a garden on the rooftops near the Arc de Triomphe, this exclusive bar is a favorite with Parisian celebs.

The Scene: Wooden decking, roses, fruit trees, and a giant chessboard set the scene for this unique bar where a glamorous crowd of TV and music stars is often seen. Feels like an oasis from the traffic madness of the Etoile down below. *May-Sept daily 3:30-9:30pm.*

Hot Tip: Time your visit so that you are here for the magical sunset over the Arc de Triomphe.

Kong*
1 rue du Pont Neuf, 1st, 01.40.39.09.00 • Hot & Cool

The Draw: Funky manga-inspired décor and cool music makes this bar/restaurant the current hot spot for a youthful international crowd.

The Scene: Used for the filming of *Sex and the City*, this place rocks from early evening to late at night. On the top floor of the Kenzo building, Philippe Starck's created a kitsch extravaganza with manga faces, life-size geisha panels, and an upper-floor Plexiglas dome. Happy-hour cocktails and the Saturday night parties are the best time to come. *Daily 10:30am-2am.*

Hot Tip: The dome has the best view over the Pont Neuf, while the main room is the hottest place to mix and mingle.

Best

Concept Stores

#25–27: When Colette opened in 1997, a new trend in shopping was born. These labs of cool, midway between art gallery and fashion boutique, expose the very latest clothes, gizmos, magazines, and music, and are always ahead of the press. No need to worry if it's hot or not, the fact that it's here is enough.

Colette
213 rue St-Honoré, 1st, 01.55.35.33.90 • Hot & Cool

The Draw: The original concept store, now with a branch in Tokyo, Colette is an essential stop on any cool-hunter's itinerary.

The Scene: Fashion forerunners and design junkies circulate around the store, browsing hipster electronics and funky accessories in glass cases and checking out the cutting-edge clothes on the upper floor. Take a break in the water bar downstairs where your choice of H_2O makes a statement about you. *Mon-Sat 11am-7pm.*

Hot Tip: Check out the iPods on the Wall of Sound—they're the fast track to music credibility.

Spree
16 rue de la Vieuville, 18th, 01.42.23.41.40 • Bobo

The Draw: This one-stop shop has everything you need to get that Montmartre bobo-chic look and lifestyle.

The Scene: The joint project of a fashion designer and an artist, Spree is both shop and gallery. There's a good selection of London designers and retro furniture and objects for the home, as well as books, accessories, and CDs. *Mon 2-7:30pm, Tue-Sat 11am-7:30pm.*

Hot Tip: Lyié van Ricke's simple, multistrand jewelry is très à la mode.

Surface to Air
46 rue de l'Arbre-Sec, 1st, 01.49.27.04.54 • Bobo

The Draw: Get well ahead of the trends at Surface to Air, the most cutting-edge and daring of all the concept shops.

The Scene: Ready to knock Colette off its pedestal, Surface to Air has fingers in every pie from DJ and artist "happenings" to graphic design commissions. A great place to hang out and gen up on what's going on. *Mon-Sat 12:30-7:30pm.*

Hot Tip: The store throws its own party once a month at the very hip club Le Paris Paris. Try to get yourself on the guest list.

Contemporary Art

#28–30: Paris has always been the home of the avant-garde, and its contemporary art scene took on a new dimension with the opening of the Palais de Tokyo, whose huge volumes spectacularly display installation art, and Maison Rouge, which gives space for private collectors to commission large-scale new works. Not since the 1920s has Paris seen such an explosion of the new.

Centre Pompidou
pl. Georges Pompidou, 4th, 01.44.78.12.33 • Hot & Cool

The Draw: As well as offering a huge 20th-century art collection, which it rehangs every couple of years, the Centre Pompidou holds large temporary exhibitions devoted to the contemporary scene.

The Scene: The Centre draws on its own massive collection and loans to bring together contemporary art on huge themes, such as *Big Bang, Destruction and Creation in 20th-Century Art*. Single-artist shows are held on the ground and first floor, including Espace 315, for which specific installations are commissioned. *Daily Wed-Mon 11am-9pm; some temporary exhibitions open Thu until 11pm. €–*

Hot Tip: Look out for the Prix Marcel Duchamp, which rewards the winner with a commission for the museum.

La Maison Rouge (Fondation Antoine de Galbert)
10 bd. de la Bastille, 12th, 01.40.01.08.81 • Bobo

The Draw: New private art foundation encourages private collectors to show and commission contemporary artists.

The Scene: This space has quickly become a hipster address due to its exciting programming. Its size enables specially commissioned installations and interventions, in the spirit of New York in the '70s. *Wed, Fri-Sun 11am-7pm, Thu 11am-9pm. €–*

Hot Tip: You can brunch on the terrace of the little red house inside.

Palais de Tokyo
13 av. du Président Wilson, 16th, 01.47.23.54.01 • Bobo

The Draw: The most exciting thing to happen in Paris since the Centre Pompidou, Palais de Tokyo exhibits sensational installations, while a hip scene revolves around its bar and restaurant.

The Scene: The gallerygoers here sport Converse sneakers and combat pants, and chat about the clubs they'll be going to afterward. The art has notably introduced the hot new generation of Chinese and Taiwanese artists, and includes large-scale and interactive work and video, all exhibited in an impressive, hangar-like space. *Tue-Sun noon-midnight. €–*

Hot Tip: Make the most of the fashionably late opening hours.

Dance Clubs

#31–33: Paris nightlife is now polarizing into small-scale venues with a luxurious, retro ambiance, where looking good is key, and those that are still devoted to pushing the boundaries of house. At the following three you can be sure of fast bpms and hot DJ names for your pure dancing pleasure.

Batofar
Facing 11 quai François Mauriac, 13th, 01.53.60.17.30 • Bobo

The Draw: Partying on a lighthouse boat on the Seine complete with its red lighthouse lamp.

The Scene: Hipsters crowd on deck for mojitos on summer nights or groove to funky house down below. There's also live music and a popular Sunday afternoon chillout with deck chairs. *Wed-Sun midnight-6am, some Sundays 4am-noon and 4-10pm, though times vary according to the event.*

Hot Tip: If you're looking for a Sunday morning after-party, Batofar's Miniboum is one of the best.

Rex Club
5 bd. Poissonnière, 2nd, 01.42.36.10.96 • Bobo

The Draw: The temple of techno, the Rex has been providing sound sustenance for a dance-happy crowd for over a decade and is now at the very pinnacle of its success.

The Scene: "No dress code, no attitude, just great music" is the maxim here. DJ Laurent Garnier is king of the Rex and gives it his all at Friday's Automatik. For the gay crowd, Saturday's Eyes Need Sugar fills up with the kind of fit bodies that can take this pace of workout. *Thu-Sat midnight-6am.*

Hot Tip: Don't make plans for the day after.

Le Triptyque
142 rue Montmartre, 2nd, 01.40.28.05.55 • Bobo

The Draw: Hot programming of live and mixed music makes this a premier clubbers' address.

The Scene: The crowd here is sexy, lithe, and hip, whether it's coming for the live soul, hip-hop, and drum and bass, or late-night electro parties. The club moves effortlessly between its chill area with comfortable seating, inner bar, and steamy dance floor. *Wed 8pm-3am, Thu-Sat 11pm-6am.*

Hot Tip: Avant-garde DJs are promoted by their record labels here, so come here if you want to be able to say "I heard it first."

Best

Eiffel Tower Views

#34–36: Had Paris been like other cities the Eiffel Tower would long ago have been dwarfed by taller buildings, but height restrictions have kept it as prominent on the Paris skyline as it was in 1889. At night, nothing beats dining with a view of the Eiffel Tower's sparkling lights for pure, scintillating glamour.

Café de l'Homme
Musée de l'Homme, 17 pl. du Trocadéro, 16th, 01.44.05.30.15 • Hot & Cool

The Draw: The beautiful people are eclipsed only by the Iron Lady herself.

The Scene: Although the high-ceilinged dining room hung with color-changing strings of crystal is just as full of stylish diners, it's the terrace that takes the prize. From this VIP spot walled in by topiary, the Tower's light show is so close it's like the monumental version of a table dance. *Daily noon-2am.* €€

Hot Tip: Reserve well in advance for a terrace table; the only view from inside is of the sparkling crowd.

R
8 rue de la Cavalerie, 8th fl., 15th, 01.45.67.06.85 • Romantic

The Draw: A fabulous penthouse location from which to enjoy sunset and a view of the tower by night.

The Scene: Upscale young professionals and romantic couples tipped off by their concierges have discovered this unusual loft that looks across the rooftops to the Eiffel Tower and has a small, glassed-in clapboard terrace. A gasp goes around each night when the Eiffel Tower's lights are switched on. *Mon-Sat 8-11pm. Bar open till 2am (6am Sat).* €€

Hot Tip: Demonstrate your chivalrous side and be sure your partner takes the seat facing the tower.

Tokyo Eat
13 av. du Président Wilson, 16th, 01.47.20.00.29 • Bobo

The Draw: The summer terrace scene of the Palais de Tokyo's restaurant is like a fabulous beach party illuminated by the Eiffel Tower backdrop.

The Scene: Fairy lights are strung between two 1930s megaliths, a DJ spins '70s funk and soul, passing bateaux-mouches send a "Super Trouper" beam over the groups of velvet-jacketed men and waifish girls that people this hip and gorgeous summer scene. To see it is to want to be part of it. *May-Sept Tue-Sun noon-3pm and 8-11:30pm. Fine weather only (the inside restaurant has no view).* €

Hot Tip: After dinner, make a point of snagging one of the rubber-band deck chairs to gaze at the Tower and the moon in a trance-like state.

Best

Fine Dining

#37-39: In the most gastronomic city in the world, it is hard to choose among the wealth of five-star establishments. With food that is guaranteed to be sublime and service that is impeccable, setting and atmosphere are the defining factors. These places stop at nothing to ensure a meal that pleases all the senses.

Alain Ducasse au Plaza Athénée
Hôtel Plaza Athénée, 25 av. Montaigne, 8th, 01.53.67.65.00 • Hot & Cool

The Draw: Patrick Nuel's magical updating of this palace dining room attracts a young ultra-glamorous crowd to splash out on haute cuisine.

The Scene: 10,000 loose crystal drops hang as if in midair, and Nehru-jacketed staff glide around like models, performing their silver-service functions with impeccable ease. Chef Christophe Moret, who trained at Spoon, has brought a contemporary style to the luxury menu, enjoyed by an elite of gastronomes, upscale professionals, and the heads of the luxury brands that line this fashion avenue. *Mon-Wed 7:45-10:15pm, Thu-Fri 12:45-2:15pm and 7:45-10:15pm. €€€€*

Hot Tip: One word: truffles.

Guy Savoy
18 rue Troyon, 17th, 01.43.80.40.61 • Hot & Cool

The Draw: Many think Guy Savoy is Paris', if not the world's, top chef. Despite his fame, he's right here, every night, cooking in the restaurant he loves.

The Scene: Savoy's two passions of food and art are combined in the contemporary dining room, decorated with paintings and African statuary. Pleasure rather than business is the principle here, and the warm welcome and relaxed atmosphere fill the tables with special-occasion diners. *Tue-Fri noon-2pm and 7-10:30pm, Sat 7-10:30pm. €€€€*

Hot Tip: Go for the dégustation menu to savor the scope of Savoy's creativity.

Taillevent
15 rue Lamennais, 8th, 01.44.95.15.01 • Classic

The Draw: A stunning setting and top-rated cuisine by an exciting young chef.

The Scene: Financiers, wine connoisseurs, and well-heeled leisure travelers settle into the beautiful townhouse setting to enjoy the finest cuisine, performed by young talent Alain Solivérès, and wines from the famous Taillevent cellar. *Mon-Fri 12:15-2pm and 7:30-10pm. €€€€*

Hot Tip: Try the caillette de porcelet, a re-creation of a medieval pork dish by the original chef, who was known as "Taillevent."

Gay Bars

#40–42: Gay Paris centers around the Marais, whose quaint historic streets come alive at night. It's easy to hop from bar to bar and the crowds spilling out on the street give a foretaste of what kind of scene to expect within. These favorites are a must for gay visitors.

L'Amnésia Café
42 rue Vieille-du-Temple, 4th, 01.42.72.16.94 • Hot & Cool

The Draw: A stylish, sophisticated, gorgeous crowd can always be found checking out the scene here.

The Scene: Tasteful and trendy, this is the place to make a fashion statement while flirting with the androgynous bartenders. Three floors cater to every mood: a happening cocktail bar on the ground floor, cozy nooks upstairs, and a camp mini-disco downstairs for energetic pre-club voguing to Madonna. *Daily 11am-2am.*

Hot Tip: The Pink Russian cocktails for la vie en rose.

Open Café
17 rue des Archives, 4th, 01.42.72.26.18 • Bobo

The Draw: Checking out the passing talent from the see-and-be-seen terrace.

The Scene: This central meeting place, a large and airy café, is open all day long. A preened and beautiful clientele shows itself off on the terrace and the waiters are drop-dead gorgeous. *Daily 11am-2am, Fri-Sat till 4am.*

Hot Tip: If you're ready to face the daylight, make a coffee here your first port of call.

Raidd Bar
23 rue du Temple, 4th, 01.48.87.80.25 • Hot & Cool

The Draw: The topless, musclebound barmen.

The Scene: Gym queens pack this club-like space where the techno is loud and the cruising unabashed. The arrival of a new bartender is a much-publicized event as these guys bare all under the shower on Sundays—and almost all as they pull pints behind the bar. An ideal halfway house between bar and club with a chilled-out lounge downstairs. *Daily 6pm-5am.*

Hot Tip: On Wednesdays you too can perform a striptease under the shower. Hot, hot, hot!

Guided Tours

#43–45: Forget the umbrella-toting tour guide regurgitating historical facts. These three tour companies combine expert knowledge with an entertaining or interactive style, and one is in a Citroën 2CV.

4 Roues sous 1 Parapluie
08.00.80.06.31 (free phone from within France), 06.67.32.26.68 • Romantic

The Draw: Whizzing around Paris in a Citroën 2CV.

The Scene: Perfect for lovers and classic-car freaks, this tour re-creates the romance of the '50s as your cloth-capped chauffeur weaves between the narrow lanes of Paris traffic while showing you the sights. Cuddled up under a blanket with the convertible hood down, you'll be amazed at just how close the monuments seem, while the distinctive engine purr is positively sexy. This car makes passers-by smile and wave, and you feel like a film star. €€€€

Hot Tip: As well as the standard tours, the company can build a tailor-made itinerary around what you want to see. Wrap up warmly for the open top.

Paris Muse
06.73.77.33.52 • Classic

The Draw: Your own private art historian will reveal the mysteries of the great artworks, and you can ask as many questions as you like.

The Scene: American art historians studying for their PhDs take groups of no more than four around the great art museums. Tailor-made and interactive, these tours go far beyond the superficial and anecdotal to reveal the deeper significance behind what you see. *Tours 1.5-2.5 hours long.* €€€€

Hot Tip: Paris Muse's Da Vinci Code tour reveals that even a bestseller can raise some fascinating questions about art.

Paris Walks
01.48.09.21.40 • Classic

The Draw: This long-established operation provides some of the best and most entertaining walking tours in Paris.

The Scene: A gaggle of assorted visitors gathers at the designated Metro stop before being led on an anecdote-packed walk on whatever theme they have chosen. The guides are great raconteurs and pepper the walks with spicy historical and local gossip. €–

Hot Tip: Check out some of the more unusual walks, such as Paris Under the Occupation and the Paris Fashion Walk.

Hipster Hangouts

#46-48: Far from the packaged cool of the Costes empire, Paris hipsters congregate in roughly done-up zinc bars and resurrected strip clubs. If you want to fraternize with a real French crowd at the cutting edge of cool, try one of these three über-spots.

Le Baron
6 av. Marceau, 8th, 01.47.20.04.01 • Bobo

The Draw: This is the place to be in with the in-crowd.

The Scene: Early in 2005 a renegade group of 20-somethings who'd gathered momentum with one-off parties took over this former strip club in the posh 16th and turned the tables on house and the superclubs. Beautiful people strut their stuff to retro funk, disco, and '80s in a euphoric Studio 54 throwback. *Daily midnight-6am.*

Hot Tip: Getting in is difficult. Dress sexily and insist that you are on the guest list; even better, get into conversation with some Baronites at the Palais de Tokyo (spottable by their aristo-chic look) and ask them to take you with them.

Café Chéri(e)
44 bd. la Villette, 19th, 01.42.02.07.87 • Bobo

The Draw: A lively bar scene and live DJs epitomize the off-the-cuff vibe. The outdoor terrace is hipster central.

The Scene: A beacon in this down-at-the-heel area, the Café Chéri(e) is like a pulsating red box. Hip and laid-back, it's a local rendezvous for artists, musicians, and idlers who like to dress down with industrial chic. Posers sit out on the terrace, while inside, it's easy to get into conversation with complete strangers at the bar while the DJs get people moving to electro sounds at the back. *Daily 8am-2am.*

Hot Tip: A hip crowd flits between here and the neighboring Ile Enchantée.

La Perle
78 rue Vieille-du-Temple, 4th, 01.42.72.69.93 • Bobo

The Draw: The beautiful bobos who have colonized this old bar.

The Scene: Up the road from the gay bars and the more sedate cafés, La Perle has ushered a new era of hipness into the North Marais. The owners have left the '70s décor untouched, just cranked up the music, and it's packed, especially on weekend nights, with a cruisey, mainly hetero crowd. *Daily 8am-2am.*

Hot Tip: Don't wait on the terrace to be served—it might never happen—but fight your way to the bar.

Jazz Clubs

#49–51: From the '30s on, Paris was the mecca for jazz musicians from across the pond. By the '50s, St-Germain was hosting nightly some of the greatest names of the 20th century. Though the fury of those hot nights has cooled, there is still plenty of jazz to go around, divided between those clubs that deal in nostalgia and other, more contemporary venues.

Le Bilboquet
13 rue St-Benoît, 6th, 01.45.48.81.84 • Classic

The Draw: This legendary spot where Miles Davis, Art Blakey, and Duke Ellington used to play keeps the flame burning for classic jazz fans.

The Scene: A nostalgia-hungry crowd comes here to relive the glory days of jazz in St-Germain, fostered by moody black-and-white photos of the greats, and musicians who tend to imitate the style of the American pioneers rather than offer anything radical. In the intimate cellar atmosphere, the crowd is hugely appreciative. *Daily 8pm-1:30am.*

Hot Tip: No need to dine—you can come just for the concert.

New Morning
7-9 rue des Petites-Ecuries, 10th, 01.45.23.51.41 • Classic

The Draw: Paris' premier jazz venue for big names and new jazz forms.

The Scene: This is a concert rather than a dining venue, and serious jazz fans mass on the pavement early to get front-row seats for the big names that play here, among them Pharaoh Sanders, James Taylor Quartet, and Carlos Esposito. *Concerts daily 9pm.*

Hot Tip: JVC Jazz Festival the second half of October is a chance to sample the new jazz scene coming out of France.

Le Sabot
6 rue du Sabot, 6th, 01.42.22.21.56 • Classic

The Draw: Energetic atmosphere and music at this vibrant new club run by a young sax maestro.

The Scene: The beamed ground-floor room fills up with an eclectic crowd of all ages, from arty St-Germain types in their sixties to groups of young professionals. All get caught up in the synergy of this place, where friends of the owner drop in unexpectedly and start jamming. Chanson and world music are also programmed. *Live music Tue-Fri from 8pm.*

Hot Tip: Don't miss Wednesday night's free jazz improv sessions that roll on late into the night.

Best

Late-Night Eats

#52-54: Paris is quaintly not a 24-hour city in so many ways. But when it comes to food it's a different matter. Why resort to fast food when brasseries offer the whole works served by silver-service waiters in gilded surroundings? Modern restaurants too are making a tentative inroad into nocturnal dining.

Music Hall*
63 av. Franklin D. Roosevelt, 8th, 01.45.61.03.63 • Hot & Cool

The Draw: Luxury all-night dining in a fantasy color-changing setting.

The Scene: Music Hall was the first place in the Champs-Elysées area to keep its kitchens open till 6am, and with so many bars and clubs around, it's a hit with smart young nightowls who come to eat or chill out to lounge sounds in the ambient mood lighting before cruising off in their BMWs. *Daily 11am-4am. €€*

Hot Tip: Insist on the main room unless you really feel like zoning out to Fashion TV.

Au Pied de Cochon
6 rue Coquillière, 1st, 01.40.13.77.00 • Classic

The Draw: The magnificent surroundings, service, and gargantuan servings of brasserie food make a midnight feast here a real occasion.

The Scene: Au Pied de Cochon's Belle Epoque décor of mirrors, chrome, and painted panels dates from the days when Les Halles was "the belly of Paris," housing the wholesale market that fed the whole city—and its opening hours are unchanged from those days. During the day it feeds tourists; by night rowdy clubbers, theater folk, and insomniacs feast on oysters, pig's feet, and profiteroles served by waiters who take great pride in upholding tradition. *24/7. €*

Hot Tip: To feel like a true Parisian, come at 4am and order a towering platter of oysters.

Le Tambour
41 rue Montmartre, 2nd, 01.42.33.06.90 • Bobo

The Draw: A fun, unpretentious night-owl haunt that feeds the hungry hordes with delicious French classics.

The Scene: Minutes from Café Noir and the Triptyque, Le Tambour is at its most buzzing at 3am, when high-spirited young clubbers and bar-crawlers trip in to fuel up on plates of charcuterie, salads, steaks, and cigarettes. Something like a Toulouse-Lautrec scene for the 21st century. *Tue-Sat noon-3pm and 6pm-6am, Sun-Mon 6pm-6am. €*

Hot Tip: The salade landaise and the profiteroles, dripping with steaming hot chocolate sauce.

Literary Bars

#55–57: The literary bar in Paris has become an art form in itself. Now that writers don't have to huddle in cafés to keep warm, the descendants of the Flore and the Deux Magots are stylish rendezvous with their own well-stocked libraries for literary types to peruse between drinks and conversation.

La Belle Hortense
31 rue Vieille-du-Temple, 4th, 01.48.04.71.60 • Bobo

The Draw: Guzzling fine wines in a bookshop feels naughty, like sneaking a bottle of booze into the college library.

The Scene: Trendy intellectuals are the patrons of this small Marais bar devoted to the cult of the book and the bottle. All the books are for sale, and all the patrons are very willing to talk about their latest work in progress. *Daily 5pm-2am.*

Hot Tip: Try Guigal's fruity red Côte du Rhônes and Monique Ayoun's fruity read, "L'histoire de mes seins" ("The Story of My Breasts").

Les Editeurs
4 carrefour de l'Odéon, 6th, 01.43.26.67.76 • Classic

The Draw: A modern café that draws a very chic, literary, Left Bank crowd.

The Scene: Editors from the nearby publishing houses, Left Bank celebrities like singer Benjamin Biolay, and other sleek 30-somethings while away their time over proofs, books, and newspapers ensconced in velvet chairs, or casually people-watch on the terrace. The food and drinks are of a high quality and you'll never be rushed—this is a literary joint, after all. *Daily 8am-2am.*

Hot Tip: Does a mighty fine brunch.

Le Fumoir
6 rue de l'Amiral-de-Coligny, 1st, 01.42.92.00.24 • Hot & Cool

The Draw: Leather armchairs, newspapers, cigars, cocktails, an old-world décor, and a trendy crowd.

The Scene: Crossing the language barrier, Le Fumoir stocks English- and French-language press and books, and its young, cosmopolitan clientele reflects the reading matter. Speaking of cosmopolitans, it does a very good one, as well as excellent plats du jour and brunches in a '30s cigar lounge setting. *Daily 11am-2am.* €€

Hot Tip: Operates a leave-one, take-one book service for backpackers who have grown up.

Best

Live Music

#58–60: Big venues are booked out months in advance for world-class names, but it's well worth checking out the smaller concert halls where you're closer to the music and the atmosphere is often electric. Paris has many crossover venues where live performers are followed up with DJs for a crowd that's mad to dance, as well as bars hosting live music in a truly intimate setting.

Elysée Montmartre
72 bd. Rochechouart, 18th, 01.41.57.32.33 • Bobo

The Draw: A great concert venue in a former Belle Epoque cabaret hall, where hot international rock bands are interspersed with big-name French acts.

The Scene: Aimed at a young public, the Elysée hosts big names such as Röyksopp, the Dandy Warhols, and Black Rebel Motorcycle Club, but in this 1900s music hall complete with stucco ceiling, you are much nearer to the band than in a stadium-size venue. Live music concerts are followed by house-led club nights.

Hot Tip: Tap "Elysée Montmartre" into fnac.com's ticket-booking site to see who's on during your visit.

Jokko Bar
5 rue Elzévir, 3rd, 01.42.74.35.96 • Bobo

The Draw: Soft-voiced Senegalese musicians weave their magic at this Marais bar/club, providing the inside track on this cross-continent world music scene.

The Scene: A young crowd of Europeans and Africans lounges on low cushioned seating to chill to fabulous Senegalese music and drinks specialty cocktails made with hibiscus flower and rum. *Tue-Sun 5pm-2am. Live music Thu-Sat.*

Hot Tip: Eat beforehand at sister restaurant Le Petit Dakar opposite.

La Scène Bastille
2 bis rue des Taillandiers, 12th, 01.48.06.50.70 • Bobo

The Draw: Rooted in the French and world music scene, La Scène is an intimate and friendly concert venue where it's pretty much impossible not to have a good time.

The Scene: A local bobo crowd lines up to get into this converted warehouse whose live scene ranges from chanson to reggae to Paul Weller. The front bistro/bar provides a buzzing chill-out zone, and live shows are followed by funk, R&B, and house dance parties. *Mon-Sat live music 8pm. Clubbing: midnight-6am. Sunday gay tea dance 6pm-2am.*

Hot Tip: On Fridays Radio Nova hosts Les Nuits Zébrées, a free party with invited live acts. Pick up tickets in advance from the nearby Nova offices (01.53.33.33.15).

Best

Lounge Bars

#61–63: Paris lounge is as much a musical style as a bar phenomenon. The compilations of Buddha Bar, Mezzanine de l'Alcazar, and other, even non-existent lounges, spread the fame of Paris as lounge capital. Here's where to sip and slink in the most seductive surroundings.

La Cantine du Faubourg*
105 rue du Fbg. St-Honoré, 8th, 01.42.56.22.22 • Hot & Cool

The Draw: Mingle with a fashionable and showbiz clientele, all enjoying the sophisticated ambiance.

The Scene: Everything seems to have been stage-managed to perfection here—the light projections marbling gauzy curtains with soothing patterns, just the right tempo of music to set the mood, and huge deep leather sofas. It's an altogether classier and more exclusive lounge than Buddha Bar or Man Ray, drawing throngs of sleek young professionals and stars like Isabelle Adjani. *Daily noon-4am.* C B =

Hot Tip: Late opening hours make this the perfect place to finish the evening in the company of beautiful lounge aficionados.

China Club
50 rue de Charenton, 12th, 01.43.43.82.02 • Bobo

The Draw: The seductive ambiance of a Shanghai gentlemen's club in the '30s.

The Scene: Young and lovely boys and girls sit up at the bar to watch their martinis taking shape, or lounge on leather Chesterfields in the red lacquer interior. Upstairs, the Hemingwayesque fumoir and whisky bar is a roaring success. *Daily 7pm-2am.* C B =

Hot Tip: Check out the basement jazz club, Sing Song, which takes place here Thursday through Saturday.

Mezzanine de l'Alcazar
62 rue Mazarine, 6th, 01.53.10.19.99 • Romantic

The Draw: The crowds come for the excellent musical programming spun by live DJs.

The Scene: The only lounge bar on the Left Bank, the Mezzanine has been pulling a stylish 30-something international crowd since it released its own best-selling compilations. The décor is minimalist, with black-and-white photos, taupe banquettes, and an impressive view down onto the restaurant below. *Daily 7pm-2am.* B =

Hot Tip: Come on Thursdays for the funky grooves.

Markets

#64–66: Paris' four flea markets and its dozens of food markets are enshrined in ancient charters, many going back to the Middle Ages. The atmosphere is always vibrant, whether it's a noisy, colorful street market, a covered market selling specialty produce, or the world's greatest flea market.

Marché des Enfants Rouges
39 rue de Bretagne, 3rd • Bobo

The Draw: Organic wines and produce, with plenty of places to sit down and enjoy a glass of something.

The Scene: Marais bobos do their weekly shopping at this covered market. Aside from fish and vegetables, there are plenty of things for the visitor to take home—olive oils, honeys, and of course wine. The atmosphere is Provençal in the chic sense of the word.

Hot Tip: Stop for fresh oysters and a glass of something crisp and white at L'Estaminet wine bar.

Marché Mouffetard
Rue Mouffetard, 5th • Classic

The Draw: Vegetables piled high in elaborate displays on the cobbled street described by Hemingway in *A Moveable Feast*.

The Scene: Though it's justly famous, Mouffetard is still a locals' market where traders shout out their wares and reward their regulars by throwing in an extra few figs or a melon. Behind the stalls are dedicated food shops selling cheese, wine, and so forth. *Tue-Sun 8am-2pm.*

Hot Tip: An accordion sing-along happens at the bottom of the market on Sunday mornings.

Marché aux Puces de St-Ouen
Rue des Rosiers, St-Ouen • Bobo

The Draw: The flea market to end all flea markets, with everything from Louis XIV furniture to buttons and badges.

The Scene: Parisians fitting out their homes, tourists, and serious antiques hunters flock to this weekend market on the northern edge of Paris. It is many markets in one—each has a name and a different specialty. Part of the appeal is the atmosphere, with market traders sitting down to plates of charcuterie and wine outside their stands. *Sat-Mon 9am-6pm.*

Hot Tip: Marché Paul Bert has some of the most interesting and eclectic objects, from street signs to steel cutlery molds.

Meet Markets

#67–69: The singles scene has boomed in the past couple of years with speed dating, "quiet parties" where the flirtation is done on paper, and even supermarket dating where special baskets advertise who's shopping for love. But French men have never been shy about coming forward. At these three places the interchange is free and easy.

Drôle d'Endroit pour une Rencontre*
46 rue Caulaincourt, 18th, 01.42.55.14.25 • Bobo

The Draw: Footloose Montmartre bobos just love the *Sex and the City* ambiance and flirty theme nights at this bar.

The Scene: Raw brick walls, nifty lighting, and a cute bartender who knows how to mix a fine cosmopolitan draw a sexy crowd that sits at the bar or at the window seats, or among friends in the restaurant at the back. Budding DJs hit the decks on Thursday nights, and there's a popular non-smoking brunch on Sundays. Singles can register for the matchmaking service or study the posted ads. *Tue-Sat 10am-1:30am, Sun noon-midnight.*

Hot Tip: Key vocabulary to get you started: "célibataire" means single; "draguer" means to chat someone up.

Pershing Lounge*
49 rue Pierre Charron, 8th, 01.58.36.58.36 • Hot & Cool

The Draw: Pershing Hall's glamorous lounge bar is the place to meet the sexiest singles east of New York.

The Scene: With its dramatic staircase, vertical garden, and red lanterns over the mezzanine bar, the Pershing provides a seductive setting, and while couples settle in the romantic terrace alcoves, a vibrant singles scene goes on in the two stucco-ceilinged rooms behind. DJs crank up the pheromones with lounge music, and fruity cocktails flow. *Daily 6pm-2am.*

Hot Tip: Tuesday night's Girls' Party offers free drinks and massages for the ladies to get them in the mood.

Le Progrès
7 rue des Trois-Frères, 18th, 01.42.64.07.37 • Bobo

The Draw: No standing on ceremony at this fun-filled Montmartre bar where you'll end up knowing everyone in the room.

The Scene: Hipster artists, musicians, and boutique owners congregate in this glass box of a bar where the liberally flowing beer and pots of red wine aid the uninhibited atmosphere. If you vacate your chair, you'll return to find a stranger telling your best friend she or he has beautiful eyes. *Daily 9am-2am.*

Hot Tip: People tend to move around—keep track of your drinks to avoid confusion at the end of the evening.

North African Dining

#70–72: As curries are to London and fajitas are to LA, so are couscous and tagine to Paris. Their purveyors range from cheap Algerian dives in the Arab quarters to refined Moroccan eateries filled with intricate tiles and a hot fashion crowd. These three are sumptuous in food and atmosphere alike.

Le 404
69 rue des Gravilliers, 3rd, 01.42.74.57.81 • Bobo

The Draw: With a party always in full swing, this is the ultimate place to rock the casbah.

The Scene: Fashion designers, Rolex-wearing bachelor boys, and extroverted girls in stilettos and strass pile in for mojitos and steaming tagines, then get up on the tables and dance. The Arabic music is right on the pulse and the *Arabian Nights* décor is stunning. *Mon-Fri noon-2:30pm and 8pm-midnight, Sat 8pm-midnight, Sun noon-4pm.* €€

Hot Tip: Book the second seating for the greatest party atmosphere, and then carry on next door at the Andy Wahloo bar annex.

Le Martel
3 rue Martel, 10th, 01.47.70.67.56 • Bobo

The Draw: This old zinc bar turned restaurant looks like a sepia photo and draws a designer crowd.

The Scene: Flash fashion barons from this manufacturing area mix with trendy loft dwellers to enjoy steaming couscous, tagines, or equally good French cuisine. It's a hot spot in this burgeoning and fascinating neighborhood. *Mon-Fri 11am-3pm and 6pm-1am, Sat 6pm-1am.* €

Hot Tip: Skip the apéritifs, which are outlandishly priced, and go for a bottle of pale pink gris de Guerrouane from Morocco.

Le Ziryab
Institut du Monde Arabe, 9th fl., 1 rue des Fossés St-Bernard, 5th, 01.53.10.10.16 • Romantic

The Draw: A fantastic view over the Seine and sublime North African cooking.

The Scene: Red lamps, crisp white tablecloths, and the penthouse setting make this restaurant atop the Institut du Monde Arabe look like it could be anywhere in the world. The cuisine, however, is rooted in the finest Moroccan tradition of mixing luscious fruits and tender meats. Sophisticated North African and European diners enjoy some of the best tagines in Paris. *Tue-Sat noon-2pm and 7:30pm-midnight, Sun noon-2pm.* €€

Hot Tip: Try the chicken and pineapple tagine, spiced with cinnamon.

Of-the-Moment Dining

#73–75: Spectacular décor, creative food, and a glamorous crowd combine to make these the restaurants that everyone's talking about. Strike while the oven is still hot.

Bon
25 rue de la Pompe, 16th, 01.40.72.70.00 • Hot & Cool

The Draw: The glamorous Philippe Starck décor and even more glamorous crowd.

The Scene: Fashionable young professionals roll up in Porsches to this Belle Epoque building that houses a wonderland of mirrors, quilted panels, and candelabras. Clubby background music and rounded banquettes on multiple levels set the scene for well-presented Asian-Mediterranean cuisine. *Mon-Fri noon-3pm and 8pm-midnight, Sat 8pm-midnight.* €€

Hot Tip: Come early and have a cocktail at the revolving bar.

Le Cristal Room
11 pl. des Etats-Unis, 16th, 01.40.22.11.10 • Hot & Cool

The Draw: Celebrity diners in close proximity in what feels like Marie Antoinette's private dining room.

The Scene: History is repeating itself in the mansion house where hostess the Vicomtesse de Noailles held flamboyant dinner parties, only luminaries such as Jean Cocteau and Coco Chanel have been replaced by the likes of Tom Cruise. The Philippe Starck décor is a kitsch tribute to 18th-century decadence, and just when you thought it couldn't get much hotter, they brought in the fashion crowd's favorite chef, Thierry Burlot, to do fabulous things with lobster. *Mon-Sat 8:30am-1am.* €€€

Hot Tip: For the ultimate decadent experience, reserve the private room seating four, which is lit by a fabulous black chandelier.

Murano
Murano Urban Resort, 13 bd. du Temple, 3rd, 01.42.71.20.00 • Hot & Cool

The Draw: The Murano's sleek dining room draws a buzzing and beautiful fashion and media crowd.

The Scene: High ceilings, tubular lights, and cranberry velvet banquettes attract design groupies, while the bouncy runway-style music makes the fashion crowd feel at home as they greet each other with air kisses. This restaurant has almost topped Costes as Fashion Week favorite. *Daily 12:30-2pm and 8-11pm.* €€€

Hot Tip: In summer, ask to be seated in the atrium for see-and-be-seen kudos.

Best

Outdoor Dining

#76–78: The fact that it's not a year-round treat makes outdoor dining in the summer feel particularly festive. And we're not talking roadside terraces here—these three restaurants have exclusive and secluded private gardens far from the madding crowd.

Le Chalet des Iles
Carrefour des Cascades, Lac Inférieur, Bois de Boulogne, 01.42.88.04.69 • Romantic

The Draw: Dining on an island reached by boat in the Bois de Boulogne creates the perfect illusion that you are in the French countryside.

The Scene: As the launch takes you across the Lac Inférieur you feel like you're crossing over to another world. Honeymooners and family groups with something to celebrate sit under the large green sunshades, sometimes woken from their reverie by the cry of a peacock. The summer menu is fresh and light and the service warm and welcoming. *Tue-Fri noon-2:30pm and 8-10pm, Sat noon-3:30pm and 8-10pm, Sun noon-3:30pm.* €€

Hot Tip: Ask for a table with a lakeside view.

Laurent
41 av. Gabriel, 8th, 01.42.25.00.39 • Classic

The Draw: This walled garden a stone's throw from the presidential palace feels exquisitely exclusive.

The Scene: The distant honking of horns on the Champs-Elysées combined with silver-service dining in the garden of a 19th-century pavilion makes lunch or dinner here an unforgettably Parisian experience. Heads of industry and government ministers are regulars, with the occasional celebrity sighting. *Mon-Fri 12:30-2pm and 7:30-10:30pm, Sat 7:30-10:30pm.* €€€€

Hot Tip: Don't hold back on the excellent cheese cart.

Le Relais du Parc
Sofitel le Parc, 51 av. Raymond-Poincaré, 16th, 01.44.05.66.10 • Hot & Cool

The Draw: The St-Tropez atmosphere in the lush courtyard of an elegant manor-house hotel.

The Scene: Business associates and couples relax in this oasis of a courtyard where lush flowers and trees and cushioned wrought-iron chairs re-create summer in Provence. The menu is overseen by Ducasse. *Daily from early May to end Sept Tue-Fri noon-2:30pm and 7-10:30pm, Sat 7-10:30pm.* €€€

Hot Tip: Try the unusual Caesar salad variant with king prawns and capers.

Parks

#79–81: The greenery of Paris is underrated. While it doesn't have a large expanse of park within the city limits, the city is peppered with utterly charming smaller squares and gardens whose appeal ranges from 19th-century nostalgia to contemporary garden design.

Jardin du Luxembourg
Rue de Vaugirard, pl. Edmond Rostand, 6th • Romantic

The Draw: Elegant, chic, and filled with Renaissance statuary, this park resembles the Boboli Gardens in Florence.

The Scene: Pensioners with poodles, smart tennis partners, children with their nannies playing with quaint old-fashioned sailboats, and Russian émigrés playing chess are part of the Proustian scene at the Luxembourg. *Daily 7:30am (summer), 8:15am (winter); closing varies 4:30-9pm according to the season.*

Hot Tip: Ice cream at the café is a nostalgic treat.

Parc André Citroën
Rue St-Charles, 15th, 01.44.26.20.00 • Romantic

The Draw: Imaginative modern landscaping and the chance to go up in a tethered hot-air balloon.

The Scene: A favorite with children and couples who picnic on the large expanse of lawn, this contemporary take on a formal French garden has water jets and several gardens focusing on different scents and sounds. *Mon-Fri 8am-dusk, Sat-Sun 9am-dusk.*

Hot Tip: One Sunday a month in summer the park hosts Sous La Plage, a Seine-side chill-out with electronic music and sizzling food stalls.

Parc des Buttes Chaumont
Rue Botzaris, 19th • Bobo

The Draw: Grottoes, a temple, and acres of grassy slopes.

The Scene: Up in the northeastern part of Paris, this fabulous 19th-century park is rarely visited by out-of-towners, but local families and bobos make good use of its sunny slopes and a maze of paths through wooded areas. Circus performers can often be seen practicing here. *Daily 7am-dusk (around 10pm in summer).*

Hot Tip: With a relaxed policy on sitting on the grass, this is the perfect park for a Sunday picnic.

THE 99 BEST OF PARIS

Power Lunches

#82–84: Knowing the right address to impress will set the barometer in your favor when you meet that important client. Chew the figures with the movers and shakers at these three on-the-ball choices.

Bon 2
2 rue du Quatre-Septembre, 2nd, 01.44.55.51.55

The Draw: Right in the heart of the financial district, Bon 2 is a witty choice for number crunchers.

The Scene: Traders sit up at the oyster bar with half an eye on the stock market info running in an electronic stream, while corporates seal the deal seated on leather chairs at the widely spaced tables. Philosophical quotations interspersing the Dow Jones and tongue-in-cheek doctor's orders on the menu (green beans "aid memory and concentration" while the pâtisseries are "good for morale") keep things light and upbeat. *Mon-Fri noon-3pm and 8pm-2am, Sat 8pm-2am.* €€

Hot Tip: There's a private room seating five for privacy and VIP kudos.

Le Chiberta
3 rue Arsène-Houssaye, 8th, 01.53.53.42.00 • Hot & Cool

The Draw: Dramatic black, spotlit décor for dash and panache.

The Scene: This long-standing business address has been pulling in a young, dynamic business clientele since its decorative revamp and takeover by top chef Guy Savoy. Corporate colleagues with busy schedules snack at the cool tapas bar, while serious lunching takes place in the two sleek dining rooms, one of which is lined with wines in temperature-controlled cabinets. *Mon-Thu noon-2:30pm and 7-11pm, Fri noon-2:30pm and 7-11:30pm, Sat 7-11:30pm.* €€€

Hot Tip: Choose the room according to the mood you wish to convey: Le Salon is black and uncompromising; La Salle is more open to discussion with white walls and red canvases.

Hiramatsu
52 rue de Longchamp, 16th, 01.56.81.08.80 • Hot & Cool

The Draw: Polished French cooking by a Japanese chef in a refined setting.

The Scene: CEOs who appreciate the finer things in life fill the tables of this top gastronomic address, smoothing their napkins in preparation for Hajime Nakagawa's exquisite cuisine. Everything's perfectly orchestrated, from the food to the service to the Baccarat and Limoges table settings. *Mon-Fri 12:30-2pm and 7:30-9:30pm.* €€€€

Hot Tip: There's a €70 "menu d'affaires," but the €180 "délice gastronomique" shows you really mean business.

Best Seafood Feasts

#85–87: Don't come to Paris without indulging in at least one of these slap-up seafood feasts. Multitiered platters are brought to the table laden with oysters, prawns, mussels, and sea urchins nestling on their bed of ice. Remember, though, for oysters, there must be an "r" in the current month for freshness (the rule works just as well in French).

La Coupole
102 bd. du Montparnasse, 14th, 01.43.20.14.20 • Classic

The Draw: The lively atmosphere at this bustling Art Deco brasserie in the heart of the Montparnasse action.

The Scene: Everybody from tourists from the Midwest to eccentric Montparnasse locals to movie stars loves La Coupole. The huge hall glints with chrome and mirrors, and waiters perform their ballet of maneuvers, while bearing aloft the festive platters. *Daily 8:30am-10:30pm.* €€

Hot Tip: The glassed-in terrace is where Parisians sit and allows you to avoid having to wait in line.

La Mascotte
52 rue des Abbesses, 18th, 01.46.06.28.15 • Classic

The Draw: This locals' spot draws a colorful crowd you'd only find in Paris.

The Scene: Noisy, smoky, and totally eccentric, La Mascotte is home to a cast of regulars who were probably the dandiest people in town in the '60s. They hold court from the dining room and the bar, sometimes breaking into song. Seafood and Sancerre and alcoholic sundaes are the order of the day. *Tue-Sun noon-3pm and 7-11pm. Bar 7am-midnight.* €

Hot Tip: Great for a winter Sunday lunch.

La Méditerranée
2 pl. de l'Odéon, 6th, 01.43.26.02.30 • Classic

The Draw: Artists' murals and Riviera atmosphere.

The Scene: In the heart of St-Germain, La Méditerranée draws a relaxed, older crowd of intellectuals, publishers, and art dealers for its sunny ambiance and great fish cooking. Artwork by Vertès, Bérard, and Cocteau decorate the walls and the plates. *Daily noon-2:30pm and 7:30-11pm.* €€

Hot Tip: Start with oysters and follow with royal sea bream or Marseillaise bouillabaisse fish soup.

See-and-Be-Seen Clubs

#88–90: Cannes has got nothing on the attitude at these Paris clubs, where the rich show off their plastic surgery like it's a new Ferrari. Happily, being foreign pays off here, and talking loudly in English may convince the guest-list queens you're really someone.

L'Etoile*
12 rue de Presbourg, 16th, 01.45.00.78.70 • Hot & Cool

The Draw: A-listers are never cordoned off here as everyone who gets in is a VIP.

The Scene: Even the bouncers are more like male models at the entrance to this townhouse on the Etoile; once inside, you'll discover the place is a stage for showing off. Those who haven't got the looks have definitely got the yacht. Celebrity birthdays are celebrated in the restaurant. *Mon-Fri noon-3pm and 8pm-1am, Sat 8pm-1am. Lounge bar from midnight Thu-Sat. Club from 11pm Tue-Sat.*

Hot Tip: The door is more relaxed in August, but the crowd is less scintillating.

Le Néo
23 rue de Ponthieu, 8th, 01.42.25.57.14 • Hot & Cool

The Draw: The very select fashion and celebrity clientele and über-cool black disco décor.

The Scene: Hollywood stars when in town, Dior fashion boys, and top models decorate the black leather crystal-studded banquettes and black marble dance floor of this intimate private club. The Sunday tea dance gathers up the most beautiful and best-dressed gay clubbers in Paris. *Tue-Sat midnight-6am, Sun gay tea dance 9pm-2am.*

Hot Tip: Dressing fashionably à la John Galliano will work wonders at the door.

La Suite*
40 av. George V, 8th, 01.53.57.49.49 • Hot & Cool

The Draw: Reality TV stars, models, heiresses, and wannabes bop the night away at Cathy Guetta's kitsch-to-the-max night spot.

The Scene: See or be seen? For the former, dine in the Penthouse Suite with its view over Avenue George V; for the latter, strut your stuff in the bar while nonchalantly watching Fashion TV on the screens dotted around. Like crowds at a cotton candy stall, which is one of the inspirations for this pink-bedecked club, the patrons just can't wait to get past the door to sample the eye-candy here. It's crushed, but at least these people use expensive cologne. *Restaurant Mon-Fri 12:30pm-3pm and 8:30-11pm, Sat-Sun 8:30-11pm. Bar Mon-Wed 8pm-2am, Thu-Sat 8pm-5am.*

Hot Tip: Booking a table in the restaurant ensures your stairway to pink heaven.

Spas

#91–93: It takes effort for French women to look so polished. In the fabulously luxurious spas of the top hotels it's not unusual to cross paths with the likes of Catherine Deneuve benefiting from the exquisite pampering treatments on offer. A new trend is the contemporary day spas offering treatments culled from around the world.

L'Espace Bien-Etre at the Meurice
Hôtel Meurice, 228 rue de Rivoli, 1st, 01.44.58.10.77 • Romantic

The Draw: Specializes in Caudalie treatments using grape seed extracts to combat free radicals.

The Scene: Many top models swear by the anti-aging properties of Caudalie, which was scientifically developed in Bordeaux. This calming contemporary spa is designed around a small vineyard and has a beautiful marble Jacuzzi overlooking the garden area. *Daily 7:30am-10pm; treatments 9am-8pm. €€€€*

Hot Tip: Reserve 24 hours in advance for the Pulp Friction massage, which uses fresh grapes.

Le Spa at the Four Seasons George V
Four Seasons Hôtel George V, 31 av. George V, 8th, 01.49.52.72.10 • Classic

The Draw: Luxurious surroundings of marble and toile de Jouy and a private suite for treatments à deux.

The Scene: Screen stars, couture clients, and well-groomed gentlemen book in for the delectable skin and body treatments using Fresh and Anne Sémonin preparations. The private treatment rooms are lulled by soft classical music. *Open for non-guests Mon-Fri 10am-4pm; for guests daily 6:30am-10pm. €€€€*

Hot Tip: Chocolate body scrubs, wraps, and massages pamper body and soul come autumn.

Spa Nuxe 32 Montorgueil
32 rue Montorgueil, 1st, 01.55.80.71.40 • Hot & Cool

The Draw: This cool contemporary day spa is in a stunning space and uses Nuxe's excellent plant-based products.

The Scene: Vanessa Paradis and Audrey Tautou are among the celebrity clients of this new beauty space offering hairdressing, beauty treatments, and massage on two floors. A stream runs through the 4,000-square-foot former wine warehouse, where exposed stone walls combine with concrete, steel, and relaxing soft lighting. *Mon, Tue, and Sat 9am-7:30pm, Wed-Fri 9am-9pm. €€€€*

Hot Tip: In need of an instant lift to sparkle tonight? Try the Soin Eclat Immédiat using aquatic plants and flowers.

Best

Statuary

#94–96: No wonder the French are such a sensual bunch, when even a walk in the park means you are surrounded by writhing bodies, marble goddesses, and heroic physiques. Here's where to find some of the most unabashedly over-the-top statuary.

Jardin des Tuileries
Rue de Rivoli, 1st • Hot & Cool

The Draw: Five centuries of statuary people the Tuileries with heroes, villains, and dreamy nudes.

The Scene: Statues seem to spring upon you as you stroll through the Tuileries' avenues of trees. Dramatic rearing horses, heroes battling wild animals, and writhing river gods are all near the fountain, while modern sculptures by Moore, Ernst, Giacometti, and Dubuffet hide in the woodland walkways. Check out too the Jardin du Carrousel near the Louvre with 18 huge nudes by Maillol. *Daily 7:30am. Closes 7:30pm-midnight depending on the season.*

Hot Tip: If you're lucky enough to be in Paris when it snows, drop whatever you're doing and race to the Tuileries with your camera to capture the surreal beauty of these statues in snow before the authorities shut the park.

Musée du Louvre
Rue de Rivoli, 1st, 01.40.20.50.50 • Classic

The Draw: The magnificent Marly horseback statues are housed in a specially created glass-roofed gallery, the Cour Marly.

The Scene: Light pours into the sandstone courtyard where Cousteau's two enormous rearing horses and Coysevox's horseback *Fame and Mercury* dwarf awestruck visitors. The statues were each hewn from a single gigantic block of marble. Another highlight is the Italian sculpture gallery in the Denon Wing, with Michelangelo's slaves and the *Winged Victory of Samothrace*. *Wed-Mon 9am-6pm, Wed, Fri 9am-9:45pm.* €–

Hot Tip: Follow brown wall signs to locate the famous highlights.

Musée Rodin
77 rue de Varenne, 7th, 01.44.18.61.10 • Romantic

The Draw: Masterworks by France's greatest sculptor are arranged around the house and garden where he lived.

The Scene: While copies are scattered around the world, all the greats are here in one place: *The Kiss, Cathedral, Walking Man,* and the lovely *Danaïde* inside, and *The Burghers of Calais, Gates of Hell, Orpheus,* and *The Thinker* in the enchanting garden. *Tue-Sun 9:30am-5:45pm, Oct.-Mar. 9:30am-4:45pm. Gardens: 9:30am-6:45pm (summer).* €–

Hot Tip: The best time to appreciate its sights and smells is after a rainfall.

Vodka Cocktails

#97-99: Whether it's a perfect martini or a fruity of-the-moment concoction, Paris' elite bartenders are currently mixing magic with the purest spirit of them all. *Santé!*

Le Bar at the George V
Four Seasons Hôtel George V, 31 av. George V, 8th, 01.49.52.70.00 • Hot & Cool

The Draw: Did the beautiful young things or the colored martinis come first? Whichever way, the combination makes this sultry hotel bar cocktail heaven.

The Scene: The gilded youth of the 8th arrondissement comes late to this luxurious English-style bar with its leather chairs and sofas. The unique flavored martinis are served in individual cocktail shakers, shaken at your table, and poured into cone-shaped stemless glasses that stay icy cold wedged into their beds of ice. *Sun-Fri 10am-1am, Sat 10am-2am.*

Hot Tip: The decadent Purple Martini flavored with violet and cassis liqueurs is a rare wonder.

Le Bar du Plaza
Hôtel Plaza Athénée, 25 av. Montaigne, 8th, 01.53.67.66.00 • Hot & Cool

The Draw: The most see-and-be-seen of any hotel bar, the Plaza thrills the fashion crowd with cocktail innovations.

The Scene: Sexy singles and fashion luminaries pose at the ice-cool illuminated bar or lounge in the leather chairs under works of art. Cocktails are often whipped up with fresh fruit coulis and served with designer nibbles. Try the Royal Martini, made with vodka, raspberry liqueur, and a purée of red fruits. *Daily 6pm-2am.*

Hot Tip: Order a side plate of vodka jellies, which look like sweets but are deceptively wicked.

Murano Bar
Murano Urban Resort, 13 bd. du Temple, 3rd, 01.42.71.20.00 • Hot & Cool

The Draw: This temple to vodka has 150 varieties as shots and a range of explosive cocktails.

The Scene: Live DJs playing lounge, groove, and R&B and '70s pop art décor set the funky scene at this hot hotel bar, where the long vodka bar fills up pre-dinner and after 10pm with a rock-chic crowd. Try the Pa Pa Paa, a mixture of puréed strawberries, strawberry liqueur, white chocolate liqueur, and strawberry vodka. *Daily 7am-2am.*

Hot Tip: Live jazz on Tuesday nights.

EXPERIENCE PARIS

Dive into the Paris of your choice with one of four themed itineraries: *Hot & Cool* (p.50), *Classic* (p.84), *Bobo* (p.116), and *Romantic* (p.148). Each is designed to heighten your experience by putting you in the right place at the right time—the best restaurants, nightlife, and attractions, and even the best days to go there. While the itineraries, each followed by detailed descriptions of our top choices, reflect our very top picks, the listings include a number of additional noteworthy options. So, whether you're looking to indulge in a decadent meal at one of Paris' top restaurants or hit the dance floor late into the night, you'll find it all right here.

Hot & Cool Paris

The March and October Fashion Weeks are when Hot & Cool Paris reaches its hysterical high. Models, designers, and celebrity clients pack the sceniest bars, nibble at salads in the hottest restaurants, and flit from party to party, making the swanky 8th arrondissement feel like one big after-show. The downside is that all the hotels and restaurants are booked and there isn't a taxi in sight. So, if you're not a model and not likely to befriend one before the collections, here's the fast track to what's newly hot and genetically cool. We've checked out the latest addresses, kept our ear to the ground for the gossip, and sussed out the door policy so you can just swan in as if you own the place. Pack your glad rags and your gold card, because glamour is the name of the game.

Note: Venues in bold in the itinerary are described in detail in the listings that follow. Venues followed by an * asterisk are those we recommend as both a restaurant and a destination bar.

Hot & Cool Paris:
The Perfect Plan (3 Days and Nights)

Your Hotel: Murano Urban Resort, whose location, long vodka bar, and rooms bathed in any color you like, is pulling the youngest, most gorgeous crowd of any five-star hotel.

Thursday

Highlights

Thursday
Morning	Musée Picasso
Lunch	Café Baci
Afternoon	Marais, La Bulle Kenzo
Cocktails	Kong*
Dinner	Georges
Nighttime	Costes*
Late-Night	Le Cab

Friday
Breakfast	Les Deux Magots
Morning	St-Germain
Lunch	Emporio Armani Caffé
Afternoon	Musée d'Orsay
Cocktails	Jardin Plein Ciel
Dinner	Bon
Nighttime	Pershing Lounge*
Late-Night	VIP Room

Saturday
Breakfast	Le Village
Morning	Faubourg St-Honoré
Lunch	Le Cristal Room
Afternoon	Musée Baccarat
Cocktails	Le Bar at the George V
Dinner	Café de l'Homme
Nighttime	La Suite*
Late-Night	Music Hall*

The Morning After
Morning	Jardin des Tuileries
Brunch	Les Orchidées

10am After a light breakfast at your hotel, celebrate your arrival with a visit to the Marais. The **Musée Picasso**, in a beautiful *hôtel particulier* (mansion house) located in the heart of this neighborhood, is filled with paintings and sculptures covering the whole of Picasso's career.

Noon Check what's on at the **Maison Européenne de la Photographie**, which runs wide-ranging exhibitions.

1pm Lunch Snag a table for lunch at one of the Marais' hottest new cafés, **Café Baci**, for some Italian antipasti under Murano chandeliers. If you're longing to get out on a café terrace and eat French food, check out the posey, predominantly gay lunch scene at **Les Marronniers**.

3pm Afterward, take a walk around the Marais' charming and narrow 17th-century streets filled with fashion, jewelry, and houseware boutiques, especially along the rue des Francs-Bourgeois, not forgetting to dip into its many accessible private galleries. Wrap up your walking tour with a spin around the beautiful Place des Vosges, one of the city's loveliest squares.

5pm If you feel a slump coming on at this stage, we hope you'll have planned ahead and booked a massage at **La Bulle Kenzo** at the Kenzo flagship store. Even if you haven't, try to line up a siesta in one of its "bulles"—the bubble-like treatment rooms. Relaxing images and music soothe you and herbal tea awaits when you awake.

7pm After your massage, levitate one floor up to the manga-inspired restaurant **Kong*** for your first cocktail of the trip, with a view of the Pont Neuf.

8pm Make your way to the **Centre Pompidou** to check out a Pollock and a Rothko or two before dinner—the galleries are open until 9pm and sometimes midnight.

9pm Dinner Once you've had your fill of art, head up to the buzzing **Georges** on the 6th floor, which continues to pull the in-crowd; in summer, be sure to get a table on the terrace. Alternatively, this could be the night to dine at the **Murano**. This is a see-and-be-seen scene to the max, bubbling over with an excitable crowd talking over the DJ-spun lounge music. For a more baroque experience that draws the best of the fashion crowd, settle in at the trendy **Costes***.

11pm Sparkling company is guaranteed after dinner at both **Costes*** and the **Murano Bar**. Secrete yourself in the black velvet bar at the former, keeping an eye out for Kate Moss, or experiment with flavored vodkas at the latter.

1am It's time to hit the club scene. If dancing is what you're after, head to nightclub **Le Cab**. If lounging is really what you'd rather be doing, head to **La Cantine du Faubourg*** and chill with beautiful people till 4am.

Friday

9:30am This morning it's all about Left Bank chic. St-Germain, famous for beatniks and jazz, is now an upscale fashion hub. Get your bearings over breakfast on the terrace to end all terraces—that of **Les Deux Magots**.

10:30am You may have spotted some fabulous footwear on the parade that passes you by: go search for it in the boutiques of rue de Grenelle and rue des Sts-Pères. All the big designer names are here, while rue de Seine is packed with art galleries. Before lunch, you might have time to fit in a look at the **Fondation Cartier**'s contemporary art gallery.

1pm Lunch Designers, models, and film stars lunch at **Emporio Armani Caffé**, above the St-Germain Emporio store, where you can also browse the latest fashion press. Or, if following food rather than fashion trends is what moves you, get in line for the sensational French tapas at **L'Atelier de Joël Robuchon**.

3pm You might want to select a cultural activity from another itinerary here. Stay on the Left Bank for the Impressionists at the Musée d'Orsay; or, at the other end of the spectrum, check out the ground-breaking installations (and the concept shop) at the Palais de Tokyo.

5pm Relax and gear up for the evening with a health-giving treatment at the fashionable **Spa Nuxe 32 Montorgueil**.

7:30pm Drink a cocktail with the stars at the exclusive **Jardin Plein Ciel** bar on the top of the Hôtel Raphael, or the sophisticated, of-the-moment **Bar du Plaza**.

9pm Dinner Dress to impress for any of tonight's dinner options, where both the setting and the company are spectacular. **Bon** is the hot rendezvous of the moment for TV producers, starlets, and upscale professionals. If you want to try Paris' high-echelon gastronomy with a fashionable crowd, choose **Alain Ducasse au Plaza Athénée**. From its chandeliers to the chic waiters' garb to the truffle-rich menu, this is one of the ultimate Paris experiences. Or compare yachts with the St-Tropez set at **L'Etoile***, whose dining room looks out on the Arc de Triomphe.

11:30pm Stay on at **L'Etoile*** as the dance floor heats up and owner Tony Gomez's celebrity friends drop in. A younger crowd congregates at the seductive **Pershing Lounge*** with its vertical garden. Lovers should book a table on the balcony; singles mingle in the two lounges behind it.

1am Dance till dawn at the swanky, celeb-infested **VIP Room**, or show off your moves at the grande dame of clubs, the legendary **Le Queen**, on the Champs-Elysées.

Saturday

9:30am A pair of Chanel sunglasses is essential, not just to hide your hangover but for the terrace scene at the newest Costes spot, **Le Village**, where you'll be very visibly having breakfast.

11am You are ideally situated for checking out the St-Honoré shopping district. Among the designer shops, getting progressively more exclusive as you go west, is essential port-of-call **Colette**. If you're not in the spending mood, see what high-fashion creations are on display at the **Musée de la Mode et du Textile**.

1pm Lunch Congratulate yourself if you've secured a table at **Le Cristal Room**, as Baccarat's restaurant is one of Paris' most popular addresses. Otherwise try the restaurant that revolutionized the French food scene, Ducasse's **Spoon, Food & Wine**.

3pm Even if you didn't eat here, the **Musée Baccarat** is not to be missed. Here, Philippe Starck has created a fantasy showcase for Baccarat's crystal collections. While in this area fashion fans can pay homage to their patron saint at the **Fondation Pierre Bergé Yves Saint Laurent** in the designer's former couture house. From modern to ancient artifice is only a block away at the **Musée des Arts Asiatiques-Guimet**. This airy museum displays a breathtaking collection of Asian art, including the Giant's Way from Angkor Wat.

7pm After the visual overload, sink into one of the leather armchairs at **Le Bar at the George V** and wait for your cocktail to be brought to you on a silver platter.

8:30pm Dinner Never mind if you haven't been up the Eiffel Tower yet—tonight she'll be sparkling just for you on the terrace of **Café de l'Homme**. You may find yourself distracted too by the fabulous fauna at this maximum-glamour location. The same might be said of **Maison Blanche**, where beautiful people gaze nonchalantly out at the rooftop view of Paris by night. If you prefer Rive Gauche, join the select crowd at the **Café de l'Esplanade** overlooking the Esplanade des Invalides.

Midnight Pull out all the stops for a last-night party at **La Suite***, the candy-colored boudoir of upscale clubbing supremos the Guettas. Or try to get through the exclusive door of **Le Néo**. Gay clubbers should not miss the scene at **Les Bains Douches**. A different mood is found in the drinking den **Mathi's Bar**, where French film stars like to relax.

3am Luxury snacks can be had at **Music Hall***, an ideal last port of call before sinking into those crisp white sheets.

The Morning After

Revive yourself with a stroll through the **Jardin des Tuileries**. Then join the stylish, black-clad crowd for the best brunch in Paris at **Les Orchidées**. Raise a glass of Champagne to the next time.

Hot & Cool Paris:
The Key Neighborhoods

In the **1st arrondissement**, hot gets even hotter on the smart rue St-Honoré, where Hôtel Costes and the concept store Colette are the first ports of call for fashionistas, while rue Montorgueil in the fashion manufacturing district is sprouting day spas and designer boutiques.

The northeast of the **Marais (3rd** and **4th arrondissements)** is the newest area to merit attention. The southern part of this enclave of 17th-century mansions and narrow, winding streets has long been popular and is filled with gay bars and kitsch boutiques, but a chicer scene has opened up around the Murano Urban Resort, whose bar and restaurant are hot for the fashion and new media crowd.

The itinerary also takes in the hot spots in the **6th arrondissement** the Left Bank, centering around the designer names and celebrity-spotting tables of St-Germain, which left Existentialism behind when Dior moved in. And aren't we glad!

The **8th arrondissement** is the BMW-cruising, Versace-wearing, martini-sipping glamour zone that spills out from the Champs-Elysées. Never mind the tourists gawping at the Arc de Triomphe—you are here to wrap those perfectly manicured fingers around a cocktail at one of the hotel bars that cluster here, and to flash your gold card in the luxury boutiques of the "Golden Triangle" carved out by avenue George V and avenue Montaigne.

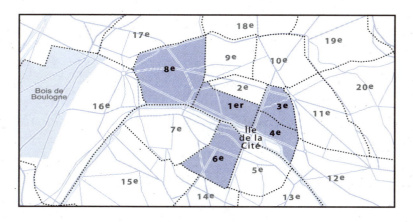

Hot & Cool Paris: The Shopping Blocks

The Marais

Rue des Rosiers and rue des Francs-Bourgeois are full of trendsetting French and foreign designers, while rues Charlot, Poitou, and the upper part of Vieille-du-Temple have emerging fashion names, contemporary design, and retro furniture.

A-Poc Issey Miyake's lab-style boutique where rolls of tubular cloth are cut to form apparel. 47 rue des Francs-Bourgeois (M° St-Paul), 01.44.54.07.05

Barbara Bui Understated, beautifully cut separates to make a statement in the workplace. 43 rue des Francs Bourgeois (M° St-Paul), 01.44.59.94.06

Martin Grant Womenswear designer favored by Cate Blanchett and Lauren Hutton. 44 rue Vieille-du-Temple (M° St-Paul), 01.42.71.39.49

Pressing Shop The hottest designs from the menswear collections for a preened clientele. 13 rue du Roi-de-Sicile (M° St-Paul), 01.40.29.16.96

St-Germain

International fashion names have colonized this area, mainly along the rue de Grenelle. Rue des Sts-Pères boasts the trio of lingerie, perfume, and chocolate.

Iris Iris' minimalist white store stocks only five labels, but they are top of the line. 28 rue de Grenelle (M° St-Germain-des-Prés), 7th, 01.42.22.89.81

Pierre Marcolini A chocolatier who has become the fashionistas' darling. 89 rue de Seine (M° Mabillon), 01.44.07.39.07

Vanessa Bruno Popular sequined bags and sleek separates. 25 rue St-Sulpice (M° Mabillon), 01.43.54.41.04

Vannina Vesperini Exquisite lingerie. 63 rue des Sts-Pères (M° St-Germain-des-Prés), 01.42.84.37.62

Rue St-Honoré

One of Paris' ultimate fashion stops, it moves from established big names on rue du Fbg. St-Honoré to a hotter, younger scene on rue St-Honoré and rue Cambon.

Colette The world-famous concept store is hot for everything from iPods to eyewear. (p.79) 213 rue St-Honoré (M° Tuileries), 01.55.35.33.90

Fifi Chachnil Froufrou lingerie in the '50s pinup style. 231 rue St-Honoré (M° Tuileries), 01.42.61.21.83

Maria Luisa Buyer with an eye for rising stars stocks Galliano and McQueen. (p.81) Main store 2 rue Cambon (M° Concorde), 01.47.03.48.08

Oscar Carvallo Venezuelan designer who shows his sizzling creations in a red and black boutique. 10 Rue Cambon (M° Concorde), 01.40.20.12.13

Hot & Cool Paris:
The Hotels

Esprit St-Germain • 6th • Trendy (31 rms)
Behind a discreet entrance is one of St-Germain's newest boutique hotels, whose cool style has a bit of an edge, with changing mood lights and chilled hip-hop playing in the lobby. To the left of the minimalist reception (one man standing behind a tiny box who whips out a laptop to check you in) is the comfortable bar, candlelit in the evenings, where guests can feel at home as they help themselves to free drinks and a novel. This spirit of home-away-from-home is exactly what owner Laurence Tafanel was looking for when she set out to create the perfect hotel drawn from her own travels. All-pervading calm is what you'll find in the rooms, with a chic décor of taupe, gray, mauve, and beige, in textures of velvet, suede, and leather. As the hotel was created out of an 18th-century building, many of the rooms have character. The magnificent beamed suite, Prestige room 502 with a terrace overlooking St-Sulpice, and 404, with its funky leopard-skin carpet, are highlights. Breakfast is taken in your room or the vaulted breakfast room. There is a small fitness room, with a sauna and hammam that can be privately booked, on the top floor overlooking the rooftops.
€€ 22 rue St-Sulpice (M° Mabillon), 01.53.10.55.55, espritsaintgermain.com

Hôtel Costes • 1st • Trendy (82 rms)
The jewel in the crown of the Costes brothers' empire is still pulling in the A-list over a decade after it opened. It's easy to see why: the décor is drop-dead gorgeous, and seemingly acres of space have been given over to socializing in what feels like an aristocrat's home that's a cross between Marrakech and Tuscany. Around the courtyard filled with tables is a little velvet-and-damask lounge with the reception desk at one end, a library, Colonnades bar, and two sexy nighttime bars. One perk is that you can eat or drink downstairs at any time of the day or night. Filled at all hours with a fashion-conscious crowd, it's not for shrinking violets, but the rooms are cozy hideaways. TVs and minibars seem incongruous in rooms with old-fashioned décor—damask fabrics, antique desks, and 19th-century portraits. The ten first-floor rooms with private, leafy terraces are the first to go, but Classic room 206 is attractive, with its own entrance hall and a draped curtain over the bed, as is De Luxe 410, with a view into a secret courtyard. In the basement is Paris' most beautiful pool, 65 feet long and candlelit, with loungers separated by muslin drapes. Costes' famous soundtrack plays throughout, except in the rooms. €€€€ 239 rue St-Honoré (M° Tuileries), 01.42.44.50.00, hotelcostes.com

Hôtel Costes K • 16th • Trendy (83 rms)
The sister to neo-rococo Costes is the antithesis of its design ethos: icy-cool, minimalist, zen. Its reputation for steely coolness seems unfounded, however—as the staff are both welcoming and helpful. The creation of Spanish postmodernist Ricardo Bofill, it oozes calm, and the hush-hush extends to its antihype approach: no website, little press—it's more like a private club whose address travels by word of mouth. Actors, advertising and film people, top lawyers, and financiers can be seen lounging on the designer leather sofas in the light-filled

lobby/bar, where you can snack on a typical Costes menu of Caesars and beef tartare and browse design magazines. Dotted around the hotel are pieces of contemporary furniture, which form part of Jean-Louis Costes' private collection. One of Costes K's great pluses is the size of its rooms, which are huge by Paris standards, with queen-size beds even in the singles. All have a leather window seat, and Deluxe rooms have a walk-in closet and separate shower. At 375 square feet, Deluxe room 326 feels like a suite. Its seating area is arranged around the curved window, which, though street-side, is quite peaceful. The hotel's gym has two rooms of cardiovascular apparatus, a yoga studio, and a wonderful black pool, which can be turned into a huge Jacuzzi and is floodlit at night until 9pm. €€€ 81 av. Kléber (M° Trocadéro), 01.44.05.75.75

Hôtel Montalembert • 7th • Trendy (56 rms)

Originally the home of the Left Bank literati, the Montalembert has managed to keep its intellectual reputation while becoming very chic indeed. There is a very Left Bank type of sophistication about its comfort: like St-Germain itself, it doesn't have to prove itself anymore, which is why fashion editors prefer to congregate here. Look around the eternally fashionable bar, chilled by a soft jazz soundtrack, and you'll see a wonderful mix of old St-Germain types, fashion designers, publishers, and stylish international travelers. The library area, behind an Art Deco screen with a real fire roaring in winter, is a cozy spot to have a cocktail. A menu of simple dishes is available all day and there's a lovely street-side terrace. When the hotel was redecorated, a few rooms retained their Louis Philippe–style furniture, but go for one of the modern ones, which are far more stylish. Their uncluttered taupe and beige furnishings and dreamy black-and-white photographs of Paris say "relax"—even the high-tech elements are hidden from view. Rooms higher up in the building are the best, as they benefit most from the light flooding in through plentiful windows. The small Junior suite 82 in the eaves is charming, with a double terrace view of the Eiffel Tower, Invalides, and rooftops making it the ultimate luxury Paris garret. €€€ 3 rue de Montalembert (M° Rue du Bac), 01.45.49.68.68, montalembert.com

Hôtel Plaza Athénée • 8th • Grand (188 rms)

Chosen for *Sex and the City*'s Paris dénouement, and by couture clients during the collections (you can watch fashion TV on a four-foot-wide screen in your suite), the Plaza oozes glamour. Despite the stunning cocktail bar, which looks like a huge block of ice, there is still something roaring '20s about the hotel with its red awnings and the piano-tinkling decadence of the Galerie des Gobelins. Indeed, the hotel's second restaurant, the Relais, is still decked out in pink Lalique crystal, as it was in Josephine Baker's day. It's worth paying extra for a Deluxe with 430 square feet of luxury with a seating area. Be sure to ask for one overlooking the ivy-walled Cour Jardin. Sumptuous fabrics in pastel tones, antique furniture, and paneling make these feel like a mini-apartment. All the rooms are in classic 19th-century salon style, with the exception of one wing of Art Deco suites decorated with reissues of original 1930s fabrics and Dior fashion sketches. One has its own terrace with a view of the Eiffel Tower. Eiffel Tower views are also found in some of the other suites. Small touches include Diptyque candles in the rooms, so you can take home the scent of your stay. The Plaza's bar and Alain Ducasse restaurant are among the top addresses in the city, and Prada, Dior, and Vuitton are but a skip away. €€€€ 25 av. Montaigne (M° Alma-Marceau), 01.53.67.66.65, plaza-athenee-paris.com

Hôtel de Sers • 8th • Trendy (52 rms)
The Vidalenc cousins, Thibault and Thomas, are set to be the next Costes. When Thibault's mother handed over the management of the former Hôtel Elizabeth II, he transformed the 19th-century mansion and made it smoking hot. Architect Thomas has made the most of an architectural playground—he also designed some of the cool, Scandinavian-style made-to-measure furniture. Walls were knocked down to create rooms and suites with enfilade, allowing guests to move from bedroom through lobby/bar through lounge through bathroom. Mirrors are strategically placed to give an impression of even more space. The brilliance of the décor is in the way it mixes old and new: a wrought-iron spiral staircase in a minimalist lobby; 19th-century portraits hung over Eames-inspired armchairs; a funky Missoni fabric on a Third Empire chair. The two suites are magnificent, one with a double balcony and the other with a large deck that can be opened out to make the skylit salon one outdoor room and party on the rooftops. Both have an unbeatable view extending from the Eiffel Tower to Sacré-Coeur. There's a sauna, hammam, and mini-gym, and a courtyard restaurant packed with trendsters. If the suites are booked, get a 320-square-foot Deluxe room on the fourth floor with an Eiffel Tower view. €€€ 41 av. Pierre-1er-de-Serbie (M° George V), 01.53.23.75.75, hotel-de-sers.com

Hôtel Sezz • 16th • Trendy (27 rms)
Passy is Paris at its most pearls and poodles, but behind closed doors all is not what it seems. With a wink at Bertolucci's *Last Tango in Paris,* filmed in this very street, this realm of cool modernity is somewhere between a science fiction fantasy and a zen architect's bedroom. The glass doors open and you are greeted by a walkie-talkie–carrying personal assistant in a *Star Trek*–ish designer black tracksuit who whisks you to a pod seating booth in the bar. A cocktail appears. This is check-in, and in addition to allocating your room, your PA will attempt to garner all sorts of personal information about you, which he enters into a PDA with the aim of catering to your every need. The impression that you are actually in *The Matrix* continues as you progress to your room. The walls are slatey concrete slabs, the bathrooms real slate, and beds are placed bang in the middle of the room, facing a flat-screen TV. Most extraordinarily, some of the bathrooms are separated from the bedroom by only a wall of glass, so there are no secrets here if you are checking in with a date. Room 72 has a double bath where you can lie in yin and yang formation. 69 and 75 have Eiffel Tower views, but our favorite is spacious single room 62 with its own curved balcony. Room service serves such delights as Petrossian caviar and sushi. €€ 6 av. Frémiet (M° Passy), 01.56.75.26.26, hotelsezz.com

Murano Urban Resort • 3rd • Trendy (52 rms)
Pundits were divided as to whether this hotel would be a hit when it opened in 2004, so new was its formula to the Paris scene. Would those who can afford five-star drop the luxury of Louis XVI furniture and white-aproned chambermaids in the 8th in favor of rock-star chic just off République? It's now clear it has made its mark, both in terms of its A-list bar and restaurant and its fabulous rooms, which fill up quickly with fashion, media, and music business professionals. The lobby features a stretch-limo of a white leather Chesterfield facing an equally elongated real-effect fire. The rooms are entered by fingerprint technology, and designed for as much fun as you dare indulge in. The white walls can be any color you want: from the bed, you program electronic lighting accord-

ing to your mood. Huge flowers are printed on some of the furniture, while chairs are based on '60s molded design, and a Warhol-style portrait of a 20th-century icon is the focus of each room. In the slate bathrooms is a kit of gizmos to spice up your love life. While the 645-square-foot Murano Suite is the ultimate luxury with its own small swimming pool, all the rooms are equipped with similar décor, lighting, and accessories. The best non-suite is the Angelo, with a raised bed under a portrait of Marilyn Monroe. €€€ 13 bd. du Temple (M° Filles du Calvaire), 01.42.71.20.00, muranoresort.com

Park Hyatt Paris Vendôme • 2nd • Modern (177 rms)

This Park Hyatt prides itself on being Paris' first contemporary palace hotel. You'll find discreet, not ostentatious, luxury here, which is why publicity-shy stars such as Sting, Janet Jackson, and Isabelle Adjani prefer it, arriving by the secret back entrance. So reassured are they by the coolness of the staff and setting that you're more than likely to see A-listers lounging about the lobby and bar. The whole ground floor is lined with pale French limestone. As you enter through silently opening doors, you are greeted by the two concierges in their tailcoats. Sweep through the polished enfilade peppered with black-clad guests and staff to find the check-in at the end. With expert feng shui, the cloistered area, inner bar, and chic Les Orchidées restaurant are all arranged around a courtyard where you can eat in fine weather. There are two categories of non-suite rooms, differing mainly in size, from the smallest, at 230 square feet, to the Deluxe category, at 430 square feet, which has a separate dressing area. Decorated in warm shades of brown and prune with rich mahogany panels, sculptures, and mood-enhancing lighting, the rooms also have spacious limestone bathrooms with under-floor heating and rain showers. A private spa sports the same cool look. €€€€ 5 rue de la Paix (M° Opéra), 01.58.71.12.34, paris.hyatt.com

Renaissance Paris Vendôme Hôtel • 1st • Trendy (97 rms)

This stylish hotel entered the scene quietly, but its inveterate chic has traveled through word of mouth. During fashion weeks it is chockablock with models, designers, and journalists, but even during such hectic periods, this hotel exudes warmth and serenity as staff in gray Nehru suits perform their duties with a smile. Everything is understated, from the Japanese and Art Deco–influenced décor to the discreet service to the teak and slate-walled 60-foot-long pool that is one of the gems of Paris. Under a glass skylight, comfortable sofas greet you in the lounge lobby, which is enhanced by orchids and bamboo artfully arranged in Chinese ginger jars. To the right is the library, where you can peruse newspapers and photography books around a fire. The four ground-floor Prestige rooms, 001 to 004, are exceptional, with their own private garden terraces for breakfasting under large sunshades. All the rooms are superbly decorated with pale or dark wood, honey- and tobacco-colored textiles, sandstone bathrooms, and flat-screen TVs. The discreet, contemporary Pinxo restaurant is a favorite with stars and politicians. The Chinese bar is also a treasure. €€€€ 4 rue du Mont Thabor (M° Tuileries), 01.40.20.20.00, plazaparisvendome.com

Hot & Cool Paris: The Restaurants

Alain Ducasse au Plaza Athénée • 8th • Gastronomic
Best Fine Dining Designer-clad staff form a guard of honor outside, and only those with reservations are admitted. Once inside, the theater commences. Patrick Jouin has redone the décor in a spirit of "magic and poetry": the chandeliers are surrounded by a cloud of 10,000 loose crystal drops that seem to float in the air. Instead of entrée, plat, dessert, one selects from specialties, which feature crustaceans and black truffles, or the less pricey (though we're still talking €80 for asparagus) Pleasures of the Table, seasonal dishes using the very best French produce. Ducasse strikes a balance between informality and grand hotel dining, attracting not just gastronomes and the rich but younger trendsetters out to celebrate a deal or impress a date. *Mon-Wed 7:45-10:15pm, Thu-Fri 12:45-2:15pm and 7:45-10:15pm.* €€€€ Hôtel Plaza Athénée, 25 av. Montaigne (M° Alma-Marceau), 01.53.67.65.00, alain-ducasse.com

Apollo • 14th • Trendy
A see-and-be-seen crowd gravitates to Apollo as soon as the first rays of sun appear, as its large terrace is a prime spot to show off your new Guccis. The restaurant is located in the 1846 pavilion that also houses an RER station. Inside, sunlight floods in from the high windows onto a loft-like space. Around the walls are convex mirrors, color-coded installations of plastic paraphernalia, and white leatherette banquettes. The modern brasserie menu has a light, healthy aspect with lots of raw food (sushi, tuna steaks, and salads), and baby spring vegetables bursting with flavor. A lunch menu attracts a chic Left Bank office crowd. In the evenings, a more glamorous crowd descends. *Daily noon-3pm and 8pm-midnight. Bar open all day until 2am.* €€ 3 pl. Denfert-Rochereau (M° Denfert-Rochereau), 01.45.38.76.77

L'Arpège • 7th • Gastronomic
Chef Alain Passard hit the headlines when he dared to pare down haute cuisine to a mere vegetable: a beetroot or potatoes at €60 apiece—was this a case of the Emperor's new clothes? Those who have tasted his cuisine swear it is alchemy, the minutiae of his cooking methods and artful use of aromatic herbs and seasoning revealing hitherto unknown flavors. The vegetables are not your run-of-the-mill market produce, but grown in organic conditions in a garden where horses plow the soil. There are luxury ingredients too: osciètre caviar, lobster, langoustine; red meat is eschewed in favor of poultry. The dining room has an undulating pearwood wall and discreet Lalique glass. It's a seriously foodie place, but if modern gastronomy is your pleasure, don't miss this experience. *Mon-Fri 12:30-2:30pm and 8-10:30pm.* €€€€ 84 rue de Varenne (M° Sèvres-Babylone), 01.47.05.09.06, alain-passard.com

L'Astrance • 16th • Gastronomic
This is as young and as sexy as haute cuisine gets. Pascal Barbot's aim in opening his split-level, silver-walled restaurant seating only 25 was to serve top-quality, creative food without stuffiness, and he quickly gained a fan club of urbane

diners. They come because Barbot's food is a trendsetter: his signature dishes appear months later on the menus of other restaurants. Fruits and earthy flavors are the grace notes of Barbot's cuisine. Try lobster with candied grapefruit peel, or pigeon with bilberry chutney and quince confit. Barbot's business partner combs the countryside for wine discoveries. In this intimate setting there is plenty of opportunity to chat with the dynamic duo. *Tue-Fri 12:15-1:45pm and 8:15-9:45pm.* €€€ 4 rue Beethoven (M° Passy), 01.40.50.84.40

L'Atelier de Joël Robuchon • 7th • Contemporary
Robuchon was the first chef to throw away his Michelin stars and reopen a few years later with this sensational gourmet tapas bar, drawing a more youthful, relaxed crowd. Diners perch on red leather stools at two counters, and the chefs work in an open kitchen. This promotes an informal, convivial atmosphere, equally good for lone diners or couples. The concept is the best of the world's cuisine, served simply. Skip the menu of entrées, plats, and desserts, and go for the tapas to sample an array of delicacies. Marinated anchovies with an eggplant confit and clams stuffed with garlic are among the mouthwatering specialties. You can only reserve for 11:30am and 6:30pm, so be prepared to wait if you come later—it's worth it. *Daily 12:30-3:30pm and 6:30pm-midnight.* €€ 5 rue de Montalembert (M° Rue du Bac), 01.42.22.56.56, robuchon.com

L'Avenue • 8th • Trendy
With a terrace jutting out into the Avenue Montaigne, this Costes-run brasserie offers maximum exposure for those who want to be seen. Indeed, it is difficult to differentiate between the model-like serving staff and the genuine runway gazelles who eat here. At lunch you may see the entire Dior staff and designers popping in for a bite; in the evening French TV stars and sports celebrities; and you can lounge around with a drink until 2am. The menu has clearly been devised with fashion people in mind as it's strong on salads and fish, and portions veer on minimalist, although you can order coarse-cut fries with your tuna steak. Service is efficient during the bustling lunchtime, making it a good choice in this area for a quick, light lunch. *Daily 8am-2am.* €€ 41 av. Montaigne (M° Alma-Marceau), 01.40.70.14.91

Bioboa • 1st • Trendy
Bio means organic in French, and this chic café has become the lunchtime cafeteria for the press attachés and shop assistants of this fashionable area. You order at the counter from a selection of dishes such as vegetable tagines, soups, and fat paninis filled with basil, Parma ham, mozzarella, and sun-dried tomatoes, and it comes to your table on a tray decorated with birds. The same bird life features in a mural on one wall of the otherwise white and minimalist interior with molded Eames-style chairs and pale wood tables. Health freaks can get their kick from Guarana fizz and other herbal pick-me-ups, although the place does a mean cup of organic coffee. *Mon-Sat 11am-6pm.* €– 3 rue Danielle Casanova (M° Pyramides), 01.42.61.17.67

Bon • 16th • Trendy
Best Of-the-Moment Dining Bon is bon again. The Philippe Starck–designed restaurant went through a slump, but has been rescued by the Flora Danica and Copenhague team, and so much the better, as the setting is fabulous. Entering the Belle Epoque pavilion, you are confronted by a silver quilted wall, mirrors,

bottles, and a conveyor-belt bar where you can enjoy sublime cocktails. The main, skylit dining room fills up toward 9:30pm with upscale professionals on a date, suave producers from Radio France entertaining their minions, and smart birthday parties taking advantage of the stunning private rooms. Couples should ask to be seated in the yellow leather alcove next to the rhinoceros' head. The menu is big on fish. Steer clear of Japanese hybrids—the Mediterranean dishes are better. *Mon-Fri noon-3pm and 8pm-midnight, Sat 8pm-midnight, Sun noon-4pm.* €€ 25 rue de la Pompe (M° La Muette), 01.40.72.70.00

Les Bouquinistes • 6th • Contemporary
With a gorgeous setting overlooking the Seine and the quayside booksellers from which it draws its name, this Guy Savoy satellite is popular with both tourists and intellectual Left Bankers—the antique dealers and publishers who work in the quarter. The room is bright and modern by day, while at night low lighting creates a more romantic atmosphere. Guy Savoy fills all his restaurants with the modern art he collects, and the paintings displayed on white walls give the impression of a gallery. The cooking is influenced by Savoy's own kitchen and a market-led prix fixe at lunch offers especially good value. The chilled tomato soup is a must for summer, as are the fluffy, fruity desserts, rounding out the expertly prepared fish and meat dishes. *Mon-Thu noon-2:30pm and 7-11pm, Fri noon-2:30pm and 7-11:30pm, Sat 7-11:30pm.* €€ 53 quai des Grands-Augustins (M° St-Michel), 01.43.25.45.94, lesbouquinistes.com

Cabaret • 1st • Trendy
The food at this club lounge is pretty good, combining Asian and Mediterranean influences. *See Le Cab in Hot & Cool Nightlife, p.74, for details.* €€ 2 pl. du Palais Royal (M° Palais Royal-Musée du Louvre), 01.58.62.56.25, cabaret.fr

Café Baci • 3rd • Trendy
This hot spot is at the center of the East Marais renaissance. Owned by actor and screenwriter Jean-Pierre Bacri, it is a favorite meeting place for his show-biz friends. Christian Lacroix likes to take his morning coffee here. Choose from the streetside terrace, high black tables, the back snug on the ground floor, or the upstairs dining room, more conducive to a dinner with friends. Huge black chandeliers and carnival prints are part of the cool décor and the pretty-boy waiters look the part. The menu of modern Italian food includes copious plates of antipasti, salads, and pasta dishes, with wines by the glass. *Daily 8am-2am.* € 36 rue de Turenne (M° St-Sébastien-Froissart), 01.42.71.36.70

Café de l'Esplanade • 7th • Trendy
You know the formula: rows of white-clothed terrace tables with maximum see-and-be-seen status; slim, beautiful servers with a haughty attitude; Jacques Garcia's neo-rococo décor; and a menu of simple, light fare such as rocket and parmesan salad, seared tuna, and steak tartare. Overlooking the majestic esplanade of the Invalides with its immense lawn and serried rows of lime trees, this is grown-up Costes in a very grown-up quarter. Smart 7th-arrondissement residents (this is government official territory), expats, and the occasional rock star sit themselves down here, enjoying the Cartesian perfection of it all. Napoléon would no doubt have approved. *Daily 8am-2am.* €€ 52 rue Fabert (M° La Tour-Maubourg), 01.47.05.38.80

Café de l'Homme • 16th • Trendy

Best Eiffel Tower Views The two 1930s megaliths at Trocadéro stand sentinel between the esplanade looking across to the Tour Eiffel. Gustav Eiffel's great-great-granddaughter, Coco Couperie, has restored the glamour with her starry restaurant on the ground floor of Musée de l'Homme. The high-ceilinged room has plenty of wow factor, packed with scenesters lounging on the leather sofas under chandeliers made from long strings of crystal that change color. But it's the terrace that takes your breath away. Under a mega statue, surrounded by topiary and with cushions on stone slabs, it feels like an exclusive Sunset Boulevard hotel, only where the pool should be is the Eiffel Tower. Amazing to think you can have all this and great food, with a menu divided into three themes: At Homme (traditional French), Equilibre (balanced), and Influence (fusion). Steer clear of the latter and order the foie gras with quince chutney. *Daily noon-2am.* €€ Musée de l'Homme, 17 pl. du Trocadéro (M° Trocadéro), 01.44.05.30.15, cafedelhomme.com

La Cantine du Faubourg* • 8th • Trendy

Excellent modern French food is served at this nightlife hot spot. *See Hot & Cool Nightlife, p.74, for details.* €€ 105 rue du Fbg. St-Honoré (M° St-Philippe-du-Roule), 01.42.56.22.32

Le Chiberta • 8th • Contemporary

Best Power Lunches The dramatic black décor here spells business, and the power brokers are in their element. When Guy Savoy took over this address, his makeover shocked the critics. The effect is sharp and chic, with a tapas bar and spotlighting reminiscent of the Galerie des Bijoux, only here the jewels are on your plate. Savoy describes the menu as "countrified," referring to the use of herbs, truffles, and other earthy ingredients, but in reality this is sophisticated, urban fare. Precision timing is highlighted, with fish lightly pan-fried, and yet slow-cooked meats such as jarret de veau are also on offer. While lunchtime is a masculine domain, at night the presence of some sophisticated female diners makes this a more glamorous show. *Mon-Thu noon-2:30pm and 7-11pm, Fri noon-2:30pm and 7-11:30pm, Sat 7-11:30pm.* €€€ 3 rue Arsène-Houssaye (M° Charles de Gaulle-Etoile), 01.53.53.42.00, lechiberta.com

Costes* • 1st • Hotel Bar

Best Always-Trendy Tables Sitting in the lobby area is like theater as through the brocade curtains you can watch the parade of fashion people, and the flurry of bowing and scraping when an A-lister arrives. There isn't a restaurant as such—you can eat almost anywhere. Choose the courtyard, if you want to be visible, or the more hidden-away Cheminée room or library. The menu is fashion grazing fare—you can even order a lettuce for €14, though more substantial appetites will appreciate the "weeping tiger" (marinated grilled beef). The servers never seem to know what's in the cocktails, but through trial and error we have found out that the martinis are best, especially the French martini (with pineapple and raspberry liqueur) and the creamy Coco Chanel. After dinner, it has to be the black Salon Chinois or the Fumoir with a huge monstrosity of a bar on six enormous griffin feet, both because the cool people hang out here, and because the bartenders know what's in the cocktails—they invented them. *Daily 7am-2am. Salon Chinois and Fumoir bars open at 7pm.* €€ Hôtel Costes, 239 rue St-Honoré (M° Tuileries), 01.42.44.50.25

Le Cristal Room • 16th • Trendy
Best Of-the-Moment Dining It was a stroke of brilliance on the part of Baccarat to invite Philippe Starck to decorate its new headquarters, transforming the distinguished crystal house into a fashion magnet. You ascend the sweeping staircase and glide through rooms of crystal before settling into pink silk-covered seats printed with cameo portraits. Chef Thierry Burlot, already a favorite with the fashion set, has devised a light, luxury menu entirely in tune with the surroundings: langoustine in a fine tulle with braised eggplant and caviar on sea bream carpaccio are among the delights. The restaurant, at its most scintillating at night, has a two-week waiting list, but lunch is available without reservation on the gallery around the staircase, and it's also open for breakfast. *Mon-Sat 8:30-10:30am, noon-2pm, and 8pm-midnight.* €€€ 11 pl. des Etats-Unis (M° Boissière), 01.40.22.11.10

Davé • 2nd • Trendy
Best Celebrity Spotting "My job is to make fabulous people feel fabulous. I mean, really, anybody can serve a spring roll," says Davé Cheung. You won't find this restaurant in many guidebooks—the patrons don't generally read them, but are introduced personally by their friends who just happen to be called Leo, Naomi, Keanu, Lulu, and Karl. It all started with Helmut Newton, who brought Grace Coddington to this dark little Chinese restaurant in its previous location near the fashion shows, and since then every A-lister in the book has stopped in and eaten bok choy. Getting a table isn't easy, but if it's any consolation, even Leo and Gisele had to wait 20 minutes on the pavement. *Mon-Fri noon-2:15pm and 7-11:15pm, Sat-Sun 7-11:15pm.* €€ 12 rue de Richelieu (M° Palais Royal-Musée du Louvre), 01.42.61.49.48

Les Deux Magots • 6th • Café
Best Café Terraces Les Deux Magots was one of the hottest addresses in Paris before and after World War II, when it attracted first the Surrealists and later the Existentialists, led by Jean-Paul Sartre. What the philosopher would have made of the area now, with its profusion of international fashion names, we will never know, but Les Deux Magots remains an unmissable port of call for any visitor, its terrace the best people-watching spot in Paris. Breakfast is the best bet and provides an excuse to eyeball models, designers, rich shoppers, television talk-show hosts, and the odd intellectual among the touristy hordes. The hot chocolate is divine. *Daily 7:30am-1am.* €€ 6 pl. St-Germain-des-Prés (M° St-Germain-des-Prés), 01.45.48.55.25, lesdeuxmagots.fr

Emporio Armani Caffé • 6th • Trendy
Best Celebrity Spotting Expect air-kissing galore at this fashionable spot. The bustling eatery above the Emporio Armani store epitomizes the international chic of this area and is the most successful of Armani's global cafés. It is decorated in keeping with the Italian couturier's style, has racks of fashion press and its own CD compilation, and the patrons come straight out of the pages of *Vogue*. The chef, hot from Milan, is wowing the lunch crowd with a superb menu of antipasti and pasta dishes. The origin of every product is cited: mullet roe from Cabras, artichokes from Albenga, and in season Alba white truffles. Wines are enticingly described, though all this provides but a minor diversion from the fashion show unfolding around you. *Mon-Sat noon-midnight.* €€ 149 bd. St-Germain (M° St-Germain-des-Prés), 01.45.48.62.15

L'Etoile* • 16th • Gastronomic
Best See-and-Be-Seen Clubs Tony Gomez' address book reads like *Vanity Fair*, and he treats the celebs and millionaires that throng his prestigious club/restaurant as his personal guests. The great thing is, the place stays open during star birthday parties and product launches with a very selective door policy, so if you make the cut, you too could be partying with Robbie Williams or Pamela Anderson. Inside there's a sexy upper-floor restaurant with bay windows onto the Arc de Triomphe, and downstairs a swanky club with a garden terrace. The menu doesn't spring surprises but has surprised critics with its quality. The Star Club prix fixe menu is available at lunch or in the bar Monday through Thursday. Themed soirées in the club include Disco Deluxe on Mondays and Girls' Privilege on Tuesday with an open bar for ladies, attracting beautiful gazelles to party with tan yacht-owning men. *Mon-Fri noon-3pm and 8pm-1am, Sat 8pm-1am. Lounge bar from midnight Thu-Sat. Club from 11pm Tue-Sat.* €€€€ 12 rue de Presbourg (M° Charles de Gaulle-Etoile), 01.45.00.78.70, letoileparis.com

Flora Danica • 8th • Contemporary
Flora Danica is a living design museum featuring classics like Jacobsen's egg chair, Boje Estermann chairs, and Nanna Ditzel's round banquette crested by a sculpture of cylindrical lights. There's an outdoor canvas-covered dining room and a mezzanine wooden terrace with a jungle of plants that makes it one of the lushest gardens in the area. The food is no less impressive, and portions are truly Viking, with wild smoked salmon from the Baltic sea available seasonally. Meat eaters should not miss the tender reindeer steak. You'll be encouraged to drink beer or vodka, but wines are also served by the glass. At 1pm the place fills up with cigar-smoking heads of industry, so come late, or, better still, in the evening when a trendier crowd enjoys the garden atmosphere. *Daily noon-2:30pm and 7:15-11pm.* €€ 142 av. des Champs-Elysées (M° Charles de Gaulle-Etoile), 01.44.13.86.26, maisondudanemark.dk

Le Fumoir • 1st • Trendy
Best Literary Bars Hemingwayesque without being a theme bar, Le Fumoir is a good call at any time of day. You can take your morning coffee with a copy of the *Herald Trib* bound onto a wooden pole, drop in for lunch or tea after the Louvre, sip cocktails snuggled into an armchair or on the heated terrace, or dine in the large, coffee-colored dining area at the back. It plays host to a mixed crowd of tourists, trendies, and young professionals. As any literary bar should, it has its own library, and if you get stuck on something you can't put down, you can borrow it or exchange it for another book. The chef turns out some tasty fare—the artichoke and lemon risotto and the rack of lamb are particularly succulent. *Daily 11am-2am.* €€ 6 rue de l'Amiral-de-Coligny (M° Louvre-Rivoli), 01.42.92.00.24, lefumoir.com

Georges • 4th • Trendy
Best Always-Trendy Tables Restaurants with great views are not in short supply in Paris, but Georges has its own magic. Taking up the whole top floor of the Centre Pompidou, it has a panoramic spread across the entire city. The interior design takes the outside-in theme of the building to a new sphere. Since its Millennium opening it's been hot, and it shows no sign of cooling down. The food is a typical Costes Mediterranean-Asian cross—chicken nems with Thai basil, risotto

with pata negra ham, and the melting chocolate moelleux. The glamour of the Paris night and the see-and-be-seen crowd make this a definite evening choice. House music keeps the chatter levels high. Be sure to ask for a table with a view. *Wed-Mon noon-3pm and 7:30pm-1am.* €€ Centre Pompidou, 6th fl. Entry by red elevator to left of main entrance; after 8:45pm entry opposite 50 rue Rambuteau (M° Rambuteau), 01.44.78.47.99

Guy Savoy • 17th • Gastronomic

Best Fine Dining While so many signature restaurants no longer have the chef in question in the kitchen, this is not so for Guy Savoy. Despite having a mini-empire of Paris restaurants, this genial bon viveur is here, in person, cooking and shaking the hands of diners at the end of the meal. In the intriguing modern space, sliding screens can change the configuration of the space according to the number of diners, and Yoruba statues and Bozo tribal masks are displayed alongside canvases by artist friends. The brilliance of the cuisine is in simple ideas masterfully carried out—don't miss the artichoke and black truffle soup, a Savoy classic. The relaxed atmosphere adds to the enjoyment, though it's still worth turning up in jacket and tie. *Tue-Fri noon-2pm and 7-10:30pm, Sat 7-10:30pm.* €€€€ 18 rue Troyon (M° Charles de Gaulle-Etoile), 01.43.80.40.61, guysavoy.com

Hiramatsu • 16th • Gastronomic

Best Power Lunches This Japanese restaurateur wields a French haute cuisine spoon with boundless creativity. With an empire of French and Italian restaurants in Japan, he opened a tiny restaurant on the Ile St-Louis with Hajime Nakagawa at the helm, to test out ingredients for export to Japan and train his staff. It was a phenomenal success, and having won its first Michelin star and acquired many fans, Hiramatsu moved into this larger, lighter space. In the elegant dark-wood and pale-stone interior, everything is perfectly orchestrated, from the gliding staff to the Baccarat crystal and Limoges porcelain. Go for the tasting menu and sit back and enjoy perfection on a plate among high-powered executives and international food-lovers. *Mon-Fri 12:30-2pm and 7:30-9:30pm.* €€€€ 52 rue de Longchamp (M° Trocadéro), 01.56.81.08.80

Kong* • 1st • Trendy

The Japanese-French fusion food at this trendy spot has had more panning than praise, but it's worth it for the setting. *See Hot & Cool Nightlife, p.75, for details.* €€ 1 rue du Pont Neuf (M° Pont Neuf), 01.40.39.09.00, kong.fr

Maison Blanche • 8th • Trendy

Best Always-Trendy Tables One of Paris' premier see-and-be-seen restaurants, this penthouse hot spot has embraced its intrinsic glamour. Depending on how insouciant you are feeling, choose between silk-clad booths, the main room with its bay window, or the upstairs mezzanine with wider views and a color-changing bar. Some claim the modern French cuisine doesn't measure up to the Pourcel twins' original restaurant in Montpellier, but this doesn't stop a starry clientele from the worlds of film, TV, and fashion from peppering the 200-seater restaurant. Nighttime is the best time to come for the spectacle inside and out: watch the lights sparkle on the Tour Eiffel from the mezzanine. *Mon-Fri noon-1:45pm and 8-10:45pm, Sat-Sun 8-10:45pm.* €€€€ 15 av. Montaigne (M° Alma-Marceau), 01.47.23.55.99, maison-blanche.fr

Market • 8th • Contemporary

Jean-Georges Vongerichten was the darling of New York in the '90s when he won a total of 12 stars from the *New York Times*. In 2001 he returned to France and opened Market, causing just as much of a splash with his raw food and seasonal vegetable-led cuisine. Screen stars and politicos are regulars in the sober dining room with its different food stations, the raw bar, pizza oven, and kitchen. You could go no further than the celebrated raw tuna pizza with wasabi sauce, but it's fun also to try the "black plate," which follows the tapas craze with an assortment of delicacies to share, and there's a full à la carte menu too. There is a choice of three wines by the glass to accompany the lunchtime prix fixe. A weekday breakfast or weekend brunch is also a fine idea. *Daily 8-11am, noon-3pm, and 7pm-1am.* €€ 15 av. Matignon (M° Champs-Elysées-Clémenceau), 01.56.43.40.90, jean-georges.com

Les Marronniers • 4th • Café

No terrace is quite like this one—four tables deep and covered with a large red awning, it's packed night and day, rain or shine, summer and winter (when it's warmed by heat lamps). It doesn't take long to figure out why the diners here are 90 percent good-looking and male—this is the cruisiest street in the Marais, but it's also convenient to the Centre Pompidou, which is right out front. It serves updated bistro fare including chicken biryani and a burger named after France's most famous environmental protester. The posiest time of all is Sunday brunch. This was one of the first places in Paris to do it and is still one of the best. *Daily 9am-2am.* € 18 rue des Archives (M° Hôtel de Ville), 01.40.27.87.72

Murano • 3rd • Trendy

Best Of-the-Moment Dining The restaurant of the design hotel Murano Urban Resort, and its bar, have been overrun with excitable fashion folk since it opened. The high-ceilinged white room is hung with a forest of tubular lights and decked with loungy cranberry banquettes and cushions, creating a perfect stage for a see-and-be-seen crowd. In summer a long banquette is open to the sky under the tall, narrow atrium. Quiet dining is not an option, as bouncy trip-hop spun by a DJ keeps the atmosphere buzzing. The food is as well dressed as the clientele, with a langoustine tataki in a soup of cocoa beans, foie gras with chutney and green tomatoes, and saffron risotto coming up trumps. Afterward, pop next door for the happening scene at the long vodka bar. *Daily noon-2pm and 8-11pm, Sun brunch noon-4:30pm.* €€€ Murano Urban Resort, 13 bd. du Temple (M° Filles du Calvaire), 01.42.71.20.00, muranoresort.com

Music Hall* • 8th • Trendy

A hot address for luxury nighttime snacks in a contemporary setting. *See Hot & Cool Nightlife, p.76, for details.* € 63 av. Franklin D. Roosevelt (M° Franklin D. Roosevelt), 01.45.61.03.63

Les Orchidées • 2nd • Contemporary

Best Brunches The most sophisticated brunch in Paris is to be found under the glass roof of the Park Hyatt Paris Vendôme. It's low-key, but you may well spot Isabelle Adjani, French crooner Garou, or Sting. Stars aside, young, upscale professionals have discovered the sleek setting and superlative brunch menu, and many make this a regular weekend event. The décor features a kind of insect's-eye of refracting glass behind the breakfast bar, which is laden with Champagne, fruit juices, croissants, and smoked salmon. For the second course you choose from the lunch menu, ranging from Caesar salad, oyster and potato velouté, and truffle omelette to lobster. Low seating promotes a relaxed atmosphere, and in summer you can move out to the terrace in the hotel courtyard. *Daily 6:30am-7pm.* €€ Park Hyatt Paris Vendôme, 3-5 rue de la Paix (M° Opéra), 01.58.71.12.34, paris.vendome.hyatt.fr

Pershing Hall* • 8th • Trendy
An enchanting setting where you can dine under the sky in good weather. Follow it up with a drink at the buzzing lounge. *See Pershing Lounge in Hot & Cool Nightlife, p.76, for details. Mon-Sat 7-10:30am, noon-3pm, 8-11:30pm, Sun 11am-6pm.* €€ 49 rue Pierre-Charron (M° Charles de Gaulle-Etoile), 01.58.36.58.00, pershinghall.com

Pierre Gagnaire • 8th • Gastronomic
"Risk gives life to cooking" is the maxim of Pierre Gagnaire, the mad scientist of haute cuisine—he actually works with a molecular biologist. You'll be treated to a show of culinary acrobatics, which could include a 25-year-old oyster cooked tableside in goose fat, or John Dory with spices, scallops, and sea urchin concoctions. The originality of the cuisine attracts dedicated foodies, adventurous expense-account diners, and the occasional star to the contemporary dining room where the table settings are a work of art. Each course comprises many dishes, as if deconstructing cuisine. The lobster, for example (it costs €137, be forewarned), is presented raw with pear juice, nashi, and nougatine; grilled with basil leaves; pan-fried and in a parsley-flavored mousseline. Madness or genius? You decide. *Mon-Fri noon-2pm and 7:30-10pm, Sun 7:30-10pm.* €€€€ 6 rue Balzac (M° George V), 01.58.36.12.50, pierre-gagnaire.com

Le Quinzième • 15th • Trendy
Le Quinzième's birth in 2005 was followed avidly by French TV viewers, as chef Cyril Lignac picked 15 wannabes and taught them the ropes of running a successful restaurant. You may have the impression that the cameras are still rolling as you see the young team working in the kitchen through a window that looks onto the street. The dark mosaic tiles and low lighting are very chic, and despite the out-of-the-way location the restaurant draws a trendy crowd of urbane 30-somethings. Among the tasty, well-presented dishes are a densely flavored tart of girolles and sea bass with purple artichokes and Bellota chorizo. The dessert smorgasbord featuring shot glasses of sweet concoctions is too much—go for something simpler. Terrace tables beckon after a summer walk in the Parc André Citroën. *Mon-Fri noon-2:30pm and 8-11pm, Sat 8-11pm.* €€€ 14 rue Cauchy (M° Javel), 01.45.54.43.43

Le Relais du Parc • 16th • Gastronomic
Best Outdoor Dining This was where Alain Ducasse made his name and the star chef still consults on the menu. The main attraction, however, between May and September, is the gorgeous terrace courtyard of this manor-house hotel, one of the most delightful summer dining locations in Paris. Business associates and romancing couples relax among the lush flowers and trees, canvas cushions on wrought-iron chairs, and settings of blue glass and orange faience that create a St-Tropez atmosphere in the city. Providing you don't have to weather a summer

storm, this is a real al fresco treat. *Daily from early May to end Sept Tue-Fri noon-2:30pm and 7-10:30pm, Sat 7-10:30pm.* €€€ ▱ Sofitel le Parc, 51 av. Raymond-Poincaré (M° Boissière), 01.44.05.66.10, sofitel.com

Senderens • 8th • Trendy

In 2005 top chef Alain Senderens threw down his Michelin stars and announced he would be reopening Lucas Carton as a new style of restaurant. Its successor would be "more sensual, more feminine, and more open" with the sky-high prices of his gastronomy reduced to no more than €100 a head. The change has been more radical than even expected. The listed Art Nouveau interior now has a false ceiling like a moon crater and Corian-topped bare tables. The inventor of nouvelle cuisine has embraced fusion with a global menu of creative dishes, each accompanied by a local drink, although you have to beware of choosing weird combinations—the Scottish salmon comes with whisky, which could leave you feeling queasy if your next courses are accompanied by Champagne. But the crowd loves it, and the affordable prices and mezzanine cocktail and tapas bar are pulling in city slickers and their leggy dates, who crow that it's like New York. *Daily noon-3pm, dinner 7-11:30pm.* €€€ ▱ 9 pl. de la Madeleine (M° Madeleine), 01.42.65.22.90, lucascarton.com

Le Sers • 8th • Trendy

A former Hôtel Costes employee has been consulting on the menu of this hot new hotel's terrace restaurant, which is often packed with a savvy 8th-arrondissement lunch crowd. This is the kind of haunt that attracts film, advertising, and media types who feel at ease pulling out their laptops to discuss their latest projects while grazing on a minimalist menu based on top-quality produce. Bellota ham, caviar, foie gras, and smoked salmon are among the one-ingredient plates, followed by high-quality pasta, risotto, or a simple steak or grilled fish. The terrace has custom-made teak furniture and is shaded by leafy catalpa trees. In winter the scene moves indoors to the artfully lit contemporary bar area. *Daily 8am-2am.* € ▱ Hôtel de Sers, 41 av. Pierre 1er de Serbie (M° George V), 01.53.23.75.75, hotel-de-sers.com

Sora Lena • 17th • Trendy

This relaxed and chic Italian restaurant has been a showbiz haunt since it was run by Coco Couperie, who now presides over Café de l'Homme. Her circle (she is married to singer Julien Clerc) has stuck around now that it's under new management, and it seems everyone is on a first-name basis here. The Giorgi brothers have created a welcoming atmosphere with colorful cushions, fairy lights, and a skylit dining room at the back, and there's also an upstairs dining room that feels like a private party in the evenings when they turn up the '70s disco soundtrack. The lunch menu is a really good value and includes not only pasta but dishes such as rabbit with olives. *Mon-Thu noon-2pm and 8-11:30pm, Fri-Sat 8-11:30pm.* €€ ▱ 18 rue Bayen (M° Ternes), 01.45.74.73.73

Spoon, Food & Wine • 8th • Trendy

Imagine the shock to the gastronomic elite when Alain Ducasse decided to let diners choose for themselves. The first Spoon has spawned others around the world with its menu of flavors collected on the chef's travels, and it remains a favorite with fashion and food PRs and international trendies. In a Philippe Starck décor in shades of prune and mauve, you choose your staple (pasta, fish pan-fried, roasted or steamed, meat or salads), condiment, and accompaniment. There are suggestions to help you avoid a culinary faux pas, or, even easier, try the Spoonsum lunch menu with a selection composed by the chef. *Mon-Fri noon-2pm and 7-10:30pm.* €€€ 14 rue de Marignan (M° Franklin D. Roosevelt), 01.40.76.34.44, spoon.tm.fr

Stella Maris • 8th • Gastronomic
For a long time Tateru Yoshino's restaurant was a hidden pearl where the Japanese chef delivered his cultivated take on classic French cuisine to a knowing few. Now, following a decorative revamp, he's everyone's favorite secret address, and John Galliano and Christian Lacroix are among his fans. Of course it's no secret anymore, but this is all the more reason to try one of the best-value gastronomic treats in town. The décor that has brought the style crowd running strikes a balance between minimalism and Art Deco. The light, high-ceilinged salon is lit from above by tubular lamps and has a clubby mezzanine area. Defying culinary stereotypes, it is with game that Yoshino shines the most. Try his exquisite tête de veau (calf's head), hare pie, or pheasant pot-au-feu. *Mon-Fri 12:30-2:15pm and 7:30-10:30pm, Sat 7:30-10:30pm.* €€€€ 4 rue Arsène-Houssaye (M° Charles de Gaulle-Etoile), 01.42.89.16.22

Le Stresa • 8th • Italian
Le Stresa makes you think of *La Dolce Vita,* and if Marcello Mastroianni were still around, he would undoubtedly still be eating here. The place never goes out of style. French star Jean-Paul Belmondo has been coming here for years, but you're just as likely to be sitting next to a Hollywood star. And when we say sitting next to, that's no exaggeration, as this place is cozy in the extreme. No effort has been made to cultivate trendiness, it's just one of those wonderful old-fashioned Italian places with red banquettes, a fug of cigarette smoke, and ingredients imported from Italy that make everything taste authentic. Though the pasta shows how it should be done, this is the place to order those Italian meat dishes that tend to be a letdown elsewhere: veal saltimbocca or anything with white truffles. *Mon-Fri 12:15-2:15pm and 7:30-10:30pm.* €€€ 7 rue Chambiges (M° Alma-Marceau), 01.47.23.51.62

La Suite* • 8th • Trendy
Reserve one of the suites for a delicious dinner, which will guarantee you entry to the club. *See Hot & Cool Nightlife, p.77, for details. Mon-Fri 12:30-3pm and 8:30-11pm, Sat-Sun 8:30-11pm.* €€ 40 av. George V (M° George V), 01.53.57.49.49, lasuite.fr

La Table de Joël Robuchon • 16th • Contemporary
There's no stopping Robuchon now that he's in the driver's seat again. He's taken over the successful restaurant 16 au 16, complete with its chef and a pâtissier he considers the best in France. The atmosphere is in keeping with this ultra-smart area, with gilt, dark wood, and Robuchon's trademark blood red. The clientele is too, which comes with the more elevated prices, but you can still choose the tapas-style dishes as an alternative to à la carte. The sensational cuisine makes this an essential for any food-lover's itinerary. *Daily noon-2:30pm and 7-10:30pm.* €€€€ 16 av. Bugeaud (M° Victor Hugo), 01.56.28.16.16

Thiou • 7th • Trendy
Petite Thai chef Thiou's fan club of fashion and showbiz stars throngs her signature restaurant in the upscale 7th arrondissement. On the menu are the spicy Thai treats that made her name and that never lose their charm, such as the famous "weeping tiger" (marinated grilled beef), spaghetti tossed with squid and spices, and Thai-style stuffed tomatoes. The honey-roasted mango dessert is to die for. Younger aficionados throng the Petit Thiou annex at 3 rue Surcouf and the new Comptoir de Thiou at 12 av. George V. Keeping hands on, Mme. Thiou cooks at all three. *Mon-Fri noon-2:30pm and 8-10:30pm, Sat 8-10:30pm.* €€ 49 quai d'Orsay (M° Invalides), 01.40.62.96.50

Toi • 8th • Trendy
You can eat well at this sceney lounge, with huge steaks and sashimi among the offerings. *See Hot & Cool Nightlife, p.78, for details. Daily noon-2am.* € 27 rue du Colisée (M° Franklin D. Roosevelt), 01.42.56.56.58, restaurant-toi.com

Le Village • 8th • Trendy
The latest hit from the Costes dynasty is this café on a pedestrian shopping passageway, the Village Royale, just behind the rue du Faubourg St-Honoré. Lined with chic boutiques, this is prime fashionista territory and a perfect little oasis for a coffee or a kir between Hôtel Costes, Colette, and Place Vendôme. Light lunches are on offer, but the whole point is the long, two-tables-deep heated terrace with comfy, cushioned chairs, where you can speak into your cell phone and actually be *heard,* darling (so no need to bellow). *Mon-Sat 8am-8pm.* €€ 25 rue Royale (M° Madeleine), 01.40.17.02.19

Ze Kitchen Galerie • 6th • Contemporary
This restaurant's minimalist, loft-style décor, open kitchen, and art-gallery feel attracts a young crowd. The chef mixes and matches flavors and techniques from around the world. You have a starter choice of soup, pasta, or raw fish, followed by meat or fish speed-grilled "a la plancha" (on an iron plaque). The simply grilled sea bass with a citrus and ginger sauce, accompanied by tempura and grilled vegetables, is typical of the fare, and desserts combine fruit, chocolate, and sorbets in contrasting temperatures and textures. The tables are rather close together, but this place has a real buzz. *Mon-Fri noon-2pm and 7:30-11pm, Sat 7-11pm.* €€ 4 rue des Grands-Augustins (M° St-Michel), 01.44.32.00.32

Hot & Cool Paris: The Nightlife

L'Amnésia Café • 4th • Gay Bar
Best Gay Bars This cozy and chic gay bar attracts gorgeous guys like bees to a honeypot. Slim-hipped waiters shimmy between the tables and leather chairs, serving delicious cocktails like the Pink Russian (a vodka and rose liqueur concoction), while a stylish crowd clusters at the bar. Upstairs is a small, chilled-out space for intimate conversation, while downstairs there's a hot and crowded dance floor with camp French classics on the decks. Around midnight the place is packed. *Daily 11am-2am.* 42 rue Vieille du Temple (M° Hôtel de Ville), 01.42.72.16.94, amnesia-cafe.com

Les Bains Douches • 3rd • Dance Club
Like all good rock stars, Les Bains hit its high in the '80s and '90s, then went through a rocky period. Happily it's now out of rehab with an all-new décor that keeps the unique former swimming pool that made it so special, a supersonic sound system, and the former artistic director of Le Queen at the helm. Les Bains aims to be the hottest gay club in the capital—which just means it's party-tastic, as gays and straights mix happily in this town. DJs renowned for their cracking house, such as Tommy Marcus, Jérôme Pacman, and Jef K, and soirées organized by the likes of Cream Fresh and Hed Kandi, are on the agenda, with a fabulous Sunday morning after too. Forget the lacquered teenagers of some gay clubs—this one is aimed at the buffed and beautiful 25-to-35 age group. *Fri-Sun 11pm-6am, Sun after-party 6am-noon.* 7 rue du Bourg-l'Abbé (M° Etienne Marcel), 01.48.87.01.80, lesbainsdouches.net

Le Bar at the George V • 8th • Hotel Bar
Best Vodka Cocktails Known as Le Bar by its Golden Triangle habitués, the classy English-style bar in the George V hotel has become an essential stop-off for sophisticated young things out on the town in the 8th. It offers perhaps the most sublime martini moment you will ever experience. The 14 martinis are all named for colors. The risqué Purple Martini has a base of violet and cassis liqueurs; the Red is made from watermelon and peach; the Brown with a touch of Amaretto. They come to your table on a silver tray loaded with luxury nibbles, in an individual mini-shaker, which is shaken (not stirred) in front of you, and poured into a stemless crystal cone resting on a bed of ice. Nestle in a Havana leather chair or pose among the avant-garde orchid displays in the Galerie. *Sun-Fri 10am-1am, Sat 10am-2am.* Four Seasons George V, 31 av. George V (M° Alma-Marceau), 01.49.52.70.00, fourseasons.com

Le Bar du Plaza • 8th • Hotel Bar
Best Vodka Cocktails Patrick Nuel's ice-cool bar has transformed the Hôtel Plaza Athénée into the most sophisticated cocktail joint in town. In high contrast to the tinkling tearoom you walk through to get here, it's low-lit and very sexy, with mini Murano chandeliers. You sit perched up at ridiculously high tables to peruse the cocktails menu with its many surprises. Men in black will bring you the Rose Royale at the drop of a hat—a delicious blend of Champagne and

crushed raspberry that you can smell before it even arrives. There are also the vodka jellies (Jell-O formed into alcoholic melt-in-the mouth squares), the Fashion Ice (a peach Bellini on a stick), cocktails involving spices and vegetables, and even a designer water that comes lit up from below. The whole multi-sensory experience is so absorbing that you can forget you came here to see and be seen. *Daily 6pm-2am.* B≡ Hôtel Plaza Athénée, 25 av. Montaigne (M° Alma-Marceau), 01.53.67.66.00, plaza-athenee-paris.com

Le Bound • 8th • Cocktail Bar
The former Barfly has changed its name to highlight the arrival of a stylish new makeover, but attracts the same sexy and affluent crowd with its hint at exclusivity (velvet ropes and bouncers at the entrance), aphrodisiac cocktails, and good-time ambiance. In summer, terrace dining is an attractive proposition before joining the crush around the curved long bar behind which wannabe Tom Cruises do their stuff. Around midnight the place is really hopping, and the fact that there is no dance floor does not stop the party. Be ready for plenty of flirtatious interaction between the English-speaking bartenders, leggy female clientele, and male ones waving their Ferrari keys to the beat of the house soundtrack. *Daily noon-2am.* B≡ 49 av. George V (M° George V), 01.53.67.84.60, buddhabar.com

Le Cab • 1st • Lounge/Club
Appearances by Tom Cruise and Penelope Cruz, Vincent Cassel, Juliette Lewis, and Toby Maguire put this swank club on the map, and though the A-list is less continually present, it has not lost its appeal. The restaurant, Cabaret, is in the original cabaret theater with cream décor by Jacques Garcia. In the rest of the vast space, the *Clockwork Orange*–inspired décor creates one of the most user-friendly clubs in Paris, with plenty of seating in leather-clad alcoves and a separate enclosed lounge area with round banquettes. The dance floor, where you can shake your booty on low podiums, attracts a well-dressed but fun-loving crowd grooving to mainstream sounds such as funk (Tue & Wed), house, and hip-hop. Big plus: the air-conditioning here really works. *Restaurant: Tue-Sat 8-11:30pm; Clubbing: Tue-Sat 11:30pm-6am.* C≡ 2 pl. du Palais-Royal (M° Palais Royal-Musée du Louvre), 01.58.62.56.25, cabaret.fr

La Cantine du Faubourg* • 8th • Lounge Bar
Best Lounge Bars "Ma cantine" is a chic way of saying my local hub, and though this spacious bar/restaurant has never quite achieved the status it was aiming at in the Faubourg St-Honoré—this honor will always go to Costes—it still attracts a moneyed, showbiz clientele to dine and lounge. Comfortable sofas and spectacular lighting with floor-to-ceiling wicker sculptures and video art projected onto the walls, plus a high-quality sound system and laid-back mixing, create a luxury, cosseted ambiance. There's an option to have a VIP table where you are served by the cooks—and late opening means this is a good address for winding down at the end of an evening. *Daily noon-4am.* C B≡ 105 rue du Fbg. St-Honoré (M° St-Philippe-du-Roule), 01.42.56.22.22

Costes* • 1st • Hotel Bar
Come at any hour to lounge to fabulous music, see and be seen, and drink expertly mixed cocktails with an A-list crowd. *See Hot & Cool Restaurants, p.64, for details.* F≡ 239 rue St-Honoré (M° Tuileries), 01.42.44.50.25

L'Etoile* • 16th • Private Club
Themed soirées at this club include Disco Deluxe on Mondays and Girls' Privilege on Tuesday. *See Hot & Cool Restaurants, p.66, for details.* 12 rue de Presbourg (M° Charles de Gaulle-Etoile), 01.45.00.78.70, letoileparis.com

Jardin Plein Ciel • 16th • Hotel Bar
Best Cocktails with a View Glide through the lobby of the Hôtel Raphaël and take an elevator straight to the seventh floor for this celebrity favorite rooftop bar. With wooden decking, trailing roses, fruit trees, and deck chairs, it's a real summer oasis, and the panoramic views extend from the Arc de Triomphe right beside it to the Eiffel Tower and Sacré-Coeur. Johnny Hallyday, TV presenter Thierry Ardisson, and a host of other French music and showbiz stars apéro here when the weather turns warm, and cocktails at €20 a pop have the pleasing effect of keeping hoi polloi at ground level. Watching the sun set here is a perfect Paris moment, but if you're feeling blasé you can always play chess on the gigantic board with 2-foot-high pieces. *Mar-Oct daily 3:30-9:30pm (depending on weather).* Hôtel Raphael, 17 av. Kléber (M° Kléber), 01.53.64.32.00, raphael-hotel.com

Kong* • 1st • Bar/Restaurant
Best Cocktails with a View Philippe Starck's extravaganza is a manga madness penthouse on top of the Kenzo building overlooking the Pont Neuf. Kitsch to the max, it has disembodied manga faces staring out of transparent perspex chairs, life-size geisha panels, candy-colored lighting, a pebble floor, and Pokémon cushions. Happy hour 6-8pm sets the ball rolling with colorful cocktails as an eclectic selection of music responds to electronic votes cast by the happy crowd. Arrive early to grab a coveted stool at the bar or come back later on Friday or Saturday when beautiful people flock here for the live DJ sounds. *Sex and the City* filmed its Paris dénouement right here. *Restaurant: daily 10:30am-2am. Clubbing: Fri-Sat 11pm-3am.* 1 rue du Pont Neuf (M° Pont Neuf), 01.40.39.09.00, kong.fr

Mathi's Bar • 8th • Hotel Bar
Mathi's is simply a gorgeous little jewel of a bar. TV talk-show hosts, actors, and girls who, without putting too fine a point on it, know how to look good after 4am have made their home in this cozy, dandified interior, which is Costes-like without having ever made the effort to be so. Pull back the velvet curtain and you'll be greeted by Madame X, who will seat you or not depending on whether there are any seats and whether she likes the look of you. A somewhat intimidating initiation, but well worth a try. *Mon-Sat 10pm-5am.* Hôtel Elysées Matignon, 3 rue de Ponthieu (M° Franklin D. Roosevelt), 01.53.76.01.62

Le Milliardaire • 8th • Private Club
The "millionaire" puts its cards right on the table: if you're rich and famous, or look like you are, you're welcome for a night of no-holds-barred hedonism. But it's small and they are very selective. P. Diddy and Leonardo di Caprio have been known to drop in; otherwise it's the playground of Paris' golden youth, with a penchant for Russian beauties who come on Fridays for the "before" Paris-Moscou. The former cabaret has kept its Art Deco bar and red and purple interior, encouraging bad behavior as the girls kick off their heels to dance on the banquettes amid popping Champagne corks. You'll be expected to order a bot-

tle of spirits and mixers to get a table. Thursday's "before" hypes up the crowd with Motown, soul, and hip hop; Saturdays are disco heaven. *Mon-Sat 11pm-5am.* C≡ 68 rue Pierre Charron (M° Franklin D. Roosevelt), 01.42.89.44.14, lemilliardaire.com

Murano Bar • 3rd • Hotel Bar
Best Vodka Cocktails The bar in the rock-star chic Murano Urban Resort looks like a colorful recording studio with its red, purple, and orange studded wall panels and circular ceiling plates. There's a choice of high and low seating, the best being up at the 50-foot-long bar from which you can survey the 130 vodkas on offer. With something this plush sorely lacking in the vicinity, Murano's been a big hit with trendy Parisians, and is even drawing the fashion crowd away from the Costes during the collections. House music and video screens create a pre-club ambiance in the evening, but the bar is also open for breakfast, coffee, and snacks during the day. *Daily 7am-2am.* B≡ Murano Urban Resort, 13 bd. du Temple (M° Filles du Calvaire), 01.42.71.20.00, muranoresort.com

Music Hall* • 8th • Late-Night Restaurant
Best Late-Night Eats This newcomer to the Elysées area attempts to bring late-night culture to Paris. Its USP, aside from that, is an ambient lighting system that switches from blue to pink to orange every few minutes, casting different moods over the room. More mood is provided by a pianist at the white grand (there are even opera evenings at the beginning of the week) and a DJ spinning excellent lounge music. The food plays with sweet and sour to mixed success, but the young clientele seems to dig it. A good address for luxury nighttime snacks or a post-clubbing chill-out rather than for dinner. Make sure you are seated in the main room as the back lounge and upper room can feel like Siberia. *Daily 11am-4am.* B≡ 63 av. Franklin D. Roosevelt (M° Franklin D. Roosevelt), 01.45.61.03.63, music-hallparis.com

Le Néo • 8th • Private Club
Best See-and-Be-Seen Clubs This latest hot spot has the likes of Bruce Willis and John Galliano on the guest list, along with other film, fashion, and music luminaries, making this intimate space something like a private club. The décor is black and very luxe, with velvet-covered walls, a black marble floor, black leather jewel-studded banquettes, a luminous bar that changes color, and screens showing specially designed video art. House is passé, say these tastemeisters: here they groove to strictly rock, '80s, and hip-hop, and since Nine Inch Nails and Audioslave have had their after-show parties here, it seems like that's cool. Sunday's gay tea dance, Club Sandwich, is a favorite with chic boys who work in fashion. *Tue-Sat midnight-6am, Sun gay tea dance 9pm-2am.* ≡ 23 rue de Ponthieu (M° Franklin D. Roosevelt), 01.42.25.57.14

Pershing Lounge* • 8th • Hotel Bar
Best Meet Markets The glory of this Andrée Putman–designed hotel is its vertical garden cascading down an entire wall of the inner courtyard. In this enchanting environment you can dine under the sky in good weather and under canvas with heat lamps in the winter. The setting is hard to beat, especially as the place attracts a trendy crowd of 30-somethings who love this urban oasis. Climb the glamorous spiral staircase and you'll find the Lounge with high, stucco-ceilinged rooms lit by red lanterns and lounge music that strikes just the right tempo. The

main room feels a little like a swish private party, while the terrace is ideal for a romantic cocktail overlooking the vertical garden (these tables are coveted, so do reserve, even for a drink). *Daily 6pm-2am.* B≡ Hôtel Pershing Hall, 49 rue Pierre Charron (M° Charles de Gaulle-Etoile), 01.58.36.58.36, pershinghall.com

Pink Paradise • 8th • Strip Club
In their own inimitable style, the Guettas managed to convince Parisians that lap-dancing was chic, making this the premier address for those who want to hand over their euros for high-class titillation. The place is very luxe with a transparent staircase, pink leopard-skin carpet, Murano glass chandeliers, and the lit-up runway, which sees high-rolling executives virtually crawling onto it to get a closer look at the all-American eye candy. No surprise, then, that it also gets used for fashion shows. The look-but-don't-touch formulas range from €25 for a table dance to €400 for a half-hour show in a private room, and if you order a bottle in advance (€200) the entry is free. Following the New York model, girls get to learn to pole-dance and watch male strippers one Sunday a month at Girls & the City. *Mon-Sat 10:30pm-5am, Thu from 8:30pm; girls' night one Sunday a month.* C≡ 49 rue de Ponthieu (M° George V), 01.58.36.19.20, pinkparadise.fr

Le Queen • 8th • Dance Club
Long live the Queen! This grande dame of the Paris night is still pumping bpms nightly on the Champs-Elysées. Though it's known as a gay club, it is by no means exclusive. Wednesdays (featuring gay R&B), Saturdays, and Sundays are the most popular gay nights, and weekends have the best DJs, including the excellent house night, Pure, on Fridays. Monday's disco night is still the best Monday clubbing option, though the crowd is tamer these days. The club regularly welcomes foreign talent such as DTPM from London's Fabric. It's a very professional act, with a great sound system, scintillating lighting effects around the giant glitter ball, and a balcony for surveying the scene. *Daily midnight-6am.* ≡ 102 av. des Champs-Elysées (M° George V), 08.92.70.73.30, queen.fr

Raidd Bar • 4th • Gay Bar
Best Gay Bars The bartenders are the stars at this hot venue on the Paris gay scene. They work four-day shifts, then have three days of gym time, keeping those pecs at peak perfection. If the sight of their topless bods is not enough, come on Sundays when the boys bare all in performance shower cubicles. On Wednesdays the punters can do likewise as the showers are open to the floor. If you want to draw attention to yourself here, wear a white T-shirt—as half the patrons seem to do—to be spotlighted in the strobe lights. The warehouse-like ground floor is filled with hard pumping house, and downstairs is a lounging area with videos of yet more body-beautiful men having fun around a pool. Around 2-3am is the best time to come for a club-like atmosphere. *Daily 6pm-5am.* ≡ 23 rue du Temple (M° Hôtel de Ville), 01.48.87.80.25, raiddbar.com

La Suite* • 8th • Bar/Club
Best See-and-Be-Seen Clubs Launched by the reigning king and queen of Paris posh nightlife, the Guettas, La Suite is plush and pink: you are greeted by a bimbette in a tutu and ascend the stairs. To the left are the four dining "suites" and to the right the bar. For the view over Avenue George V, ask for a window in the Penthouse Suite. The Honeymoon Suite is a sexy boudoir for two or four

where you can close the curtains between courses. Reserving a table for dinner guarantees entry into the bar, which is packed on weekends, with banquettes, mini TV screens showing fashion footage, and a fish tank where tropical sea life swims among bottles of Bombay Sapphire. The fauna is almost as exotic: universally tanned, tall gorgeous men in silk shirts mingling with leggy girls—a St-Tropez slice of life all bopping to the soundtrack. So hot it's scorching. *Mon-Wed 8pm-2am, Thu-Sat 8pm-5am.* 40 av. George V (M° George V), 01.53.57.49.49, lasuite.fr

Toi • 8th • Lounge

This attractive lounge/bar and restaurant has '60s-inspired pink walls and brown velvet and orange cushions on which a young, very suntanned clientele drapes itself. Cunning orange-pink light is diffused everywhere, and there is an upstairs room from which you can look down on the entrance through a tear-shaped hole in the floor. The best seating, however, is in the cozy niche in the back. The cocktails get mixed reviews: the Cosmopolitan-variant "pomme empoisonné" is excellent and the Caipirinhas are pretty good. You can eat well here, with huge steaks and sashimi among the offerings. It's packed at lunchtime with a smart office crowd and sceney at night, especially Saturdays when a DJ spins soul and disco till 4am. *Thu-Sat noon-4am.* 27 rue du Colisée (M° Franklin D. Roosevelt), 01.42.56.56.58, restaurant-toi.com

Le VIP Room • 8th • Private Club

Best Celebrity Spotting Famous people have fan clubs; Jean Roch has a fan club composed of famous people: Gwen Stefani, Grace Jones, Bono, Oliver Stone, Paris Hilton, Dita von Teese, and the list goes on. Admittedly, events like Roch's own birthday bash are pretty much a closed shop to mere mortals, but on any Saturday night the German and Italian cars massing outside his club and the long line of Armani-clad revelers on the street testify to who wants to get in on the action. In summer Roch and his celebrity friends decamp to St-Tropez, but at other times of the year you never know who might be sipping Champagne in the VIP of the VIP. A new makeover by star decorator Andrée Putman is reminiscent of *The Matrix. Tue-Sun midnight-5am.* 78 av. des Champs-Elysées (M° George V), 01.56.69.16.66, viproom.fr

Hot & Cool Paris:
The Attractions

La Bulle Kenzo • 1st • Spa
This adorable little spa in the Kenzo building is quite unlike anything you'll find elsewhere. The beautiful white space is designed for you to touch, feel, and smell Kenzo's exclusive scents designed around colors, and fun relaxation toys such as the must-have head-massager and T-shirts with holes in them to encourage wandering hands. At the back of the room are the massage bubbles, one covered in white plastic hair and bathed in yellow light and the other a cocoon enveloping you in a mauve mood. The menu of massages promises to leave you in various states from "floating and gracious" to "amnesiac." For that jet-lag slump, check in without an appointment for a 30-minute siesta with images, music, and a murmuring wake-up call followed by tea. *Mon-Sat 10am-10pm.* €€€€ 1 rue du Pont Neuf (M° Châtelet), 01.73.04.20.04, labullekenzo.com

Centre Pompidou • 4th • Art Museum
Best Contemporary Art It's ugly, it's funky, and it's Paris' best-loved monument aside from the Eiffel Tower. Renzo Piano and Richard Rogers' giant shoebox with its inside-out transparent escalators, primary-colored pipes, and huge air ducts contains the largest collection of modern art in Europe, only a fraction of which can be shown at one time. Levels 4 and 5 cover the two periods up to and after 1960, with partial rehangs every year, and there are seven temporary exhibition spaces. Don't miss the room devoted to Yves Klein with videos of his Anthropométrie performance art in action, and the Dubuffet cave. The center also houses cinemas, a massive library, and Georges restaurant on the top floor. *Daily Wed-Mon 11am-9pm; some temporary exhibitions open Thu till 11pm.* € pl. Georges Pompidou (M° Rambuteau), 01.44.78.12.33, centrepompidou.fr

Colette • 1st • Store
Best Concept Stores The first ever concept store, Colette is a cultural phenomenon that generates tourism in its own right, but even with this influx of gawkers, it always adheres to its pure style maxim. Displays that are midway between merchandise and contemporary art might include Alexander McQueen's leather bodices or the latest robotic gizmo. Venture inside and you'll find hipster electronics, limited-edition style and manga mags, photographic and art tomes, cool cosmetics, music and DVDs, the selection constantly changing as the store predicts and makes trends. The latest draw is the "wall of sound" where suspended iPods allow you to listen to the entire musical selection, chosen by Michel Gaubert, who programs the music for runway shows. The upper floor is devoted to cutting-edge fashion. The basement café is best known for its water bar. *Mon-Sat 11am-7pm.* 213 rue St-Honoré (M° Tuileries), 01.55.35.33.90, colette.fr

Drugstore Publicis • 8th • Store
The Drugstore is a long-running love affair for the French, who remember its 1960s incarnation when it was the place to be seen for swingers like Jacques Dutronc and Jane Birkin. Fast-forward to 2004 when the advertising company opened a contemporary version with fiber-optic lighting and futuristic glass cladding. Inside is a brasserie, a cinema, and a selection of shops selling luxu-

ry foods, wines, cigars, cosmetics, cigarettes, and newspapers, right by the Etoile and open till 2am. Impossible to recapture the spirit of the '60s, when this French take on American culture was the Colette of its day, but it's useful to stock up on foreign press, New World wines to take back to your hotel room, and nifty food gifts for the folks back home. *Mon-Fri 8am-2am, Sat-Sun 10am-2am.* 133 av. des Champs-Elysées (M° Charles de Gaulle-Etoile), 01.44.43.79.00, publicisdrugstore.com

Fondation Cartier • 14th • Photography Gallery

The watchmaker's swanky offices, a masterpiece of light and transparency, house a foundation that has become an important player in the contemporary art world. Five exhibitions a year either focus on one artist or take a theme *(The Desert, Fragility)* and commission works in various media. Recently J'en Rêve paired up 58 artists under 30 exhibiting for the first time with established names. Imaginatively curated by Hervé Chandès, the Fondation makes contemporary art accessible and intriguing rather than highbrow. A program of musical and other performance events inspired by the exhibitions, *Les Soirées Nomades*, happens in the evenings. *Tue-Sun noon-8pm. Closed for 3 weeks between exhibitions.* €– 261 bd. Raspail (M° Raspail), 01.42.18.56.72, fondation.cartier.fr

Fondation Pierre Bergé Yves Saint Laurent • 16th • Fashion Museum

Best Chic Museums Fans of the couturier will love this small foundation in the building where Yves Saint Laurent formerly measured his couture clients. It's very classy, as are the people who come here, friends of the designer and blue-blooded former clients among them, as many of the dresses have been lent or donated by their original owners. Twice-yearly exhibitions draw from the Fondation's collection, which is stored at a perfect temperature and hygrometric level on the building's upper floors, or are devoted to friends and muses of the designer. A glimpse into a rarified world that is rapidly becoming a museum piece itself. *Tue-Sun 11am-6pm. Closed Aug and between exhibitions.* €– 1 rue Léonce-Reynaud (M° Alma-Marceau), 01.44.31.64.00, ysl-hautecouture.com

Jardin des Tuileries • 1st • Park

Best Statuary The Tuileries were the royal gardens before the Revolution and later became a fashionable place for a promenade. There is still something wonderfully chic about the green metal chairs arranged around the fountain and the tearoom hidden in the center of the park as if for a romantic tryst. Plenty of hopefuls are looking for just that here—single women will not be left alone for long so are advised to brush up on their brush-off phrases. Don't be put off, it's still a gorgeous place for a stroll under the chestnut trees or to watch the sun go down. *Daily 7:30am. Closes 7:30pm-midnight depending on the season.* Rue de Rivoli (M° Tuileries)

Jeu de Paume • 8th • Photography Gallery

The 17th-century royal tennis courts now house the Centre National de la Photographie with a varied program of exhibitions covering big-name photographers or themed shows covering the entire century and a half of photographic creation. There are two large, airy galleries, a hip café, and a basement video art and cinema suite, as the institution aims to forge links between photography and video art. *Tue noon-9pm, Wed-Fri noon-7pm, Sat-Sun 10am-7pm.* €– 1 pl. de la Concorde (M° Concorde), 01.47.03.12.50, jeudepaume.org

Maison Européenne de la Photographie • 4th • Art Gallery
The Marais has two photography galleries, the small offshoot of the Jeu de Paume in the Hôtel de Sully (62 rue St-Antoine, 4th, 01.47.03.12.50) showing documentary and political photography, and the MEP, also in a Marais mansion with a modern annex. This institution, devoted to post–World War II photography, is the most international of the lot with a varied program of exhibitions, films, and lectures. You might find anything here from William Klein to experimental art photography. *Wed-Sun 11am-8pm. €-* 5-7 rue de Fourcy (M° St-Paul), 01.44.78.75.00, mep-fr.org

Marais private galleries • 3rd • Art Galleries
As you wander around the Marais' narrow streets, dipping in to the many fashion and interior design boutiques, take the time to explore some of its private art galleries. The Marais remains the most important stop for contemporary art collectors. Galerie Daniel Templon is one of the oldest, showing mainly painters, including young American artists and European ones. Through the courtyard of a former mansion is Yvon Lambert, probably France's most important private gallery, showing Nan Goldin, Jenny Holzer, intriguing and sometimes shocking installations, and video art. Galerie Emmanuel Perrotin has provocative art from the new Japanese generation and well-known names such as Sophie Calle, and a shop sells limited-edition books and prints. The galleries are a great way to acquaint yourself with what's new on the art scene. *Generally open Mon-Sat 10am-7pm.* Galerie Daniel Templon: 30 rue Beaubourg, 01.42.72.14.10, danieltemplon.com. Galerie Yvon Lambert: 108 rue Vieille-du-Temple, 01.42.71.09.33, yvon-lambert.com. Galerie Emmanuel Perrotin: 76 rue de Turenne, 01.42.16.79.79, galerieperrotin.com. (M° Hôtel de Ville/St-Paul)

Maria Luisa • 1st • Store
With Nicole Kidman and Cameron Diaz as her clients, Maria Luisa Poumaillou is a star in her own right and a name to drop in every fashionista's vocabulary. Since 1988 she's been selecting the crème de la crème of each season's prêt-à-porter collections for her rue Cambon boutique, which is arranged like a personal dressing room. The buyer who helped launch Galliano, McQueen, Rick Owens, and Véronique Branquinho, among others, she always has an eye for rising stars, and the stores' knowledgeable assistants will help you mix and match with fabulous results. *Mon-Sat 10:30am-7pm.* 2 rue Cambon, 01.47.03.48.08. Accessories: 4 rue Cambon. Streetwear: 38 rue du Mont-Thabor. Menswear: 19 bis rue du Mont-Thabor. (M° Concorde)

Musée d'Art Moderne de la Ville de Paris • 16th • Art Museum
This museum devoted to 20th-century art has reopened after two years of closure. It features new art spaces, including a subterranean *salle noire* (black room) for video art installation and a new café, among other renovations. Although it is perhaps best known for its blockbuster temporary exhibits highlighting one artist or artistic period, its permanent collection of some 8,000 works reveals the changing trends in contemporary art over the course of the century. Situated opposite the Palais de Tokyo, it also boasts an exceptional location overlooking the Seine with fine views of the Eiffel Tower. *Tue-Fri 10am-5:30pm, Sat-Sun 10am-7pm. €–* 11 av. du Président-Wilson (M° Iéna), 01.53.67.40.00, mam.paris.fr

Musée des Arts Asiatiques-Guimet • 16th • Art Museum

The monumental Giant's Way, part of an entrance to the temple of Angkor Wat, greets you as you enter Guimet, which brings a serene, light, and spacious layout to its galleries of Asian art. The museum grew out of a private collection, which was later merged with national collections and enriched by objects brought back from archaeological expeditions to Korea, China, and Afghanistan, to make it one of the world's greatest Asian art museums. The museum is educational, but you can also simply lose yourself in the wonder of Khmer statues, exquisite Tibetan bronzes, and Han tomb figures with their powerful spiritual significance. *Wed-Mon 10am-6pm. €–* 6 pl. d'Iéna (M° Iéna), 01.56.52.53.00, museeguimet.fr

Musée Baccarat • 16th • Design Museum

Best Chic Museums *Alice in Wonderland*, Marie-Antoinette, and Dalí all come together in the fantastical palace of the Musée Baccarat, designed by Philippe Starck. The crystal company opened its new showcase in the former mansion house of the Vicomtesse de Noailles. Red carpets, fiber-optic lighting, and a fish tank with a submerged chandelier greet you before you visit a banquet room with its gorgeous setting reflected in infinite mirrors, an "alchemy room" entirely painted by mythological artist Garouste, and a gallery of crystal masterpieces. In a word, wonderland. *Mon-Sat 10am-6:30pm. €–* 11 pl. des Etats-Unis (M° Boissière), 01.40.22.11.00, baccarat.fr

Musée de la Contrefaçon • 16th • Museum

Set up by the Union of Manufacturers to deter forgery, this small museum has acquired cult status. It seems owners of real and fake Gucci and those who care about having the LV logo on their person can't get enough of the "spot the difference" displays showing fakes alongside the originals. Reebok, Lacoste, Hermès, perfume brands, Bic biros, and Swiss Army Knives are all here, as well as more unusual objects. A Gallo-Roman amphora with its maker's mark and a copy from the same epoch show that faking it is at least as old as Paris itself. Fascinating—and kind of useful. *Tue-Sun 2-5:30pm. €–* 16 rue de la Faisanderie (M° Porte Dauphine), 01.56.26.14.00

Musée de la Mode et du Textile • 1st • Fashion Museum

Best Chic Museums Housed in a wing of the Louvre, the state fashion museum holds the most important collection in Europe. Only a little bit can be seen at one time, and the collection is shown in changing exhibitions that run from a single creator to thematics (the play of light, the handbag). Some exhibitions are devoted to contemporary designers, with life-size films of their runway shows. The dark rooms with spotlighting create an atmosphere of mystery and glamour. The same can be said of the Galerie des Bijoux, which is included in the ticket. Two rooms spotlight jewels from medieval châtelaines to contemporary pieces. *Tue-Fri 11am-6pm, Sat-Sun 10am-6pm. €–* 107 rue de Rivoli (M° Palais Royal-Musée du Louvre), 01.44.55.57.50, ucad.fr

Musée Pícasso • 3rd • Art Museum

Picasso's bequest to the French state is housed in a beautiful Marais hôtel particulier that serves as a wonderful backdrop for the artist's work. As you wander around, among stylish international gallerygoers and Marais residents popping in for a cultural breather, you may feel as if you have been invited to a private viewing in a gorgeous, art-filled house. The museum covers every phase of Picasso's life and work, from the Blue period through Cubism and classicism, and the ribald, crude later work. The artist's collection of tribal art juxtaposed with his own sculptures shows direct influence. *Wed-Mon 9:30am-5:30pm (till 6pm in summer).* €– Hôtel Salé, 5 rue de Thorigny (M° St-Sébastien-Froissart), 01.42.71.25.21, musee-picasso.fr

Spa Nuxe 32 Montorgueil • 1st • Spa

Best Spas The sveltest Parisian stars are favoring Nuxe's contemporary spa, which hides behind a bamboo-planted courtyard. Here you can be coiffed like French beauties Vanessa Paradis, Audrey Tautou, and Emmanuelle Béart, who are all clients of John Nollet. A glass elevator takes you down to the 4,000-square-foot treatment and relaxation rooms. Medieval stone vaults and beams combine with polished concrete, steel, and Japanese paper screens, all sepulchrally lit by the architects. The Nuxe products, based on plants and essential oils, really work. Treatments include an hour-long pedicure using rose petals (Fridays only) and the Rêve de Miel honey body scrub and envelopment, anti-cellulite treatments, and massages. €€€€ *Mon, Tue, Sat 9am-7:30pm, Wed-Fri 9am-9pm.* 32 rue Montorgueil (M° Les Halles), 01.55.80.71.40, nuxe.com

Classic Paris

Don't be shy about it: you're dying to see the Eiffel Tower, visit the Louvre, soak up the atmosphere of the Latin Quarter. They're not famous for nothing, but you certainly don't want to waste your valuable time standing in line with the rest of the world, and you won't be going home with an "all I got was this lousy T-shirt" gift pack either. This itinerary fits in all the classics, but in a different way. Take a unique tour led by an art expert, go up the Eiffel Tower at night, see the singing nun at the Sacré-Coeur, and eat in restaurants where you really feel like you're in that Paris movie and not the made-for-TV version.

*Note: Venues in bold in the itinerary are described in detail in the listings that follow. Venues followed by an * asterisk are those we recommend as both a restaurant and a destination bar.*

Classic Paris:
The Perfect Plan (3 Days and Nights)

Your Hotel: Hôtel de Crillon, because this sumptuous palace hotel has a superb location, a splendidly decadent décor, and a gorgeous bar and restaurant.

Thursday

Highlights

Thursday
Breakfast	Angelina
Morning	Louvre
Lunch	Café Marly
Afternoon	Bateaux Vedette, Invalides
Cocktails	Café du Marché
Dinner	Jules Verne
Nighttime	Le Tourville
Late-Night	Bar du Marché

Friday
Breakfast	Le Rostand
Morning	Latin Quarter
Lunch	Les Papilles
Afternoon	Musée d'Orsay
Cocktails	Les Editeurs
Dinner	La Coupole
Nighttime	La Coupole
Late-Night	Chez Castel

Saturday
Breakfast	At hotel
Morning	Père Lachaise
Lunch	La Mascotte
Afternoon	Ile de la Cité
Cocktails	Concert
Dinner	La Truffière
Nighttime	Bar Hemingway
Late-Night	Ritz Club, Au Pied de Cochon

The Morning After
Brunch	Les Ambassadeurs

9am Begin your visit in royal splendor with breakfast at **Angelina**, the ornate tearoom that used to be the rendezvous for society English and Americans in Paris.

10am That luxury breakfast should give you what you need to tackle that behemoth, the **Louvre**. Don't join the lines outside the I.M. Pei pyramid; you can scoot in with a prebooked ticket through a relatively secret entrance in passage Richelieu, or via the Cour des Lions. Choose your pleasure—Renaissance masters and the *Mona Lisa*, French painting, Dutch masters, sculpture, Egyptians and the Middle East, or the impressive gallery of Primitive Arts. You won't be able to cover it all, so just pick two or three. Consider opting for an expert and interactive guided tour in English by **Paris Muse**.

1pm Lunch After taking in as much world-class art as you can, snag a prime seat on the cloistered terrace of **Café Marly** overlooking the glass pyramid, where some of the best-dressed waiters in Paris serve delicious salads and Italian antipasti. Or for historical

CLASSIC

85

atmosphere, make your way to **La Table d'Hôte du Palais Royal**, in a 17th-century vaulted cellar located opposite the writer Colette's former apartment.

3pm After lunch, relax on a riverboat cruise offered by **Bateaux Vedette du Pont Neuf**. Handily departing from near the Louvre, it does a well-narrated hour-long tour that takes in major riverside sites. Suitably refreshed, walk across the Ile de la Cité and take the RER from St-Michel to arrive at Invalides. If you want to skip the narration, simply take a one-way trip on the **Batobus** river transport from the Louvre directly to the Invalides.

4:30pm The impressive golden-domed building of **Les Invalides**, the church of a military hospital, houses Napoléon's porphyry tomb. You can also visit the Musée de l'Armée, which is full of military pomp and good exhibitions on the two World Wars.

6pm Take a walk around the Champ de Mars, where the Mur de la Paix makes a brave attempt to promote world peace in several languages. Then relax and enjoy an early evening apéritif at **Café du Marché**. Then return to your hotel to primp for the evening.

9pm Dinner There are two good reasons to book the **Jules Verne**: the fabulous view and the special VIP elevator that spirits you over 400 feet up to level two of the Eiffel Tower without forcing you to stand in line. At the last count the waiting list was four months long, however, so if you're the spontaneous type, save the tower for after and sample the Mauritian-tinged cuisine of **Le Chamarré** or elevated bistro food with an Eiffel Tower view at **Au Bon Accueil**.

Midnight The **Eiffel Tower** by night offers one of Paris' magical moments, as you are encased in the glittering structure while surveying Paris below. Afterward, have a drink on the superb terrace of **Le Tourville** before heading into St-Germain.

1am **Bar du Marché** is one of the most lively late-night venues with a strategic terrace and waiters dressed in overalls and cloth caps. If you're hankering for live jazz, make your way to **Le Sabot** for great atmosphere and a genuine St-Germain crowd, or **Le Bilboquet**, celebrating a half-century of swing.

Friday

9:30am Breakfast at the elegant **Le Rostand** next to the lovely Jardin du Luxembourg.

10:30am Soak up the spirit of medieval Paris at the nearby **Musée Nationale du Moyen Age-**

Thermes et Hôtel de Cluny. From here you can stroll around the medieval heart of the Latin Quarter, taking in quaint cobbled roads, the oldest church in Paris, St-Julien-le-Pauvre, the famed English bookshop Shakespeare and Co., the Sorbonne, and the **Panthéon**. The colorful food markets of rue Mouffetard and place Monge should whet your appetite for a fine lunch.

1:30pm Lunch A bustling local spot at lunchtime is the bistro **Le Pré Verre**, full of academics, journalists, and other Left Bank folk tucking into the great-value prix fixe. Or try the great food and atmosphere at the award-winning wine bar **Les Papilles**.

3:30pm Take bus 24, which runs to the **Musée d'Orsay**. While its Impressionist collection is the main draw, Orsay, housed in a grandiose former railway station, also has sculpture, furniture, and photography dating from the years 1848–1914.

6pm After all that art you deserve a terrace break, so head back into St-Germain and hobnob with editors and writers at **Les Editeurs** or philosophers and nostalgists at **Café de Flore**. Then consider a little cat nap back at the hotel before dinner.

9pm Dinner It wouldn't be Paris without a slap-up, multistoried seafood platter borne to your table by bow-tied waiters, and there's nowhere better to order it than **La Coupole**, the legendary Montparnasse brasserie that's enjoying a fashionable comeback. The other brasserie classic is the Alsatian choucroute garnie, which is served at the equally famous **Brasserie Lipp** in St-Germain. Vintage French film stars and politicians treat this place like their cafeteria. For something more low-key, soak up the south of France atmosphere complete with Cocteau paintings at **La Méditerranée**.

11pm After dinner, check what's going down in the basement of **La Coupole**, where the club that once played host to Josephine Baker now holds nights devoted to salsa, R&B, broken beats, and house. If a quiet drink is more what you're after, have a martini at the wonderfully arcane **Rosebud** or the piano bar **La Closerie des Lilas**, where Hemingway wrote *The Sun Also Rises*.

1am Put on a knowing look to get past the door at **Chez Castel**, a private club where the jet set has been partying for 30 years.

Saturday

10am Ease into the day with a leisurely breakfast at your hotel. Then it's time to visit the mother of all celebrity burial grounds,

Cimetière de Père Lachaise. Don't be surprised if you see a few strange black-clad figures walking around—they are looking for Jim Morrison's grave. Other famous names run into the hundreds. If cemeteries aren't your thing, start your day at **Le Spa at the Four Seasons George V**.

Noon From Père Lachaise, move up to Montmartre to see the **Basilique du Sacré-Coeur** and check out the area's artistic and political history at the charming **Musée de Montmartre**.

1pm Lunch Montmartre is a higgledy-piggledy mix of tourist junk, trendiness, and old-world eccentricity. The latter is enshrined by **La Mascotte**, a brasserie where some of the area's most colorful characters gather for lunch. A quieter ambiance is found at **Le Poulbot Gourmet**, a high-quality bistro named after the cartoon ragamuffin of Montmartre.

3pm Then head south to the city center on the Ile de la Cité to stroll the narrow cobbled lanes and see the **Cathédrale Notre Dame**, the **Conciergerie**, and the stained glass of **Ste-Chapelle**.

7pm For early evening, consider a concert. Many of Paris' churches have classical music or gospel concerts. Ste-Chapelle or St-Julien-le-Pauvre provide a beautiful setting. If classical's not your style, see who's starring at **l'Olympia**, the mythic concert hall where all the greats (Sinatra, Piaf) have played. Or choose jazz at Paris' highest-profile jazz address, **New Morning**.

9pm Dinner If you've attended a concert in a church, come down to earth in the most heavenly way with a truffle feast at **La Truffière**. After l'Olympia try **Aux Lyonnais**, Alain Ducasse and Thierry de la Brosse's regional eatery. New Morning will leave you looking for a late dinner. Try **Julien**, an Art Nouveau brasserie.

11pm It's your last night, so celebrate with a cocktail at the Ritz's classy **Bar Hemingway**, or the Crillon's piano bar, **Bar César**.

1am Then join the exclusive party scene at the **Ritz Club** or stroll down the Champs-Elysées to long-standing **Régine's Club**.

4am Wrap up your visit in suitable style with a towering platter of oysters at the perennially popular **Au Pied de Cochon**.

The Morning After
The World Brunch is a great way to experience the Crillon's chandelier-and-marble dining room, **Les Ambassadeurs**, and a splendid finale to your visit.

Classic Paris:
The Key Neighborhoods

The **Ile de la Cité** (**1st** and **4th arrondissements**), with Notre-Dame, the Conciergerie Revolutionary prison, and Ste-Chapelle, is where Paris began. North of this on the Right Bank is the immense Louvre and lovely formal Tuileries gardens, the former pleasure gardens of the Palais Royal, and the historic Bourse area.

The **5th** and **6th arrondissements** are filled with historical and literary associations. In St-Germain you can soak up the spirit of its famous jazz clubs and café terraces, while Montparnasse, the artists' quarter in the '20s and '30s, still has a host of Art Deco brasseries serving platters of shellfish with lots of atmosphere. The Latin Quarter in the 5th arrondissement is still a student area where bookshops and medieval churches vie for attention and you can trace the path of Hemingway's *A Moveable Feast* as you shop at the rue Mouffetard market.

The **7th arrondissement** is an elegant district that houses many good restaurants as well as the Eiffel Tower and the imposing Invalides, where Napoléon is buried. The Champ de Mars and Esplanade des Invalides, both designed for military parades, are filled with picnickers and frisbee-players at other times.

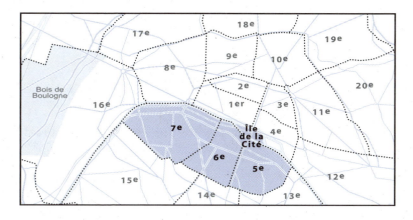

Classic Paris: The Shopping Blocks

The Grands Boulevards

This is the birthplace of the department store's twin *grands magasins,* which vie for attention like two spoiled children. Around them are international chains such as Zara and Benetton, though the streets to the north contain some more unusual curiosities as well.

Détaille Step back in time in this museum piece of a perfume shop, which sells its original scents. 10 rue St-Lazare (M° Notre-Dame-de-Lorette), 01.48.78.68.50

Galeries Lafayette Glittering behemoth of a department store. (p.110) 40 bd. Haussmann (M° Chaussée d'Antin), 01.42.82.34.56

A la Mère de Famille Old-fashioned épicerie that sells jams and other delicacies. 35 rue du Fbg. Montmartre (M° Grands-Boulevards), 901.47.70.83.69

Papeterie Laffitte More than just a stationer, this papeterie has a large selection of high-quality gifts, leather bags, wooden toys, and artists' materials. 27 rue Laffitte (M° Le Peletier), 01.47.70.38.83

Printemps This department store's Art Nouveau cupola and the biggest beauty department in the world are two of its claims to fame. (p.113) 64 bd. Haussmann (M° Havre-Caumartin), 01.42.82.57.87

The Latin Quarter and Odéon

Joyce's and Hemingway's former stomping-ground is the heartland of secondhand bookshops and specialist tea merchants.

Abbey Bookshop This tiny, packed bookshop on a pretty street also runs a Canadian club. 29 rue de la Parcheminerie (M° St-Michel), 01.46.33.16.24

La Maison des Trois Thés The largest tea collection in the world, presided over by the gracious Maître Tseng. 1 rue St-Médard (M° Place Monge), 01.43.36.93.84

San Francisco Book Co. Well-stocked American secondhand bookshop. 17 rue Monsieur le Prince (M° Odéon), 01.43.29.15.70

Shakespeare & Co. Literary landmark around since 1951, with young writers (and a cat) living on the premises. (p.114) 37 rue de la Bûcherie (M° Maubert-Mutualité), 01.43.25.40.93

Village Voice 25-year-old English-language bookstore with literary magazines and a lively program of readings. 6 rue Princesse (M° Mabillon), 01.46.33.36.47

Classic Paris: The Hotels

Four Seasons George V • 8th • Grand (245 rms)
　The George V has been a favorite for Americans in Paris since it opened in 1928. In less carefree times General Eisenhower set up his wartime HQ here. The hotel is decorated with a wealth of antiques, tapestries, and carpets so thick it's like skating in snow. This isn't your typical Four Seasons, therefore, but the 2002 takeover by the luxury chain enabled it to shine up the silverware in a big way. Echoing the Plaza Athénée's bar and restaurant shock treatment, the George V has brought in Jeff Leatham, florist to Ian Schrager, to inject some avant-garde accents with his contemporary art–style floral displays. Rooms, among the largest in Paris hotels, are traditionally decorated in yellow, blue, and green Louis XVI style, Napoléonic, or English décor. The bar is a fashionable cocktail rendezvous, the Le Cinq restaurant among the top five in the city, and the summer terrace restaurant has a *Great Gatsby* atmosphere with piped jazz and waiters in beige flannel suits. But the real draw is the spa. With statues, chandeliers, and murals of the gardens of Versailles around the pool, this is where the Sun King would get pampered if he were still around. €€€€ 31 av. George V (M° Alma-Marceau), 01.49.52.70.00, fourseasons.com

Hôtel Le Bristol • 8th • Grand (175 rms)
　There's a certain self-assuredness about the Bristol. It doesn't need fads or flashy gilding to keep its clients happy, and it is this, together with the incredibly large Presidential suites and the hotel's famous discretion, that makes it the number one choice for visiting heads of state. Situated on the fashionable rue du Faubourg St-Honoré, the 18th-century building has been a hotel since 1925. The two-Michelin-starred chef Eric Frechon creates fabulous cuisine served in an oval former private theater, or in the summer dining room overlooking the largest garden of any Paris hotel. The Bristol has an exceptional collection of Gobelin tapestries, period furniture, and paintings. The rooms are decorated in a fresh and uncluttered way, using floral chintzes from the famous French fabric houses. Another perk is the biggest bathrooms in town. The new Prestige rooms, at 538 square feet, have two! And up on the Paris rooftops, the pool is designed to make you feel like you're on a luxury yacht. €€€€ 112 rue du Fbg. St-Honoré (M° Miromesnil), 01.53.43.43.00, hotel-bristol.com

Hôtel de Crillon • 8th • Grand (127 rms)
　The Crillon's fab location attracts a galaxy of stars including Uma Thurman, Michael Jackson, and J-Lo, as well as royalty and heads of state. Calling this a palace is no understatement—it was the private residence of the Counts of Crillon, and in its first-floor salons you could imagine yourself at Versailles. There is also a rococo inner courtyard, where three centuries drop away in the crystalline acoustics. The Crillon seems to contain more marble than all the other hotels together—acres of the stuff in shades of toffee, cream, and black are polished to perfection in the lobby, Winter Garden, and Les Ambassadeurs restaurant, not to mention the spacious bathrooms. The redecorated Louis XV–style rooms have sumptuous brocade fabrics. Ask for one in purple and gold

in the older front part of the hotel, which retains its elaborate moldings, or, if money is no object, the Duc de Crillon suite—the duke's private chapel, decorated with 17th-century painted panels of fruit and flowers. The Crillon is currently on a drive to attract a new generation of sybarites, and its utterly dreamy 18th-century dining room is enlivened by chill-out grooves for the Sunday brunch, while fashion types crowd into the snazzy mosaic-trimmed bar. €€€€ 10 pl. de la Concorde (M° Concorde), 01.44.71.15.00, crillon.com

Hôtel Edouard VII • 2nd • Modern (69 rms)

One step down from a palace, the Edouard VII is a well-appointed classic sleep. In the entrance you'll step over the mosaic unicorn insignia of the Prince of Wales, which refers to the future Edward VII of England, who stayed here on his forays to Paris to visit the opera and the city's famous courtesans in the 1890s. Next door is the Angl'Opéra restaurant where film, theater, and media types enjoy hot chef Gilles Choukroun's culinary creativity. A wrought-iron lift takes you up to the rooms, decorated in sunny Provençal colors or chocolate and burgundy stripes, antiques, and oil paintings. Plush marble and mosaic bathrooms and fluffy monogrammed robes await guests. Ask for the third or fourth floor for the most recently updated rooms; 304 has a great view of the Opera Garnier from its balcony. €€€ 39 av. de l'Opéra (M° Opéra), 01.42.61.56.90, edouard7hotel.com

Hôtel Lutetia • 14th • Grand (259 rms)

Staying at the Lutetia is all about nostalgia for the jazz age in Paris. The city's first Art Deco hotel, it was built in 1910 specifically to house shoppers at the prestigious Bon Marché department store and became a focus for the Left Bank artistic community. Picasso, Matisse, André Gide, and Josephine Baker all stayed here or partied in its sumptuous bar and restaurant, and General de Gaulle spent his wedding night here. Carved stone Art Deco lettering proclaims the name of this historic monument, and the gastronomic restaurant, brasserie, and two bars glitter with chrome, zinc, and mirrors. At night the Ernest bar fills up with journalists, showbiz personalities, and Left Bank intellectuals just as it always has, with live jazz Wed-Sat. Ask for one of the newly decorated Deluxe rooms with a balcony view of the Eiffel Tower. Guests who've gone for Internet deals have often ended up with the disappointing courtyard rooms. €€€€ 45 bd. Raspail (M° Rue du Bac), 01.49.54.46.46, lutetia-paris.com

Hôtel Ritz • 1st • Grand (175 rms)

There is only one Ritz, all others are just imitators. When César Ritz opened his hotel in 1898, his friends provided the fantasy guest list of the age. The Ritz's gilded décor, its palms and mirrors, lush garden and cozy bars are merely the trappings: it's the ghosts of so many famous guests that give staying here its frisson. In the dusky pink Espadon restaurant it is easy to imagine Fred Astaire "putting on the Ritz" at an afternoon tea dance; the rue Cambon entrance was Coco Chanel's private door (she lived here for over 30 years); Cole Porter began the beguine in the bar Vendôme; and Hemingway is nowhere more present than in the bar named after him. The Windsors' and Chanel's suites are just as they left them; others evoke Hemingway, F. Scott Fitzgerald, Chopin, and Elton John. Even the classic rooms are delightful, with floral or silken fabrics and the bathrooms designed by César Ritz's wife. Those overlooking the garden are sunniest, with Proust's room an extra-special Deluxe—it has a summer sky painted on the ceiling. €€€€ 15 pl. Vendôme (M° Tuileries), 01.43.16.30.70, ritzparis.com

Classic Paris: The Restaurants

Allard • 6th • Traditional
Tucked behind the fashion boutiques and bustle of the Carrefour de Buci, Allard is the sort of place where time stands still. The 1940s feel of the place, with its mustard-yellow walls, brown-leather banquettes, and lace curtains at the window, is loved by locals and visitors alike, and you'll find a mixed crowd of all ages partaking in the nostalgic experience. Waistcoated waiters rush around serving the classics that make this place worth searching out: duck with olives, boeuf bourguignon, and Bresse chicken with mushrooms. If you're looking for the perfect Parisian bistro experience, go no further. *Mon-Sat noon-2:30pm and 7-11:30pm.* € 41 rue St-André-des-Arts (M° Odéon), 01.43.26.48.23

Les Ambassadeurs • 8th • Gastronomic
Best Brunches Freshened up for its Emmy-winning and fashion-world clientele without scaring off the traditionalists, the restaurant of the Crillon has had a subtle nip and tuck that's injected a mere glimmer of trendiness here. It's a feast of pink marble and chandeliers, rendered more staid by pale décor and formal waiters gliding about in designer suits. DJ Béatrice Ardisson has devised a chic soundtrack for the modish Sunday World Brunch. The world bit refers to the extravagant buffet drawn from four countries, and you can select from smoked salmon, cured ham, poached eggs, and fabulous French pastries. Snag a table in the window for a view of Place de la Concorde. *Mon 7-10:30am and 7:30-10pm, Tue-Sat 7-10:30am, 12:30-2pm, and 7:30-10pm, Sun noon-3pm.* €€€€ Hôtel de Crillon, 10 pl. de la Concorde (M° Concorde), 01.44.71.16.16, crillon.com

Angelina • 1st • Tearoom
This classic tea salon, originally known as Rumpelmeyer's, once formed part of an upper-crust English and American enclave here, along with the Hôtel Meurice and bookshops Gallignani and W.H. Smith. Though gaudy gift shops have now invaded rue de Rivoli, Angelina remains pristine with its green marble-topped tables, leather armchairs, flamboyant murals, and courteous staff. The fact that it is now a tourist attraction has not harmed the quality of the fare, particularly the sticky pastries and superlative hot chocolate. There are two breakfast formulas, the pastries and coffee (or chocolate) version, or the full works with eggs, smoked salmon, and so on. Expensive, but worth it. *Mon-Fri 9:45am-6:45pm, Sat-Sun 9am-7pm.* € 226 rue de Rivoli (M° Tuileries), 01.42.60.82.00

L'Angle du Faubourg • 8th • Contemporary
Taillevent, one of Paris' most prestigious restaurants, has an incredible cellar containing some 5,000 bottles. For diners who love the finer things in life but don't want to splash out on a €400 meal, the restaurant's proprietor has opened this smaller, more affordable place with the aim of perfectly matching food and wine. Wine lovers are therefore the most regular patrons, as well as businesspeople at lunch. The modern interior is warmly decorated with terra-cotta walls

and velvet chairs. The talented female sommelier will guide you through the various vintages and will match a wine by the glass to each course. If wine's your thing, a visit to the cave, where you can also buy wine to take home, will be a highlight of your trip. *Mon-Fri noon-2:15pm and 7-10:15pm.* €€ 195 rue du Fbg. St-Honoré (M° Charles de Gaulle-Etoile), 01.40.74.20.20, taillevent.com

L'Avant-Goût • 13th • Bistro
Ask any foodie what his favorite bistro is and he'll probably go into raptures about L'Avant-Goût. On a busy avenue near the cobbled streets of the Butte-aux-Cailles, it's the king of this bistro quarter, and journalists, chefs, and intellectuals pack its tight tables. The atmosphere is noisy and convivial. Thursday night's "chef's choice" always generates excitement, and the lunch menu is a great deal. The suckling pig, a brimming pot au feu flavored with fennel, sweet potato, and ginger, is unforgettable. *Tue-Fri 12:15-2pm and 7:45-11pm.* € 26 rue Bobillot (M° Place d'Italie), 01.53.80.24.00

Le Bistrot d'à Coté Flaubert • 17th • Bistro
Michel Rostang's baby bistro next to his gastronomic restaurant attracts an intriguing mix of distinguished old dames in fur coats, posh sons and daughters entertaining their parents, and courting couples. The former Belle Epoque épicerie has great ambiance, with a tongue-in-cheek décor of Toby jugs caricaturing world leaders and old Michelin guides. The delicious food uses the freshest ingredients and a mixture of Granny's pantry satisfiers (the wild duck and foie gras pâté en croûte) and international touches (lobster salad with tiny ravioli and sea bass in a Thai-style sauce). You have to order the fondant au chocolat before the meal: do it. The servers seem to be on a training program, inexperienced but eager to please. *Tue-Fri 12:30-2:30pm and 7:30-11pm.* €€ 10 rue Gustave-Flaubert (M° Ternes), 01.42.67.05.81, michelrostang.com

Au Bon Accueil • 7th • Bistro
Best Bistros An address well worth knowing, this excellent bistro has a view of the Eiffel Tower from its outside tables, but it doesn't stint on quality just because out-of-towners have discovered it. If you sit inside you won't have the tower, but you can enjoy the trendified décor of paneled walls and rush-backed curved banquettes. Jacques Lacipière takes traditional French dishes and adds a bit of modern dash, such as braised beef cheek with rhubarb or veal and rice stew with crayfish. There's a choice of fresh, fruity desserts or cheeses, and an interesting wine list, and the welcome couldn't be warmer. *Mon-Fri noon-2:30pm and 7:30-10:30pm.* € 14 rue Monttessuy (M° Alma-Marceau), 01.47.05.46.11

Brasserie Lipp • 6th • Brasserie
The brasserie established by Léopold Lipp in 1890 is so integral a part of the St-Germain scene that the restaurant is now classed as a "place of memory" by the Ministry of Culture. Hemingway, St-Exupéry, Camus, Gide, politicos of all sides (Mitterrand virtually lived here), and actors such as Lauren Bacall and Jack Nicholson have eaten here, and it continues to pull in a distinguished A-list, which means that unknowns who don't protest often get seated in social Siberia upstairs. The menu and service haven't changed a jot. Expect steaming plates of choucroute garnie, pig's trotter, beef tartare, and blanquette de veau borne aloft by black-tied waiters. *Daily 10am-1am.* €€ 151 bd. St-Germain (M° Rue du Bac), 01.45.48.53.91, brasserie-lipp.fr

CLASSIC • RESTAURANTS

Le Bristol • 8th • Gastronomic
Though many cite Le Bristol's summer quarters—in or overlooking its large, neatly manicured garden—as one of the most outstanding outdoor dining experiences in the city, it's the paneled, oval winter dining room with its painted ceiling that is the real star. A former private theater, this setting is so intimate and privileged that the summer dining room feels a little like a wedding marquee in comparison. Wherever you dine, you'll get Eric Frechon's superlative cuisine with a luxury menu where all the seasonal highlights have their opportunity to shine, from mushrooms to lobster to truffles. *Daily noon-2:30pm and 7-10:30pm. Summer dining room open May-Oct.* €€€€ ▯ Hôtel Bristol, 112 rue du Fbg. St-Honoré (Mº Miromesnil), 01.53.43.43.00, lebristolparis.com

Café Marly • 1st • Trendy
Best Café Terraces Join fashionistas and art lovers at this Costes café in the Cour Napoléon of the Louvre. Seated under the elegant cloister, you can't help but feel superior as you watch the line snaking patiently round I.M. Pei's pyramid to descend into the world-famous museum. The dandified waiters are plentiful, though it is hard to get their attention, so choose what you want from the light and tasty menu of antipasti, large salads, and plats du jour and start waving. It doesn't really matter what you order as a chance to linger in this prime spot can only be a good thing. *Daily 8am-2am.* € ▯ Cour Napoléon du Louvre, 93 rue de Rivoli (Mº Palais Royal-Musée du Louvre), 01.49.26.06.60

Le Chamarré • 7th • Contemporary
A unique dining experience awaits at this cozy-chic, cushion-and-velvet restaurant near the Eiffel Tower. Go for the "carte blanche" tasting menu and sit back as a procession of plates is brought to the table. Many of the dishes use a European base—Scottish grouse, Breton lobster, or sea bass—enhanced by Mauritian spices and fruit condiments, which are arranged on the plate as on a painter's palette; others present three variants on one meat or fish with varying degrees of exoticism. At the end of the meal, the chefs come and chat with guests to hear what you think of their creations. *Tue-Fri noon-2:30pm and 7:30-10:30pm, Sat 7:30-10:30pm.* €€€€ ▯ 13 bd. de la Tour-Maubourg (Mº La Tour-Maubourg), 01.47.05.50.18

Chez Marianne • 4th • Jewish
A Jewish brunch in the Marais has become a favorite Sunday rendezvous, and the welcome is always genuine at this Sephardic spot. You can choose from a variety of ambiances, from the grown-up right-hand dining room lined with wines to the ethnically decorated left-hand one, which has a lot of character. In summer the restaurant takes over a little courtyard, and there's also the deli at the far end where you can buy pastries to go. Wherever you choose, you'll find it bustling with a young and lively scene. The idea's simple: you make up your own plate from the many kemia on offer: chopped liver, hummus, tabouli, roast eggplant, and so on, and finish with a sticky, honey-covered pastry. No scrambled eggs, but the mint tea does wonders for a delicate head. *Daily 11am-midnight.* € ▯ 2 rue des Hospitalières-St-Gervais (Mº St-Paul), 01.42.72.18.86

Le Cinq • 8th • Gastronomic
The George V's luxurious dining room offers everything you'd want from a Paris palace—pearly gray and gilt surroundings, huge flower displays and palms,

impeccable service, and the ultimate luxury ingredients metamorphosed into polished dishes. A distinguished older crowd tends to dine here, with suited CEOs at lunch, though the setting is perfect for a special meal à deux. Philippe Legendre was the chef at Taillevent before coming here, and he adds a dash of invention to classical French cuisine. The wood-smoked lobster with morels is unforgettable. Le Cinq's cellar is curated by two winners of the Best World Wine Steward award. *Mon-Fri 7-10am, noon-2:30pm, and 6:30-11pm, Sat-Sun 7-10:30am, 12:30-2:30pm, and 6:30-11pm.* €€€€ Four Seasons George V, 31 av. George V (M° Alma-Marceau), 01.49.52.70.00, fourseasons.com

La Coupole • 14th • Brasserie
Best Seafood Feasts There's no better place for a slap-up seafood feast than this historic but still buzzing Montparnasse brasserie. Despite its fame, La Coupole manages to absorb out-of-towners into a purely Parisian atmosphere, aided by the fact that it's still a prime address for locals. The people-watching is fantastic—old dames with mad hair, cravatted gents, cinema stars, artists from the nearby Fondation Cartier, and Montparnasse-ophiles from everywhere in the world. If slurping fresh oysters from a towering cake-stand isn't your style, there's a menu of fish and meat classics. The huge main room is all chrome and glass, with 32 columns painted by artists from Montparnasse's heyday. To skip the wait, opt for the glassed-in terrace. *Daily 8:30am-10:30pm.* €€ 102 bd. du Montparnasse (M° Duroc), 01.43.20.14.20, coupoleparis.com

Da Rosa • 6th • Café
Chic shoppers around Carrefour de Buci like to stop in to Da Rosa for a glass of wine and a quick bite drawn from the gourmet selection on sale in this luxury épicerie. With its *tomettes* (terra-cotta tiles) on the floor and gilded Belle Epoque front panels advertising "charcuterie, fromages, vins," you'd never guess that this place hadn't been going for a century or so, but it's all the work of Jacques Garcia. Choose from the red cushioned chairs on the terrace or the cozy upstairs room to enjoy plates of smoked salmon, Bellota ham and caviar, or Pierre Hermé macaroons at teatime with a young, well-dressed crowd. Don't leave without a trip down to the cellars and charcuterie room where smoky hams hang like a scene from a Dutch old master. *Daily 10am-10pm.* € 62 rue de Seine (M° Mabillon), 01.40.51.00.09, darosa.fr

L'Equitable • 5th • Bistro
Some of Paris' most talented chefs prefer serving an appreciative local crowd in their own small bistros to the international fame of a hotel dining room, and Yves Mutin is one of them. His excellent cooking makes this one of the great deals of the area. Neighborhood academics and Latin Quarter 30-somethings deconstructing their friends' love lives are regulars here, as well as the odd discerning tourist who has heard about this hidden gem. The décor has all the innocence of a country inn—exposed stone walls, antique scales, and figurative paintings—but the cuisine is sophisticated. Asparagus with a poached egg and mousseline, veal steak with baby vegetables, and crêpes flambéed at the table are the kind of food you'll get here. *Tue-Sat noon-2:30pm and 7:30-11pm.* € 1 rue des Fossés-St-Marcel (M° Censier-Daubenton), 01.43.31.69.20

CLASSIC • RESTAURANTS

L'Espadon • 1st • Gastronomic
Palms, swags, a ceiling painted with fluffy clouds, and a four-piece chamber orchestra set the scene for this Ritzy experience, as enjoyed by the Duke and Duchess of Windsor, Coco Chanel, and Di and Dodi on their fateful last night. The current crowd is pretty much the same, comprised of celebrities and the very rich, and the price tag puts it pretty much in the older age bracket. Put on your glad rags to sweep into the grandiose dining room with its rose-colored velvet banquettes or the summer courtyard, for this is the most see-and-be-seen of all the hotel dining rooms in the city. Michel Roth executes classic cuisine with the expected panache. Dishes that Proust might have enjoyed (a salad of Breton lobster with truffled rémoulade and apple) are joined by exotic notes (sea urchin with mango and passion fruit jus) and Italian additions. If the €180 tasting menu seems too extravagant, come for lunch when you can put on the Ritz for just €75 plus wine. *Daily 7-11am, noon-2pm, and 7-10pm.* €€€€ Hôtel Ritz, 15 pl. Vendôme (M° Tuileries), 01.43.16.30.80, ritzparis.com

Fogón St Julien • 5th • Spanish
Why not go south of the border for a meal at what's universally acclaimed as the best Spanish restaurant in Paris? Saffron-colored paneled walls and wrought-iron furniture set the scene for fabulous, moist paella (for two) and excellent seasonal tapas. Owner-chef Alberto Herraiz seeks out the very best ingredients for each—try the paella Valenciana with chicken, rabbit, snails, and vegetables. This may be the student quarter, but with its crisp white tablecloths, the Fogón feels very much like a grown-up restaurant, and service is both warm and professional. It's popular with a 30-something crowd that loves the Catalan authenticity. *Tue-Fri 7pm-midnight, Sat-Sun noon-2:30pm and 7pm-midnight.* € 10 rue St-Julien-le-Pauvre (M° Maubert-Mutualité), 01.43.54.31.33

Le Jules Verne • 7th • Gastronomic
The unique experience of dining some 400 feet up on the second level of the Eiffel Tower is quite sought after, so you'll need to book well in advance for the spectacular nighttime scene. It's thrilling, but vertiginous, so only book a window seat if you can take it. This gastronomic restaurant draws plenty of Parisians celebrating a special birthday or a business deal with a blowout. Alan Reix's cuisine is luxurious and creative. Tiny squid combined with melted foie gras, lobster with fennel, and Challans duck are always good. As an extra privilege, you can walk out onto the terrace after the last tourists have gone and have the Paris skyline all to yourself. *Daily 12:15-1:45pm and 7:15-9:45pm.* €€€€ Eiffel Tower, Champ de Mars (M° Bir-Hakeim), 01.45.55.61.44, tour-eiffel.fr

Julien • 10th • Brasserie
Julien is full of Belle Epoque charm. Through red velvet curtains you enter the long room with its magnificent stained-glass ceiling, a Majorelle carved mahogany bar, tiled panels of Art Nouveau maidens, and potted palms reflecting in mirrors. The buttoned-up waiters look and act the part, fluffing out starched tablecloths and flambéeing expertly. The menu does not shock or surprise, with the requisite beef tartare, entrecôtes, gigot of lamb, sole meunière, and profiteroles for dessert, all executed to the letter. One of the best choices is the classic roast John Dory with fennel. Come late for the animated post-theater crowd. *Daily noon-3pm and 7pm-1am.* €€ 16 rue du Fbg. St-Denis (M° Strasbourg-St-Denis), 01.47.70.12.06, julienparis.com

Laurent • 8th • Gastronomic

Best Outdoor Dining Government ministers and heads of industry have their power lunches here, but it's not all suits—we spotted Mick Jagger and Charlie Watts lunching with the ex-boss of Vivendi-Universal. The walled garden of this 19th-century pavilion near the Elysées Palace makes you feel like the bee's knees as you are catered to by formal waiters wheeling carts. The food is on the heavy side, as loved by the cigar-chomping patrons: a supreme caramelized rack of lamb, Corrèze veal with marrowbone, pigeon with foie-gras–flavored turnips. Partake of the excellent cheese cart, and peek into the historic salons. The €70 lunch menu makes Laurent affordable but it doesn't allow the chef to shine as he does à la carte. *Mon-Fri 12:30-2pm and 7:30-10:30pm, Sat 7:30-10:30pm.* €€€€ 41 av. Gabriel (M° Champs-Elysées-Clemenceau), 01.42.25.00.39, le-laurent.com

Aux Lyonnais • 2nd • Traditional

Alain Ducasse and Thierry de la Brosse have made this one of the best bistros in Paris. Situated in the Bourse area, it's so successful with the local bankers, auctioneers, and foodies that it doesn't even open on weekends. The setting is picture perfect, with flowery tiles, a mahogany bar with red leather-topped stools, and classic red-striped tea cloths on the tables. Christophe Saintagne, a star at only 26, has adapted heavy Lyon specialties for modern tastes, so the sabodet sausage is finely chopped and accompanied by a light gribiche sauce, the roast chicken deglazed with vinegar, and even the quenelles are light enough to enable you to get up from the table and enjoy some afternoon activity. Not before tasting the Cointreau soufflé, though, which is a must. *Tue-Fri noon-2pm and 7:30-11pm.* €€ 32 rue St-Marc (M° Bourse), 01.42.96.65.04

La Mascotte • 18th • Brasserie

Best Seafood Feasts Untouched by the Flo Group's painters and polishers, and indeed by the 21st century, La Mascotte revels in its '70s brasserie allure. Take your place by the zinc counter or squeeze up on a banquette inside and watch a carnival of Montmartre's most colorful characters take up their places. Drag queen Michou is here most Sundays, as is a Zandra Rhodes look-alike who holds court in a haze of smoke as all her friends drop in for a gossip, and whole families with infants unfettered by bourgeois good behavior. Despite the chaos, the food is just as it should be: platters of oysters, entrecôtes, and ice cream desserts suffused with alcohol. *Tue-Sun noon-3pm and 7-11pm. Bar: 7pm-midnight.* € 52 rue des Abbesses (M° Abbesses), 01.46.06.28.15

La Méditerranée • 6th • Gastronomic

Best Seafood Feasts Welcome to the Riviera, Paris-style. Not only is the menu redolent of chic seasides at this restaurant just off the Odéon, but the décor was painted by the artists who hung out in the south. In the three salons there are mythological murals by Vertès and Bérard, photos of Picasso, and drawings by Cocteau. Going since 1944, La Méditerranée was a favorite of jet-setters like Princess Margaret and Jackie Onassis, and still pulls in a stylish crowd. Seated on pale blue velvet chairs with curtains hanging on brass rails, you can revel in such delights as oyster platters and Marseillaise bouillabaisse. There are a few meat dishes, but it's the fish that shines. *Daily noon-2:30pm and 7:30-11pm.* €€ 2 pl. de l'Odéon (M° Odéon), 01.43.26.02.30, la-mediterranee.com

CLASSIC • RESTAURANTS

Les Papilles • 5th • Wine Bar
Winner of the 2005 Fooding prize for best wine bar, Les Papilles was opened by Bertrand Bluy, whose talents already included playing rugby and being chef pâtissier at Taillevent. His dream was to create a wine bar with the flavor of his native southwest, and with his Lot-et-Garonne accent, sunny colors, and shelves stacked with delicious wines and produce, it certainly has that. In the kitchen Laetitia Cosnier, a former second at Taillevent, produces wonderful regional cuisine: a velouté of tomatoes whipped with mustard grains and confit de canard à l'ancienne. Come during a rugby match and you'll really taste the southwest, as friends crowd into the basement with a TV and sports photos lining the walls to cheer "Allez la France!" *Mon-Sat noon-2:30pm and 7:30-10:30pm. Shop: 8pm-1am.* € 30 rue Gay-Lussac (RER Luxembourg), 01.43.25.20.79, lespapilles.fr

Pères et Filles • 6th • Café
Pères et Filles looks almost like a themed French restaurant in New York or London with its checked floor, Gitanes posters, and antique dresser in the center. But the good-looking waiters and clientele of St-Germain trendies and trustfunders are definitely French, and the designer Gallic look combined with jazz and Latin music keeps it jiving with a young crowd. In summer the entire front of the restaurant opens up to the street, with a large and noisy terrace too, while the wallpapered back room filled with books is a quieter option. The menu draws on many sources, with French classics like beef tartare as well as tagines and pasta dishes. *Sun-Thu noon-2:30pm and 7:30-11pm. Fri-Sat noon-2:30pm and 7:30-11:30pm.* € 81 rue de Seine (M° Mabillon), 01.43.25.00.28

Au Pied de Cochon • 1st • Brasserie
Best Late-Night Eats Night owls of all stripes crowd in to this lively 24/7 brasserie to quell the midnight—or 4am—munchies, making it a fun place to meet "le tout Paris" in jovial spirits. Coming here at an unearthly hour definitely throws up a more interesting crowd, as the restaurant's beautiful Belle Epoque interior has put it on many tour party itineraries during the day, but these decent folk are tucked up in bed by the time you'll get there. Feast decadently on seafood platters, steak and frites, snails, or the eponymous pig's feet. The brasserie is a last vestige of the Les Halles market, which has now moved out of town, and the place still has masses of atmosphere. *24/7.* € 6 rue Coquillière (M° Les Halles), pieddecochon.com, 01.40.13.77.00

Le Poulbot Gourmet • 18th • Bistro
This quiet bistro takes its food seriously. In decorous surroundings of studded leather banquettes, frosted glass, and crisp white tablecloths, with Commune pamphlets and black-and-white photos on the walls, you can enjoy foie gras and oysters in season, authentic tête de veau, or a beautiful starter of endives, dried beef, artichoke, and goat's cheese, followed by pan-fried scallops in garlic or veal kidneys with morels. The terrine of bitter chocolate with cherries soaked in eau de vie is divine. *Mon-Sat noon-2pm and 7:30-10:30pm.* € 39 rue Lamarck (M° Lamarck-Caulaincourt), 01.46.06.86.00

Le Pré Verre • 5th • Bistro
Best Bistros A phenomenal success since it opened, this modern bistro is packed with local publishers, shop owners, and academics having noisy lunches on its sunny terrace and in its eggplant-colored interior. The tables are tiny and you're

virtually sitting in your neighbor's lap, but nobody's complaining with food this good at this price. Chef Philippe Delacourcelle has traveled the world and delicately spices his food, but not so much as to scare away French palates. You'll find rabbit with cumin, salt cod with cassia bark, and then parsley in the strawberry dessert and figs with olives. Try not to sit in the downstairs room as you'll miss the buzzing atmosphere. *Tue-Sat noon-2pm and 7:30-10:30pm.* € 8 rue Thenard (M° Maubert-Mutualité), 01.43.54.59.47

Le Rostand • 6th • Café

A very Parisian scene unfolds at this Belle Epoque café with its huge terrace extending around two sides. Grab a seat in the glassed-in winter garden where you are shielded by potted palms but still have a view of the Jardin du Luxembourg. Ensconced here, with your paper, your breakfast, espresso or glass of chilled white, is the perfect place to watch a parade of ladies in fur coats with small dogs, dapper gents, surgically enhanced divorcees, and cute young couples. For winter, there's a cozy interior of mahogany, mustard walls and Orientalist paintings. *Daily 8am-2am.* € 6 pl. Edmond-Rostand (RER Luxembourg), 01.43.54.61.58

La Table d'Hôte du Palais Royal • 1st • Bistro

Chef Caroll Sinclair is quite a character on the Paris food scene. Her new restaurant, called "table d'hôte" to reflect her ethos of making guests feel like they've been invited to an intimate dinner of friends, is in the 17th-century vaulted cellars of the Palais Royal. Two of the four cozy underground salons are like railway carriages, lined with paneling from the Orient Express, so expect to find cooing couples in the evenings. At lunchtime it attracts a lively crowd of gourmands from the nearby stock exchange and elegant shoppers from the Palais Royal arcades. Sinclair adds a touch of North African color to the intrinsically French menu, all cooked with organic ingredients: the scallops marinated in citronelle and served in their shells are simply divine. Early opening makes this a good choice for pre-theater. *Daily 11:30am-2:30pm and 6pm-midnight.* € 8 rue du Beaujolais (M° Bourse), 01.42.61.25.30, carollsinclair.com

La Table Lauriston • 16th • Bistro

At this prize-winning bistro, you are likely to see French food writers, other journalists, and relaxed locals. The cuisine is defined by its simplicity. A pungent foie gras maison, tuna carpaccio, and spring asparagus are among the starters, while mains are quite heavy, including a peppery onglet de veau or delicious seared scallops with tiny leeks. Beware: the dessert specialty is rum babas with a choice of three rums—deliciously naughty, but you may need a siesta to recover. *Mon-Fri noon-2:30pm and 7-10:30pm, Sat 7-10:30pm.* €€ 129 rue de Lauriston (M° Trocadéro), 01.47.27.00.07

Taillevent • 8th • Gastronomic

Best Fine Dining Despite the competition, Taillevent consistently ranks as among the best, if not the best, fine dining experiences in Paris. The setting in a beautiful townhouse; the charming owner Jean-Pierre Vrinat; Alan Solivérès' elevated cooking; and the famous Taillevent cellar all conspire to approach perfection. Solivérès has made his reputation reinventing southern French cuisine. You'll find ingredients stuffed and wrapped, hiding distinct flavors one inside the other, such as the red mullet with a spider crab filling. More classic preparations include the trademark "épautre"—a spelt risotto with bone marrow, black truffle, and frogs' legs—and a medieval pork dish taken from the recipe book of Guillaume Tirel, the chef known as "Taillevent." Ask for the second room, which is far more lively. Taillevent has a reasonably priced lunch menu, but for the best atmosphere, come for dinner. *Mon-Fri 12:15-2pm and 7:30-10pm.* €€€€ 15 rue Lamennais (M° Charles de Gaulle-Etoile), 01.44.95.15.01, taillevent.com

La Tour d'Argent • 5th • Gastronomic

If you can't decide which gastronomic restaurant to make the pinnacle of your trip, it's easy to know what you're getting at the Tour d'Argent: a fabulous view of the cathedral of Notre-Dame, illuminated at night, and the chance to eat the famous mallard, around which much ceremony revolves. The duck is carved at your table, and to mark the occasion, you'll be given a numbered postcard which you can keep or get the waiters to send off to food-loving friends. Who ate which duck is noted in a leather-bound book—thus Emperor Hirohito at number 53,211 and Edward VII at 328. If all this sounds strangely gimmicky, it's more akin to some of the more bizarre traditions found at old universities, as this place really is redolent with history—it's been going since the 16th century. The €70 lunch menu includes the duck, but at night you get the Paris-by-night view. *Tue 7:30-9:30pm, Wed-Sun noon-1:30pm and 7:30-9:30pm.* €€€€ 15-17 quai de la Tournelle (M° Pont Marie), 01.43.54.23.31, tourdargent.com

La Truffière • 5th • Traditional

La Truffière is housed in the beamed, stone vaults of a 17th-century building, made even more atmospheric by candlelight. Of course, it specializes in truffles, and there is no better place to taste them, though there are plenty of non-truffle choices on the menu. The presence of truffles will depend on the season—when they are not freshly available they appear in the form of truffle oil, or dried, enriching potato preparations or terrines. One of the most unusual dishes is the truffle soufflé with caramelized custard cream and truffle-honey-flavored frozen yogurt. Service is charming and the clients here tend to be dressed-up and distinguished. *Tue-Sat noon-2pm and 7-10:30pm.* €€€ 4 rue Blainville (M° Place Monge), 01.46.33.29.82, latruffiere.com

Le Voltaire • 7th • Traditional

Le Voltaire is a seductive little restaurant whose perfect location has done nothing to quell the warmth of its welcome for celebrities and nobodies alike. Ladies often get a kiss on the hand from maître d' Antoine after they swish through the velvet curtains. All ages are welcome here, not to mention the lapdogs that accompany many of its regulars. The huge salads can be followed by country dishes such as sautéed rabbit or luxury city fare like the lobster omelette. It's so cozy and Parisian you'll want to stay all day. *Tue-Sat 12:30-2:30pm and 7:30-10:15pm.* €€€ 27 quai Voltaire (M° Rue du Bac), 01.42.61.17.49

Willi's Wine Bar • 1st • Bistro

A cozy wine bar serving superb bistro food, along with a fine cellar of wines. *See Classic Nightlife, p.106, for details.* € 13 rue des Petits-Champs (M° Pyramides), 01.42.61.05.09, williswinebar.com

Classic Paris:
The Nightlife

Bar César • 8th • Hotel Bar
Best Classic Hotel Bars A pianist stroking the keys like velvet and two bartenders who seem to have been waiting just for you welcome you into the civilized world of the Hôtel Crillon's bar. This is a traditional piano bar with jazzy mirror mosaics designed by the sculptor César and boudoir fabrics chosen by Sonia Rykiel. Another name to consider here is Baccarat, who supplied the crystal glasses for the Baccarat cocktail, a sublime mix of rosé Champagne, cranberry juice, Grand Marnier, and lime, which is served after dinner with wickedly dark, pink-speckled chocolates. Or choose from the rich selection of Cognacs. During fashion week, the place buzzes with wild conversation and even wilder outfits; at other times, this is a relaxing place to retreat for a taste of unsurpassed refinement. *Daily 11am-2am.* Hôtel de Crillon, 10 pl. de la Concorde or 6 rue Boissy d'Anglas (M° Concorde), 01.44.71.15.39, crillon.com

Bar Hemingway • 1st • Hotel Bar
Best Classic Hotel Bars This cozy spot is one of three bars in the Ritz, but the only one worth visiting. Walking the length of the shopping arcade is somewhat daunting, but those in the know enter via the discreet back entrance on rue Cambon. Bar Hemingway was "liberated" by the writer during World War II and is full of Hemingway memorabilia. Today, however, it's bartender Colin Peter Field who is the living legend here. As well as mixing the perfect martini, at the perfect temperature (17.5 degrees Fahrenheit), he knows how to make guests feel comfortable, finding a space for everyone in the cocoon-like bar, regaling guests with anecdotes about the Old Man and the origins of cocktails. You'll find a wonderful cross-section of people, from awestruck business travelers to models and their entourage. After midnight it gets very crowded and cigar-smoky; pre-dinner cocktails are more enjoyable. *Mon-Sat. 6:30pm-2am.* Semiformal dress. Hôtel Ritz, 15 pl. Vendôme or 28 rue Cambon (M° Tuileries), 01.43.16.33.65, ritzparis.com

Bar du Marché • 6th • Bar
The Bar du Marché is always full, winter and summer, night and day. Its strategic position at this St-Germain junction and the fact that it's got loads of character make it a magnet for anyone living or staying in the area. Dressed-up locals on their way to the boulangerie have a coffee, shoppers and tourists idle away the afternoon, and international trendies gather on the terrace late at night. The interior's an attractive mix of old posters, neon and mirrors, and its carnivalesque look is heightened by the waiters dressed in Parisian uniform of dungarees and flat caps. Sit back and enjoy the great people-watching here. *Daily 8am-2am.* 75 rue de Seine (M° Mabillon), 01.43.26.55.15

Le Bilboquet • 6th • Jazz Club
Best Jazz Clubs Formed by Boris Vian and friends in 1947, this jazz club was one of the main haunts of the party crowd of the '50s known as the "troglodytes" for their midnight Lindy-hopping antics. Jazz was the music and

all the greats played here: Miles Davis, Bud Powell, Bobby Jaspar, Django Reinhardt, Duke Ellington, and so on. The crowd has grown up and overseas jazz fans now chill to dinner jazz and reminisce as young imitators revive the swing of days gone by. Big names still play, and the intimate cellar atmosphere with black-and-white photographs of Miles and Billie Holiday is intact. If you miss dinner, you can catch the end of a concert until 1:30am. *Daily 8pm-1:30am. Jazz 9pm-1:30am.* C⌐ 13 rue St-Benoît (M° St-Germain-des-Prés), 01.45.48.81.84

Café Delmas • 5th • Café
If Hemingway's what's led you to place de la Contrescarpe, you can dip into *A Moveable Feast* here while enjoying a petit déjeuner complet (with eggs) or lunch on its sunny terrace. The cobbled square with its fountain at the top of rue Mouffetard always has plenty going on. In late afternoon it is noisy with Vespa-riding youth, not to mention gypsy violinists, and an apéritif here is always fun if you like a bit of a scene. The interior is comfortable and contemporary with Art Deco–style seating and glistening lights, but the people-watching terrace is the place to be. Smooth lounge music creates a happening atmosphere that goes on until late into the night. *Sun-Thu 7:30am-2am, Fri-Sat 7:30am-5am.* ⌐ 2-4 pl. de la Contrescarpe (M° Place Monge), 01.43.26.51.26

Café de Flore • 6th • Café
The wartime home of the Lost Generation, the Café de Flore was favored by Simone de Beauvoir, Jean-Paul Sartre, and their acolytes in part because it shunned the occupying Germans. The couple set up shop here, working, having meetings, and expounding their Existentialist philosophy. Nowadays there is still plenty of intellectual activity: the café hosts its own literary prize and has play readings and philosophy sessions in English on the first Wednesday of the month in the upstairs room. Recently it's been enjoying a youthful renaissance. Philosopher Bernard Henri-Levy and Karl Lagerfeld, as well as international celebs, from time to time give an extra frisson to the see-and-be-seen terrace. *Daily 7:30am-1:30am.* ⌐ 172 bd. St-Germain (M° St-Germain-des-Prés), 01.45.48.55.26, cafe-de-flore.com

Café du Marché • 7th • Café
Soak up a bit of market atmosphere on the terrace of this perennially popular café not far from the Eiffel Tower. At the center of the action, it has a lively mix of market traders, local trendies, and eccentric oldies with small dogs in tow. Sit back in front of a kir as the vegetable sellers shout out bargain prices in an attempt to lighten their load, but make sure you leave before the army of green cleaning lorries moves in after 7:30pm. *Mon-Sat 7am-midnight, Sun 7am-5pm.* ⌐ 38 rue Cler (M° Ecole-Militaire), 01.47.05.51.27

Chez Castel • 6th • Private Club
Old and new money, real tans and fake, dapper millionaires with young mistresses and vice versa, all can be found at this legendary St-Germain club. Something about Castel has kept it classy after all these years, and now the dandy young writers, actors, and chanson stars who are the in-crowd are knocking at its door. Intimate, and styled like a private club—which it is, though chic out-of-towners will always get in—it has two upstairs dining rooms, one lively and bistro-like with checked tablecloths and the other more intimate and clubby.

Most of its habitués will be found lolling in the Oscar-Wilde-style smoking chairs or strutting their stuff till dawn on the tiny disco dance floor downstairs. *Tue-Sat. 9pm-6am.* 15 rue Princesse (M° Mabillon), 01.40.51.52.80

La Closerie des Lilas • 6th • Bar/Brasserie
One of the great brasseries of Montparnasse's heyday, La Closerie has fed everyone from Trotsky to Apollinaire, Picasso to Hemingway (who wrote the first draft of *The Sun Also Rises* right here as his café-crème famously got cold). Though it is proud of its literary legacy, the Closerie doesn't live in the past—even today, it's likely that you'll spot a famous face among the mainly French regulars. There is a more formal restaurant and a glassed-in terrace surrounded by shrubbery, but it's the dark and sultry mahogany-and-chrome bar that attracts late-night barflies who cluster around the piano. *Daily noon-1am.* 171 bd. du Montparnasse (M° Vavin), 01.40.51.34.50.

Crazy Horse • 8th • Cabaret
In the days of digital technology, the Crazy Horse looks innocently retro, like arty '70s soft porn. The "art of the nude" dresses almost-naked girls with saucy names like Nooka Karamel and Misty Flashback in patterns shed by lighting gels as they gyrate on the too-small stage. No longer "taboo" despite the show's name, it is tacky in parts, artistic in others, and attracts whole families and even post-modern bachelorette parties. The ticket gets you two very strong drinks. *Tue-Fri, Sun 8:30 and 11pm, Sat 7:30, 9:45 and 11:50pm.* 12 av. George V (M° George V), 01.47.23.32.32, crazyhorse.fr

Dancing at La Coupole • 14th • Brasserie
The Art Deco ballroom under the brasserie is having a revival. "Dancing à La Coupole" was where high-kicking Josephine Baker and a jazz crowd swung in the '20s. Now, after decades in the wilderness, the sunburst mirror is all shined up again for club nights and attracting 21st-century dance-lovers. Salsa, broken beats, electro-soul, and deep house rotate according to the night. So Happy In Paris and Bodylingus are popular on Thursdays, as well as Friday's Cheers with DJs from Le Queen. *Wed-Sat 11pm-5am, though hours can vary.* 104 bd. du Montparnasse (M° Vavin), 01.43.27.56.00, flobrasseries.com/coupoleparis

Les Editeurs • 6th • Café
Best Literary Bars The Left Bank literary café is brought up to date at this stylish intellectual spot. Donations of the latest hot titles from nearby publishing houses fill the shelves and it hosts its own literary prize. Seated on velvet banquettes or the heated terrace is a stylish crowd in linen suits chatting—naturally—about the book trade while jazz creates a smooth atmosphere. It's the perfect place to start your memoirs over coffee. Les Editeurs serves its own moveable feast running from breakfast to some chic and tasty lunch dishes (grilled tuna with pesto and piperade). It's great at any time of day, and the brunch attracts the cream of smart, good-looking young singles. *Daily 8am-2am.* 4 carrefour de l'Odéon (M° Odéon), 01.43.26.67.76, lesediteurs.fr

Moulin Rouge • 18th • Cabaret
As long as you're not expecting the sensual carnival of Baz Luhrmann's film or Toulouse-Lautrec's posters, the Moulin Rouge still offers a great night out with its polished cabaret show. As well as the can-can dancers dressed in tricolor costumes and feather headdresses, there are other perfectly synchronized dance

items, acrobats, and magicians. The costumes are fabulous and the choreography is slick. Some consider this a family show since sequins cover just about anything risqué—though there are a few topless bits. Book for the late show, when you're not obliged to dine. *Daily 9 and 11pm.* C≡ 82 bd. de Clichy (M° Blanche), 01.53.09.82.82, moulin-rouge.com

New Morning • 10th • Jazz Club
Best Jazz Clubs Paris' premier jazz venue has little to do with the troglodytic cellars of the bebopping days. Here, in a large, black-walled auditorium in the souk-like Faubourg St-Denis, an exciting program attracts serious jazz fans to hear greats like Pharaoh Sanders and John McLaughlin and modern new-jazz pioneers like Julien Lorau. Quality guaranteed. *Concerts daily 9pm.* CB≡ 7-9 rue des Petites-Ecuries (M° Château d'Eau), 01.45.23.51.41, newmorning.com

L'Olympia • 9th • Concert Hall
This legendary concert hall certainly isn't lacking for atmosphere. You descend a long red carpet deep beneath the Grands Boulevards, where the former Art Deco cinema has been hosting world-famous musicians since the '50s. Sinatra, Piaf, the Beatles, the Stones, Aznavour all played here; these days it hosts French chanson stars and international names such as Sting and Cristina Branco. The acoustics and the view are fantastic and there is not a bad seat in the house. *Concerts daily 8:30pm.* C≡ 28 bd. des Capucines (M° Opéra), 01.55.27.10.00, olympiahall.com

La Palette • 6th • Café
La Palette retains a bohemian vibe with its unbelievably pretty terrace. Paintings are crammed into the two-room interior with its traditional Parisian décor of mirrors and leather banquettes, and art students, art dealers, and even the occasional artist mingle with expensively dressed young mothers and distinguished older couples. The patron is famously rude, shouting at people who sit down without asking and spilling their drinks in his mania for shoving the tables up close to one another. Next thing, he'll be dandling someone's baby in the most charming way. Infuriating, but all is forgiven once the strawberry tart arrives and you'll find yourself inexplicably wanting to return. The terrace is sought after for lunch. *Mon-Sat 9am-2am.* ≡ 43 rue de Seine (M° Mabillon), 01.43.26.68.15

Régine's Club • 8th • Private Club
Régine's is one of the mythic names of the Paris night. Its heyday was the '60s and '70s, and stars of that era still come here. It's drawing a younger crowd again along with wealthy businessmen and their dates who boogie to Donna Summer and swill pricey Champagne. With its multiple-mirrored ceiling, red velvet chairs, and tiny dance floor, Régine's décor is quite fabulous. Thursday from 9-11pm is a bachelorette party with strippers and makeup lessons, but afterward the guys are let in. Independent promoters take over the club outside its regular days, such as Sunday's funky house Orange Party. The door policy is strict on attire, so check your footwear and wear a jacket. *Thu-Sat 11pm-6am.* ≡ 49-51 rue de Ponthieu (M° George V), 01.43.59.21.13, regine-paris.com

Ritz Club • 1st • Private Club
It's been a well-kept secret for years that the Ritz has its own nightclub, opposite the Bar Hemingway and accessed by the hotel's back entrance. Since Kate Moss and friends made Bar Hemingway one of the coolest places on earth to sip

cocktails, the club has benefited from a fashionable spillover effect. A young in-crowd has woken the cigar-smoking middle-aged habitués from their stupor, leaving them wondering if they've died and gone to disco heaven. The cozy, retro space with alcoves, carpet, and a tiny dance floor is especially full during Supernature nights, which alternate between here and Maxim's. Officially a private club, it will allocate free membership cards to anyone who looks right in these surroundings. *Fri-Sat 12:30am-6am.* C (sometimes, other nights free) 38 rue Cambon (M° Madeleine), 01.43.16.30.90, ritzparis.com

Le Rosebud • 14th • Cocktail Bar
With a name drawn from *Citizen Kane* and former habitués including Sartre and de Beauvoir, Ionesco and Duras, the Rosebud is a classic piano bar that you'll love for its authenticity. The pianist tinkles jazz and white-jacketed bartenders mix impeccable martinis and provide small talk or a listening ear, just as a good bartender should. The atmosphere is intimate and aristocratic; the patrons eclectic and often eccentric. A pure slice of Montparnasse. *Daily 7pm-2am.* 11 bis rue Delambre (M° Vavin), 01.43.20.44.13

Le Sabot • 6th • Jazz Club
Best Jazz Clubs Wild man of the sax Mathias Luszpinski owns this funky little jazz club, which has all the spirit of St-Germain without wallowing in nostalgia. You enter through a kind of kitsch gallery with changing exhibitions run by Mathias' sister, while his artist father and a whole collection of bohemian friends are always among the patrons. In a beamed medieval room is the bar/restaurant and music stage. Treat it like a restaurant (the plats du jour and salades géantes are pretty good), a bar (try unusual cocktails with Get 27 and Manzana), or just come for the music, which ranges from jazz to chanson to Afro-beat. Wednesday nights are always free jazz improv with Mathias' quartet and invited guests roaring on into the night. *Live music Tue-Fri from 8pm.* 6 rue du Sabot (M° St-Germain-des-Prés), 01.42.22.21.56

Le Tourville • 7th • Café/Bar
Vying with the Café de l'Esplanade for best terrace around the Invalides is the less exclusive Tourville, which still has loads of style. Rich boys in velvet jackets, girls in Gucci, and American exchange students congregate under its heated lamps for an apéritif at sundown or an animated late-night drink. The décor is superbly done, with tassel lamps, a quilted staircase, and velvet chairs. Nighttime DJs create an ambiance akin to that of the Hôtel Costes, but with less attitude and a younger crowd, and food is served at any time of day. *Daily 7am-2am.* 43 av. de la Motte Picquet (M° Ecole Militaire), 01.44.18.05.08

Willi's Wine Bar • 1st • Wine Bar
Every now and then an Englishman like Mark Williamson astonishes the French by doing what they do, only better. Since he opened this cozy wine bar in 1980 it's become an established player, serving superb bistro food, along with a fine cellar of wines. Some customers have been coming here for years, and a younger crowd is constantly discovering it. At lunch the local French business crowd eats here; in the evenings it attracts English and American bons vivants. Sit up at the long bar and join the banter, or at tables in the beamed back room. *Mon-Sat noon-2:30pm and 7-11pm. Bar open till midnight.* 13 rue des Petits-Champs (M° Pyramides), 01.42.61.05.09, williswinebar.com

Classic Paris: The Attractions

Basilique du Sacré-Coeur • 18th • Monument
It's surprising when you discover just how recent an addition to the Paris skyline the basilica of Sacré-Coeur is—it was not completed until 1914. After World War I, the edifice was finally consecrated in 1919 as a basilica—a place of pilgrimage. The mount of Montmartre had been a sacred hill since Roman times, when it held a temple to Mars and Mercury. Inside, a shining gold and blue mosaic is also neo-Byzantine in style. At 785 feet above sea level, with a dome 272 feet high, it commands a wonderful view across Paris. It is also a place of fervent and popular worship with three Masses a day, four on Fridays. Sunday's 4pm vespers fill the basilica with singing led, as if in some kind of beatific karaoke, by a beaming, gesticulating nun. *Daily 6am-11pm. Summer: 9am-7pm; Winter: 9am-6pm. Dome €-* 35 rue du Chevalier-de-la-Barre (M° Abbesses), 01.53.41.89.00, sacre-coeur-montmartre.com

Basilique St-Denis • St-Denis • Monument
Strange to find Paris' equivalent of Westminster Abbey in the middle of depressed St-Denis, five Métro stops north of Paris, but such are the quirks of history. Saint Denis, officially the first Christian martyr in France, is said to have picked up his head and marched all the way here from Montmartre (a good two miles). His grave, in a Gallo-Roman cemetery, became a place of pilgrimage, and in the 12th and 13th centuries a basilica was built that became a manifesto of the wonders of Gothic architecture. It includes the first-ever rose window and the first use of ogival vaulting, later enhanced by flying buttresses to make the arches soar even higher. The abbey was the burial place of kings from the 10th century to the end of the monarchy, and is filled with exquisitely crafted effigies. One of the most magnificent is that of François I who lies naked next to his queen, with their clothed figures enthroned on top of the huge tomb. Down in the vaults you can see the Bourbon sepulchral vault, where Louis XVI and Marie-Antoinette are buried, as well as cenotaphs and statues erected by Louis XVIII in a desperate attempt to keep the cult of the monarchy alive. *Mon-Sat 10am-6:15pm, Sun noon-6:15pm (5:45pm Oct-Mar). €-* 1 rue de la Légion d'Honneur (M° Basilique de St-Denis), 01.48.09.83.54, monum.fr

Bateaux Vedette du Pont Neuf • 1st • Boat Trip
This variant on the bateaux-mouches sets off handily from the Pont Neuf in the center of town, rather than from further downriver near the Eiffel Tower. Its one-hour tour spirits you around the Ile de la Cité, past the Musée d'Orsay and down to the Eiffel Tower, then up the other side of the islands as far as the Institut du Monde Arabe and back, passing under 16 of Paris' famous bridges, including Pont Alexandre III with its shining gold statues. The live commentary is well informed and you can sit inside almost at water level or outside on the top deck. *Tours: daily every half-hour Mar.-Oct. 10am-10:30pm; every 45 mins Nov.-Feb. 10:30am-10pm. €-* Square du Vert Galant (M° Pont Neuf), 01.46.33.98.38, vedettesdupontneuf.com

Batobus • Various • Boat Trip
The river transport that plies up and down the Seine stops at eight places between the Eiffel Tower and Jardin des Plantes in the Latin Quarter, including Musée d'Orsay, St-Germain and Notre-Dame. Some lucky Parisians take the Batobus to work. If it's serving your destination, it's far more enjoyable than the Métro, passing all the same spots as the bateaux-mouches but without a commentary. The staff are happy to offer sightseeing information, however. Short-hop, day, two-day, and monthly passes are available. *Daily every 25-35 mins 10:30am-4:30pm. €–* 08.25.05.01.01, batobus.fr

Les Catacombes • 14th • Sight
Paris's eerie underground attraction contains the bones of 6 million people transferred here by wheelbarrow after the Revolution, when the cemetery of St-Eustache burst its banks. The bones are piled up to bust height and artfully arranged so that skulls and femurs form patterns in the mass of horizontally stacked leg bones. With the 19th-century cult of death came quotations carved in stone: "Stop! This is the empire of death!" at the entrance and others with the theme of carpe diem or death as the great leveler. The latter is certainly true as Marat, Robespierre, and many of the aristocrats guillotined in the Revolution are anonymously interred with nameless ordinary Parisians. Only a small portion of the 3,000 kilometers of tunnels is open to visitors so it is not possible to get lost—unless you join the "cataphiles," illegal underground party-people who devote themselves to finding secret entrances. *Tue-Sun 10am-5pm. €–* 1 pl. Denfert Rochereau (M° Denfert-Rochereau), 01.43.22.47.63

Cathédrale Notre Dame de Paris • 4th • Monument
Ranking number one in popularity among all Paris' monuments is this Gothic edifice that lords over the Ile de la Cité. Constructed on the site of a Gallo-Roman temple to Jupiter and an earlier Christian basilica, it was begun in 1163 and not finished until 1334. Napoléon crowned himself here in 1805, but the cathedral was already falling into severe disrepair and it took Victor Hugo's novel featuring the fictional hunchback to wake people up to its plight, resulting in a large-scale restoration. Its sheer scale is awesome, as is the west front's rose window and doorways and the long nave. Climbing the towers is well worth it for the view of Paris and close-up of the mythological beasts that peer down. You can also visit the archaeological crypt containing layer after layer of Paris history. The cathedral is a working church with masses at 6:30pm on Saturday and 11am and 6:30pm Sunday. *Daily 7:45am-6:45pm. Towers from 9am (10am-4:45pm Oct-Mar.)* Pl. du Parvis Notre-Dame (M° Cité), 01.42.34.56.10, cathedraledeparis.com

Cimetière de Père Lachaise • 20th • Cemetery
The most impressive of Paris' three celebrated cemeteries (the others are Montmartre and Montparnasse), Père Lachaise was landscaped as a place for strolling at the end of the 18th century. It was only when the authorities moved Héloïse and Abelard, Molière and La Fontaine here that people cottoned on to the celebrity value of being buried in the Père, and things really moved on from there. Now two of the most visited graves are those of Jim Morrison and Oscar Wilde, both of which have to be protected from the crazed behavior of their fans (graffiti and getting high for the Lizard King; lipstick kisses for the playwright). There's also the journalist Victor Noir, whose prominent manhood has been

rubbed shiny by women hoping to conceive. Playing hunt-the-celebrity is fun, even without a map, though these are available free at the entrance. You may stumble on the tomb of Chopin, Balzac, Colette, Sarah Bernhardt, or Edith Piaf as you wander round—there are hundreds of celebrities buried here. There is also the Mur des Fédérés, where 147 members of the Paris Commune were shot in 1871, and a powerful series of Holocaust memorials further up. Give yourself at least two hours here. *Mon-Fri 8am-6pm, Sat 8:30am-6pm, Sun 9am-6pm; Winter: closes at 5:30pm.* Bd. du Ménilmontant (M° Père-Lachaise), 01.55.25.82.10

Concerts in Churches • Various • Event
With their wonderful acoustics and ancient paintings and pillars lit by candles, Paris churches provide a magical setting for concerts. Let yourself drift away to ethereal Ave Marias, baroque masterpieces, or Chopin nocturnes as you soak up the magnificent architecture and centuries of history. Various groups organize the concerts: Amp Concerts (ampconcerts.com) covers a spectrum of classical music in Ste-Chapelle, the Madeleine, Eglise St-Germain-des-Prés, and the pretty, jewel-like Syrian Orthodox church of St-Ephrem. Rousing gospel is performed in many churches by the acclaimed group Gospel Dream (gospeldream.com). For a full selection of what's on, check in the listings magazine *Pariscope* or tap "eglise" and choose "spectacles" on the Fnac website. Tickets can be booked from branches of Fnac, or pop into any church to find a selection of flyers for forthcoming concerts. *Concert times vary.* 01.42.50.96.18, ampconcerts.com, gospeldream.com, or fnac.com

La Conciergerie • 1st • Monument
The Conciergerie was a royal palace until the 15th century, when the kings moved into the Louvre. The 13th-century Bonbec Tower, 14th-century César and Argent towers, and clock tower are what remains from the Capetian palace; the pseudo-medieval façade was added in the 19th century. But it is the part that it played in the Revolution and the Terror that makes the Conciergerie redolent of fear and treachery. Both Marie-Antoinette and her tormentors Danton and Robespierre were held here. The tour takes you through the huge kitchens, a vaulted Gothic hall, the women's courtyard, and the re-created cell of Marie-Antoinette with waxwork models and a guillotine blade. The ticket includes entry to Ste-Chapelle. *Daily 9:30am-6pm.* €– 2-4 bd. du Palais (M° Cité), 01.53.40.60.93, monum.fr/m_conciergerie

Edible Paris • Various • Guided Tour
For true foodies who want a Paris itinerary built around their passion, food writer Rosa Jackson will create an exclusive tailor-made tour and email it to you. Stipulate whether French cheeses, wine, chocolates, or all these and more are what you are most interested in and you will be directed to the best purveyors with a personal recommendation. She can also make restaurant reservations at hard-to-get-into places. €€€€ edible-paris.com

Eiffel Tower • 7th • Monument
A symbol of Paris the world over, the tower was built in 1889 for the World Fair that celebrated the centenary of the French Revolution. As well as being the world's tallest structure at 1,023 feet—a glory that it held for four decades until the Empire State was built—it showed off French engineering prowess with its iron frame held together with 2.5 million rivets. You can ascend by elevator or,

for stair-climber enthusiasts, on foot, to three levels. The first has a bistro restaurant, the second the Jules Verne restaurant and the third a reconstruction of Eiffel's tower-top salon and views 40 miles out on a clear day. For science buffs, there are a variety of machines that explain the working of the elevator and the tower's construction on the ground, first, and second floors. The tower even has its own winter ice rink on the first floor. Night is the least busy time to come and the most magical, as 20,000 flashbulbs glitter for ten minutes on the hour. *Daily 9am-midnight (14 June-31 Aug.), 9:30am-11pm (Sept-13 June).* €– Champ de Mars (M° Bir-Hakeim), 01.44.11.23.23, tour-eiffel.fr

Fondation Henri Cartier-Bresson • 14th • Photography Gallery
Opened shortly before the death of Cartier-Bresson at the age of 96, the foundation holds the great photographer's archive of "defining moments" of the 20th century, captured on his Leica. It is housed in a tall, narrow studio designed by the architect Molinié that is evocative of the Montparnasse artists' quarter at the beginning of the century. Three exhibitions a year include one devoted to Cartier Bresson and one to the winner of the prestigious annual prize awarded by the foundation. Do go up to the top floor lounge where you can watch a film about Cartier-Bresson. *Wed 1-8:30pm, Thu-Fri, Sun 1-6:30pm, Sat 11am-6:45pm.* €– 2 impasse Lebouis (M° Gaîté), 01.56.80.27.00, henri-cartierbresson.org

Galeries Lafayette • 9th • Store
This giant retailer and its neighbor Printemps are in hot competition. Luxury though it is, Lafayette has a gaudy, souk-like quality, with stalls lined up at the front to remind one of the novelty bazaar it once was. This can be frustrating when you're trying to make a beeline for something, as the store is arranged to divert and confuse at every turn. Cutting-edge fashion is on 1, and in the biggest lingerie department in the world on 3, you're bound to find something delectable. Lafayette Homme woos men with designer corners and a "clubroom" with internet access. The Lafayette Maison store opposite is almost as big as the main store. The best thing about Galeries Lafayette, however, is its gourmet food hall, incorporating a wine cellar with its own bar where you can buy at store prices and enjoy on the premises. *Mon-Sat 9:30am-7:30pm. Late-night shopping until 9pm Thu.* 40 bd. Haussmann (M° Chaussée d'Antin-Lafayette), 01.42.82.34.56, galerieslafayette.com

Le Grand Palais • 8th • Art Museum
Blockbuster exhibitions are held in this ornate palace built for the 1900 Exposition Universelle. Shows range from Gold of the Scythian Kings to the Arts of the Brazilian Indians to monograph art shows (Gauguin, Vuillard) and multi-artist collections, and many go on to other galleries around the world. They draw huge crowds, so reserve tickets in advance to avoid waiting in long lines. *Wed 10am-10pm, Thu-Mon 10am-8pm. Pre-booking compulsory before 1pm.* €– 3 av. du Général-Eisenhower (M° Champs-Elysées-Clemenceau), 01.44.13.17.30, rmn.fr/galeriesnationalesdugrandpalais

Ile de la Cité • 1st and 4th • Island
This island in the Seine was the origin of Paris itself when a Celtic tribe called the Parisii formed a settlement here around 250 BC. It remained the center of government until Philippe-Auguste built the Louvre. Originally a teeming island

of medieval streets and churches, it was cleared of its 25,000 inhabitants as part of Baron Haussmann's urban planning, which left only the monumental buildings of the Conciergerie, Ste-Chapelle, Notre-Dame, and a handful of other institutions. Place Louis-Lépine houses a flower market. On Sundays this is joined by a squawking bird and small animal market, which has existed since the Middle Ages. A quieter place to stroll is the pretty 17th-century place Dauphine near the Pont Neuf and the triangular garden of Square du Vert-Galant at the tip, which André Malraux described as "the sex of Paris." Approached by the Pont Neuf, Pont au Change, Pont St-Michel, or Pont Notre-Dame (M° Cité)

Les Invalides • 7th • Monument/Museum

The complex that houses Napoléon's tomb was built as a military hospital in the 17th century by two of Paris' greatest architects, and still in part fulfills that function. Glorying the Sun King, it has serried ranks of topiarized yews and cannons, arcades and sundials, which no doubt assuaged the war wounded lucky enough to be here. The two churches, one for the soldiers and one for the king, are connected behind the altar. The baroque Eglise du Dôme is now dedicated to the cult of Napoléon, who achieved massive heroic status almost immediately after his death. His body was brought here and installed in a porphyry tomb in the crypt, surrounded by eulogizing friezes and texts. Your ticket also gives access to the Musée de l'Armée, which is well worth a visit, not just for the sumptuous uniforms and arms of the Napoléonic era, but for fine portraiture and its moving coverage of the two World Wars. *Daily 10am-6pm, Oct.-Mar. 10am-5pm. €–* Esplanade des Invalides (M° Invalides), 01.44.42.38.77, invalides.org

Marché Mouffetard • 5th • Food Market

Best Markets "That wonderful narrow crowded market street, beloved of bohemians," wrote Hemingway, who lived just a street away from rue Mouffetard. Too famous to be bohemian now, and cluttered with Greek restaurants and accessories shops, it still has a popular morning food market characterized by some of the most elaborate vegetable displays at any Paris market. Behind the noisy stalls with their raucous-voiced traders are specialized food shops selling cheese, wine, bread, and pastries. At the top of the street is café-filled place de la Contrescarpe and at the bottom Eglise St-Médard, in front of which an accordion sing-along of French popular songs takes place on Sunday mornings. *Tue-Sun 8am-2pm.* Rue Mouffetard (M° Censier-Daubenton)

Musée Carnavalet • 3rd • Museum

This museum dedicated to the "memory of Paris" is housed in two Marais mansions, one of which was the home of the prolific 18th-century letter-writer Mme. de Sévigné. The building itself, with its beautiful interiors, is one of the most important exhibits, and other entire rooms have been transplanted here, including Proust's cork-lined bedroom, a jewelry shop decorated by Alphonse Mucha, and a room of exquisite 17th-century painted paneling done for the Duke of Uzès. Exhibits cover Paris' entire existence from Gaulish kayaks to the early 20th century. Renaissance art and furniture is in the original 16th-century rooms, and the Revolutionary collection is fascinating. *Tue-Sun 10am-6pm.* 23 rue de Sévigné (M° St-Paul), 01.44.59.58.58, carnavalet.paris.fr

Musée du Louvre • 1st • Art Museum
Best Statuary Even before Dan Brown set a murder scene inside it, the world's biggest art museum was pretty intimidating. With 12 miles of corridors and 300,000 works of art, where do you start? In fact, this is many museums in one, as well as being a former stately home, with its décor left intact in some places (Louis XIV's bedchamber is in the Egyptian department). Pick what you really want to see, whether it's clocking all the major masterpieces or losing yourself in the detail of one collection, and locate it on the free map. Ancient Egypt, Mesopotamia, and classical civilizations each have their own extensive galleries with magnificent oversize exhibits like the giant sphinx or the reconstructions of the palaces of Sargon II and Darius I (Oriental Antiquities). It's hard to beat the statuary here, from the *Winged Victory of Samothrace* at the top of the grand staircase of the Denon wing and the *Venus de Milo* to the two Renaissance sculpture courts housing the nostril-flaring Marly horses. Renaissance painting or French masterpieces would take you half a day and there is much, much more. For a refreshingly new experience, visit the African, Asian, Oceanic, and American arts, a precursor to the huge new museum due to open on Quai Branly. *Wed-Mon 9am-6pm (Wed, Fri till 9:45pm).* €– Rue de Rivoli (M° Palais Royal-Musée du Louvre), 01.40.20.50.50, louvre.fr

Musée de Montmartre • 18th • Museum
Just behind Sacré-Coeur, a house with its own rambling garden recounts the colorful history of the Butte. An artists' studio above the entrance pavilion was once occupied by Suzanne Valadon, Renoir, Raoul Dufy, and Maurice Utrillo. Over five floors, each room is devoted to a different aspect of the historic hill, which was annexed to Paris in 1860 but retains its village character even today. Learn about revolutionary Louise Michel, composer Gustave Charpentier, Suzanne Valadon, and the Lapin Agile cabaret (with original Toulouse-Lautrec posters) in this intriguing museum. *Tue-Sun 10am-12:30pm and 1:30-6pm.* €– 12 rue Cortot (M° Abbesses), 01.46.06.61.11, museedemontmartre.com

Musée Nationale du Moyen Age-Thermes et Hôtel de Cluny • 5th • Museum
This museum is housed in the 6th-century mansion of the Abbots of Cluny, and also comprises the 1st-to-3rd-century Gallo-Roman baths, one of the most complete Roman remains in the whole of Gaul. Its frigidarium (cold room) features a mosaic of "Love riding a dolphin." The museum's medieval treasures include the celebrated *Lady and the Unicorn* tapestry cycle displayed in its own circular room, Gothic sculpture from Notre-Dame, ecclesiastical goldwork, and an exhibition on daily life in the Middle Ages. In front of the museum a formal garden has been planted with medicinal and aromatic plants inspired by the museum collections. *Wed-Mon 9:15am-5:45pm.* €– 6 pl. Paul Painlevé (M° Cluny-La Sorbonne), 01.53.73.78.00, musee-moyenage.fr

Musée d'Orsay • 7th • Art Museum
Famous for its Impressionist paintings, the Musée d'Orsay is devoted to the pivotal period in art from 1848 (the Paris Commune) to 1914 (World War I). It is housed in a former train station, a masterpiece of Beaux Arts style that was built for the 1900 Exposition Universelle. The galleries run along either side of a central, light-filled sculpture aisle where the tracks once were. On the first floor are Impressionism's precursors among works by Ingres, Delacroix, Cabanel, the Symbolists, Barbizon painters, and Courbet, whose *L'Origine du Monde* is here.

Then head upstairs for the crowded Impressionist galleries with masterworks by Pissaro, Renoir, Caillebotte, Monet, Degas, Van Gogh, and Cézanne. The gallery of mystical pastel drawings by Odilon Redon is worth a look, and the mezzanine is devoted to the Nabis painters. There are also furniture galleries and exhibits displaying early photography. *Tue, Wed, Sat, Sun 9:30am-6pm, Thu 9:30am-9:45pm.* €– 1 rue de la Légion d'Honneur (RER Musée d'Orsay/M° Solférino), 01.40.49.49.78, musee-orsay.fr

Le Panthéon • 5th • Monument

Though it looks like a church and was originally conceived as one by Louis XV, the domed Panthéon ended up the great white elephant of the French Revolution. It was finished in 1790, just as a new era of atheism began, and was rededicated as a "temple of reason." Today it is a mausoleum to France's "great men," although a single woman, Marie Curie, was interred here in 1995, to lie alongside Voltaire, Rousseau, Victor Hugo, and Zola. New additions, such as Alexandre Dumas, who was moved here from his native village in 2002, are fêted with much pomp and ceremony. Soufflot's architecture, influenced by St-Paul's in London, is neo-classical with its Greek columns. From the dome hangs a replica of Foucault's pendulum, designed to prove by its swinging movement that the earth revolves on its axis. Climbing the steep spiral steps to the colonnade provides good views over the city. *Daily 10am-5:15pm.* €– Pl. du Panthéon (M° Cardinal Lemoine), 01.44.32.18.00

Paris Muse • Various • Guided Tour

Best Guided Tours American art historian Ellen McBreen and her team of experts offer personalized guided tours of Paris art museums and monuments that are the very antithesis of being herded around by an umbrella-toting guide, or the didacticism of an audio guide. With groups no larger than four, the tours are tailor-made to what you want to see and make art appreciation the contemplative and interactive experience it was meant to be. Four different facets of the Louvre are offered, from *The Da Vinci Code* to hidden treasures, and most of the other major museums as well as Notre-Dame can be visited in this way. *Tours 1.5-2.5 hrs long.* €€€€ 06.73.77.33.52, parismuse.com

Paris Walks • Various • Guided Tour

Best Guided Tours English couple Peter and Oriel Caine have been running guided walks in Paris for more than a decade and know the city inside out. They have developed about 100 different themes for discovering Paris and call on a bank of experts to give tours ranging from *The Da Vinci Code* to Americans in Paris, from Opera, Fashion, and World War II to the Paris Sewers. The walks are accessible and entertaining, full of nuggets of Paris gossip as well as sound historical fact. Hemingway's Paris, every Friday morning, is one of the most popular. *Daily 2hr tours start at 10:30am and 2:30pm Apr-Oct, less regularly in winter.* €– 01.48.09.21.40, paris-walks.com

Printemps • 9th • Store

For stylish midrange fashion, Printemps is definitely the leader. Its second-floor trend collection is more classy and better organized than Lafayette's with a strong emphasis on French designers such as Paule Ka, Vanessa Bruno, and Paul et Joe, alongside the likes of Stella McCartney and Alexander McQueen. There are free fashion shows at 10am on Tuesdays. The first-floor Luxury Store has "all of place Vendôme, Avenue Montaigne, and rue St-Honoré in one place." Another highlight is the biggest beauty department in the world, now with a Nuxe salon, Shiseido offering Qi massage, and the Nickel male grooming institute. You can snack under the '20s glass dome, or on the open-air rooftop café. Foreign travelers can save a lot of money here by asking for the 10% discount card at the Welcome Service, in addition to 12 percent tax refunds. *Mon-Sat 9:35am-7pm. Late-night shopping until 10pm Thu.* 64 bd. Haussmann (M° Havre-Caumartin), 01.42.82.57.87, printemps.com

La Ste-Chapelle • 1st • Monument

Taking the same entrance as for the Conciergerie, follow signs to the chapel of Ste-Chapelle. This 13th-century structure is one of the jewels of French sacred architecture and reveals the richness and religious fervor of the medieval court. The flamboyant Gothic chapel was built by the devout Saint Louis in the 1240s to house his relic of the Crown of Thorns. The upper chapel, for the use of the royal family, consists almost entirely of 50-foot-high stained-glass windows depicting hundreds of Biblical scenes. It rivals Chartres Cathedral in the intricacy and depth of color of the work. Try to pick a sunny day to see it in its full glory. For classical music concerts in the chapel, see Concerts in Churches (p.109). *Daily 9:30am-6pm. €–* 4 bd. du Palais (M° Cité), 01.53.40.60.80

Shakespeare & Co. • 5th • Store

Though this isn't the bookshop that published *Ulysses*—George Whitman, who opened in 1951, took the name in homage to the Sylvia Beach shop—this Shakespeare & Co. has become just as famous thanks to the generations of "struggling" writers who have taken rooms here in exchange for staffing the bookshop. And if Hemingway never stopped in here, the Beat poets did when they lived in rue Gît-le-Coeur. Now run by Whitman's daughter and a knowledgeable staff of young, romantic types with glasses, it's a fantastic, higgledy-piggledy warren of thousands of English-language books and an expats' institution. *Daily noon-midnight.* 37 rue de la Bûcherie (M° Maubert-Mutualité), 01.43.25.40.93

Le Spa at the Four Seasons George V • 8th • Spa

Best Spas The George V has one of the most luxurious spas in Paris, decorated like a palatial private home with classical statues, marble, floral arrangements, and toile de Jouy fabrics on the walls of the treatment rooms. The reception and relaxation area, outfitted with a juice bar, overlooks the magnificent pool, although day spa guests can only dream—it's reserved for the use of the hotel's guests. There are, however, some very special treatments on offer here. In autumn and winter a whole sequence of facials and body scrubs revolves around chocolate. In spring and summer, mint, cucumber, and lotus flower come to the fore. The spa is also a forerunner in male grooming, with massages and four male facials. Equally unique are the two double treatment rooms for couples to enjoy side-by-side treatments. *Non-guests Mon-Fri 10am-4pm. Guests daily 6:30am-10pm. €€€€* Four Seasons Hôtel George V, 31 av. George V (M° George V), 01.49.52.72.00, fourseasons.com

Les Thermes • 8th • Spa
This is is one of the few hotel spas that opens up all its facilities to non-guests, including its superb pool overlooking the hotel garden. Day membership (€100) also gives you access to classes, from yoga to aqua gym, making this a great choice for a half-day of fitness and relaxation. It is also one of the most beautiful settings for relaxing on loungers around the pool or a light lunch at the poolside restaurant. The spa specializes in slimming treatments and aromatherapy massage, and you can get an instant spray-tan to be ready for that fabulous party. Though it gets busy after work—the spa has become quite the place for chic Parisians to work out—come on a weekday afternoon and you will likely have the pool to yourself. *Daily 9am-8pm.* €€€€ Hôtel Royal Monceau, 13 av. Hoche (M° Charles de Gaulle-Etoile), 01.42.99.88.00, royalmonceau.com

Bobo Paris

It was an American who coined the term, but the French invented the words—bourgeois(e)-bohème. These hipsters love to be at the forefront, converting old workshops into lofts, hanging out in artists' squats, discussing fair trade in old zinc bars that look artfully decayed. The epicenter of bobo life is the Canal St-Martin, a stretch of bars, bistros, and boutiques by the water, featured in the film *Amélie* (the bobo style manual). We've also included the new hipster scene that's infiltrating the posh heartland of the Champs-Elysées. Bobo is today what beatnik was before—intellectual, avant-garde, and cool, though not giving a damn (or pretending not to). Want to be on the cutting edge? Then these are the places you belong. But first gen up on your art house cinema—and lose the tie.

Note: Venues in bold in the itinerary are described in detail in the listings that follow. Venues followed by an * asterisk are those we recommend as both a restaurant and a destination bar.

Bobo Paris:
The Perfect Plan (3 Days and Nights)

Your Hotel: **Hôtel du Petit Moulin**, because it's designed by Christian Lacroix and is within striking distance of the Canal St-Martin.

Thursday

Highlights

Thursday (Night)
Cocktails	La Belle Hortense
Dinner	Le 404
Nighttime	Andy Wahloo
Late-Night	L'Etoile Manquante

Friday
Breakfast	Viaduc Café*
Morning	La Bastille
Lunch	Pause Café
Afternoon	Montmartre
Cocktails	Drôle d'Endroit*
Dinner	La Famille
Nighttime	Le Progrès
Late-Night	Au Soleil de la Butte, Le Tambour

Saturday
Breakfast	Hotel
Morning	Marché aux Puces
Lunch	Le Soleil
Afternoon	India & Spa
Cocktails	Palais de Tokyo
Dinner	Tokyo Eat
Nighttime	Tokyo Idem
Late-Night	Le Baron

Sunday (Day)
Morning	Marché des Enfants Rouges
Brunch	L'Estaminet
Afternoon	Canal St-Martin
Cocktails	Les Jemmapes

5pm The northeastern side of the Marais, centering around rue Charlot, is less busy and less chichi than the southern end. Start your bobo weekend by exploring its fascinating streets where new design boutiques and cafés are springing up beside old-style workshops and tabacs.

7pm Then stop in for a glass of wine and a browse in literary wine bar **La Belle Hortense** or **Les Philosophes*** café on happening rue Vieille-du-Temple.

9pm Dinner Moroccan spice and all things nice are found in **Le 404**, a fashion hangout where steaming tagines are brought forth by waiters who then get up on the bar to dance. Just as the rhythms of tango are more mysterious and measured, so is **Anahi**, an authentic Argentinian restaurant with cracked tiles and cacti that attracts film stars and bohemians of all ages to dine on steaks flown in from the pampas. Or grab a terrace table and order a pastis for some southern-French hospitality at **Chez Janou**.

BOBO

117

11pm It's easy to bar-crawl in the Marais. Just beside Le 404, its sister-bar **Andy Wahloo** does pop art, North African style, and a lively crowd and strong cocktails keep it grooving till the small hours. **Jokko Bar** has live West African music Thursday to Saturday in a lounge/bar atmosphere. Head up to **La Perle** to meet the area's hippest crowd, or, for the gay scene, rue des Archives, where **Open Café** is a good starting point.

1am Later on there's always a party atmosphere at **Banana Café**, with its male go-go dancers, and **Le Tropic Café**, while **Chez Richard** heats up with a more hetero clientele, and **L'Etoile Manquante** is perfect for a late terrace drink.

Friday

9:30am Head out to the Faubourg St-Antoine, which was a traditional working-class area until the Opéra Bastille opened in 1989. Even today, the quarter has retained a lot of its artisan charm. On avenue Daumesnil, craftsmen's studios are housed under the arches of an old viaduct. With its large open terrace, **Viaduc Café*** is the perfect place to breakfast.

11am Afterward, climb the steps to reach the walkway above, the **Promenade Plantée**, which takes you back to place de la Bastille. Walking south by the Port de l'Arsenal you'll come to the city's latest contemporary art gallery, **La Maison Rouge**, while crossing over by one of the footbridges gives you the chance to survey new architectural projects and a history of Paris at the **Pavillon de l'Arsenal**. The **Musée du Fumeur** has displays of opium pipes and growing plants, but leave time for wandering around the Faubourg itself.

1pm Lunch There's a huge choice here for lunch. **Pause Café** is a hip hangout with a see-and-be-seen terrace beloved of film people. The bistro **Le Square Trousseau** is like a film set itself, and you can't do better if you're looking for a steak Béarnaise in Art Nouveau surroundings. Italian food enthusiasts will be in heaven at **Sardegna a Tavola**, whose spaghetti with squid ink is utter perfection.

3pm Head up to multicultural Montmartre, making your way to the Abbesses quarter, where many young designers' boutiques are now situated. There's plenty to do here, from shopping for a handmade creation to lounging on the grass in front of Sacré-Coeur to lingering on one of the café terraces overlooking rue des Abbesses. More legwork will take you to the Cimetière de Montmartre and west into the bobo quarter of Batignolles.

BOBO · ITINERARY

6pm You may also want to visit the **Musée de l'Erotisme**, a huge collection of historical eroticism in saucy Pigalle.

7pm Stop for a drink at the New York–style singles bar **Drôle d'Endroit pour une Rencontre*** ("a funny place to meet").

9pm Dinner Choose from three bobo favorites among the many small restaurants on the Butte Montmartre. **La Famille** is a very hip place serving adventurous cuisine; **Café Burq** a lively neighborhood café that draws a pre-clubbing crowd; or for a cozier, more old-fashioned atmosphere, try **Chez Toinette**.

11pm Stay in Abbesses to take advantage of its lively bar scene. At the neo-bohemian **Le Progrès** you'll meet the artists, musicians, and designers who live nearby, while **Le Sancerre*** is a happy mix of locals and hip tourists, sometimes with live music. If you're feeling adventurous, go off the beaten track to two bars where DJs mix, **L'Ile Enchantée** and **Café Chéri(e)**. If you're in the mood for dancing, Brazilian club **Favela Chic** always has a party crowd, while the **Elysée Montmartre** is a cabaret with some good house nights.

1am Late-nighters can carry on at the club **Au Soleil de la Butte** then head on to one of **Folies Pigalle**'s legendary after-parties.

4am Late-night hunger can be satisfied at the lively all-night café **Le Tambour**.

9:30am Treat yourself to breakfast in bed—you'll appreciate the time you've saved when you get to Paris' largest flea market, the **Marché aux Puces de St-Ouen**. With many markets in one, it ranges from antiques priced in the thousands to buttons and badges that can be had for a song and has a great atmosphere.

1pm Lunch A calm haven away from the frenetic flea market is found at bistro **Le Soleil**, where you'll find antique dealers celebrating a good sale with foie gras and excellent wines. Or, if you're up to it, sample a Parisian "guingette" with accordion music and dancing at **Chez Louisette**.

3pm After heading back to the hotel with your flea-market finds, a massage is in order. **India & Spa** offers a range of restorative massages. Alternatively choose a cultural activity from another itinerary—the Musée Picasso and Musée Carnavalet, about the history of Paris, are both in the Marais. Or simply relax under the chestnut trees of the Place des Vosges.

7pm Head to the **Palais de Tokyo**, a contemporary art space that is now a major scene with its concept shop, bar, and restaurant.

9pm Dinner Stay for dinner at **Tokyo Eat**. In summer, the restaurant moves outside, complete with fairy lights and a DJ. In winter, everyone stays inside and it's still quite a scene. A more low-key option is the Italian eatery **Swann et Vincent** by the Bastille.

11pm Have a drink at the downstairs bar, **Tokyo Idem**, which sets out deck chairs in summer.

1am Many hipsters go on to dance at **Le Baron** or **Le Paris Paris**. The former re-creates a Studio 54 ambiance, while the latter programs live music and DJs. Across town, a less exclusive but equally enjoyable scene is found at the **Batofar**, a club on a lighthouse boat. Alternatively, bar-crawl by the Bastille, where the upbeat **Sans Sanz** and **China Club** are two of the best bets.

4am To keep the party going, try **Le Triptyque** or **La Scène Bastille**, both of which have live music followed by DJs.

Sunday

10am Head to the **Marché des Enfants Rouges** to stock up on organic wines and wonderful olives. You could choose to picnic if the weather's fine, as many Parisian bobos do, in the **Parc des Buttes Chaumont**. Or select a brunch option below.

11am Brunch L'Estaminet, a wine bar in the Marché des Enfants Rouges, has a Provençal atmosphere and attracts a very bobo crowd. If an eggs-and-pancakes brunch is what you hanker for, choose **Le Loir dans la Théière**.

1pm On sunny days in June, July, and September, the Canal St-Martin is the place to be—the quayside is lined with bobos soaking up the sun and picnicking. **Chez Prune*** and **Canal 96*** are two of the best cafés.

2:30pm People-watch by the water, then take a leisurely stroll among the boutiques on rue Beaurepaire and quai de Valmy, which stock everything that goes with this lifestyle. Another option is to take a cruise up the Canal, starting from Bastille and going up to La Villette, with **Canauxrama**. From there, wrap up your day with a walk down the eastern quay of the Canal d'Ourcq to find another Sunday afternoon scene, where hipsters chill while DJs spin at **Bar Ourcq**.

5pm If you're still at the Canal St-Martin at apéritif time **Le Jemmapes** does a roaring trade in take-out drinks to be enjoyed by the water.

Bobo Paris:
The Key Neighborhoods

The **Marais (3rd** and **4th arrondissements)** has a happening gay and hetero bar scene, small designer boutiques, and a slew of hipster restaurants along its narrow, cobbled streets.

To experience the true bobo vibe you have to hang out on the **Canal St-Martin (10th arrondissement)**, especially on a Sunday afternoon, when the canal's quayside is lined with bobo scenesters and you can pick up original fashion and books at the boutiques on rue Beaurepaire and rue de Lancry. Further up the canal in the 19th arrondissement former dive bars host live DJs and throng with hipsters.

The bobo scene can also be found in the **Bastille (11th arrondissement)** along the Faubourg St-Antoine. Colonized a decade ago by young artists and designers who converted industrial buildings into lofts, this area still houses some traditional craft workers restoring furniture and houses a concentration of great bistros and a wonderful market, as well as a thriving nightlife scene and some interesting art and museum spaces.

Abbesses (18th arrondissement) is the hip part of Montmartre, where small boutiques, great bars, and bistros spill out onto the sloping cobbled streets with an edgy bobo crowd.

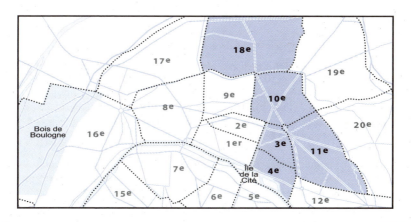

Bobo Paris: The Shopping Blocks

Abbesses

The pretty cobbled streets below the Sacré-Coeur are awash with young designers.

Base One Hip concept store with limited-edition clubwear, CDs, and fanzines. 47 bis rue d'Orsel (M° Abbesses), 01.53.28.04.52

Les Filles à l'Anis Atelier-boutique carrying simply cut dresses in cool colors and funky bags. 19 rue Houdon (M° Abbesses), 01.42.64.40.54

Lili Perpink The Japanese owner has an eye for upcoming designers and vintage clothing. 22 rue de la Vieuville (M° Abbesses), 01.42.52.37.24

Patricia Louisor Delicate knits and elegant tailoring from this young designer. 16 rue Houdon (M° Abbesses), 01.42.62.10.42

Spree Concept shop with iconic furniture, cutting-edge fashion, books, and art exhibitions. (p.147) 16 rue de la Vieuville (M° Abbesses), 01.42.23.41.40

Canal St-Martin

Everything for the bobo lifestyle can be found in the boutiques by the Canal.

Antoine et Lili Separates in puce and pink, and kitsch ethnic objets. (p.143) 95 quai de Valmy (M° Jacques Bonsergent), 01.40.37.41.55

Artazart Hipster bookstore selling rare photography and design tomes, with its own art gallery. 83 quai de Valmy (M° Jacques Bonsergent), 01.40.40.24.00

Coin Canal '60s furniture, Plexiglas lamps, and paintings arranged in room sets. 1 rue de Marseille (M° Jacques Bonsergent), 01.42.38.00.30

Ginger Lyly An ever-changing stock of funky fashion, jewelry, and knickknacks. 33 rue Beaurepaire (M° Jacques Bonsergent), 01.42.06.07.73

Viveka Bergström Swedish jeweler selling her unusual creations. 23 rue de la Grange-aux-Belles (M° Jacques Bonsergent), 01.40.03.04.92

The Marais

A window-shopper's heaven full of small boutiques selling gorgeous creations.

AB33 Multilabel shop with a delicious array of feminine fashion. 33 rue Charlot (M° Filles du Calvaire), 01.42.71.02.82

Code 3 Jazzed-up old furniture, amid retro lights and funky art. 2 rue Froissart (M° St-Sébastien-Froissart), 01.32.71.41.90

Galerie Simone A truly original selection of young designers' one-off creations. (p.144) 124 rue Vieille-du-Temple (M° St-Sébastien Froissart), 01.42.74.21.28

Jacenko A beautiful menswear shop. 38 rue de Poitou (M° Filles du Calvaire), 01.42.71.80.38

Quidam de Revel By appointment only, this vintage shop stocks clothing dating from 1900–1970. 24 rue de Poitou (M° Filles du Calvaire), 06.15.95.74.83

Bobo Paris:
The Hotels

Le Général • 11th • Trendy (47 rms)
There is nothing military about Le Général except its name. Inside this boutique hotel, everything is a bit funky. This is a hotel that looks even better in the flesh than in pictures, with much attention paid to the lighting, textures, and patterns in the décor. The large lobby opens into an attractive bar. The disco soundtrack and good-looking bartenders dressed in ties that match the huge pink flower print on the wall hint at the hipster clientele that hangs out here, sampling designer alcohols like Bombay Sapphire and Havana Club rum during the 7-9pm happy hour. A huge bowl of Jelly Babies is on the bar; glass backgammon sets are set up between the '60s pod chairs, mauve tweed armchairs, and white PVC pouffes; and optical light boards show changing mood colors. The rooms are more soothing, decorated in white and taupe with wood headboards, a shot of color coming from a fuchsia chair and matching orchids. The modern bathrooms have round basins set into wooden counters. Wi-Fi and a small gym and sauna are all you need to complete the bobo idyll. This is a bit like a junior Murano, fun but less flashy and a tad more tasteful—aside from the bartenders' ties. € 5-7 rue Rampon (M° Oberkampf), 01.47.00.41.57, legeneralhotel.com

Hôtel Le A • 8th • Trendy (25 rms)
This minimalist hotel offers contemporary style just off the Champs-Elysées. The well-stocked library in the white, chocolate, and metal lounge bar gives a clue to the clientele: floor to ceiling are stocked with the kind of books you'll find in an architect's, photographer's, or contemporary art critic's home, and there is original art on a massive scale by Fabrice Hybert. A tapestry of tree trunks echoing the pendulous lamps fills an entire wall of the glass-roofed breakfast room, and cartoons, sketches, and drawings line the walls elsewhere. Stripe-mad designer Frédéric Mechiche has been remarkably restrained here, with just a striped carpet and bathroom tiles as his trademark. Think all-white rooms, complete with starched white slipcovers on the furniture that are changed after each guest. Bathrooms are granite with designer taps and orchids. It all looks designed to fit around your iBook, though Wi-Fi, be warned, is an additional expense. If space is important, book a deluxe rather than superior room, though with suites the price of a room elsewhere in the vicinity, why not splash out? €€ 4 rue d'Artois (M° St-Philippe-du-Roule), 01.42.56.99.99, paris-hotel-a.com

Hôtel Bourg Tibourg • 4th • Trendy (31 rms)
Welcome to Costes junior. This boutique hotel is owned by Guy Costes, brother of Jean-Louis, whose Hôtel Costes needs no introduction. Here you won't find the same see-and-be-seen crowd as it doesn't have a restaurant, but young models making their first runway appearance, and bobo fashion hounds who love its cosseting environment and aristo-chic Jacques Garcia décor. There's a Gothic theme going on here, in the wrought-iron door, lobby furniture, and pale blue turreted top-flight staircase. You can imagine yourself in Lewis Carroll's Oxford rooms, and the *Through the Looking Glass* fantasy continues with the impres-

sion that some of the rooms have shrunk around their large beds, and the amusing discovery that some doors are visual jokes, leading to nothing but a piece of tapestry. Some don't have space to swing a Cheshire cat, but who cares when you're surrounded by striped taffeta, crisp white sheets, and a single orchid in its vase? Bathrooms are also tiny but exquisite, with ebony-colored mosaic tiles. Thirteen rooms overlook the leafy little patio. The lower ones are rather dark—ask for 55, which is light with a streetside terrace, or 56, which has a warm terra-cotta color scheme. Downstairs is a crypt breakfast room and lounge where the Gothic thing gets truly funky with throne chairs in a blue leopard-skin print. The reception area is often manned by Guy's daughters, who are utterly charming and offer lots of great tips for enjoying the area. €€ 19 rue du Bourg-Tibourg (M° St-Paul), 01.42.78.47.39, hotelbourgtibourg.com

Hôtel du Petit Moulin • 3rd • Trendy (17 rms)

This boutique hotel was the fashion hit of 2005. When Christian Lacroix noticed that the low-grade hotel in this 17th-century building was being renovated, he offered his services as decorator, resulting in the hotel equivalent of one of his flamboyant womenswear collections. The former bakery on the ground floor is now the reception area, complete with its boulangerie lettering. Next door is the chic little bar open only to hotel guests, decorated with a nod to the '50s with brightly colored panels and chairs. A labyrinth of staircases leads to the curiously shaped rooms, which make up for smallness in their bespoke décor and spacious bathrooms. Each one is as individual as a couture creation, made up of a collage of fabulous colors, textures, and photographic murals. The delightful ground-floor single 04 has a zingy combination of stripes of huge pink carnations on the walls and a black-and-white polka-dot carpet; Superior room 205 has a spectacular wall motif of blown-up coral formations and a black-tiled bathroom with a Victorian bath; 204 is the ultimate fashion groupie's choice with Lacroix fashion sketches covering the walls. If that's all too frenetic, choose soothing Junior suite 301 where a starry night sky with planets will help you sink into a deep sleep. All this for less than the price of a pair of denims chez Lacroix—it's the best fashion deal out there. €€ 29-31 rue de Poitou (M° Filles du Calvaire), 01.42.74.10.10, hoteldupetitmoulin.com

Kube Rooms • 18th • Trendy (40 rms)

From the makers of Murano Urban Resort comes this latest out-there venture, a design hotel right in the middle of the edgy La Chapelle area to the east of Montmartre. If outside is all Arab street hawkers crying "Marlborrrro" and shops selling everything for €1, inside, the sleek cube is a cosseting environment designed to soothe and stimulate the senses. You check in in the glass cube in the middle of the courtyard and proceed through the dark and sultry lounge bar with its faux fur sofas and soft, almost fetishistic cushions. On the mezzanine is the Ice Kube, a bar built of solid ice and maintained at 21 degrees Fahrenheit. Fingerprint recognition opens the door to rooms that have a similar look to those at the Murano, only here it's touch, not color, that is the defining sense. Slip on a pair of yeti-like slippers, fondle the curtains of faux polar-bear fur, or lounge in the silky-smooth cube-shaped tub hidden behind a wall of glass blocks that echoes the Ice Kube. The Duplex room is exceptional for its hanging bed. The techno needs of the urban nomads who stay here are met by the Sony Vaio entertainment system into which you plug your laptop for Internet access, and Wi-Fi in the lounge bar. Rough-edged though the neighborhood is,

Kube is brilliantly placed for access to Roissy airport and the Eurostar terminal, and lest the environs should offend your gentle sensibilities, a fleet of cars is on hand to chauffeur you to the Murano restaurant, station, or airport. €€ 1-5 passage Ruelle (M° La Chapelle), 01.42.05.20.00, kubehotel.com

Pavillon de Paris • 9th • Trendy (30 rms)
Zen is the operative word here, in this feng shui–designed hotel. When it opened in 1998, this was one of the first boutique hotels, and its style has not dated. The reception desk is a gold cube that opens like a Pandora's box, revealing laptop and key cards for the friendly staff to check you in. The rooms are all around the same compact size, but the four junior executive rooms on the sixth floor have exposed beams lending them extra appeal. Room 66 is particularly sunny and quiet, overlooking the courtyard and rooftops. Streetside rooms, such as 44, have their own Parisian charm as they look out at the shuttered windows and geranium boxes of this pretty, small street. The décor is also uniform, a soothing scheme of mushroom, chocolate, and cream. Dark wood headboards have cream padded backrests for reading. The hotel was designed with savvy business travelers in mind and has direct-dial telephones and free Wi-Fi, though the guestbook testifies to plenty of leisure travelers who rave about the helpfulness of staff. Breakfast is served in a glass-roofed room next to a tiny courtyard, and the cute, Japanese-influenced bar hosts photographic exhibitions. €€ 7 rue de Parme (M° Place-de-Clichy), 01.55.31.60.00, pavillondeparis.com

Villa Royale • 9th • Trendy (31 rms)
If you yearn for the glory days of the Moulin Rouge, place yourself in the rock-rococo Villa Royale, whose rooms have oodles of ooh-là-là. As well as having garter-twinging credentials, this little enclave just south of Montmartre is the music district—where else could you find a sax shop and a sex shop right opposite each other?—and DJs and bands often check into this hotel. From the rooms of this pristine white 19th-century villa you can choose between a view of the transvestites emerging from wild nights of go-go dancing at Folies Pigalle or the heavenly domes of the Sacré-Coeur. The Jean Marais room on the sixth (named after Cocteau's lover) has both, and you can view the Basilica from the double-size round Jacuzzi. The lobby is like a boudoir with chaises longues, many-shaded lamps, and a canopied ceiling. From here you ascend the staircase to the rooms, which combine flamboyant décor with mod cons. Flat-screen TVs are framed by gold rococo frames and the minibar is hidden behind a studded silk door. The overwhelming color scheme is pink, with curtain canopies over the beds, swirly carpet patterns, and punky papier-mâché lamps, though one room is done out in midnight-blue velvet with stars on the ceiling. The four Chambres Royales have a Jacuzzi in the marble bathrooms, which sport taps that would not look out of place in Graceland, and a cozy real-effect fire; Deluxes also have a Jacuzzi. The breakfast room with a circus theme is perfect for the morning after. Not for minimalists, but a lot of fun. €€ 2 rue Duperré (M° Pigalle), 01.55.31.78.78, leshotelsdeparis.com

Bobo Paris: The Restaurants

Le 404 • 3rd • North African
Best North African Dining Stepping into this North African restaurant in the Marais is like walking into a wicked party in Marrakech. The minute you're through the door the booty-shaking Asian beats shake you up, and it's hard to stay seated long enough to eat. Momo, the owner, is a bit of a celebrity in Paris and London, where he has Sketch and Momo's, but often drops in, as do his Channel-hopping friends. The place is always packed with a fun-loving crowd. Order the house cocktail, a variant on the Mojito, and briques (triangles of pastry filled with tuna) or a spicy dip as you wait for your tagine to arrive. As the terra-cotta dome comes off, delicious aromas waft, whether it's the lamb and prune or the wonderful fish version. Then the lithe waiters get up on the bar and start the dancing. Book the late seating for the best party atmosphere. *Mon-Fri noon-2:30pm and 8pm-midnight, Sat 8pm-midnight, Sun noon-4pm. €€* 69 rue des Gravilliers (M° Arts-et-Métiers), 01.42.74.57.81

Anahi• 3rd • Argentinian
Argentinian sisters started a restaurant in this old butcher's shop more than 20 years ago. They didn't redecorate, just stuck some arty black-and-white photos of themselves up over the cracked white tiles, put some cacti on the windowsill, and were open for business. Since then Johnny Depp, Quentin Tarantino, and Thierry Mugler have been in, but still nothing has changed. The same succulent slabs of beef (choose from French or Argentinian, flown in from the pampas) are served up on wooden boards with a simple, copious green salad. Don't miss out on the starters, which are really something, especially the chunky sea bass ceviche. Fellow diners of all ages tend toward the flamboyant. The restaurant tables are close, to say the least. Do ask to be seated in the front room. *Daily 8pm-midnight. €€* 49 rue Volta (M° Arts-et-Métiers), 01.48.87.88.24

Le Baron Rouge • 12th • Wine Bar
A wine bar like in the good old days, Le Baron Rouge is lined with full barrels and has a real atmosphere of conviviality around the zinc bar. Workers from the Marché d'Aligre stop in for a sharpener at hours when other people are just blinking over their morning coffee. Sunday mornings have become a real institution as this is when (in season, from October to March) an oyster stall sets up outside. Bobo locals, Japanese tourists, children, and dogs all mix with the marketers to enjoy the festive atmosphere, spilling out onto the pavement where you balance your glass and plate on upturned barrels. There are plates of robust charcuterie behind the bar and wines by the glass up on a blackboard. *Tue-Thu 10am-2pm and 5-10pm, Fri-Sat 10am-10pm, Sun 10am-3pm. €-* 1 rue Théophile-Roussel (M° Ledru-Rollin), 01.43.43.14.32

Le Bistrot du Peintre • 11th • Bistro
The "painter's bistro" is quite an oil painting itself. With its 1907 Art Nouveau windows and interior it could be the setting for a Toulouse-Lautrec drawing, and you can imagine a boozy crowd of misfits carousing here a century ago. Now the

customers are distinctly trendy as many of the neighboring workshops now house film production companies, recording studios, and small publishers. Though there is a spillover from the hip Pause Café across the road, the Peintre is a less hyped address, enjoyable for its confit de canard, grilled lamb, and profiteroles. The terrace is always crowded, as is the small downstairs room. Up the winding staircase it's a little more chilled out and you can linger over lunch as it's open all day. *Mon-Sat 7am-2am, Sun 10am-2am.* € 116 av. Ledru-Rollin (M° Bastille), 01.47.00.34.39

Café Burq • 18th • Bistro
Since an architect and an actor took over a dyed-in-the-wool rustic bistro, replaced the red checked tablecloths with shiny black tables, added orange Plexiglas lighting, and brought in some truly inventive bistro cooking, this place has been the talk of the Butte. It's hip, but it's also villagey, as the locals are fashion designers, actors, and other laid-back trendsters. Everyone raves about the food, whether it's the onglet of beef with red onion and balsamic sauce or seared salmon on semolina with fennel and black olives. There's an excellent wine selection too, which you can sample as you wait at the bar. It's smoky and noisy, but great if you want to sample the new energy of Montmartre. *Mon-Sat 8pm-midnight.* € 6 rue Burq (M° Abbesses), 01.42.52.81.27

Café Charbon • 11th • Café/Bar
A longtime hipster scene, Charbon still has abundant character with its stucco ceiling and mirrors, making lunch here plenty atmospheric. *See Bobo Nightlife, p.135, for details.* € 109 rue Oberkampf (M° Parmentier), 01.43.57.55.13

Canal 96* • 10th • Café
Parisian hipsters can't get enough of the Canal St-Martin, and when this aging café with its long canalside terrace came up for grabs, the new owners knew just what to do. Velvet-covered chairs and banquettes inside; comfortable terrace seating outside; a selection of smoothies, coffee, and alcoholic drinks; and simple, delicious plates of charcuterie or cheese served throughout the day. In the mornings they are ready with mounds of croissants and pains au chocolat piled up on the bar. On a summer night this is one of the best terraces to soak up the Canal vibe, and the fresh raspberry juice or artisanal ice cream works as a zingy pep-me-up if you're flagging. More than anything, though, the place is to be loved for its delightful staff. *Mon-Fri 7:30am-2am, Sat-Sun 9:30am-2am.* €– 96 quai de Jemmapes (M° Jacques Bonsergent), 01.42.02.87.95

Chai 33 • 12th • Trendy
Bercy shopping village has been converted out of old stone wine warehouses, and this is its flagship restaurant. Chai 33 pulls in a classy clientele, which isn't surprising as it all revolves around wine. The brilliant design encompasses a sleek modern lounge bar where a younger crowd sample wine-based cocktails, a dining room with thick wooden tables in the shapes of wine regions, a screen of suspended bottles, and a "cave paradis" containing dreamed-of vintages. Wine lovers rejoice: if you eat here you can choose a wine from the cellar at a reduced price. The terrace bistro is lovely for Sunday brunch and is neatly combined with a stroll through the Bercy gardens and visit to the Cinémathèque Française. *Sun-Mon noon-midnight, Tue-Sat noon-2am.* €€ 33 cour St-Emilion (M° Cour St-Emilion), 01.53.44.01.01, chai33.com

Le Chateaubriand • 11th • Bistro
This bistro is worth a detour for its fabulous food and wine. The setting is gorgeous too—a '30s interior that's been cleared of clutter, highlighting the beauty of its zinc bar and tiled floor. Bobo foodies and trendsters fill the small wooden tables, ordering from the blackboard such dishes as pike perch with Swiss chard, crispy beef cheek, and saddle of rabbit with gourmet peas. Wines are a treat—ask for Susan's recommendations from the sulphur-free, small-producer selection. Even by the carafe they are outstanding. A meal here can be followed by a drink on Oberkampf or the Canal St-Martin. *Tue-Fri noon-2pm and 8-11pm, Sat 8-11pm.* € ▤ 129 av. Parmentier (M° Goncourt), 01.43.57.45.95

Chez Janou • 3rd • Bistro
Daniel Auteuil and Jean-Paul Gaultier have both been spotted eating at this southern-flavored bistro, which just shows that simple things are sometimes the best. Get there early to snag a table on its tiny terrace hemmed in by greenery, but even if you don't, the wait at the zinc bar is a sociable affair as the bartenders hand rounds of pastis over the heads of the patrons as if they were back in Marseilles. The tuna steak and the risotto with scallops have the taste of the sun, and meat dishes are succulent, but it's the atmosphere that keeps people coming back. *Mon-Fri noon-3pm and 8pm-midnight, Sat-Sun noon-4pm and 8pm-midnight.* € ▤ 2 rue Roger-Verlomme (M° Chemin Vert), 01.42.72.28.41

Chez Louisette • St-Ouen • Brasserie
Hidden at the back of Marché Vernaison is the chance to sample a French "guingette" dance hall. At lunchtime on market days you'll find it in full flow, with anything from a camp heavy-metal act to singers crooning Trenet and Brel. Later the accordions come on for waltzes, fox-trots, and tangos to numbers such as "La Romance de Paris." Brasserie classics such as sweetbreads and pungent andouillette sausage are served, but the food is irrelevant as soon you'll be waltzing with a market trader or bawling your eyes out to Piaf songs in a boozy sentimental haze. Guaranteed bonhomie! *Sat-Mon noon-6pm.* € ▤ 130 av. Michelet (M° Porte de Clignancourt), 01.40.12.10.14

Chez Prune* • 10th • Café
"Meet me at Prune" is what everyone says when they're arranging a rendezvous on the Canal, as this café is the epicenter of bobo life. In itself it's nothing special—the wine can be a tad rough and the only evening eating choices are large cold plates of charcuterie, cheese, and salads, but the hipsters who congregate here don't care. With poets perched up at the zinc bar and chicks on the terrace dressed in vintage and pearls, this is boho Paris as you dreamed it. Snag a mosaic table and make as though you're reading a Michel Houellebecq novel and you'll fit in just fine. Sunday brunch is the time to see the fauna at its best. The lunch menu is pretty good if you can get a table. *Mon-Sat 8am-2am, Sun 10am-2am.* € ▤ 71 quai de Valmy (M° République), 01.42.41.30.47

Chez Toinette • 18th • Bistro
Noel treats his patrons like dinner-party guests in this dark red room on a Montmartre side street, promoting laughter between tables with his over-the-top banter. He reels off the menu with an enthusiastic air of "you're gonna love this," which you will provided you're a dedicated carnivore—the one fish dish is often off the menu. In season it does game such as wild boar and venison,

accompanied by fruity sauces. A short list of red wines has been specially chosen. Plates of radishes and tomatoes are a nice touch. From the CD player, your ears will be assaulted by French crooners massacring Frank Sinatra hits, and the evening has been known to end with a sing-along. *Mon-Sat 7:15-11:15pm.* € 20 rue Germain-Pilon (M° Abbesses), 01.42.54.44.36, chez-toinette.com

Djoon • 13th • Restaurant/Club
The 13th is a windswept wasteland currently under construction to become a 21st-century Latin Quarter. Coming here right now, you may feel like you're in some science-fiction movie, but Afshin Assadian has created a lounge bar as an outpost of hipness among the cranes. On the ceiling, a copy of Da Vinci's Sistine Chapel is covered with gold and silver balloons, while the walls are painted with trompe l'oeil columns. Long, cushion-stacked banquettes line the two facing walls. The place moves effortlessly from bar to restaurant to club, with tables set out of the way and a DJ moving in as slick, black-clad diners tuck into seared tuna on eggplant purée and imaginative desserts. The dance floor fills up with a young crowd after midnight. Sunday's non-smoking Dance Culture is a chance to boogie out the weekend. *Mon-Thu 10am-2am (food served until 10:30pm), Fri 10am-4am, Sat 6pm-4am, Sun (club only) 6pm-1am.* €€ 22-24 bd. Vincent-Auriol (M° Quai de la Gare), 01.45.70.83.49, djoon.fr

Drôle d'Endroit pour une Rencontre* • 18th • Bar/Restaurant
Popular for its non-smoking brunch, bistro classics, and friendly scene. *See Bobo Nightlife, p.137, for details.* € 46 rue Caulaincourt (M° Lamarck-Caulaincourt), 01.42.55.14.25

L'Estaminet • 3rd • Wine Bar
L'Estaminet has become the life and soul of this trendy food market. Marketers, foodie locals, and well-heeled Londoners over on the Eurostar drop in to sample Thierry's latest discoveries—he specializes in natural wines produced without sulfur or chemicals so you can even tipple at 10am without fear of a headache! With that come plates of charcuterie, fish tartiflette, and seafood platters brought in by the fishmonger himself. Everything's incredibly fresh, as it's just been plucked from soil and sea and landed on your plate. The brunch falls into the French trap of too much salad and not enough eggs—better to opt for the dish of the day and a glass of wine. When the terrace tables are out in summer you'll feel like you're in Provence. *Tue-Thu 9am-2pm and 4-8pm, Fri-Sat 9am-8pm, Sun 9am-4pm.* € Marché des Enfants Rouges, 39 rue de Bretagne (M° Temple), 01.42.72.34.85, aromes-et-cepages.com

La Famille • 18th • Bistro
This great little restaurant was the first to do something modern in the cutesy cobbled streets of Montmartre, and it's hip to the max. Make sure you've booked a table, preferably the large one on the ground floor just behind the bar, from where you can eavesdrop on the banter and groove to the upbeat sounds as you sip a mojito. The menu from the new chef has been dubbed "playful." There are two seatings and if you can wait till 10pm, go for the second, when the atmosphere really rocks as friends of the owners and even aging rock stars drop in to prop up the bar. *Tue-Sat 8pm-2am (last serving 11:15pm).* € 41 rue des Trois-Frères (M° Abbesses), 01.42.52.11.12

Le Loir dans la Théière • 4th • Tearoom
Branchitude (trendiness) gives way to brunchitude at this laid-back Marais tearoom where a distinctly bobo set packs in for weekend scrambled eggs. Young French screen heartthrob Romain Duris is a regular, blending in with the sexy, 30-something international types who like to lounge around on weekends. The setting is rather English, with a mismatched clutter of chairs and tables (try to snag the roomy leather armchairs), posters on the walls, and books. The only problem, especially if there are more than two of you, is getting a seat, as you can't reserve. Arrive early and once you've got one, don't move until they throw you out. *Mon-Fri 11:30am-7pm, Sat-Sun 10am-7pm.* € ≡ 3 rue des Rosiers (M° St-Paul), 01.42.72.90.61

La Madonnina • 10th • Italian
When every new kitchen opening in Paris these days seems to think it's Italian, it's great to know there's La Madonnina: authentic, youthful, and wonderfully boho. Just behind the Canal St-Martin, it's a favorite with local 30-somethings and a smattering of fashion designers, presumably attracted by the Catholic kitsch. Patrons arrive late, so if you're there around 8pm, you may find yourselves the only ones to watch Gianni and his French wife setting up the antipasti bar near the Madonna with fairy lights. About an hour later, a stampede of ebullient diners arrives, and the noise level rises as the night goes on. Great antipasti and pasta make use of fabulous mozzarella, fresh tomatoes, and herbs in copious amounts. *Mon-Thu 12:15-2:30pm and 8-11pm, Fri-Sat 12:15-2:30pm and 8-11:30pm.* € ≡ 10 rue Marie-et-Louise (M° Goncourt), 01.42.01.25.26

Aux Marches du Palais • 16th • Bistro
This bistro was quietly minding its own business, serving up egg mayonnaise, veal liver, and crêpes Suzette, when along came the Palais de Tokyo and a whole wave of hipness descended. The spillover from Tokyo Eat meant trendsters soon discovered its more modest neighbor for an inexpensive bite after a launch party or before the Baron, and 16th-arrondissement regulars now share the space with the Colette- and Converse-clad. Despite its grandiose name, it's still a *troquet* (a small, traditional café) with '30s décor, polite waiters, and jazz, and long may it remain so. *Mon-Fri noon-5pm and 8-10:30pm, Sat 8-11pm.* € ≡ 5 rue de la Manutention (M° Alma-Marceau), 01.47.23.52.80

La Marine • 10th • Bistro
By far the best café-bistro along the Canal St-Martin, this place has been going in its present incarnation since 1996 and before that was a café-charbon fueling the mariners who worked on the barges. From the mustard cornices, brass rails, and banquettes jazzed up with red fiber-optic lights, to the good-natured service, this place promotes a sense of joie de vivre. The great-value €12 lunch menu pulls in a noisy crowd of all ages, and you'll be amazed by the quality of the food, such as a pintade in a caramel sauce on a mound of potato purée and the ultra-creamy crème caramel. *Mon-Sat 8:30-11am, noon-2:30pm, and 8-11:30pm.* € ≡ 55 bis quai de Valmy (M° République), 01.42.39.69.81

Le Martel • 10th • North African
Best North African Dining The edgy, souk-like Faubourg St-Denis is a neighborhood on the cusp of trendiness, and Le Martel is emblematic of the change. A couscous restaurant created out of an old French café, it looks like a sepia photo

of Casablanca in the '30s, and the beauty of the zinc bar and plain walls with black-and-white photos has not gone unnoticed by the aesthetically minded newcomers to the area. Both French and North African food are served here. The ubiquitous sesame-seared tuna and sweetbreads are on offer, but it would be a shame not to go native with a couscous Royale—fluffy couscous, broth, and grilled meats—followed by Algerian sweets. Come late to enjoy the mix of flamboyant rag-trade types and local loft-dwellers. *Mon-Fri 11am-3pm and 6pm-1am, Sat 6pm-1am.* € 3 rue Martel (M° Château d'Eau), 01.47.70.67.56

Pause Café • 11th • Café
Best Café Terraces Ever since it featured in Cedric Klapisch's zeitgeist film *Chacun cherche son chat*, the Pause has been hipster central. When the first summer sun hits Paris at the end of May, it's lights, camera, action for a terrace scene transplanted from Cannes. Eavesdrop on screenplay discussions, recording contracts, and other pretentious sound bites as you soak up the rays and play "spot the French actor." In winter black turtlenecks are de rigueur, and the scene moves inside to the red Formica tables. Food includes a wicked cod cooked in olive oil, steaks, and magret de canard accompanied by carafes of house red. The espresso machine is in constant overdrive. *Mon-Sat 7:30am-2am, Sun 9am-8pm.* € 41 rue de Charonne (M° Ledru-Rollin), 01.48.06.08.33

Les Philosophes* • 4th • Café
A happening scene at any time of day, it does a roaring trade at lunch and in the evening with its good café food. *See Bobo Nightlife, p.140, for details.* € 28 rue Vieille-du-Temple (M° St-Paul), 01.48.87.49.64, cafeine.com

Polichinelle Café • 11th • Bistro
The Polichinelle has Pause Café appeal with its pretty, colorful '50s interior, but a cozier, less hyped ambiance. It's a locals' favorite, either for coffee at the zinc bar or the extensive bistro menu, and the small streetside terrace is a sun trap. Warmhearted manageress Hélène is like a mother hen fussing over her chicks when regulars come in, and will help explain the specialties. Tempted though you may be by an "épigramme" or a "capuccino of ..." it's best to stick to standards like onglet de boeuf and noisettes of lamb, though the "tiptop" of Cuban chocolate with a lavender and orange coulis is delicious. A fun atmosphere as it fills up with noisy groups of friends catching up on the gossip. *Daily 10am-1am.* € 64-66 rue de Charonne (M° Ledru-Rollin), 01.58.30.63.52

Le Sancerre* • 18th • Café/Bar
At the heart of the Abbesses scene with a popular terrace. *See Bobo Nightlife, p.141, for details.* € 35 rue des Abbesses (M° Abbesses), 01.42.58.08.20

Sardegna a Tavola • 12th • Italian
Food lovers will schlep across town to taste the specialties at this Sardinian restaurant. If the Parisian weather's been unkind, all you need is to step inside the yellow and stone room with gentle piped music to feel like you're on the sun-baked isle. Garlic, chilies, and hams hang from the ceiling, goading the appetite for homemade antipasti and superb pasta dishes as well as game in season. A must is the black spaghetti prepared with squid ink and farfalle with Sardinian flavorings of almonds, mint, chili, and olive oil. Taste an ambrosial sweet wine with almond cake to finish. *Mon 7:30-11:30pm, Tue-Sat noon-2:30pm and 7:30-11:30pm.* € 1 rue de Cotte (M° Ledru-Rollin), 01.44.75.03.28

Le Soleil • St-Ouen • Bistro
The only good place to eat at the vast Clignancourt flea market, Le Soleil's success will hopefully spawn others. Formerly a smoky café, it is now a roomy bistro with a sunny atmosphere generated by a glassed-in terrace and the jolly proprietor's welcome. The décor is in tune with the flea market (old '30s café table bases, a piano) without being over-the-top, and, seated between antiques dealers discussing their latest finds, you can enjoy some wonderful food: marbled foie gras, expertly prepared fish dishes, and a Chateaubriand for two. A great excuse to make a trip to the puces into a proper day out. *Mon-Wed noon-2:30pm, Thu-Sat noon-2:30pm and 8-10pm, Sun noon-4pm.* €€ 109 av. Michelet (M° Porte de Clignancourt), 01.40.10.08.08

Somo • 2nd • Lounge Bar
A great place to fuel up. *See Bobo Nightlife, p.141, for details.* € 168 rue Montmartre (M° Sentier), 01.40.13.08.80, hip-bars.com/somo

Le Sporting • 10th • Café
One of the most popular cafés along the Canal, Le Sporting has gone for the *Elle Decor* version of Parisian café. You swish through velvet curtains to a high-ceilinged room with fashionable taupe-painted walls, black-and-white photos, colonial-style plants, and nicely spaced wooden tables. A beautiful zinc bar sadly no longer fulfills its original use as the owners insist on sit-down service. Those who appreciate aesthetics are regulars here: magazine editors, fashion designers, and other style-mongers. The prix fixe menu has some tasty choices, though portions tend to be small. Sunday lunch is a popular scene. *Daily noon-1am.* € 3 rue des Récollets (M° Gare de l'Est), 01.46.07.02.00

Le Square • 18th • Bistro
New restaurants are springing up like daisies in this pretty quarter behind the Cimetière de Montmartre, responding to the influx of 30-somethings buying up apartments in the area. Here a former café has transformed into a trendy modern bistro with the added charm of a bamboo-enclosed garden with heated lamps. The beige and brown interior is attractive too, with a curtain of pearly beads, tiny lamps, and Chesterfields opposite the bar. Groups of friends congregate for the French cuisine with a modern twist: mozzarella and eggplant mille-feuille, cream of lentils with melted foie gras, and a delicious magret de canard. *Tue-Thu noon-2:30pm and 8-10:30pm, Fri-Sat noon-2:30pm and 8-11pm.* € 227 bis rue Marcadet (M° Guy Moquet), 01.53.11.08.41

Le Square Trousseau • 12th • Bistro
Best Bistros A dream bistro this, with its 1900s interior, outside tables looking onto a leafy square, and jocular staff dressed in white butchers' aprons. This area boboized some 20 years ago and rotund middle-aged bohemians as well as younger trendies patronize the restaurant, among them many film people, as the restaurant itself is often used as a set. At lunchtime screen and book deals are clinched, while in the evening it's a chattery mêlée as the wine flows freely. Dishes are also rooted in the 1900s, with one of the best steak tartares in the city, lamb braised for seven hours, and andouillette. *Tue-Sat noon-2:30pm and 8-11:30pm.* €€ 1 rue Antoine-Vollon (M° Ledru-Rollin), 01.43.43.06.00

Swann et Vincent • 12th • Italian
This Bastille Italian is a favorite of Christian Lacroix and Jean-Paul Gaultier, and it's easy to see why they love it. Opening the door, you are swept into a flurry of delicious smells and tremendous noise, with a jovial man at the bar turning away diners who haven't booked ahead. A confident local crowd of all ages is crammed into a space that seems more tall than it is wide with huge mirrors and an antipasti counter in the middle, which the spunky waiters seem to shimmy around. You choose from the gigantic blackboard menu, and there are always specials of the day and wines of the month. The food is old school and not exceptional, but the atmosphere is unbeatable. *Daily noon-2:30pm and 7:45-11:30pm.* € 7 rue St-Nicolas (M° Ledru-Rollin), 01.43.43.49.40

Le Tambour • 2nd • All-Night Café
Best Late-Night Eats This Paris night institution is a café, tabac, brasserie, and general beacon in the small hours, always filled with a young and happy, interactive (as far as you can be after three bottles of red) crowd. "It's like a Renoir painting," exclaimed one patron when we visited at 4am. More dissolute perhaps, but colorful and animated. The décor is something like a Swiss chalet with iron helmets, chains, a mural of an astronaut, and old metal signs. But best of all is the amazing food. The salade landaise has two chunks of foie gras on toast, a duck leg, chunks of smoked duck, beetroot and lettuce, copious comfort food all for a song. *Tue-Sat noon-3pm and 6pm-6am, Sun-Mon 6pm-6am.* € 41 rue Montmartre (M° Sentier), 01.42.33.06.90

Tokyo Eat • 16th • Trendy
Best Eiffel Tower Views The restaurant of hip contemporary art museum the Palais de Tokyo has two scenes, and both of them rock. In winter you're in the hangar-like inside space with its flying-saucer lamps, open kitchen, and gigantic photographic portraits on the walls. In summer the whole caboodle moves out to the terrace facing the Eiffel Tower. Lit up by fairy lights and clubby light projections on the 1930s edifice, it feels like a fabulous beach party. In between the restaurant tables and the deck chairs of the Tokyo Idem bar, which also moves outside, are mixing decks with a DJ spinning funky music between the restaurant and the deck chairs of the bar/chill-out area. Along with the food menu comes a menu of eclectic hits so you can order a tataki de boeuf and David Bowie or croustillant de chocolat with Coldplay and suddenly they're playing your song. *Tue-Sun noon-3pm and 8-11:30pm.* € 13 av. du Président Wilson (M° Alma-Marceau), 01.47.20.00.29

Viaduc Café* • 12th • Café
Created out of the stone arches of this former railway viaduct, this spacious modern café feeds the artists and artisans who work in the viaduct's studios as well as visitors to the area. Start the day in a leisurely way with breakfast at the teak tables and chairs on the terrace shaded by olive trees before a walk along the Promenade Plantée that runs above it. The large vaulted main room has a giant palm growing inside it and a huge canvas of the café in action painted from life by Hippolyte Romain. It serves lunch and dinner, a popular brunch with live jazz, and on weekends turns into a club with DJs until 4am. *Daily 8am-4am.* € 43 av. Daumesnil (M° Ledru-Rollin), 01.44.74.70.70

Bobo Paris:
The Nightlife

Andy Wahloo • 3rd • Bar
This offshoot bar to the 404 reveals the Pop Art potential of Marrakech. Huge garish Arabic posters, recycled signs as tables, Warhol-style portraits, and a rather sinister montage of women in Louis Vuitton veils are the décor, but by the time this bar fills up around 10pm you won't even notice, as it's full to bursting. Marais hipsters and rowdy groups of English girls downing cocktails rub shoulders with dressed-up French locals ordering Champagne in buckets, and if there were more space on the tiled floor they'd be shimmying to Momo's funky Arabic compilations. The cocktails are killer concoctions of alcohol, fruit, and pick-me-ups like ginger: try the Wahloo Spécial. Book if you want a table, although the bar stools are a fine place to perch as well. *Mon-Sat 4pm-2am.* 69 rue des Gravilliers (M° Arts-et-Métiers), 01.42.71.20.38

Banana Café • 1st • Gay Bar
The best-known bar in the whole of gay Paris, Banana Café is a sure bet for party people of all persuasions who want to carry on till dawn. Veteran disco divas, television stars, and just about anyone else piles in to watch the go-go dancers on the bar. As the night rolls on, head downstairs to the piano bar for campy themed entertainment. *Tue-Sat 5:30pm-6am. Piano bar midnight-6am.* 13 rue de la Ferronnerie (M° Châtelet), 01.42.33.35.31, bananacafeparis.com

Bar Ourcq • 19th • DJ Bar
The Canal d'Ourcq, running north from the Canal St-Martin, is the new Sunday chill-out zone for Parisian hipsters, and it all revolves around this small blue bar. DJs spin trip-hop and breakin' beats as the bar staff keep up a constant stream of beer and rum punch. A small lounge area is at the back of the bar, but the main scene runs all along the quayside where deck chairs are set out for soaking up the rays and watching the scullers and canal boats pass. You can also hire boules from the bar to play a laid-back game on the sandy boulodromes. *Wed, Thu, Sun 3pm-midnight, Fri, Sat 3pm-2am.* 68 quai de la Loire (M° Laumière), 01.42.40.12.26

Le Baron • 8th • Private Club
Best Hipster Hangouts The Parisian nightspot of the moment, this former strip joint was taken over by La Johnson collective, which made its name organizing fabulous one-off parties and the Calvi on the Rocks festival in Corsica. The cool clique, which counts DJs and record producers among its number, has created a Studio 54 for the 21st century. Entry is normally by personal recommendation, though if you are prepared to stand in line and look hip enough you may get in. Groups of debs with the privileged but debauched look of rock stars' children cluster and canoodle in the red velvet snugs. Before long the tiny dance floor is deluged with gorgeous Colette-clad guys and gals grooving to '60s, '70s, and '80s hits. The dance floor fever is infectious and everyone but everyone has a smile on his or her face, which is fairly unusual for Paris. *Daily 11pm-6am.* 6 av. Marceau (M° Alma-Marceau), 01.47.20.04.01, clublebaron.com

Batofar • 13th • Dance Club
Best Dance Clubs House-loving hipsters adore this unusual club venue on a former Irish lighthouse boat. Its red lighthouse beam pulsates from afar, and the scene spreads out onto the quayside where the Batofar also has a bar and tables. Up the gangplank on deck is a cocktail bar with tropical plants ideal for a summer mojito-fest, and if you don't fancy the hothouse down below you can just chill here. Down in the bowels of the ship, the club offers eclectic programming, from hip-hop to electro-jazz, with some live music concerts. DJs such as Eva Gardner and David Walters mix regularly, summer Sundays have afternoon clubbing on the quay, and the after-party Miniboum (starting at 4am) is the best in Paris. *Wed-Sun midnight-6am. Some Sundays 4am-noon and 4-10pm, though times vary according to the event.* CBE Opposite 11 quai François Mauriac (M° Quai de la Gare), 01.53.60.17.30, batofar.org

La Belle Hortense • 4th • Wine Bar
Best Literary Bars Hard to imagine this anywhere else but in Paris. Is it a wine bar in a bookshop, or a bookshop in a wine bar? Whichever way, La Belle Hortense is the perfect place to find intellectual lubrication. Sit at the bar and discuss the latest prize-winning novelists with trendy literary types or hide yourself away in the back non-smoking library and get quietly sozzled as you lose yourself in Maupassant. The friendly staff will recommend wines and books with knowledge and enthusiasm, and both are available to go. *Daily 5pm-2am.* 31 rue Vieille-du-Temple (M° St-Paul), 01.48.04.71.60

Café Charbon • 11th • Café/Bar
If you want to sample the Oberkampf bar "strip" (it bears little resemblance to Las Vegas except that there's lots of neon and you may end up staggering like Nicolas Cage on his last legs), there's no better place to start than Charbon. This café started the whole swinging scene here over a decade ago, and while the real hipsters have deserted for the Canal St-Martin and the Grands Boulevards, the youthful crowds thronging the streets, bars, and take-out joints are still massive. Created out of an old cabaret, the Charbon has abundant character with its stucco ceiling and mirrors, making an espresso or lunch here plenty atmospheric. In the evenings you may find yourself fighting for space at the bar with backpackers trying to dance with their backpacks still on. *Sun-Tue 9am-2am, Thu-Sat 9am-4am.* 109 rue Oberkampf (M° Parmentier), 01.43.57.55.13

Café Chéri(e) • 19th • DJ Bar
Best Hipster Hangouts This hipster scene in Belleville revolves around the Café Chéri(e) and Ile Enchantée on the same road. Chéri(e) is a red bar garishly lit up from the outside whose terrace is constantly packed whatever the season (in winter die-hard trendsters sit out here in parkas, so compelling is the scene). Inside Mikli eyewear and Diesel pants are the overriding style of the patrons, who prop up the bar or dance to cutting-edge DJ sounds. People are friendly and it's easy to strike up conversation in any of multiple languages. The lesbian bar staff epitomize the urban hip vibe. When it closes, follow the cool crowd next door to the Bons Amis for cheap couscous and sometimes crashable private parties. *Daily 8am-2am.* BE 44 bd. la Villette (M° Belleville), 01.42.02.07.87

Café Noir • 2nd • Café/Bar
A '50s dive bar patronized by the ultra-hip, this bar is a stepping-off point for the Triptyque club or the Rex. During the day, it's true, the *Figaro* journalists getting their espresso fix don't quite fit the bill, but at night the Formica tables fill up with bobo singles and a black-clad crew discussing their latest film and music projects. Daytime jazz also moves seamlessly into more contemporary beats as the DJs move in, with raucous conversation and the Gauloise timbre of the patronne's voice added to the mix. The terrace is a great people-watching spot for this nighttime scene. There's no polite holding back on the drinking here. *Mon-Sat 8am-2am.* F≡ 65 rue Montmartre (M° Sentier), 01.40.39.07.36

Canal 96* • 10th • Café
On a summer night this is one of the best terraces for soaking up the Canal vibe. See Bobo Restaurants, p.127, for details. 96 quai de Jemmapes (M° Jacques Bonsergent), 01.42.02.87.95

Chai 33 • 12th • Wine Bar
Lively wine bar in newly revitalized Bercy Village. *See Bobo Restaurants, p.127, for details.* B≡ 33 cour St-Emilion (M° Cour St-Emilion), 01.53.44.01.01, chai33.org

Chez Prune* • 10th • Café
The café at the epicenter of Bobo life on Canal St-Martin. *See Bobo Restaurants, p.128, for details.* F≡ 71 quai de Valmy (M° République), 01.42.41.30.47

Chez Richard • 4th • Bar
A successful bar approached through a stone archway in the Marais, Chez Richard strikes just the right balance between style-conscious and friendly. Couples having a romantic drink, Marais bar-crawlers, and clubbers revving up for the night ahead all find their niche here as there are four rooms to choose from. The cocktail crowd perches at the bar, but you might just find the mezzanine, cozy alcove, or candlelit basement bar more to your taste. Art exhibitions cover the walls, amid spiky plants, a mosaic staircase, and wrought-iron chandeliers. *Daily 5pm-2am.* B≡ 37 rue Vieille-du-Temple (M° St-Paul), 01.42.74.31.65

China Club • 12th • Lounge Bar
Best Lounge Bars This seductive lounge bar reminiscent of Shanghai in the '20s is so classy that it's hard to believe it's not a private club. Downstairs is a red lacquer interior with candlelit black tables, leather Chesterfields perfect for a smoochy tête-à-tête, and a long bar where cocktails are expertly mixed by staff straight out of a Wong Kar Wai film. They will also bring you delicious dim sum in wooden baskets. And there's more: a dark upstairs fumoir that the young, trendy crowd prefers, and a packed jazz club with a nightly program of soulful or funky jazz. We don't know whether it's the candlelight, the ambiance, or the music, but everyone here looks beautiful. *Daily 7pm-2am.* CB≡ 50 rue de Charenton (M° Bastille), 01.43.43.82.02

De la Ville Café • 10th • DJ Bar
This former cabaret hall complete with stucco ceiling has become one of the hottest pre-club rendezvous on the Grands Boulevards and is packed nightly with a hedonistic crowd. It's so popular that it's difficult to get a seat, never mind get served, though with waiting staff this sexy all is easily forgiven. Fight,

or gyrate, your way to the back or simply drape yourself on the banisters or the heated outside terrace, for this is as see-and-be-seen as the Grands Boulevards gets. Don't expect to chat, as the DJ sets are practically at club decibels. *Daily 11am-2am.* 34 bd. Bonne-Nouvelle (M° Bonne Nouvelle), 01.48.24.48.09

Djoon • 13th • Restaurant/Club
Lounge bar in an up-and-coming neighborhood. See Bobo Restaurants, p.129, for details. 22 bd. Vincent-Auriol (M° Quai de la Gare), 01.45.70.83.49, djoon.fr

Drôle d'Endroit pour une Rencontre* • 18th • Bar/Restaurant
Best Meet Markets A group of friends went to New York and came back with the idea of this bar, unabashedly based on *Sex and the City*. It's been an enormous hit, not just with singles but with the whole bobo crowd that's settled in this area. Brick walls, exposed pipes, modern lamps interspersed with chandeliers, a mixture of '50s bistro furniture, and red leather-upholstered Louis XV chairs make for a relaxed atmosphere. Perched up at the cocktail bar, sip a faultless Cosmopolitan and nibble on tasty dips, or sit at a table where you either just drink or dine on bistro classics. The non-smoking Sunday brunch with board games has been a real success, there's a DJ on weekends, and on Thursdays patrons can come with their own vinyl. There's also a matchmaking service for singles. *Tue-Sat 10am-1:30am, Sun noon-midnight.* 46 rue Caulaincourt (M° Lamarck-Caulaincourt), 01.42.55.14.25

Elysée Montmartre • 18th • Concert Hall/Dance Club
Best Live Music If you strike on the right night, you'll have a ball at the Elysée Montmartre—literally! Once a month it holds Le Bal, a nostalgia-fest led by a live band with accordions and beehives that attracts a huge crowd mad to dance to hits from the '30s to the '80s and smooch over the *quart d'heure américain*" (the slows). Aside from that, this former Belle Epoque cabaret hosts big-name rock concerts and some great house nights such as Panik and Open House. The stucco-ceilinged room, with DJs up on a stage, good lighting effects, and dance podiums, is one of the best venues to shake it on down. *Fri-Sat midnight-6am; earlier for concerts.* 72 bd. Rochechouart (M° Anvers), 01.41.57.32.33, elyseemontmartre.com

L'Etoile Manquante • 4th • Café/Bar
L'Etoile is one of four cafés on this Marais street that are owned by Xavier Denamur, who's equipped them all with extraordinary bathrooms. Here, an electric train circulates while you flush and a camera records your image on a screen as you wash your hands, along with science fiction footage. That's not its only plus point, thankfully, as it also has a superb people-watching terrace filled with an arty, mixed, and preened Marais crowd. Ideal for an espresso in the afternoon or a nightcap as the evening draws to a close. *Daily 9am-2am.* 34 rue Vieille-du-Temple (M° St-Paul), 01.42.72.48.34

La Fabrique • 12th • DJ Bar
A modern restaurant serving flammenküche (a kind of Strasbourgian pizza) during the day, La Fabrique transforms into a club-bar at night and has been so successful that it's exported the concept to Tokyo. Unless it's flammenküche you're after, it's important not to turn up too early, as the clubby scene doesn't really take off until after 1am, when hot up-and-coming DJs play thumping electro. The front bar area, with '60s-style low seating, is always packed with shaved

heads and cool chicks sipping cocktails or enjoying the microbrewery beers, though with music this loud your drink is the only thing you'll be conversing with. *Mon-Sat 11am-5am.* C (Fri & Sat only) 53 rue du Fbg. St-Antoine (M° Ledru-Rollin), 01.43.07.67.07, fabrique.fr

Favela Chic • 11th • Restaurant/Club
Forget eating in this Brazilian restaurant/club as someone might just step on your food, such is the dance frenzy it attracts. On weekends the place is heaving with a good-time crowd downing extra-strong caipirinhas and jumping around to eclectic music—anything from hip-hop to Piaf to Arabic funk, with a bit of batucada thrown in. Dancing on the benches is encouraged by the staff, who seem to be having as much fun as the patrons. *Tue-Thu 8pm-3am, Fri-Sat 8pm-5am.* B 18 rue du Fbg. du Temple (M° République), 01.40.21.38.14, favelachic.com

Folies Pigalle • 9th • Dance Club
Folies is where true hedonists end up. A relatively cozy club where no one is respectful of anyone's personal space, or indeed their chosen sexuality, it's a crazy mêlée of drag queens, prostitutes, pimps, and clubbers where however outrageously you dress or behave you'll still look like a shrinking violet compared to the exhibitionists that get up on the podium. Funky tribal house with live drumming plays all night long and there's a chilled-out mezzanine area where you can survey the colorful crowd. Best for its after-parties, though Bitchy José's Peach and Saturday's Hystory have some hot DJs. Gay clubbers shouldn't miss the Sunday tea dance Black Blanc Beur. *Mon-Thu midnight-6am, Fri-Sat midnight-noon, Sun 6pm-6am.* 11 pl. Pigalle (M° Pigalle), 01.48.78.55.25, folies-pigalle.com

L'Ile Enchantée • 10th • DJ Bar
An excellent place to edit your script or ponder world revolution by day—especially as it's a step away from Oscar Niemeyer's Communist Party HQ—the Ile morphs into a happening night scene that revolves around up-and-coming electronic music stars. Producers come here to spot talent, it has been said, and there are certainly a lot of musicians, DJs, and VJs among the groovy, self-conscious crowd. As well as the attractive bar, there's a hidden upstairs room hosting everything from DJ sets to debates. *Mon-Fri 8am-2am, Sat 4pm-2am.* B 65 bd. de la Villette (M° Colonel Fabien), 01.42.01.67.99

Le Jemmapes • 10th • Café
A tiny, tobacco-stained bar, Le Jemmapes seems nevertheless to attract the crème of boho beauties, who sit swinging their Antoine et Lili handbags and sipping raspberry juice on the terrace on sunny afternoons. If it's not this, it's groups of tall men with small beards, and presumably sometimes the two get together. The main thing is that the Jemmapes serves drinks in plastic glasses for takeout, which accounts for the fact that the entire quay is lined with bobos in the summer and is quite a scene. Killjoy government minister Nicolas Sarkozy has tried to put an end to the fun by saying no takeouts after 9pm, but you can always cram into the bar for some of the wicked rum punches. *Daily 11am-2am.* B 82 quai de Jemmapes (M° Jacques Bonsergent), 01.40.40.02.35

Jokko Bar • 3rd • Music Bar
Best Live Music A chic take on the African bar, the Jokko is spacious and modern with low, cushioned seating around recycled aluminum-covered tables that you'll want to take home with you. In fact you can—they are on sale in the shop next door which, along with a restaurant, forms this tri-part Senegalese enclave. A mixed crowd chills out to the gentle Senegalese music performed by visiting and Paris-based musicians, while a dainty waitress dressed in Xuly Bët slides between tables taking orders for the fabulous hibiscus-flavored cocktails. Sometimes if you stay late it turns into one big party as friends of the bartender pile in and hit the decks, and suddenly everyone's dancing. *Tue-Sun 5pm-2am.* 5 rue Elzévir (M° St-Sébastien-Froissart), 01.42.74.35.96, jokko.net

Kube Lounge and Ice Kube • 18th • Lounge Bar
Up a secluded passage from the shifty rue Marx Dormoy, the Kube Rooms' buzzing lounge bar is already pulling in international hipsters. Once installed in one of its fake-animal-fur sofas, grooving to the electro sounds spun by a DJ and diffused by a high-tech surround-sound system, you will *not* want to leave. The tactile cushions and red-fur-tipped gauze curtains covering the long windows are suggestive ice-breakers in the sultry lounge bar. Upstairs, however, things get hotter while they get distinctly cooler in the Ice Kube. A fixed price of €38 gets you a half-hour all-inclusive session in this bar carved out of 20 tons of solid ice which, illuminated by iridescent color-changing lights, looks like Lalique crystal. First you don snowboarding gear in a red-lit acclimatization room, then enter the arctic zone. Free-flowing flavored vodka shots served in cube-shaped ice glasses, tapas, and high-octane music make for a full-on party atmosphere. Outside the bar, hanging pod chairs allow laid-back lounge lizards to watch the frantic fraternizing action through the glass wall. *Kube Lounge daily 7am-2am. Ice Kube daily 6:30pm-1:30am (reservation required).* 1-5 passage Ruelle (M° La Chapelle), 01.42.05.20.00, kubehotel.com

Open Café • 4th • Gay Bar
Best Gay Bars See that crowd taking up half the road ahead of you? *That's* the Open Café, and even if the café disappeared, the crowd would probably still be there, so etched into the Paris gay circuit has it become. More open than some of the other places on rue des Archives, its main function is a cruising one with plenty of pretty boyz on the pavement. Start here and you're sure to find out where to go to next, and maybe meet some chums to go with. *Sun-Thu 11am-2am, Fri-Sat 11am-4am.* 17 rue des Archives (M° Hôtel de Ville), 01.42.72.26.18

Le Paris Paris • 1st • Dance Club
This delicious space hosts a spillover crowd from the exclusive Le Baron. A fiber-optic–lit stairway descends to the spacious dance floor surrounded by slinky leather seating. Live rock concerts, electro, and up-and-coming DJs are part of the scene, and arty acolytes from concept shop Colette, independent record labels, and the fashion world let their hair down—to the extent that French people can (watching Parisians move an eyebrow to Motorhead provides endless amusement). Some nights are given over to private launch parties so check the website before turning up—it also gives a foretaste in photos of the kind of fauna you'll find here. *Tue-Sat midnight-dawn.* 5 av. de l'Opéra (M° Pyramides), marco@leparisparis.com, leparisparis.com

La Perle • 4th • Café/Bar
Best Hipster Hangouts It's one of those inexplicable trend things. An ordinary corner café with a zinc bar and '70s décor changes its name and suddenly everyone's there, including bobo style-meister Romain Duris. Maybe it has to do with the mutation of the north Marais, which now has Christian Lacroix's hotel, but La Perle is far hipper than this. An ultra-hip crowd have made it theirs and fill the bar area and back seating with its bizarre op-art mural and '70s orange lamps. The staff appear to be loving it, despite the crush, and turn up the music to create a party ambiance. Grab a beer and a terrace seat to see and be seen, hipster style. *Daily 8am-2am.* B≡ 78 rue Vieille-du-Temple (M° St-Sébastien-Froissart), 01.42.72.69.93

Les Philosophes* • 4th • Café
If you feel too hidden away in the Belle Hortense, take to this philosophical terrace just around the corner, where you can pose and pontificate at the same time. A happening scene at any time of day, it does a roaring trade at lunch and in the evening with its good café food (the honey-flavored confit de canard is especially tasty). Its quintessential Parisian café ambiance, with wicker chairs and waiters in traditional garb, is not lost on an often international crowd. *Daily 9am-2am.* ≡ 28 rue Vieille-du-Temple (M° St-Paul), 01.48.87.49.64, cafeine.com

Le Progrès • 18th • Café/Bar
Best Meet Markets This glass box on a corner in happening Abbesses is one of the hippest yet friendliest spots in Montmartre. Local boutique owners, artists, musicians, and fashion designers carouse here and you'll easily be swept into conversation with the amicable crowd. Getting a seat here is musical chairs but that doesn't matter as it's all part of the fun, and your own will be swept from under you the minute you get up. The flirtation and free-flowing wine make this the modern equivalent of the artists' cafés of Montmartre legend. *Daily 9am-2am.* B≡ 7 rue des Trois-Frères (M° Abbesses), 01.42.64.07.37

Le Pulp • 2nd • Dance Club
Proving girls just wanna have fun, this lesbian club has become one of the great names of the Paris night scene, especially for its Wednesday and Thursday nights that are open to all and free (Friday is open but more girl-centric, and on Saturdays, sorry, boys, but you'll have to go elsewhere). Electro-goths, rock chicks, and disco queens find this dance-floor heaven here, and even Viktoria Abril and MC Solaar have been seen strutting their stuff. Start the week here and you'll get to sample the very best female DJ talent as well as some international stars. *Wed-Sat midnight-6am.* C (Fri & Sat only). ≡ 25 bd. Poissonnière (M° Grands Boulevards), 01.40.26.01.93, pulp-paris.com

Rex Club • 2nd • Dance Club
Best Dance Clubs Under the Art Deco Rex cinema, this club is one of the worldwide greats for pure dance music. It may not have the massive capacity of a Ministry of Sound of Space, but it's got the best sound system in Paris. Internationally renowned DJs Laurent Garnier and Ivan Smagghe are the residents, and Garnier's marathon 12-hour sets are legendary at Friday's Automatik. Thursdays can be more underground, and Saturdays have a revolving program of scintillating sounds with the phenomenally successful gay night Eyes Need

Sugar once a month. There's plenty of room to dance here, which is the point and the whole point. *Wed-Sat midnight-6am and sometimes later.* C≡ 5 bd. Poissonnière (M° Bonne Nouvelle), 01.42.36.10.95, rexclub.com

Le Sancerre* • 18th • Café/Bar
Le Sancerre is the terrace for the Abbesses people-watching scene, and is filled morning to night with arty locals and shoppers browsing in the hip boutiques on this cobbled street. One of its great plus points is that it serves breakfast with eggs every day of the week—a rarity in Paris—but it's also good for its huge plates of chicken and fries or salads. At night a flirty crowd congregates around the bar, especially for Sunday's funky jazz concerts. *Daily 7am-2am.* F≡ 35 rue des Abbesses (M° Abbesses), 01.42.58.08.20

Sanz Sans • 12th • DJ Bar
Even early in the evening, Sanz Sans is hopping as the DJ in the front bar area gets people dancing to tribal house, reggae, and R&B, jazzed up by percussion from the bar staff drumming on cymbals hanging from the ceiling. A trendy Bastille crowd likes to get in the mood here, but some never leave the place as it's funky all night long and by 12:30pm it's hard to get to the bar through the dance frenzy. Behind the bar, there are two floors of sofas and tables for lounging over cocktails. Upstairs you won't feel left out as a video screen transmits images of the madness below—unless you choose to retreat to one of the alcoves. *Mon 9am-2am, Tue-Thu 9am-4am, Fri-Sat 9am-6am, Sun 6pm-2am.* ≡ 49 rue du Fbg. St-Antoine (M° Ledru-Rollin), 01.44.75.78.78, sanzsans.com

La Scène Bastille • 12th • Concert Hall/Dance Club
Best Live Music Less attitude, more music is the maxim of this great little club with a weekly program of live rock, world, and French chanson, followed by club nights. On Fridays 8pm-midnight it hosts the free Radio Nova party, Les Nuits Zébrées, with Nova artists broadcast live (pick up tickets from the Nova offices, 01.55.33.33.15). This is followed by Who Stole the Soul (soul, funk, disco) or Groove Committee, while Saturdays hold the banging techno party Sweetpeak or gay-friendly Eyes Need Sugar (also at the Rex). Gay progressive-house fans find their heaven on Sundays. The new bistro lounge at the front is a chance to mingle with the trendy, music-biz crowd. *Mon-Sat live music 8pm; clubbing midnight-6am; Sunday gay tea dance 6pm-2am.* C≡ 2 bis rue des Taillandiers (M° Ledru-Rollin), 01.48.06.50.70, la-scene.com

Au Soleil de la Butte • 18th • DJ Bar
The basement of this Montmartre crêperie has become a weekend hoedown for nonchalant hipsters. If you fancy a boogie after a bar crawl, or simply a late-night drink, slide down to this tiny dive where dancing on carpet gives it the feel of a party in someone's living room. No need to worry about spilling your drink, though. A clubby atmosphere with no attitude and party people aplenty dancing to '80s, funk, hip-hop, and just about anything else guarantees a good time. *Daily concerts 9pm-midnight, club Fri-Sat 11pm-6am.* ≡ 32 rue Muller (M° Château Rouge), 01.46.06.18.24

Somo • 2nd • Lounge Bar
The English Cheap Blonde team that fields a number of bars around Paris has courted Manhattan ambiance here, and coined a natty title for the place, "South of Montmartre." A happy-hour or pre-club crowd lounges on leather sofas or

chats in English to the friendly bar staff as they mix mean mojitos. There's delicious food lunch and evenings and an eggs and bacon brunch on Sunday. DJs spinning '60s and soul pull in the party people on Saturdays. A good starting point for clubs on the Grands Boulevards or for a late-night drink. *Mon-Sat noon-2am, Sun noon-4:30pm.* BC= 168 rue Montmartre (M° Sentier), 01.40.13.08.80, hip-bars.com/somo

Tokyo Idem • 16th • Café
The Palais de Tokyo's basement bar is a hip place to chill after wandering around the modern art installations. Low-slung chairs are joined by temporary works of art—at one point the entire bar floor was painted by a Korean artist. In summer the deck chairs move outside, under the moon, with a view of the Eiffel Tower as DJs spin, creating a Paris version of Ibiza's Café del Mar. *Tue-Sun noon-1am.* = 13 av. du Président Wilson (M° Alma-Marceau), 01.47.20.00.29

Le Triptyque • 2nd • Dance Club
Best Dance Clubs The zeitgeisty crowd can be found grooving here at eclectic-electro club nights such as Chiennes Hi-Fi and Dirty Dancing. A very stylish club, Triptyque is at the heart of the Grands Boulevards renaissance, and style-mongers and music producers often gather here to drink in its outer lounge area outfitted with screens of the dance floor or concert action within. Live programming runs from African soul to hip-hop and drum and bass, after which DJs run the whole gamut of electro sounds with a bit of funk and '80s thrown in. Wednesday's Afterwork is a chance to hit the dance floor as early as 8pm. *Wed 8pm-3am, Thu-Sat 11pm-6am. Concerts 8pm.* C= 142 rue Montmartre (M° Grands Boulevards), 01.40.28.05.55, letriptyque.com

Le Tropic Café • 1st • Gay Bar
Boxed in by greenery and fairy lights, Le Tropic Café is an island of campy cocktail delight in Les Halles. This stalwart of the Paris gay scene has been going for years but shows no signs of flagging, and many a coming-out party has been held here. Young clubbers flock to snack on French tapas around midnight and die-hards flog it out on the heated techno terrace until dawn. It's even brought out its own compilation. *Daily noon-5am.* B= 66 rue des Lombards (M° Châtelet), 01.40.13.92.62

Viaduc Café* • 12th • Café
An airy café built under the arches of an old viaduct. *See Bobo Restaurants, p.133, for details.* = 43 av. Daumesnil (M° Ledru-Rollin), 01.44.74.70.70

Le Zinzin • 9th • Dance Club
Proving that Le Baron was just the beginning of its Paris nightlife sweepstake, the LaJohnson crew went on to open Le Paris Paris, a hot location for private parties and after-shows, and Le Zinzin. This latter club holds 600 and has a fine pedigree—none other than Edith Piaf and Jacques Brel played here when it was at the height of its '60s fame. Many incarnations thereafter, it's gone back to a wonderfully glittery '70s décor in time for Paris's renewed love affair with funk. Look out for the monthly In Funk We Trust and wait till you see how those uptight Parisians can really groove when they dig the right vibrations. An ideal place to cut loose from house with a sexy, stimulating crowd of 20- and 30-somethings. *Opening varies according to programming.* = 8 bd. de la Madeleine (M° Madeleine), lezinzin.com

Bobo Paris:
The Attractions

Antoine et Lili • 10th • Store
The shop that started it all on the Canal St-Martin, Antoine et Lili's colorful facades reflect on the water on summer afternoons. Puce green, pink, and cobalt blue are its trademark colors, made into simple, one-size-fits-all designs that are fun to wear, accessorized with the ethnic and shiny knickknacks and Moroccan slippers also on sale. Next door to the pink fashion store is the green décor one, filled with Senegalese recycled chairs, Chinese coffee flasks, Indian incense sticks, and Moroccan tea glasses, somehow made more desirable by being assembled in this kitsch setting. To complete the lifestyle picture, the yellow café serves great cheesecake in a bright setting with the same funky style. *Mon-Sat 11am-8pm.* 95 quai de Valmy (M° Jacques Bonsergent), 01.40.37.41.55, altribu.com

Canauxrama • 12th • Boat Trip
Instead of beating down the Seine on a bateau-mouche, take the slow boat up the lesser-known Paris waterways of the Canal St-Martin and Canal d'Ourcq. The journey from Bastille to the La Villette science and music park takes two and a half hours. The relaxing tour takes in a mysterious vaulted tunnel pierced with light shafts, lock gates, revolving and lifting bridges, the Hôtel du Nord of the Marcel Carné film, and the Rotonde de la Villette. Best of all is simply to glide by fishermen and chestnut trees and under romantic footbridges. Paris Canal (01.42.40.96.97, pariscanal.com) runs the same tour starting at La Villette and finishing at the Musée d'Orsay, and both also offer longer rides out to the *guinguettes* (old-style dance halls on the River Marne). *Daily, embark 9:45am and 2:30pm Port de l'Arsenal. In winter months, call in advance for schedule.* € Depart Port de l'Arsenal, opposite 50 bd. de la Bastille (M° Bastille), 01.42.39.15.00, canauxrama.com

Cinémathèque Française • 12th • Museum/Movie Theater
This fantastic Frank Gehry building lay empty for years after funding ran out for an American Center, but it now forms the new home of the Cinémathèque Française. Created in 1936 by Henri Langlois to conserve French and foreign film heritage, it has one of the world's most important collections of films, archive material, magic lanterns, cameras, costumes, and posters, much of which can now be displayed for the first time in a permanent exhibition. Four state-of-the-art screens include one with an orchestra pit for live performance of silent movie scores. The BIFI film library, with 3,150 videos and DVDs to watch in situ, is also housed here. There's an exciting program of directors' cuts and themed showcases. Look out for films labeled VO (version originale) if you want to watch them with subtitles in English (VF—version française—means they've been dubbed into French). *Exhibitions: Mon-Tue, Thu-Fri noon-7pm, Sat-Sun 10am-8pm.* €- 51 rue de Bercy (M° Bercy), 01.71.19.33.33, cinemathequefrancaise.com

Friday Night Fever • 14th • Activity
Experienced in-line skaters can see Paris whizz by in an exhilarating three-hour roller marathon that takes over the city streets every Friday night. Crowds of up to 40,000 skaters congregate near the Tour Montparnasse at 10pm and slowly move off like a swarm of bees, gathering momentum until they are humming down boulevards and across bridges, following their Pied Piper leaders who choose a different route each week. From couples on a date to exhibitionists sporting the latest wheels to '70s purists on rollerskates, it attracts all sorts, and there's plenty of whistle-blowing to keep the momentum up. As an alternative to clubbing, this puts you on a natural high. Skates can be hired from Nomades, 37 bd. Bourdon (M° Bastille), (01.44.54.94.42). *Fri 10pm.* Starts pl. Raoul Dautry (M° Montparnasse-Bienvenüe), 01.43.36.89.81, pari-roller.com

Galerie Simone • 3rd • Store
Styled as an art gallery for fashion, Simone exhibits the most original of the emerging designers in clothes, jewelry, and bags, with star pieces displayed on tailors' mannequins. The designers here use couture skills to create one-off pieces that really are works of art, such as Manon's appliquéd dresses, Eymèle Burgaud's felt skirts, and Tengu Karasu's adaptations of old kimonos. An Van Hove's stunning jewelry made from electrical connectors is a major conversation-starter. There's also a small selection of vintage apparel. *Tue-Sat noon-7pm.* 124 rue Vieille-du-Temple (M° St-Sébastien-Froissart), 01.42.74.21.28

India & Spa • 3rd • Spa
The presence of dark wood and a Murano glass chandelier reveals that we are in the trendiest part of the Marais, which seems to have established its own decorative style. This three-floor spa is beautiful, its different spaces reflecting the Indian, Asian, and North African origins of the treatments it offers. Choose a Moroccan steam bath in the turquoise-tiled hammam followed by an orange-flower–scented massage; the tempting Romance Mauricienne featuring a ylang-ylang and coconut bath and papaya scrub; or a four-handed yin and yang massage in Rajasthani-colored massage rooms on the upper floor. Note that it's possible to have a massage à deux. *Mon-Sat 11am-9pm, Sun 11am-7pm.* €€€€ 76 rue Charlot (M° Filles du Calvaire), 01.42.77.82.10

Louise Weiss galleries • 13th • Art Galleries
Though Galerie Emmanuel Perrotin has made it to the big-brother quarter of the Marais, rue Louise Weiss in the under-construction 13th arrondissement remains the place to taste the salt of daring contemporary art. Video and installations are the strong suits of the row of galleries, and Kréo and Jousse Entreprise also showcase cutting-edge furniture, blurring the boundaries between art and design. The hip scene turns into one big party during the group *vernissages* or private viewings. Check the website to find out when the next one is. *Tue-Sat 11am-7pm.* Rue Louise Weiss (M° Chevaleret), 01.48.51.33.21, louise13.fr

La Maison Rouge (Fondation Antoine de Galbert) • 12th • Art Gallery
Best Contemporary Art The little red house, almost like a child's drawing of a house, is the café at the center of this new contemporary art foundation. Lunching or brunching on its terrace is a strange inside-out experience, as the 22,000-square-foot gallery has been built around it using the shell of a former

factory. Art collector Antoine de Galbert established this ambitious new space to show art in other private collections, and it also allows collectors the space to fund and curate new work. Defiantly contemporary, it highlights how private collectors lend muscle to creation, even on a massive scale. *Wed, Fri-Sun 11am-7pm, Thu 11am-9pm.* €– 10 bd. de la Bastille (M° Bastille), 01.40.01.08.81, lamaisonrouge.org

Marché des Enfants Rouges • 3rd • Food Market
Best Markets The oldest market in Paris, named after a nearby orphanage where the children wore red uniforms, Les Enfants-Rouges was reopened in 2000 to supply Marais bobos with the organic and high-quality produce they love. Though it doesn't have the chaotic street-vending mayhem of some Paris markets, this well-behaved covered emporium has the advantage of plenty of places to sit and taste the delights on offer. Try a glass of wine and charcuterie at the convivial wine bar l'Estaminet or a Moroccan tagine at the mosaic tables opposite. Fresh fish, olive oils, organic fruit, and honeys are sold in a tranquil atmosphere more redolent of Provence than of Paris. *Tue-Thu 8:30am-1pm and 4-7:30pm, Fri-Sat 8:30am-1pm and 4-8pm, Sun 8:30am-2pm.* 39 rue de Bretagne (M° Temple)

Marché aux Puces de St-Ouen (Clignancourt) • St-Ouen • Flea Market
Best Markets The enormous market of St-Ouen north of Paris is what most people refer to as the "puces" (although the city actually has four different flea markets). Emerging from Clignancourt Métro, follow the crowds and cut through the initial African and Asian gear to reach the true heart of the market, branching off on alleys running the length of rue des Rosiers. Here ten different covered and open-air markets house 2,500 dealers. The best, and most eclectic, are Marché Paul Bert with '30s coffee sets, old glove molds, lace, tinware, and many bizarre objects; and Marché Vernaison in an attractive two-floor '20s building with Napoléon III mirrors, Art Deco, kitchenware, paintings, exquisite vintage clothes, and the entire contents of an old haberdashery. Bargain confidently, preferably in fluent French, as an American accent doubles the price. *Sat-Mon 9am-6pm.* Rue des Rosiers (M° Porte de Clignancourt), les-puces.com

Musée de l'Erotisme • 18th • Museum
A romp around the seven floors of Paris' erotic museum will either have you panting for breath or gasping for air—most visitors claim it is not an erotic experience, but then it wouldn't be cool to say it was, would it? You can certainly while away a couple of hours in this curious place, which runs the gamut from scholarly archaeological finds such as Etruscan fertility symbols to the plain ridiculous—a vaginal dinner plate? The fourth floor display on Paris' magnificent brothels, which closed after World War II, is amusing, as are the 1920s silent porn movies, many of them made by enthusiastic amateurs or professional actors having a bit of fun at the end of a shoot. *Daily 10am-2am.* €– 72 bd. de Clichy (M° Blanche), 01.42.58.28.73

Musée du Fumeur • 11th • Museum
Far from being an ode to the French love of Gauloise fug, this museum relates to smoking as a higher art or an aid to philosophical and religious contemplation. A collection of smoking-related paraphernalia includes exquisitely crafted objets d'art, while the different strains of smokable plants can be seen growing

in the "planetarium." Thematic art exhibitions have included *Women Smokers, from Geishas to George Sand.* In the beautiful café-gallery, which looks like a 19th-century apothecary's shop, you can eat organic food and drink plant-based cocktails. *Tue-Sun 1-7pm.* €– 7 rue Pache (M° Voltaire), 01.46.59.05.51, museedufumeur.net

Palais de Tokyo • 16th • Art Gallery
Best Contemporary Art The biggest thing to hit the French art scene since the Centre Pompidou, this huge contemporary art space was created out of the Japanese pavilion built for the 1937 Exposition Universelle. The deconstructed space has the huge volumes needed to display impressive installations. These are often interactive, such as Chen Zhen's circle of drums stretched over upturned beds, *Dancing Body, Drumming Mind,* which resulted in a spontaneous tribal drumming by gallerygoers; or Jota Castro's *Liberté, Egalité, Fraternité,* where non-blacks were barred by bouncers from entering a nightclub-like room. If this wasn't enough to attract a hipster crowd, there is a mini concept shop, Black Box, and the restaurant and bar Tokyo Eat and Tokyo Idem, which move out onto the terrace for a DJ-animated scene in the summer months. *Tue-Sun noon-midnight.* €– 13 av. du Président Wilson (M° Alma-Marceau), 01.47.23.54.01, palaisdetokyo.com

Parc des Buttes Chaumont • 19th • Park
Best Parks Paris' most sublime park, and one of its most relaxed, the Buttes Chaumont was landscaped in the Haussmann era out of the quarries that provided stone for the foundations of the massive building program. With grottoes, a temple, waterfalls, and a lake, it is one big fantasy, and many visitors don't believe those stalactites are actually artificial. Unlike in many other parks, here you can roll on the grassy slopes and women can sunbathe without being hassled. Daytime is the domain of joggers, tai-chi practitioners, and family picnics, while as evening falls distant drums and aromatic smells create an alternative ambiance. Watch the sun set over Sacré-Coeur from the lawn by the Weber Café. The park keepers blow whistles to show you when it's closing, though there are always some latecomers who end up climbing out. *Daily 7am-dusk (around 10pm in summer).* Rue Botzaris (M° Botzaris)

Pavillon de l'Arsenal • 4th • Museum
Run by the city of Paris, the Pavillon, in an 1880s iron-framed, glass-roofed gallery, acts as a living museum of the changing face of the city. On the ground floor, lined in industrial concrete, is a permanent exhibition on the history of Paris through architecture. While the text is unfortunately only available in French, it is still well worth a visit as timelines, scale models, and revolving screens showing the major monuments of each era provide a useful map and chronology in your head as you go out and discover the city. The upper floor has temporary exhibitions on architects or themes, and the mezzanine displays plans for future projects, such as the floating swimming pool on the Seine. There's a hip little café where local architects hang out, perusing the international press that's delivered daily. *Tue-Sat 10:30am-6:30pm, Sun 11am-7pm.* 21 bd. Morland (M° Sully-Morland), 01.42.76.33.97, pavillon-arsenal.com

Promenade Plantée • 12th • Planted Walkway
Before the Bastille Opéra was built, a little train left the station here and made its way out to the villas on the Marne. The viaduct it took has been skillfully converted into artists' and artisans' studios underneath the arches and a planted walkway on top. After checking out some of the metalworkers, furniture restorers, and jewelry and instrument makers in their workshops (29–35 has exhibitions of current work), take the high road for a walk among the rooftops through rose pergolas and lovers' seats from place de la Nation to Bastille. *Studios open Mon-Sat 11am-7pm.* Next to av. Daumesnil (M° Bastille), viaduc-des-arts.com

Spree • 18th • Store
Best Concept Stores A concept store, Montmartre-style, Spree is run by artistic director Bruno Hadjadj and fashion designer Roberta Oprandi, who have pooled their creative talents to offer a one-stop shop for Parisian bobos. In two white rooms, changing photography exhibitions decorate the walls, while collectible retro furniture—Charles Eames and George Nelson chairs, Murano disc chandeliers—is scattered with objects and accessories, books, and CDs as if you've just dropped in on someone's home. At the back of the store, fashion labels include Isabel Marant, Comme des Garçons, and the pick of London's current hot designers, plus handmade ballerina shoes from Italy and surreal jewelry. *Mon 2-7:30pm, Tue-Sat 11am-7:30pm.* 16 rue de la Vieuville (M° Abbesses), 01.42.23.41.40

Surface to Air • 1st • Store
Best Concept Stores Based in New York and Paris, this collective of four Americans, two French, and one Argentinian is now rivaling Colette for tastemaker supremacy. Their store, which they term a "public office," mounts monthly collaborations between artists and musicians such as Zero 7 and Gonzalez as well as stocking cutting-edge fashion and design. More avant-garde than its rival, it espouses the deconstructed, reconstructed, grafitti-ized, and gothicized, though that will surely have changed by the time you read this. Some of the furniture, such as the Shock Absorber Lounge Chair, has potential as modern classics. The outfit also operates as a graphic design agency whose clients include Levi's, Reebok, and Virgin. *Mon-Sat 12:30-7:30pm.* 46 rue de l'Arbre-Sec (M° Pont Neuf), 01.49.27.04.54, surface2air.com

La Villette • 19th • Park/Museum/Concert Venue
This futuristic science and entertainment park was created out of the old slaughterhouses of La Villette. Containing the Zénith concert hall, Cabaret Sauvage club and concert venue, Cité de la Musique devoted to classical music, Espace Châpiteau for avant-garde circus, Cité des Sciences et de l'Industrie, and Géode IMAX cinema, it hosts many of Paris' biggest events. The park, designed with walkways over canals that are moodily lit up at night, is the venue for summer outdoor events with a festival atmosphere. Thousands sit under the stars for open-air cinema on the biggest screen in Europe or rave in the sunshine to Brazilian and electronic music. Check the website for what's on. *Park open daily; museums closed Mon.* 211 av. Jean-Jaurès (M° Porte de Pantin), 01.40.03.75.75, villette.com

Romantic Paris

So you're in the most romantic city in the world—why do you need a guidebook? Well you've only got three days and we want you to go home with a stack of memories that will last a lifetime. Not clichés, not "well, it would have been romantic if it wasn't for the insolent waiter/traffic/hordes of children on their spring break," just the feeling of irrepressible joie de vivre. While this itinerary seeks out many seductive spots for couples in love, Paris' romantic side is for anyone who's willing to give in to it. Look up at that sky, sip that rosé, and soon you'll be singing like Josephine Baker: "J'ai deux amours, mon pays et Paris …"

Note: Venues in bold in the itinerary are described in detail in the listings that follow. Venues followed by an * asterisk are those we recommend as both a restaurant and a destination bar.

Romantic Paris: The Perfect Plan (3 Days and Nights)

Your Hotel: **L'Hôtel**, whose discreet Left Bank location, gorgeous décor, intimate bar, and seductive subterranean plunge pool are made for lovers.

Thursday

Highlights

Thursday
Breakfast	**Au Vieux Colombier**
Morning	**Jardins du Luxembourg**
Lunch	**Le Grand Véfour**
Afternoon	**Covered Passages**
Cocktails	**Café de la Paix**
Dinner	**Angl'Opéra**
Nighttime	**Le Doudingue***

Friday
Breakfast	**Jardin de Varenne Café**
Morning	**Musée Rodin**
Lunch	**Le Salon d'Hélène**
Afternoon	**4 Roues sous 1 Parapluie**
Dinner	**Le Bélier**
Nighttime	**Summer Dancing**
Late-Night	**Mezzanine de l'Alcazar**

Saturday
Breakfast	**Hotel**
Morning	**Musée Marmottan**
Lunch	**Pré Catelan**
Afternoon	**La Collection 1900**
Cocktails	**Le Dokhan's**
Dinner	**Lapérouse**
Nighttime	**Bar Fontainebleau**

The Morning After
Brunch	**Café Jacquemart-André**
Morning	**Musée Jacquemart-André**

9:30am Get your visit off to an elegant start with a stroll through the narrow streets of St-Germain, stopping for breakfast at the lovely Art Nouveau café **Au Vieux Colombier**.

10:30am Continue with a ramble around the nearby **Jardin du Luxembourg,** stopping in to view the exhibition at the **Musée du Luxembourg**. Walk up to the Seine, crossing at the Pont des Arts and through the courtyard of the Louvre. Make your way to the **Palais Royal**.

1pm Lunch Two of Paris' most romantic restaurants are built into the cloisters of the Palais Royal, the gastronomic **Le Grand Véfour** with its delicate painted panels, mirrors, and gilt, and **Le Restaurant du Palais Royal**, which has a superb terrace.

3pm After strolling the gardens, explore some of the **Covered passages** to the east and north of the Palais Royal. These 19th-century shopping arcades have a nostalgic charm and are filled with boutiques, wine and toy stores, and antiquarian booksellers.

ROMANTIC

149

4:30pm Moving north from here by foot or bus route 74, you'll find yourself in the Nouvelle Athènes, home of the artists, writers, and composers of the Romantic movement. Place Gustave Toudouze and Place St-Georges are worth a detour, as is the **Musée de la Vie Romantique**, which in summer has a rose-filled garden tearoom. In winter the nearby **Les Cakes de Bertrand** is run by the same people.

6pm Have a glass of Champagne at the **Café de la Paix** on Place de l'Opéra, whose splendid Second Empire salons glitter just as they did when this was the focus of 19th-century high society.

8pm This will get you in the mood for an evening at the opera or ballet at the **Opéra National de Paris Palais Garnier**, whose red-velvet boxes and marble staircases carry romantic to the extreme. If opera's not your thing, go for dinner on the barge **La Balle au Bond***. A deck-top meal with a view of the Seine and the Louvre can be followed by a jazz concert down below.

11pm Dinner Angl'Opera, only a few steps from the Palais Garnier, is perfect for a post-performance meal, where the chef dishes out culinary surprises in a velvet-and-Murano-lights setting. Or, for a candlelit step back in time, go to the brasserie **Gallopin**.

1am Go up to Montmartre for a late-evening walk. Look down on Paris from in front of the Sacré-Coeur, then have a drink at **Le Doudingue***, a secluded bar with painted clouds, or take the steps east of the basilica down to the quietly romantic Square Maurice Utrillo, where **Botak Café** is a relaxed open-air spot for a drink. If you want to go dancing, try **Le Divan du Monde**, a club with eclectic music and cozy seating in the original Divan Japonais that features in many Toulouse-Lautrec paintings.

Friday

9:30am For an exploration of the Left Bank's most romantic places, start with breakfast in **Le Jardin de Varenne**, in the **Musée Rodin**'s garden. Then wander around the garden itself, filled with Rodin's sculptures, planted arcades, and a pond, before visiting the museum, in an elegant former private mansion. Don't forget to take up the suggestive mood of his sculpture *The Kiss*.

11am With an early start you can also fit in a visit to the tomb of Napoléon at Les Invalides or the Eiffel Tower, covered in the Classic Itinerary.

1pm Lunch In St-Germain, **Le Salon d'Hélène** is the downstairs, less formal dining room of chef

ROMANTIC · ITINERARY

Hélène Darroze, where you can share tapas-style dishes on low, cushioned seating. Or go the exotic route with some of the best Vietnamese food in Paris at the dark and sultry **Le Palanquin**.

3pm Take a tour around Paris in a Citroën 2CV, the car that was nicknamed "the love bug," with **4 Roues sous 1 Parapluie**. You can get your chauffeur to pick you up at the restaurant before whizzing you around the sites in this most original way with an excellent commentary.

5pm Take a trip to the contemporary-style **Parc André-Citroën**, where **Le Ballon Eutelsat** will float you above Paris for a grand view. Then return to your hotel for a little cat nap and to prepare for the evening ahead.

9pm Dinner The window seats at **R** (pronounced "air") are the perfect place to be when the Eiffel Tower turns on its scintillating lights at nightfall as you enjoy excellent modern cuisine. Alternatively dine at **Le Bélier**, L'Hôtel's very special restaurant, in a Wildean décor of tasseled lamps and low armchairs. Or enjoy a candlelit meal at the intimate, family-run **Le Réminet**, in the heart of the Latin Quarter.

11pm A romantic weekend in Paris has to include a walk by the Seine. From the quays leading east or west from St-Michel you can look across to the Ile de la Cité. In summer two special attractions are Paris Plage (see Best Events, p.184) on the Right Bank, or the **Summer dancing by the Seine** in Square Tino Rossi. Salsa, tango, and other dance enthusiasts set up improvised parties in the Seine-side alcoves of this sculpture park for nightly dance fever, all summer long.

1am Go back into St-Germain for a quiet drink at L'Hôtel or the terrace of **Café de la Mairie**, overlooking Place St-Sulpice. A more upbeat atmosphere can be found at **Mezzanine de l'Alcazar**, with disco fever to follow at **Le Wagg**'s Friday night Carwash, or at the late-night lounge bar **L'Echelle de Jacob**.

Saturday

10am Enjoy a leisurely breakfast in bed at your hotel before setting off for the **Musée Marmottan**, in the far west of Paris. This Impressionist museum concentrates on Claude Monet, with his late water-lily canvases in a specially created room.

Noon You can walk from here into the **Bois de Boulogne**, the former royal hunting forest that stretches out through acres of wild open spaces and woods.

1pm Lunch The Bois has two of Paris' most romantic restaurants, **Le Pré Catelan**, in a Belle Epoque pavilion, and **Le Chalet des Iles**, on an island in a lake. For the latter you need to take a launch and can lunch on a festive terrace or in the firelit country-house interior.

3:30pm If the weather's fine, stay in the Bois and get lost among its chestnut trees, laze in the long grass, or rent a boat or bicycle. Otherwise, fit in a guided visit to **La Collection 1900** at Maxim's, an evocative re-creation of a courtesan's apartment filled with Art Nouveau treasures, or a museum from another itinerary, perhaps the Musée Guimet or Musée Baccarat, which are both on this side of town.

5pm Book a spa treatment for two in **Les Bains du Montorgueil**, a luxurious North African hammam. Alternatively, get an introduction to French wines at an English-language tasting by Olivier Magny at **O Château**.

7:30pm Begin a very special last night with a glass of Champagne at the candlelit **Champagne Bar at Le Dokhan's** or the cocktail heaven of the **Le Defender**.

9pm Dinner This evening, book your own private salon at **Lapérouse**, the historic restaurant where centuries of Frenchmen have entertained their mistresses. Or, if money's no object, savor the exquisite cuisine and surroundings of **L'Ambroisie** in a mansion house on the Place des Vosges. Or soak in the dressed-up, Belle Epoque romance of the legendary **Maxim's** restaurant.

Midnight Carry on in the spirit of rarefied luxury with a martini, surrounded by 19th-century frescoes in the **Bar Fontainebleau** of the Hôtel Meurice. Alternatively, settle into the seductive atmosphere of **Buddha Bar** or play cocktail roulette to sitar music at the Indian-themed **Le Jaipur**. For dancing, summer evenings are the time to go to the **Bateau Concorde Atlantique**, where you can stargaze on deck, while **Man Ray**'s opulent décor and beautiful people makes it a prime choice for an upscale weekend night out.

> **The Morning After**
> The **Musée Jacquemart-André** has a romantic story attached. As you wander through its lavish salons, you'll warm to the tale of how portrait painter Nélie Jacquemart and banker Edouard André traveled the world buying works of art. Afterward, brunch under one of their treasures, a Tiepolo ceiling, in the **Café Jacquemart-André**.

Romantic Paris: The Key Neighborhoods

The covered passages in the **1st** and **2nd arrondissements** are romantic leftovers from the days of shopping by gaslight, when the bourgeois would step from their carriages into these protected glass-roofed arcades, and north of here is the Nouvelle Athènes, where writers, artists, and musicians such as George Sand and Chopin created a bohemian utopia.

On the **Left Bank (5th**, **6th**, and **7th arrondissements)** you'll visit the Musée Rodin's romantic gardens, the Jardin du Luxembourg, and have the chance to soar above Paris in a balloon at the contemporary Parc André-Citroën near the Eiffel Tower, as well as dance the night away in the open air by the Seine.

The **Bois de Boulogne** can be abundantly romantic on a warm spring day, when a bucolic lunch al fresco on a small island, followed by a stroll next to one of its small lakes, provide a lovely respite from the city.

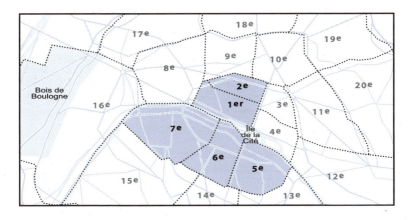

Romantic Paris: The Shopping Blocks

Palais Royal (M° Palais Royal-Musée du Louvre unless otherwise noted)

One of the most romantic spots in Paris, the 18th-century Jardin du Palais Royal is enclosed by cloistered arcades containing select boutiques selling fashion, perfume, antiquarian books, and objets d'art. The theme is continued in the elegant Galerie Vivienne just north of the Jardin.

Anna Joliet Possibly the only shop in the world to sell nothing but music boxes. 9 rue de Beaujolais, Jardin du Palais Royal, 01.49.27.98.60

Didier Ludot Specialist in vintage haute couture from the wardrobes of the Parisian elite. 19, 20, 23, 24 galerie de Montpensier; 125 galerie de Valois, Jardin du Palais Royal, 01.42.96.06.56

L'Eclaireur Beautiful store full of objects for the home and selected clothes in natural tones. (p.172) 131 galerie de Valois, Jardin du Palais Royal, 01.40.20.42.52

Emilio Robba Italian craftsman making exquisite artificial orchids in silk gesso. 29 galerie Vivienne (M° Bourse), 01.42.61.71.43

Salons du Palais-Royal Shiseido In an 18th-century salon ambiance, sample individual perfume ingredients to discover the scent that works for you. 142 Galerie de Valois, Jardin du Palais Royal, 01.49.27.09.09

Place Vendôme and the Madeleine

Cut like a big diamond itself, Place Vendôme is the world's most exclusive jewelry district. Alongside big players Chanel, Dior, Bulgari, and Chopard, check out the more unusual creations of French master jewelers. Strolling up to Place de la Madeleine, where society weddings are often held, you'll find yourself surrounded by foodshops selling delectable treats.

Boucheron Now owned by Gucci, this venerable jeweler combines some of its classic designs with voluptuously modern ones. 26 pl. Vendôme (M° Opéra), 01.42.61.58.16

Chanel Joaillerie The boutique is decorated in a style reminiscent of Coco's apartment and each design is based on her key motifs. 18 pl. Vendôme (M° Opéra), 01.55.35.50.05

Fauchon The pink and black store established in 1886 is packed with beautifully boxed chocolates, foie gras, and wines. (p.173) 26-30 pl. de la Madeleine (M° Madeleine), 01.47.42.60.11

Résonances All the contents of a housemaid's cupboard have been made utterly covetable by this shop: feather dusters, silver polish, shoe trees, cookbooks, and bathroom goodies. 3 bd. Malesherbes (M° Madeleine), 01.44.51.63.70

Romantic Paris: The Hotels

L'Hôtel • 6th • Trendy (20 rms)
L'Hôtel has long been a fabled Paris address. Before, it had a famously tacky leopard-print room for illicit affairs. In 1996 Costes decorator Jacques Garcia made it a little more respectable, but it is still deliciously decadent. The circular stairwell allows you to look up or down through several floors of curved ivory-painted banisters. Off this are the rooms and suites, each individually decorated to a theme. Oscar Wilde's is the most famous—the writer died here, his bill unpaid. Another former guest, French singer Mistinguett, has the pink Art Deco bedroom of her home at Bougival re-created with the original mirrored bed, dressing table, and clock. Romantics, however, should plump for the purple and gold Eastern promise of the Pondichéry room complete with a sensual Hindu sculpture; Madame de Merteuil's 18th-century boudoir; or Napoléon III with a huge rococo mirror over the bed. L'Hôtel's bar and restaurant, Le Bélier, is equally seductive, and below ground is the sensuous thermal bath, a small plunge pool with a perpetual wave, use of which can be followed by lounging in the cushioned rotunda. This exceptional private spa is reserved by the room so you'll have it all to yourself. Chances are you won't leave L'Hôtel till check-out time, despite its excellent St-Germain location. €€ 13 rue des Beaux-Arts (M° St-Germain-des-Prés), 01.44.41.99.00, l-hotel.com

Hôtel Lancaster • 8th • Trendy (60 rms)
Plenty of film stars stay here, but you'd have to resort to torture to get the staff to reveal their names. What we can tell you is that Marlene Dietrich lived here for several years, and she never had grounds for complaint. Each of the many public rooms has an exceptional style all its own: the cream-paneled lobby makes you think of the Astors; the fragrant Salon Berri lounge is a symphony in puce green and purple with Louis XV furniture; next door is the masculine Fontenoy room where antique toy soldiers are displayed in cabinets. On to the main lounge where high-backed chairs in mauve damask make a dramatic modern statement; the Table du Lancaster restaurant full of Japanese seduction; and the exotic bamboo garden, which is lit up at night. In contrast, the Lancaster's rooms are traditional, but done in exquisite taste, with softly hued fabrics, antique furniture, and objets d'art. Then, surprise, the bathrooms are contemporary again with square-cut pearly-gray marble sinks. All the non-suite rooms are lovely, but if you can, go for suite 76 and arrive in the late afternoon when film-set lighting floods in through an unusual frosted round window into the living room. A small gym on the top floor has views of Paris. €€€€ 7 rue de Berri (M° George V), 01.40.76.40.76, hotel-lancaster.fr

Hôtel Meurice • 1st • Grand (125 rms)
Nicknamed the "City of London" in the 19th century, the Meurice was a home away from home for British aristocrats. By the end of the 20th century, however, the old lady was looking a little faded. Cue a massive facelift: 500 artisans meticulously restored mosaics, stained glass, friezes, cornices, and antiques, revealing in time for the millennium just what a beauty this palace really is.

ROMANTIC

It's all been done with incredible taste, making it the most romantic of all the palace hotels. Sipping a pink martini under a ceiling of apricot clouds in the bar, watching the liveried concierges through gilt-framed windows, or chilling to piano music in the palm-filled winter garden, you'll have to pinch yourself to remind you that you're not in a Merchant-Ivory film. The restaurant is a full-on 19th-century ballroom, and the fashionable Caudalie spa has a marble Jacuzzi for two. But the dream doesn't stop there. Just as much care and exquisite details have been lavished on rooms. Lovers should book into the romantic Marco Polo suite in the eaves, or a prestige double on the sixth floor, such as 601. These have a heart-stopping view over the Tuileries gardens, and from the gorgeous bathroom you can step out onto a tiny balcony. €€€€ 228 rue de Rivoli (M° Concorde), 01.44.58.10.10, meuricehotel.com

Pavillon de la Reine • 3rd • Timeless (56 rms)

The Place des Vosges is one of the most romantic squares in Paris. Built at the instigation of Henri IV, its park with a fountain and chestnut trees is surrounded by elegant townhouses that were the focus of 17th-century courtly life. Now it takes years of social engineering to secure an address here, but you can have yours for a day or two in this ivy-clad villa set back behind the cloisters through a courtyard garden. The spacious ground-floor salon is like that of a country house, with exposed beams, a log fire in winter, and comfortable, chenille-covered armchairs in which to enjoy a drink, browse magazines, or play chess. The three categories of non-suite room differ in size and are decorated in warm-hued checks and subtle florals with a choice of courtyard or garden view. For something a little different, the cozy duplex rooms are like mini-lofts with study alcoves, velvet upholstery, and sleeping areas up above. Duplex suites are the ultimate in seduction with a theatrical, contemporary take on the 17th-century salon in velvet and taffeta, while some of the main suites have beams and a four-poster. Breakfast is in the richly upholstered vaulted cellar. €€€ 28 pl. des Vosges (M° Chemin Vert), 01.40.29.19.19, pavillon-de-la-reine.com

Relais Christine • 6th • Timeless (51 rms)

This haven of calm in St-Germain is entered through a courtyard with trailing ivy, rhododendrons, and statues. Inside, the comfortable salon has the atmosphere of a country house with striped velvet sofas, portraits, a chessboard laid out, and an honesty bar, and the rooms are similarly full of sophisticated home comforts. The three non-suite categories vary in size but all have light flooding in from long windows and are decorated in velvet, toile de Jouy, and striped or checked linens with harmonious, restful color schemes. Exposed beams and balconies add to the Left Bank charm. The Duplex in the eaves is delightful, and idiosyncratic ground-floor suites open onto the lush garden. As well as a majestic breakfast room in the old vaults of a 13th-century convent, complete with suit of armor and cauldron over the fire, there is a spa in the medieval vaults that provides one of the most aesthetically pleasing workouts in town. The raw sandstone walls have been beautifully lit and it includes a mosaic-tiled Jacuzzi and treatment rooms where you can summon a masseur at 45 minutes' notice any time of day or night. €€€ 3 rue Christine (M° Odéon), 01.40.51.60.80, relais-christine.com

ROMANTIC · HOTELS

Trocadéro Dokhan's • 16th • Timeless (59 rms)
The Dokhan's may be part of a chain, but it feels like your own private townhouse. Housed in a spectacular 19th-century flatiron building near the luxury shops and restaurants of the 16th arrondissement, it combines some stunning original features such as the beautiful oak parquet of the lobby and the paneled bar with Frédéric Méchiche's ultra-Romantic décor. In the rooms, luxuriously decked in stars and stripes in pale gray and midnight blue, you'll feel as though you are in a Napoleonic campaign tent. Architectural prints on the walls, antique furniture, blue and white ginger jars and candlesticks—everything is perfectly placed and harmoniously coordinated. The Ming Suite is especially charming, with a diamond-shaped window framed by curtains above the bed so you can let the morning light flood in as you enjoy breakfast in bed. Otherwise, ask for a "chambre étoilée" with a star design. The suites are in the four rooms that climb the front of the building, with windows facing in many directions. If you can tear yourself away from your room, go down to the pale green–paneled bar, which feels like a St-Petersburg salon, and enjoy a Champagne tasting by candlelight. The talented hotel manager invites opera and jazz musicians to perform from time to time. €€ 117 rue Lauriston (M° Boissière), 01.53.65.66.99, dokhans.com

Romantic Paris:
The Restaurants

A Priori Thé • 2nd • Tearoom
In the most elegant of Paris' 19th-century covered passages, American Peggy Ancock runs this tea salon whose terrace is right on the mosaic-floored thoroughfare of the glass-roofed arcade. The setting attracts a fashionable crowd—owners of galerie Vivienne's stylish boutiques at lunch and French actresses for Sunday brunch. The copious options include quiches, salads, and pasta, but the stars are the pastries, including a cheesecake with raspberry coulis. There are 25 varieties of tea on offer, from fragrant lapsang souchong to orange pekoe. Inside, you can sink into cushioned wicker chairs, but it's more fun to see and be seen in the passage. *Mon-Fri 9am-6pm, Sat 9am-6:30pm, Sun noon-6:30pm.* €– 35-37 galerie Vivienne (M° Bourse), 01.42.97.48.75

L'Ambroisie • 4th • Gastronomic
The pinnacle of romantic fine dining is found in this 17th-century townhouse on one of Paris' most beautiful squares. Step in through the cloisters to these two small salons, decorated with Aubusson tapestries and lit by antique sconces and chandeliers. The extremely high price tag means that company directors are often seen here, but the intimate, refined setting creates the illusion that you are royalty dining in your own Italian palazzo. L'Ambroisie is all about tradition, soft-footed waiters bringing small offerings between courses. Everything is done with warmth and grace. "C'est de l'Ambroisie!" means food fit for the gods, and Bernard Pacaud's cooking is worthy of the name. According to the season, forgotten flavors appear, such as the autumnal fricassée of Breton lobster with chestnuts and pumpkin. Reserve well in advance. *Tue-Sat noon-1:30pm and 8-9:30pm.* €€€€ 9 pl. des Vosges (M° Bastille), 01.42.78.51.45

Angl'Opera • 9th • Contemporary
Just minutes from the Palais Garnier and therefore perfect for a meal after the opera or ballet, this hotel dining room has been a fashionable hit since Gilles Choukroun stepped into the kitchen. Stylish couples, journalists, and media types and young opera buffs—occasionally performers too—fill the chocolate-and-red striped velvet banquettes, and it always has a lively atmosphere, particularly after nearby performances let out. At night, the warm, contemporary décor of this corniced, high-ceilinged room is lit by tiny colored lights. The welcome is warm too, but the main reason for all the excitement is Choukroun's fun approach to cuisine. He mixes French ingredients with Thai spices and adds in iconoclastic touches like Vache Qui Rit cheese, Nutella, and mint liqueur—it seems to work and there are traditional options for non–risk-takers. *Mon-Fri noon-11:30pm.* € Hôtel Edouard VII, 39 av. de l'Opéra (M° Opéra), 01.42.61.86.25, edouard7hotel.com

La Balle au Bond* • 5th and 6th • Restaurant/Jazz Club
The romance of dining on board a moored canalboat across the water from the Louvre can seduce even long-term Paris residents, and from young first-daters to Golden Ponders, many are drawn to this beloved spot. La Balle au Bond,

spruced up with marble tables, teak chairs, Astroturf underfoot, and masses of flowers, combines dining on deck with the option of going down below afterward for concerts of jazz, pop, chanson, rock, punk, or bossa nova according to the day (but Thursdays are reliably jazz). The delicious food includes items like beef tartare and sea bream with fennel, lemon, and olives. In summer there are strawberries with spiced red wine. Come at sunset to enjoy this lovely setting at its most romantic. In winter it changes its backdrop from the Louvre to Notre-Dame. *Apr-Sept daily 11am-2am. € Concerts year-round at 9pm. €–* Apr-Sept facing the Louvre, on quai Malaquais (M° St-Germain-des-Prés); Oct-Mar (concerts only) facing Notre-Dame, on quai de la Tournelle (M° Maubert-Mutualité), 01.40.46.85.12, laballeaubond.fr

Le Bélier • 6th • Trendy
At the back of this exquisite hotel, with its tasseled lamps, private snugs, and intimate bar, is its restaurant, a favorite with writers, (successful) artists and their dealers, and anyone who loves discreet decadence. With the atmosphere of a private salon from the 1880s, it is lit by a glass skylight, and at night low-hanging lights conjure up images of tête-à-têtes between courtesans and their clients in Zola's novels. There's a view over a little patio with a fountain, cornices, and marble pillars, and you sit for dinner in low armchairs. The temptation to sneak off to one of the rooms or the underground pool is strong, but the quality of the food may hold you back. The chef turns out dishes fit for these surroundings: foie gras with fig purée, lacquered lamb shank, and an excellent sole meunière. If you are not too busy gazing into each other's eyes, you may spot the odd celebrity here. *Tue-Sat 12:30-2pm and 7:30-10pm. €€* L'Hôtel, 13 rue des Beaux-Arts (M° St-Germain-des-Prés), 01.44.41.99.01, l-hotel.com

Café Jacquemart-André • 8th • Tearoom
Best Brunches Although you don't have to go to the Musée Jacquemart-André to enjoy its splendid café, it is worth touring the museum, as the romantic story of this 19th-century couple will put you in the mood for your meal. Located in the old dining room of Nélie Jacquemart and Edouard André's mansion, the café has a ceiling painted by Tiepolo for the Villa Cantarini in the 18th century, and its walls are lined with Brussels tapestries. Few tearooms can match that. This one also does an excellent brunch with fresh orange juice, coffee, tea, or hot chocolate, oeufs en cocotte (eggs baked in cream, a French specialty) with herbs, salads, smoked salmon, and dessert. Come in the afternoon to enjoy sticky pastries that make you wonder how the smartly dressed ladies who meet for tea here can still fit into their twinsets. *Daily 11:45am-5:45pm. €* Musée Jacquemart-André, 158 bd. Haussmann (M° St-Philippe-du-Roule), 01.45.62.11.59, musee-jacquemart-andre.com

Café Maure de la Mosquée de Paris • 5th • Tearoom
The beautiful Paris mosque has its own hammam (steam baths) and tearoom, which are both open to non-Muslims. Both are so popular that on Saturdays it can be difficult to get a table, or a *gommage* (body scrub) in the baths. It's the dreamy, Arabian nights environment that has made this such a fashionable spot. The baths look like an Ingres painting, and the tearoom, with its tiled interior and fig-tree–filled courtyard, like an art-film version of Marrakech. As well as the excellent mint tea and pastries, which can be enjoyed over a game of chess, come here to taste authentic tagines, the meat, vegetable, and fruit stews slow-

cooked in conical terra-cotta pots. At night, the garden smells fragrantly of jasmine. Reserve to be sure of a table if you plan to stay for dinner. *Daily 9am-midnight.* € 39 rue Geoffroy-St-Hilaire (M° Place Monge), 01.43.31.38.20

Les Cakes de Bertrand • 9th • Tearoom
This quaintly named tea shop is one of the most charming stop-offs in this quarter full of hidden treasures. The result of a collaboration between a dietitian (of the best kind—he positively encourages you to indulge in macaroons and mille-feuilles) and a decorator, it is decorated with stripy wallpaper, 19th-century portraits, candles, and curiosities. They also sell their own accessories and chocolate boxes. Cakes, of course, savory tarts, salads, teas, a glass of wine, and decadent hot chocolate can all be enjoyed in this intimate setting, and Sunday brunch includes delicious creamy oeufs en cocotte (eggs in cream) and a glass of Champagne. *Daily 9:30am-7:30pm.* €– 7 rue Bourdaloue (M° Notre-Dame-de-Lorette), 01.40.16.16.28, lescakesdebertrand.com

Le Chalet des Iles • Bois de Boulogne • Traditional
Best Outdoor Dining A peacock may suddenly appear on the hedgerow of this very special restaurant on an island in the Bois de Boulogne, and that is not the only thing that lends this place its magic. Reached by a launch, it feels a million miles from the city. In summer the mood is festive, with relaxed couples and groups of friends raising a glass of Champagne on the terrace. In winter, it is cozy, as diners move inside to the large room decorated in French country florals, with a log fire to sit by with a glass of Cognac. The food, too, changes with the seasons, from light summer dishes such as goat's cheese with lemon and fig confit, to winter warmers featuring girolles mushrooms and chestnuts. The desserts are the icing on the cake. Come in the evening to savor the moonlight. *Tue-Fri noon-2:30pm and 8-10:30pm, Sat noon-3:30pm and 8-10:30pm, Sun noon-3:30pm.* €€ Carrefour des Cascades, Lac Inférieur du Bois de Boulogne (M° La Muette, then walk or taxi), 01.42.88.04.69, lechaletdesiles.net

Le Doudingue* • 18th • Bar/Restaurant
Up a steep cobbled street from Abbesses, this jewel of a bar/restaurant seems designed for lovers. It's been dubbed a "Montmartre-style lounge" for its easy ambiance and soft electronic music, though we're talking a lounge in a shoebox as it only seats about 30. Billowy clouds and angels are painted on the walls and ceiling, cushions are scattered on the window-side banquettes, and it's lit by baroque candelabra, Morroccan lanterns, and candles on the tables. An upper level has tables for tête-à-tête dining that features a mix of flavors and colors. Otherwise, squeeze in to the lower-level banquettes for a cocktail with the artists and musicians who are regulars. *Daily 11:30am-2am.* € 24 rue Durantin (M° Abbesses), 01.42.54.88.08

Flora • 8th • Contemporary
Though it's on swanky Avenue George V, Flora attracts a clientele that's older and less brash than that of its flashier neighbors and is perfect for a civilized dinner for two. The dining room gives the impression of being in a private house, with wallpaper and a marble fireplace, made enchanting by a Murano glass chandelier, strings of glass beads, and lotus flowers and tea lights floating in bowls. Avoid the second room, which is rather formal and designed for larger groups. Chef Flora Mikula brings much warmth to the place and to her inven-

tive, contemporary cuisine. The quenelles (fish dumplings) are made with langoustine, asparagus, and truffle; sole is served with truffle butter. This perfection on a plate could prove to be the food of love. *Mon-Fri noon-2:30pm and 7-11pm, Sat 7-11pm.* €€ 36 av. George V (M° George V), 01.40.70.10.49

Gallopin • 2nd • Brasserie
Paris brasseries range from brassy, bustling seafood purveyors to the old-world calm of Gallopin. At lunch it's full of financial types who work at the nearby stock exchange, but in the evening its 1870s décor—polished mahogany paneling, brass coat hooks, and intricate tiled floor—comes into its own, dimly lit by Art Nouveau wall lights that cast a sepia glow. The waiters in their cutaway coats are proud masters of their art, bringing the whole fish for inspection before it is taken away to be served and offering spot-on wine recommendations. Classic dishes include grilled sea bass spiked with fennel seeds and stems and dribbled with olive oil, or steak Chateaubriand, followed by rhum baba or flambéed crêpes Alexandre. *Daily noon-midnight.* €€ 40 rue Notre-Dame-des-Victoires (M° Bourse), 01.42.36.45.38, brasseriegallopin.com

Le Grand Véfour • 1st • Gastronomic
Dining at this breathtakingly beautiful historical gem is one of the most romantic experiences Paris has to offer. Secreted in the shady cloisters of the Palais-Royal, it has been here since before the French Revolution. In those days it was a café; now it is one of the world's great haute cuisine restaurants. If you don't want to blow €200 on one meal, come at lunchtime and order the prix fixe. You won't experience the soaring heights of Guy Martin's cuisine, but the superlative service, the jewel-box décor, and the little extras are still there. This chef is an artist when it comes to presentation, layering ingredients and studding them with caviar or truffles, which are more prevalent in the à la carte offerings. The room is a feast for the eyes, with gilt mirrors between panels painted with classical motifs. Each table is named after a famous guest. Ask for Victor Hugo's table, which has a view over the gardens as well as the interior. *Mon-Thu 12:30-1:30pm and 8-9:30pm, Fri 12:30-2pm.* €€€€ 17 rue de Beaujolais (M° Palais Royal-Musée du Louvre), 01.42.96.56.27, relaischateaux.com

Le Jardin de Varenne • 7th • Café
Bordered by chestnut trees, in the Musée Rodin's sculpture garden, is this delightful café. In fine weather, the terrace is especially enjoyable. Come early for breakfast when there's hardly anyone here and you can hear birdsong in central Paris. Breakfast offerings are simple—tea, coffee, hot chocolate, croissants, pains au chocolat—but it's worth forgoing eggs and bacon for the setting. At lunchtime, there is a fuller menu of salads, bruschetta, antipasti, and a daily hot special. One of the secrets Paris knows best how to keep. *Tue-Sun Apr-Sept 9:30am-5:45pm; Oct-Mar 9:30am-4:30pm. Entry to garden without museum €1.* €- Musée Rodin, 77 rue de Varenne (M° Varenne), 01.44.18.61.10

Ladurée • 6th • Tearoom
Pâtissier Ladurée was the first to open a tearoom in Paris, in 1862, its novelty being that women could come here without shaming their reputation (the cafés were the notorious haunt of courtesans). The original branch, on rue Royale near the Madeleine, and the second, large one on the Champs-Elysées, both have stupendous décor but can be very crowded. The St-Germain branch, opened in

1947, is more conducive to a tête-à-tête, offering a choice of the light-filled veranda, elegant upstairs dining room, or decadent Prussian-blue salon. The family was also the inventor of the macaroon, sugary rounds with a cream filling that come in a rainbow of colors and flavors. Lunchtime delicacies include luxury omelettes, lamb cutlets, red mullet, and large salads, and afternoon tea is otherworldly. *Daily 8:30am-7:30pm.* € 21 rue Bonaparte (M° Mabillon), 01.44.07.64.87, laduree.fr

Lapérouse • 6th • Gastronomic
The upstairs private salons of this historic restaurant no longer lock from the inside (Paris has other addresses for that kind of mischief), but they still retain a sexy allure. This is where writers and politicians used to rendezvous with their mistresses. Romantic couples are in their element—they say the scratches in the mirrors are from ladies testing the quality of their rocks before saying yes. Much, anyway, can be divined from the choice of table—either in the small rooms with red divans, the larger ones with a view over the Seine, or the more animated downstairs dining room. While the low-ceilinged rooms with mahogany paneling and oil paintings are like museum pieces, the chef takes a refreshingly modern approach to French classic cooking. End with the soufflé Lapérouse, with a hot wild raspberry sauce—definitely a passion-stoker. Despite the good-value lunch menu, it is worth waiting till after dark for the candlelit ambiance here. *Mon-Fri 12:30-2:30pm and 7:30-10:30pm, Sat 7:30-10:30pm.* €€€€ 41 quai des Grands Augustins (M° Cité), 01.43.26.68.04

Macéo • 2nd • Contemporary
Sax maestro Macéo Parker is honored in the name of this buzzing contemporary restaurant, and suave jazz background music contributes to the mood. It attracts youngish English- and French-speaking professionals who love the tasty modern cuisine. The setting is atmospheric, whether you snag a window seat in the high-ceilinged Second Empire ballroom with sculpted naked ladies adorned by vines or choose the more contemporary Palais Royal room with light wood paneling and wicker chairs. The food is lovely, from the homemade foie gras with date and mango chutney to cumin-baked piglet cheeks with crunchy fennel and raisin caramel. Desserts are sumptuous. Afterward retire to the cozy bar for a drink. *Mon-Fri noon-2:30pm and 7:30-11pm, Sat 7:30-11pm.* €€ 15 rue des Petits Champs (M° Pyramides), 01.42.97.53.85, maceorestaurant.com

Maxim's • 8th • Traditional
The legendary restaurant is bridging the centuries in an extraordinary way. First, there is the restaurant experience, set in one of its stunning Belle Epoque rooms that are all red velvet and billowing furbelows. Far from being a fusty museum-piece, the place still throngs with European and entertainment royalty. The patrons may be on the mature side, aside from those entertaining their "nieces," but the old-style service, decent food, and pure drama of the setting make this an atmospheric and highly romantic dinner option. Suit and tie for men is obligatory. Then there are the soirées orchestrated by fin-de-siècle fan and owner Pierre Cardin. Every last Friday of the month, Maxim's re-creates a 1900s cabaret with gypsy violinists, the songs of Yvette Guilbert, a supper of fin-de-siècle dishes and dancing to an orchestra, which nostalgists of all ages turn up to in evening dress. Shooting right into the 21st century, private promoters have started to throw wild one-off parties here. These aren't advertised

ROMANTIC • RESTAURANTS

on Maxim's website, but if you see a late crowd at the door, try your luck. *Tue-Thu 12:30-2pm and 7:30-10pm, Fri-Sat 7:30-10:30pm.* €€€€ 3 rue Royale (M° Concorde), 01.42.65.27.94, maxims-de-paris.com

Mon Vieil Ami • 4th • Contemporary
If you're looking for somewhere to eat on this lovely island, this is the address on everyone's lips. Other places may foster romance with candlelit tables, but here in starred chef Antoine Westerman's stone-walled, beamed bistro, the loving's gone into the cooking. You'll find young international food-lovers rather than indifferent tourists at nearby tables. Anthony Clémot executes Alsatian-influenced dishes such as caramelized choucroute with pork-stuffed chicken, slow-braised shoulder of roebuck with chestnuts and quince, and updated grandma's pantry desserts. Be sure to reserve. *Wed-Sun 11:30am-2:30pm and 8-10:30pm.* €€ 69 rue St-Louis-en-l'Ile (M° Pont Marie), 01.40.46.01.35

Le Palanquin • 6th • Vietnamese
France's long history with Southeast Asia means Paris is one of the best places outside the Far East to taste the fresh herb-and-vegetable-infused food of Vietnam. Palanquin is also a little oasis where you'll never be rushed and the service is always gracious. The dark interior is decorated with wood and stones, and gentle music slows things down, promoting a feeling of well-being even before the food arrives. The specialties are the thing to go for: tamarind soup with prawns and gentle spices, green papaya salad with green herbs, and prawns cooked with sugar canes. The nems are considered to be among the best in Paris, and the moist coconut cakes are not to be missed. You'll find yourself eating among an elegant crowd of St-Germainites—editors, writers, and actors are frequent guests. *Mon 7:30-10:30pm, Tue-Sat noon-2:30pm and 7:30-10:30pm.* € 12 rue Princesse (M° Mabillon), 01.43.29.77.66, lepalanquin.com

Pétrelle • 9th • Contemporary
This is an address few people know about, but once you've discovered it, you'll be passing it on to the favored few. Among the cognoscenti are fashion designers and film stars, but still they keep it under their hats. Nighttime is the best time to come, as the romantic appeal of the dining room comes into its own in candlelight. It is decorated with eclectic flea-market finds that give it a theatrical edge and make you feel like you're in an arty friend's living room. So fascinating are the antique prints, old guides, and cookbooks that you might forget to study the menu, but you're sure to be pleased by anything you order. Seasonal foods combine to form dishes like the rosemary-scented rabbit with roasted vegetables, and unforgettable wine-poached figs. *Tue-Sat 8-10pm.* €€ 34 rue Pétrelle (M° Anvers), 01.42.82.11.02

Pomze • 8th • Contemporary
Toffee apples in French are called *pommes d'amour* (apples of love), and it's likely you'll fall for this apple-themed restaurant. It's a simple concept but executed with style. A 19th-century apartment has been converted into a restaurant with white-painted rooms decorated only with arty black-and-white photographs of apple producers in their fields. Downstairs is the gourmet shop, stocking all sorts of varieties of apples, cider, and preserves, and in the basement is a fumoir-style bar. What really gets the juices flowing is the superb cuisine, where the apple doesn't dominate but enhances the main ingredients. The

menu changes according to produce and apple varieties, but if you are here in autumn you can taste the unforgettable quail stuffed with apple, sultanas, and tiny green beans. Background jazz adds the urbane touch that completes the homely apple's image makeover. *Mon-Fri 8am-11pm, Sat 9am-11pm.* €€ 109 bd. Haussmann (M° Miromesnil), 01.42.65.65.83, pomze.com

Le Pré Catelan • Bois de Boulogne • Gastronomic

The Pré Catelan provokes that feeling of "what did I do to deserve this?"—in the best possible way. As your taxi rolls up to the mansion in the forest, staff rush to open the door and usher you to your table, which will either be in the Belle Epoque dining room or the garden dining room under festive sunshades. The house itself, which glories in a roaring fire in winter, is pleasant in summer too as the French windows are thrown open to let in the garden light. Champagne and refined appetizers arrive as you pick from the minimalist menu. On weekdays at lunch there is a good-value prix fixe. The chef goes in for one-word dishes: the Sardine, the Pigeon, the Chocolate. If the idea of ordering a sardine for €52 gives you pause, have confidence—the food is sexy. Linger over coffee and sweets, as this is heaven on a plate. *Tue-Sat noon-1:45pm and 7:30-9:30pm. Sunday lunch from May-Oct.* €€€€ Route de Suresnes, Bois de Boulogne (M° Porte Maillot then taxi), 01.44.14.41.14, lenotre.fr

R • 15th • Contemporary

Best Eiffel Tower Views It's a wonderful surprise to emerge from the elevator into this penthouse restaurant with a view of the Eiffel Tower. And it's not just the panorama that demands praise. The service is warm, the décor cool, and the food something to behold. Ask to be seated at the window or in the glassed-in, white clapboard terrace. In the main room, a young, hip crowd mixes with older out-of-towners tipped off by their hotel concierge. Choose from Asian-influenced starters such as the cylinder of crab topped with pickled cucumber and flanked by an artistic swirl of mango, or foie gras. The chef's special is like a piece of primitive art: a slab of juicy cod served on a stone from Brittany. As the evening progresses, the sun sets over the tower and suddenly, whoosh, she starts to sparkle. More hipsters arrive after midnight Thursday-Saturday when DJs mix electro-house in the lounge-bar area. *Mon-Sat 8-11pm. Bar open till 2am (6am Sat).* €€ 8 rue de la Cavalerie, 8th fl. (M° La Motte-Picquet Grenelle), 01.45.67.06.85, le-r.com

Le Réminet • 5th • Bistro

Through a velvet curtain on this pretty street is a stone-walled room with only eight crisp, white-clothed tables, the largest of which seats six. The fact that it's in the heart of a tourist area and serves excellent food means you have to reserve in advance, but do, as this is one of the most romantic little spots in the area. Locals of all ages come back time and time again. The elevated bistro food is wonderful and beautifully presented. Examples are the whiting served on a bed of moist eggplant, or guinea fowl in a cream sauce. For a romantic bistro meal by candlelight you can't do better than this. *Thu-Sun noon-2pm and 7:30-11pm.* € 3 rue des Grands-Degrès (M° Maubert-Mutualité), 01.44.07.04.24

Le Restaurant du Palais Royal • 1st • Contemporary

With its terrace tables in the cloisters overlooking the formal gardens of the Palais-Royal, this is one of the most magical and most Parisian places to dine.

ROMANTIC • RESTAURANTS

This is particularly the case in the evening when the gardens are closed to the public, lending the experience an air of exclusivity. Romancing couples share the space with officials from the Ministry of Culture who are lucky enough to work nearby. It's the garden that makes it extra-special, although the red, contemporary dining room, lit by low-standing lamps and candles, is just fine if you get a window-side table. Chef Bruno Hees serves up delicious Mediterranean cuisine. *Mon-Sat 12:15-2:15pm and 7:15-10pm.* €€ ▄ 110 galerie Valois (M° Bourse), 01.40.20.00.27

Le Salon d'Hélène • 6th • Contemporary
Haute cuisine chef Hélène Darroze has opened this more chilled-out salon downstairs from her gastronomic restaurant. Its low seating scattered with colorful cushions makes it the perfect place to get cozy, and the tapas-style menu promotes intimate eating as you can order many dishes to share. With a lower price tag, it also attracts younger, trendier patrons. This is French-style tapas, with a southwestern slant, so count on lots of foie gras and mushrooms. Try the raw marinated tuna with red-pepper sauce or Landaise daube of mushrooms and pasta baked with duck foie gras. Leave room for dessert, as these are delicious. Note that service can be slow. *Tue 7:30-10:15pm, Wed-Sat 12:30-2pm and 7:30-10:15pm.* €€ ▄ 4 rue d'Assas (M° Sèvres-Babylone), 01.42.22.00.11

Senso • 8th • Contemporary
Terence Conran's second Paris restaurant eschews his open-kitchen style in favor of an intimate Haussmannian dining room. Gray walls and ivory columns and chairs are punctuated by splashes of red in the artwork and flowers. A good-value set menu pulls in a business clientele at lunch, but it's more seductive in the evening, when it was picked for the classic first-date scene in the hit French movie *Mensonges et Trahisons* (in which the couple leave to have sex before returning to the restaurant). The modern European cooking encompasses a panaché of vegetables, a copious rocket and parmesan salad, and sea bream wrapped around a skewer of dried fennel. Desserts are disappointing. *Daily noon-2:30pm and 7-10:45pm.* €€ ▄ Hôtel Trémoille, 16 rue de la Trémoille (M° Franklin D. Roosevelt), 01.56.52.14.14, hotel-tremoille.com

Au Vieux Colombier • 6th • Café
A gorgeous old-style café that's perfect from breakfast until late-night. *See Romantic Nightlife, p.170, for details.* € ▄ 65 rue de Rennes (M° St-Sulpice), 01.45.48.53.81

Le Ziryab • 5th • North African
Best North African Dining At the top of the Institut du Monde Arabe is Paris' most elegant North African restaurant, housed in a spacious penthouse with a panoramic view over the Seine and as far as the Sacré-Coeur. Ask for a window seat, and come at night, when the scene is lit up by passing bateaux-mouches. Thick white tablecloths and red lamps make for a calm, contemporary setting, where grown-up, cosmopolitan diners enjoy the superior take on traditional Moroccan cuisine. Start with the mixed meze, and follow with one of the excellent tagines. The minty fruit salad with green tea ice cream is a refreshing end to the meal, or you can finish with mint tea and pastries. *Tue-Sat noon-2pm and 7:30-midnight, Sun noon-2pm.* €€ ▄ Institut du Monde Arabe, 9th fl., 1 rue des Fossés St-Bernard (M° Jussieu), 01.53.10.10.16, imarabe.org

Romantic Paris:
The Nightlife

La Balle au Bond* • 5th and 6th • Restaurant/Jazz Club
This boat moored on the banks of the Seine hosts concerts of jazz, pop, chanson, rock, punk, or bossa nova depending on the day. *See Romantic Restaurants, p.158, for details. Concerts daily at 9pm.* Apr-Sept facing the Louvre, on quai Malaquais (M° St-Germain-des-Prés); Oct-Mar (concerts only) facing Notre-Dame, on quai de la Tournelle (M° Maubert-Mutualité), 01.40.46.85.12, laballeaubond.fr

Bar Fontainebleau • 1st • Hotel Bar
Best Classic Hotel Bars The most beautiful bar in Paris is in the Hôtel Meurice. By dim candlelight akin to that of an Italian church, you can make out exquisite 19th-century frescos of the Forest of Fontainebleau, while peachy clouds soar above on the ceiling, so it's no surprise that dapper young Parisians bring their dates here to start an evening of seduction. One side is open to the Winter Garden where a pianist tinkles jazz. The Sicilian bartender is a gent of the old school. You won't find many innovations here, though the Meurice Millennium mix of rosé Champagne, rose liqueur, and Cointreau tastes as good as it looks. Discretion is what it's all about—yes, you may see a famous face or two, but nobody will bat an eyelid. Once cosseted here, you may want to stay all night. *Daily noon-2am.* Hôtel Meurice, 228 rue de Rivoli (M° Concorde), 01.44.58.10.10, meuricehotel.com

Bateau Concorde Atlantique • 7th • Dance Club
When other clubs close down for the summer, the action moves to this waterborne club on a canalboat. Cocktails on deck, under the Paris moon, are romantic in the extreme and you may not even feel the need to delve down below where the large dance floor fills up quickly with a young, fun-loving crowd. The music is mainly house, and Wednesday night's Respect draws anyone who's fashionably blasé about being in Paris in July and August. The Sunday morning after-party Terrassa also courts an Ibiza-style ambiance. The good news is that the fun starts early with cocktails served starting at 7pm on summer nights. In winter it's more likely to be used for private parties. *Daily 7pm-5am or 6am.* Opposite 23 quai Anatole France (M° Assemblée Nationale), 01.47.05.71.03, concorde-atlantique.com

Botak Café • 18th • Café
This laid-back café is one of three with terraces on the delectable Place Utrillo. Virtually unknown to the tourist hordes, this shady little square is reached by steps down the eastern side of Sacré-Coeur with a vertiginously steep park to the right, which, if you can avoid slipping down it, is a nice place to lounge on the grass. Botak Café, attracting a hip local crowd, is lovely for breakfast, lunch, or dinner and stays open till 2am. Huge salads, chicken and chips, or beef tartare are the order of the day. Friendly service, great mojitos, and only a few tables—but you can spill over onto the square. *Daily 10am-2am.* 1 rue Paul Albert (M° Anvers), 01.46.06.98.30, botak-cafe.com

ROMANTIC • NIGHTLIFE

Buddha Bar • 8th • Lounge Bar/Restaurant
Impressive though its décor is—and the food's not bad either—the overhyped Buddha Bar can be exasperating if you book a table to eat. Walkie-talkies galore and a charge for the coat check when you're spending €70 a head sends the zen meter down to zero. The mezzanine cocktail lounge, however, is a seductive alternative. Seated in near darkness on low colonial furniture in alcoves, you can enjoy being cocooned with your beloved and an exotic cocktail, with a ringside seat on all the action below. Groove to the Eastern-influenced lounge music that made this place famous. Great for a smoochy after-hours drink if you're in the area. *Daily noon-3pm and 4pm-2am.* 8 bis rue Boissy d'Anglas (M° Concorde), 01.53.05.90.00, buddhabar.com

Café de la Mairie • 6th • Café
The point and the whole point is to sit on the terrace overlooking St-Sulpice and its fountain, lit up at night to look like a Roman palazzo. Although the selection of wines, beers, spirits, and coffee isn't especially memorable, the view is sublime, and it's just the spot for post-dinner lingering on the Left Bank. In winter the interior has zinc bar appeal and the full gamut of eccentric characters if you like that kind of thing. *Mon-Fri 7am-2am, Sat 8am-2am, Sun 9am-9pm.* 8 pl. St-Sulpice (M° St-Sulpice), 01.43.26.67.82

Café de la Paix • 9th • Café
Rising like the phantom of the opera from its decorative overhaul is the glittering Café de la Paix. Distinguished operagoers. awestruck foreigners, and ladies who lunch and buy baubles at the Galeries Lafayette crowd in to the rejuvenated Napoléon III interior. The painted clouds on the ceiling panels are fluffier, the marble is more polished, even the palms seem to have been on a tropical holiday (and the waiters, perhaps). Get a table in the glassed-in terrace to watch the world gliding by as you sip Champagne, before or after the opera. Delicious pastries and luxury lunch snacks are also a delightful treat in this supreme setting. *Daily 7:30am-midnight.* 12 bd. des Capucines (M° Opéra), 01.40.07.30.20, paris-le-grand.intercontinental.com

Champagne Bar at Le Dokhan's • 16th • Hotel Bar
This discreet hotel has a secret that is open to non-guests: its candlelit Champagne bar. With its original verdigris paneling delicately edged in gold leaf, antique wall sconces, and chandeliers, the room is a step back in time to a more refined age that attracts romantic couples and wine connoisseurs. The bar takes its mission seriously—this is the place to discover unknown and rare Champagnes. Each Thursday a choice of three recommendations are available for tasting, often with an enologist on hand. But it's the ambiance that is most exceptional. The manager has organized a series of musical evenings that recreate the atmosphere of a salon. Jazz musicians, string quartets, and opera singers are invited to give a private performance to a select few. And to enhance your Champagne sipping, there is a menu of what could be called the foods of love—smoked salmon, caviar, and foie gras. *Daily 6pm-2am.* Trocadéro Dokhan's, 117 rue Lauriston (M° Boissière), 01.53.65.66.99, dokhans.com

Le Defender • 1st • Hotel Bar
Le Defender defines a lot of what is great about hotel bars. It's got a monumental décor of palms and gold-flecked pillars, amazing cocktails, and an eclectic

clientele ranging from ancient and Japanese hotel guests to the trendy local intellectuals who have recently colonized it. Johann Burgos, a former second at the Ritz, was largely responsible for its rise to fashion status, and now his successor, Vincent Girault, is carrying on the creative mixology. So sink into one of the enormous brocade sofas under the red lacquer ceiling and wait for him to work his magic. There is the bare minimum of classics on the menu—you are encouraged to name your spirit and tastes of choice. The disco soundtrack is a little upbeat for this low-key, intellectual locale, though it fills up with a fashionable crowd after dinner. *Daily 10am-1am.* Hôtel du Louvre, pl. André Malraux (M° Palais Royal-Musée du Louvre), 01.44.58.37.89, hoteldulouvre.com

Le Divan du Monde • 18th • Dance Club
This is the original Divan Japonais, drawn by Toulouse-Lautrec and frequented by Baudelaire and Picasso. It's now a hipster bar and live music venue that, if you strike on the right night, can be an enjoyable place to chill out to music, dance, and meet the new bohemians of Montmartre. On the stage of the main room from 7-11pm there's live music ranging from insane gypsy orchestras (great) to gentle chanson (great) by way of emerging French rock (not so great perhaps). Then the action moves up to the mezzanine bar, recognizable from Lautrec's famous poster, with a Gaudí-inspired metal bar and candles on the tables. Video art is projected onto screens lowered from the ceiling that curtain this area from the dance floor below. Most nights a dance party takes place midnight-6am. You never know what you're going to get here; it's worth taking a chance on it. *Thu-Sat 7pm-6am, though hours can vary.* 75 rue des Martyrs (M° Pigalle), 01.40.05.06.99, divandumonde.com

Le Doudingue* • 18th • Bar/Restaurant
A cozy Montmartre-style lounge where you can interact with the musicians and artists who are regulars. *See Romantic Restaurants, p.160, for details.* 24 rue Durantin (M° Abbesses), 01.42.54.88.08

L'Echelle de Jacob • 6th • Lounge Bar
Under a name synonymous with the the jazzy, existentialist hipsters of St-Germain in the '50s, a new lounge bar has opened and quite a few of Paris' "in" people have walked through its door. In a golden, vaguely Asian décor with a blackamoor candelabra and candles everywhere, Left Bank sophisticates lounge on sofas and choose from the 217 cocktails on the list. Lanterns light the way up the staircase (from whence it gets its name) to the seductive second floor. Excellent lounge music sets the mood. Ideal for a nightcap. *Daily 7pm-4am.* 12 rue Jacob (M° Mabillon), 01.46.34.00.29

Le Jaipur • 8th • Hotel Bar
Le Jaipur transports you to another realm. You could indeed be in Jaipur or in Shangri-la, as you are lulled by piped Indian music and sink into soft cushions, surrounded by elephant prints. This soporific land that time forgot is ideal for couples, though singles will also find it's easy to get into conversation with the attractive 30-something barflies here. If you are lost for something to say, the cocktail menu provides plenty of inspiration with its outlandish offerings featuring herbs and spices. As well as the suggested concoctions (number 6, the refreshing apple, cinnamon, vodka and pepper, is good, though some lack the expected bite or sufficient sugar), you can play Russian roulette with a menu of

ingredients (sage and blueberry, chili and rum, anyone?), mixed by a laconic bartender. Otherwise go for the large selection of single malts. *Daily noon-3pm and 6pm-1am.* Hôtel Vernet, 25 rue Vernet (M° George V), 01.44.31.98.06, hotelvernet.com

Man Ray • 8th • Restaurant/Club
This contemporary of the Buddha Bar with a similarly opulent Asian décor and photos by Man Ray has managed to buck the trends and keep out the tour groups. It remains one of the best lounge bars in the capital, but don't think of eating here as the food is universally bland. The clientele is largely international, with smart French habitués of the Elysées popping in for an after-work cocktail on the mezzanine. On weekends the dining tables are moved to the periphery around midnight, opening up a fabulous dance floor with plenty of places for sitting one out or sipping drinks. Themed evenings include opera on Mondays, jazz on Thursdays, and some great club nights on Fridays and Saturdays. The close of the prêt-à-porter fashion collections (January, March, July, and October) is celebrated with model-friendly Don't Tell My Booker. *Mon-Sat 6pm-2am.* bar free. 34 rue Marbeuf (M° Franklin D. Roosevelt), 01.56.88.36.36, manray.fr

Mezzanine de l'Alcazar • 6th • Lounge Bar
Best Lounge Bars Terence Conran's reworking of the historic Alcazar brasserie into a minimalist "gastrodrome" is a big success. Business lunches, Sunday brunches complete with a free masseur, and dinner, attracting Eurostar weekenders, are all popular, though you can get better French cuisine elsewhere. Upstairs, the Mezzanine bar has carved out a niche as one of the finest lounge bars in the capital, with high-quality sounds from invited DJs from both sides of La Manche. Like Man Ray, it also has its own series of compilations. Chilled-out sounds start the week on Wednesday, moving through soul, funk, hip-hop, and groove on Thursday to dance-floor Saturday house and disco, though truth be told, most of the groovers here are too cool to dance. Beautiful people lounge on the taupe banquettes or lean nonchalantly on the balcony, surveying the more frenetic scene in the open-plan dining area below. After 2am you can get more energetic at Le Wagg in the basement. *Daily 7pm-2am.* 62 rue Mazarine (M° Odéon), 01.53.10.19.99, alcazar.com

Opéra National de Paris Palais Garnier • 9th • Opera House
Paris' grand opera house was the crowning glory of the Haussmann building program, a see-and-be-seen palace for the late-19th-century bourgeoisie. Its sweeping marble staircase adorned with statues, splendid bar, and balustrades on every floor for surveying the scene provide as much theater as the stage, and even many of the seats offer a better view of the audience than the show. The opera boxes that fill all but the front stalls and the top floor form little red velvet boxes that, once closed, can only be opened from the inside (more prosaically you often have to share these with other people). The Opéra de Paris shares its lyric and ballet performances between here and the modern Opéra Bastille, but for romantic value this is by far the better experience. *Performance days vary, 7:30pm and Sun 2:30pm. Guided tours in English Tue-Sun 1pm and 2pm.* for tour and for tickets. Pl. de l'Opéra (M° Opéra), box office 08.36.69.78.68, guided tours 01.40.01.22.63, opera-de-paris.fr

Summer dancing by the Seine • 5th • Dance Scene
Starting around 6pm and going late into the night, music floats across the Seine—tango, salsa, rock 'n' roll, African, Greek even—drawing eager dance enthusiasts to this riverside scene. It's not clear how it started, but dancing in the alcoves of the Jardins Tino-Rossi sculpture park has become a summer craze, attracting thousands of people on weekends. Each group brings its own music system and some provide lessons at the start of the evening. A free expression of joie de vivre that has to be seen to be believed. *June-Sept daily from 6pm.* Jardins Tino-Rossi, quai St-Bernard (M° Jussieu)

Au Vieux Colombier • 6th • Café
A shopper's pit stop and girly gossip shop by day, a rendezvous for the pre-theater crowd by night, this gorgeous old-style café is the perfect place for an apéritif or late-night drink near St-Sulpice. If you're here by day, the lasagna and crôque-monsieur served with copious green salad are a treat. The staff are incredibly good-natured, never rushing you from your table or complaining about the shopping bags that fill every last space. At night, get a table behind the attractive Art Nouveau windows for a view of the world going by as you soak up the atmosphere with a bottle of wine or a kir amid the young Left Bank couples and groups of friends. After a stop here, you'll only wish there were more places like this. *Mon-Sat 8am-1am, Sun 11am-8pm.* 65 rue de Rennes (M° St-Sulpice), 01.45.48.53.81

Le Wagg • 6th • Dance Club
Just about the only club worth its salt on the Left Bank, Le Wagg takes over where the Mezzanine de l'Alcazar leaves off, drawing a happy dance crowd. The low-ceilinged stone vaults are equipped with slinky alcoves and Conran seating and the lighting effects and sound are good. No longer stuck in the house groove, Le Wagg also programs funk and disco, with Carwash every Friday night attracting big crowds to boogie the night away in colored Afro wigs. On Sundays salsa fans descend for the Cuban beats. Those on the trail of Jim Morrison will be interested to know this was the site of the old Whisky A Go-Go, but those dissolute days are long gone. *Fri-Sat 11:30pm-6am, Sun 3pm-midnight.* 62 rue Mazarine (M° Odéon), 01.55.42.22.01, wagg.fr

Romantic Paris: The Attractions

4 Roues sous 1 Parapluie • Various • Guided Tours
Best Guided Tours Cuddle up in the back seat of a chauffeur-driven Citroën 2CV as you tour the sights of the most beautiful city in the world. Nicknamed "the love bug," the Citroën 2CV is a French icon that sealed many a romance in the '50s and '60s. Florent Dargnies, the very model of a dashing Frenchman, had the bright idea of putting them back on the road for guided tours, and even Parisians have been booking the retro trip. A team of skilled drivers in jaunty cloth caps will take you on the Classic (1.5 hr.) or Magic (3 hr.) tour, or they can devise a route to suit you. They'll even drive you out to Versailles if you wish, and will pick you up at your hotel or any other convenient spot. *Daily, Classic tours: 9 and 11am, 1, 3, 8 and 10pm; Magic tours: 9:30am, 1:30 and 8:30pm.* €€€€ 08.00.80.06.31 (free phone from within France), 06.67.32.26.68, 4roues-sous-1parapluie.com

Les Bains du Montorgueil • 2nd • Spa
A sensuous spa experience awaits at this exceptional spot, a private hammam (steam bath) that has been opened up to the public. It is decorated with the finest materials by artisans from Morocco: jewel-colored mosaic and zélig tiles, tadelakt walls, and hand-carved moldings and fountains. A love poem in Arabic unfolds around the steam bath; the showers have aquariums in the walls, and there is a refreshing icy plunge pool surrounded by scattered rose petals. The hammam serves a maximum of 10, and is normally exclusive to women, but couples can reserve it for three hours at a time. Ask for the "Formule Mille et Une Nuits" where for an all-inclusive price of €400 you'll have the privacy of the spa together with exfoliations and massages. To ease you back into reality you'll be brought a bottle of Champagne, fruit, and pastries. *Tue-Sun 11am-9pm.* €€€€ 55 rue Montorgueil (M° Etienne-Marcel), 01.44.88.01.78

Le Ballon Eutelsat • 15th • Activity
Weather permitting, the Eutelsat balloon gently ascends and descends from its mooring in the Parc André Citroën with passengers in its huge basket, offering an amazing panoramic view of up to 25 miles in any direction. It reaches 500 feet—the same height as level two of the Eiffel Tower but is a far more zen-like experience. Hot-air balloons have a fascinating link with the history of Paris. The first one was invented here before the French Revolution, and during the Prussian siege in 1870 a politician called Gambetta made a spectacular exit from the city in a balloon. *Daily 9am-30 mins before park closing (varies).* €– Parc André-Citroën (M° Balard), 01.44.26.20.00, aeroparis.com

Bois de Boulogne • Bois de Boulogne • Park
It is worth taking an afternoon out to explore this 2,000-acre former hunting forest to the west of the 16th arrondissement. It's so huge that it's easy to feel far from the madding crowd here, whether you are tramping through the woods, boating on one of its lakes, or simply lazing in the long grass. Bikes can be rented and cycle paths are marked. The Lac Inférieur is one of the prettiest spots,

and located within walking distance from the metro stop La Muette. Grottoes and waterfalls have been created around it and one of its two islands contains the restaurant Chalet des Iles. Further west is the Pré Catelan, known for its gastronomic restaurant and gardens themed around Shakespeare plays. Further in is the Parc de Bagatelle, which surrounds a chateau with a rose garden and orangerie that hosts a summer Chopin festival. At night, it is the haunt of transsexuals working out of camper vans, so be prepared for a show if you're taking a taxi back from one of the restaurants. *24/7.* M° Porte Maillot, La Muette, or Porte d'Auteuil. Bike rentals from the Cyclobus at Porte d'Auteuil bus station (M° Avenue Henri Martin) on Sundays

La Collection 1900 • 8th • Museum

Fashion designer Pierre Cardin shows off his collection of Art Nouveau objects in the rooms above Maxim's. This intimate tour, led by an Art Nouveau expert, is like no other. Visitors are immersed in the world of a 1900s courtesan's boudoir, as room after room is filled with dreamy porcelain nymphs and dragonflies, Tiffany lamps, beds inlaid with marquetry opium flowers, and Gustav Eiffel's own dinner set, which looks just right for serving up turtle soup to a gathering of aristocrats, artists, and painted ladies. The Belle Epoque courtesans may have been selling their favors to the highest bidder, but they did it with the most exquisite taste. On Tuesdays and Saturdays you can follow the visit with a light meal and performance of opera classics. *Wed-Sun guided tour in English 2pm or by appointment, in French 3:15 and 4:30pm.* € Maxim's, 3 rue Royale (M° Concorde), 01.42.65.30.47, maxims-musee.artnouveau.com

Covered passages • 2nd, 9th, and 10th • Walk

In the 19th century, shopping was not a pleasant experience (who's to say it is now, but hey, at least you don't get a chamber pot emptied on your wig while you're browsing). Paris' elegant solution was to build glass-covered shopping streets, which are now one of its architectural treasures. Though many of the covered passages have been lost to history, 20 or so remain. Just north of Palais Royal, galerie Vivienne is the most stylish, now colonized by fashionable boutiques as well as wine merchant Legrand Filles et Fils and the tearoom A Priori Thé. Next door is Galerie Colbert with the brasserie Le Grand Colbert. Nearby is Galerie Véro-Dodat, housing toy shops and swank makeup shop By Terry. Further north, Passage Jouffroy and Passage des Panoramas have lots of eccentricity, with antiquarian books, philatelists, toys and fossils, and old-world printers Mercier and Stern. Galerie Vivienne, Galerie Colbert, 2nd (M° Bourse); Galerie Véro-Dodat (M° Palais Royal-Musée du Louvre), 2nd; Passage des Panoramas, 2nd, Passage Jouffroy, 9th (M° Grands Boulevards); parisinconnu.com/passages

L'Eclaireur • 1st • Store

L'Eclaireur's universe of tactile natural fabrics, minimalist furniture combined with sheepskin or hand-knitted throws, unusual ceramics, and deliciously scented candles just makes you want to move in. The Palais Royal store is arranged like an apartment with the bedroom upstairs and tableware and a small selection of fashion and jewelry downstairs. The two Marais stores are more fashion-based, with the jewelry on rue des Rosiers well worth a look and the menswear store stocking an exclusive collection designed by John Malkovich. Rue Hérold is another fantasy realm in a warehouse space, where a peacock stands on a plinth near rows of deconstructed linen jackets. *Mon-Sat 11am-7pm.*

131 galerie de Valois, Jardin du Palais Royal (M° Palais Royal-Musée du Louvre), 1st, 01.40.20.42.52, leclaireur.com. Other stores: 12 rue Mahler (menswear), 4th; 3 rue des Rosiers (clothes, décor, and design), 4th; 10 rue Hérold (gallery space), 1st, 26 av. des Champs-Elysées

L'Espace Bien-Etre at the Meurice • 1st • Spa

Best Spas In 1993 a professor in Bordeaux revealed a remarkable discovery to the winemakers at the Château Smith Haut Lafitte: grape seeds contain polyphenols that are a powerful combatant of the free radicals that age the skin. They patented the method of emulsifying them into lotions. Today, the Hôtel Meurice contains an exclusive Caudalie spa in Paris. At the Espace Bien-Etre vines grow in a little garden, where you can relax after your treatments. The large Jacuzzi is a wonderful place to unwind, flanked by a sauna and steam room, and there is a small gym. Various packages are on offer, lasting from 2 hours to a complete day, and include anti-aging treatments and relaxing massages. The Pulp Friction full-body massage using fresh grapes is positively Bacchanalian (reserve 24 hours in advance). *Daily 7:30am-10pm; treatments 9am-8pm.* €€€€ Hôtel Meurice, 228 rue de Rivoli (M° Concorde), 01.44.58.10.77, meuricehotel.com

Fauchon • 8th • Store

Auguste Fauchon started out selling vegetables from a cart on Place de la Madeleine in 1885. A year later he'd opened a delicatessen, whose "five o'clock tea" (the phrase was emblazoned in English) became a fashionable rendezvous. Now, with its rival and neighbor Hédiard, it's as much a monument on this square as the Madeleine itself. With their new black and pink makeover, Fauchon's windows look like chocolate boxes, precursors to the delicacies within, which run from confectionary to wines to high-class deli fare (canapés like works of art, strawberry-studded foie gras, caviar …). Everything is packaged in chic boxes, making it the next best thing to a diamond ring. *Mon-Sat 9:30am-8pm.* 26-30 pl. de la Madeleine (M° Madeleine), 01.47.42.60.11, fauchon.com

Ile St-Louis • 4th • Island

The smaller island in the Seine, joined by bridges to the Ile de la Cité and the Right and Left Banks, is a peaceful haven for walking around as, with the exception of some gift and gourmet food shops on the main rue St-Louis-en-l'Ile, it is mainly residential. The island was mainly built up from the 1630s to the 1660s and contains some magnificent private residences. On the quai d'Anjou, plaques recount the many famous people who once lived here, including, at #17, the poet Baudelaire. The island has one exceptional restaurant, Mon Vieil Ami, and the famous Berthillon ice cream shop at 31 rue St-Louis-en-l'Ile—you'll recognize it by the line stretching out the door. *Shops generally open Mon-Sat 11am-7pm, Sun noon-7pm.* Rue St-Louis-en-l'Ile, quai d'Anjou, quai d'Orléans (M° Pont Marie)

Jardin du Luxembourg • 6th • Park

Best Parks The most Parisian of the city's parks, this is where you'll find intellectuals playing chess, blue-rinsed ladies walking their dogs, lovers kissing by the fountain, dreamers dreaming, and seducers trying out the oldest lines in the book. The Italianate landscaping dates from Marie de Medici, who had the palace and gardens built in the 1620s. The palace is now home to the French Senate. There's still something aristocratic about the park, whose tennis courts draw chic players and where children play with old-fashioned sailing boats on the pond. The Fontaine de Medici is a well-known lovers' tryst, and the café is a real delight. *Daily 7:30am (summer), 8:15am (winter); closing 4:30-9pm according to season.* Rue de Vaugirard, pl. Edmond Rostand (M° Odéon)

Musée Jacquemart-André • 8th • Museum
She was a lowly portrait painter; he a rich but lonely banker; together they traveled the world in search of art. It sounds like the plot of a Barbara Cartland novel, but the story of Nélie Jacquemart and Edouard André really is a winner, told as it is in the evocative surroundings of their Boulevard Haussmann mansion. During their travels, they bought a huge number of masterpieces, including a Botticelli virgin and child, Mantegna's *Ecce Homo*, and Rembrandt's *Portrait of Doctor Tholinx*. The audio-guide is a must for this museum, as it takes you through room by room, plunging you into Second Empire bourgeois life, with gossip and music to conjure up the spirit of a ball. The double spiral staircase of the winter garden feels like the end of the tour, but there is more—upstairs a treasure trove that they stashed away in their private "Italian museum." Afterward, brunch in the café. *Daily 10am-6pm. €–* 158 bd. Haussmann (M° St-Philippe-du-Roule), 01.45.62.11.59, musee-jacquemart-andre.com

Musée du Luxembourg • 6th • Art Museum
When Marie de Medici had the Palais du Luxembourg built, she included two galleries, one expressly to house the 24 Rubens of her in various stages of undress that can now be seen in the Louvre. This second gallery, in a pavilion to the east of the palace, became the first public gallery in France in 1750 when, in a rare act of equanimity, Louis XV exposed 100 paintings to the masses. Since its collection was moved to the Louvre and the Musée d'Art Moderne, it has held temporary exhibitions, and lately has been getting some world-class shows including Raphael, Botticelli, Modigliani, and Matisse. Exhibitions alternate between Renaissance masters and artists from the late 19th and early 20th century. Reserve tickets ahead to avoid standing in line. *Mon, Fri, Sat 11am-10pm, Tue-Thu 11am-7pm, Sun 9am-7pm. €–* 19 rue de Vaugirard (M° Odéon), 01.42.34.25.95, museeduluxembourg.fr

Musée Marmottan • 16th • Art Museum
The picture that started the whole Impressionist movement, *Impression Soleil Levant*, is right here, and after all those poster reproductions, it makes sense to have a look at the real thing. The world's greatest collection of Monet, Marmottan houses 165 Monet works here, including part of the Rouen Cathedral series and late water-lily canvases, housed in their own circular room (the Nymphéas are still in the Orangerie, which is closed for archaeological work). Other Impressionists here include Renoir, Manet, Gauguin, Caillebotte, and Berthe Morisot, which gives an overview of the movement. First thing in the morning is the best time to come, as this museum is popular. *Tue-Sun 10am-6pm. €–* 2 rue Louis-Boilly (M° La Muette), 01.44.96.50.33, marmottan.com

Musée Rodin • 7th • Art Museum
Best Statuary With its enchanted garden filled with emerging nymphs and tragic muses, roses, lawns, and chestnut trees, Rodin's is undoubtedly the most

romantic of Paris museums. The sculptor of *The Kiss* was a prolific worker—between here and the out-of-town Meudon museum there are some 6,600 works. The mansion house where Rodin worked has room after room of sensual white marble bodies, hands, and heads—look out for the ethereal *Danaïde* like a sleeping swan, *Fleeting Love,* and *Man with a Broken Nose.* There are also bronzes; paintings by Monet, Renoir, and Van Gogh; and works by Rodin's mistress Camille Claudel. In the gardens are *The Thinker, The Burghers of Calais,* and *Gates of Hell,* as well as lesser known bronzes. *Tue-Sun 9:30am-5:45pm (till 4:45pm Oct-Mar). Gardens open till 6:45pm in summer.* €– 77 rue de Varenne (M° Varenne), 01.44.18.61.10, musee-rodin.fr

Musée de la Vie Romantique • 9th • Museum

Though this small museum is devoted to the Romantic movement, it is also romantic with a small *r,* especially when the garden café serving tea and Parma violets by a statue of Chopin is open. What the French call a "musée sentimentale," filled with the personal effects of a writer or artist, it mainly contains objects and paintings belonging to George Sand. Chopin and Maupassant's lover, Sand was at the center of the bohemian 19th-century circle who lived in this quarter, then dubbed the Nouvelle Athènes. The museum is quickly visited, and truth be told it doesn't reveal much of Sand's torrid affairs, though it is atmospheric and some good temporary exhibitions take place here from time to time. *Tue-Sun 10am-6pm.* 16 rue Chaptal (M° Blanche), 01.55.31.95.67, vieromantique.paris.fr

O Château • 11th • Wine Tasting

Confused by French wine? Olivier Magny's your man. This young French wine expert offers tastings in English in his trendy Paris loft that make learning about wine great fun. Having lived in California, he knows exactly why New World wine lovers are confused by the arcane French labeling system. Working his way through three to seven bottles that are carefully chosen by his tasting team, he cuts through the snobbery and demystifies one of life's great pleasures. You'll learn enough about regions and appellations to make an informed choice from a menu or supermarket, but most of all, you'll enjoy the experience itself as Olivier's a great communicator. You can take home the bottles you liked the most. There's a basic one-hour tasting or more extensive two-hour tasting, or a lunch with French cheese. *Daily, noon (wine and cheese lunch), 3pm (three-wine tasting), 5pm (seven-wine tasting).* €€€€ 100 rue de la Folie Méricourt (M° Oberkampf), 01.44.73.97.80, o-chateau.com

Palais Royal • 1st • Monument

From a cardinal's palace to a libertines' paradise, the Palais Royal has had a checkered past. It was built in the 1630s for the Machiavellian Cardinal Richelieu. When it passed on to the Duc d'Orléans, Louis XVI's fun-loving brother, he made it a pleasure garden full of mountebanks, charlatans, prostitutes, pimps, and dissolute aristocrats. Now the formal gardens are sedate enough, a quiet place to walk, while their cloisters house upscale restaurants and dealers in antique toy soldiers, stamps, and music boxes, as well as vintage haute couture shop Didier Ludot and perfumery Shiseido. The main square has since 1986 housed Daniel Buren's striped column installation. *Daily 7:30am-8:30pm.* Pl. du Palais-Royal (M° Palais Royal-Musée du Louvre)

Parc André Citroën • 15th • Park
Best Parks The only Paris park to border the Seine, André Citroën will soon be linked by a riverside walk that extends across Paris. Landscaped in the 1990s on the site of the former factory that manufactured the iconic Citroën DS, the park is a contemporary formal garden unlike any other Paris park. Wide lawns are lined with streams, and there is a maze of gardens devoted to colors, touch, and even sounds. Lose yourself in the blue garden, dedicated to rain and scents; the red garden, dedicated to waterfalls and taste; or the Jardin en Mouvement, filled with flowers and roses. In summer water jets play on a paved court in front of the glass houses. The park also boasts the world's largest tethered balloon (see Le Ballon Eutelsat). *Mon-Fri 8am-dusk, Sat-Sun 9am-dusk.* Rue St-Charles (M° Balard), 01.44.26.20.00

PRIME TIME PARIS

Everything in life is timing (with a dash of serendipity thrown in). Would you want to arrive in Pamplona, Spain, the day *after* the Running of the Bulls? Not if you have a choice and enjoy the world's most exciting experiences. With our month-by-month calendar of events, there's no excuse to miss out on any of Paris' greatest moments—when its energy is at its peak. From the classic to the whimsical, the sophisticated to the outrageous, all the events that are worth your time are right here.

Prime Time Basics

Eating, Drinking, and Clubbing

Parisians don't have much more than a croissant and coffee for breakfast. Cafés sometimes offer a *tartine* (bread, butter, and jam). At lunchtime restaurants fill up on the dot of 1pm, so get there early to snag a seat. They stop serving between 2 and 3pm. Dinner is between 8 and 10:30-11pm. Paris restaurants are divided into bistros—homely places serving traditional food—and brasseries, which serve food all day until 1 or 2am. "Restaurants" are more elevated. Cafés serve simple dishes, and in trendy districts they may serve good bistro food too.

There is not really an after-work drinks culture in France—drinking is more closely linked to eating than in English-speaking countries. Anytime between 7 and 9pm can be "l'heure de l'apéritif." This is the bars' busiest time until the after-dinner crowd comes post-10pm. Most bars stay open until 2am; a few, especially the lounge bar kind, have licenses until 4am.

No sophisticated Parisian would think of going to a club before 1am; most do not open before midnight. They stay open until at least 6am.

Weather and Tourism

Mar.–May: Springtime is when Paris looks its best, with windowboxes, parks, and gardens in bloom. The first wave of warm weather can hit anytime from March to late April; when it does café chairs go out on the pavement and watching the girls go by becomes the national pastime. Spring can also be rainy, however. Fashion week in March fills hotel rooms and prices go up but high season really starts in May.

June–Aug.: June is delightful with often perfect weather. In July and August, temperatures

Seasonal Changes

Month	Fahrenheit High/Low	Celsius High/Low	Hotel Rates
January	43/34	06/01	L
February	45/34	07/01	L
March	54/39	12/04	L
April	61/43	16/06	S
May	68/50	20/10	H
June	73/55	23/13	H
July	77/59	25/15	S
August	75/57	24/14	L
September	70/54	21/12	H
October	61/46	16/08	H
November	50/41	10/05	L
December	45/36	07/02	L

H-High Season S-Shoulder L-Low

have been known to reach the 100s, but average the mid-70s, with hot and humid spells punctuated by dramatic summer downpours. Bastille Day celebrations mark the beginning of the holiday season and Parisians decamp en masse for the month of August, leaving the city pleasantly traffic-free but with the downside that many restaurants are closed.

Sept.–Nov.: On September 1 Parisians go into a frenzy known as *la rentrée*—the return from their holidays. Books, products, new restaurants, and clubs are launched and exhibitions open. Fashion Week and a host of other salons make this a busy time to come and it may be difficult to get a hotel room. Warm weather can last until mid-October and the autumn is a strong season for arts events.

Dec.–Feb.: Nothing is more magical than Paris with a thin dusting of snow, which normally lasts only a day or two, but winter can also be bitterly cold with leaden skies. Paris by night looks beautiful with its illuminated monuments. Christmas is quite low-key but *le Réveillon*—New Year's Eve—is celebrated with feasts and fireworks.

National Holidays

New Year's Day	January 1
Easter Sunday and Monday	March or April
Fête du Travail (Labor Day)	May 1
Victory 1945	May 8
Ascension (always on a Thursday)	May (40 days after Easter)
Pentecost (always on a Monday)	May or June (7 weeks after Easter)
Bastille Day	July 14
Assumption	August 15
Toussaint (All Saint's Day)	November 1
Armistice 1918	November 11
Christmas Day	December 25
Réveillon (New Year's Eve)	December 31

Listings in blue are major celebrations but not official holidays.

The Best Events Calendar

January
- Maison & Objet

February
- Six Nations Rugby

March
- Fashion Week

April

May
- French Tennis Open
- Les Puces du Design

June
- Paris Jazz Festival
- Prix de Diane-Hermès
- Fête de la Musique
- Gay Pride (La Marche des Fiertés)

July
- Solidays
- Bastille Day
- Paris Quartier d'Eté
- Cinéma en Plein Air
- Paris Plage
- Tour de France

August
- Cinéma au Clair de Lune
- Rock en Seine

September
- Maison & Objet
- Jazz à La Villette
- Techno Parade
- Journées du Patrimoine
- Festival d'Automne

October
- Fashion Week
- Les Puces du Design
- Prix de l'Arc de Triomphe
- Nuit Blanche
- Foire Internationale d'Art Contemporain

November
- Fête du Beaujolais Nouveau
- Salon du Chocolat

December
- New Year's Eve

The Night & Day's Top Five Events are in blue.
High Season months are represented by blue background.

The Best Events

January

Maison & Objet
Parc des Expositions, Paris-Nord Villepinte, Roissy-Charles de Gaulle, 01.58.07.18.00, maison-objet.com

The Lowdown: This major European design fair showcasing future trends in furniture, interiors and what the French call "the art of living" generates the atmosphere of a fashion week for the home. The salon is trade and press only, but shops put on special exhibitions alongside (look out for the Paris Capitale de la Création logo) and magazine editors get into a frenzy.

When and How Much: Last full weekend of January and first full weekend of September. Badges cost €52 for five days; free for press.

February

Six Nations Rugby
Stade de France, St-Denis, 08.92.70.09.00, stadefrance.fr

The Lowdown: The six rugby nations of France, England, Ireland, Italy, Scotland, and Wales compete in this tournament played in each country's stadiums. Matches generate huge excitement as Paris is invaded by Scots in kilts and flag-waving Irish, Welsh, and English fans. If you can't get a stadium seat (book in advance from stadefrance.fr or 6nations.co.uk), soak up the atmosphere in a Celtic or British pub with big-screen action.

When and How Much: Saturdays and Sundays from early February to mid-March. €15-€110 depending on seating.

March

Fashion Week
Carrousel du Louvre and other venues, modeaparis.com

The Lowdown: The women's prêt-à-porter shows generate hysteria like you've never seen before. Runway shows and salons take place in the top hotels, Carrousel du Louvre, and Tuileries gardens, but the real action is in the bar and party circuit. Some parties are crashable if you look the part, or soak up the "ab-fab" atmosphere at Costes or the Murano bar.

When and How Much: Early to mid-March and early to mid-October. Runway shows are by invitation only; salon badges generally have a fee. The rest of the action is free, aside from the cost of cocktails and your knock-'em-dead outfits.

PRIME TIME

May

French Tennis Open
Stade Roland Garros, 2 av. Gordon-Bennett, 16th, 01.47.43.48.00, frenchopen.org

The Lowdown: The grand slam tournament draws socialites, celebrities, and sports fans who gather to see the world's top seeds compete.

When and How Much: Two weeks, beginning the last Sunday in May. €12.50-€67.50 per day.

Les Puces du Design
Passage du Grand Cerf, Place Goldoni, 2nd, pucesdudesign.com

The Lowdown: This 20th-century design flea-market throws up pieces such as the Charles Eames lounge chair, Arco lamp, and Philippe Starck prototypes with a fun street-market atmosphere.

When and How Much: Friday through Sunday in mid-May and mid-October. Free.

June

Paris Jazz Festival
Parc Floral de Paris, Bois de Vincennes, 08.20.00.75.75, nemomusic.com

The Lowdown: Jazz lovers will dig these free concerts by the lake of the parc Floral. Bring a picnic and chill out to big names, new jazz, blues, and world music.

When and How Much: Saturday and Sunday 3:30pm, early June to late July. Free, except for €3 park entry.

Prix de Diane-Hermès
Chantilly racecourse, Chantilly, 03.44.62.41.00, france-galop.com

The Lowdown: French, British, and Irish high society converge on Chantilly in morning dress and extravagant hats for the French Derby. The festive atmosphere is heightened by an invited horse nation such as Kazakhstan, putting on equestrian dare-devil shows, and music.

When and How Much: Second weekend of June. Free on the *pelouse* (lawn); grandstand seats €8. Plus betting costs …!

Fête de la Musique
All over Paris, fetedelamusique.fr

The Lowdown: A musical frenzy takes place on midsummer's night all over France. Big-name concerts are held at Place de la Bastille and the Hôtel de Ville, but it's best to choose an area (St-Germain, Latin Quarter, Montmartre) for more varied fare and a local crowd. Blues in bars, Brazilian bands, African sound systems, and chamber music create an unmissable party atmosphere.

When and How Much: 21 June. Free.

Gay Pride (La Marche des Fiertés)
Starts place du 18 Juin 1940, 14th, at 1:30pm, fiertes-lgbt.org

The Lowdown: More than 700,000 people mass in the streets to join the Pride parade, with extravagant floats, gorgeous transvestites, whistle-blowing, and pumping house music. The parade travels from Montparnasse through St-Michel to Bastille, followed by a Radio Nova party in the square and hedonistic nights at clubs such as Le Queen, Twins, Pulp, and Vinyl.

When and How Much: Last Saturday in June. Free.

July

Solidays
Hippodrome de Longchamp, Bois de Boulogne, 01.53.10.22.22, solidays.com

The Lowdown: Roots, rap, reggae, rock, and chanson are some of the genres covered by this energetic three-day festival to raise money for AIDS charities. There's often an international headliner—in 2005 it was Patti Smith.

When and How Much: Second full weekend in July. Day €20; weekend €35.

Bastille Day
Place de la Bastille, Champs-Elysées and around town, paris.fr

The Lowdown: France's national day kicks off the night before with *bals populaires* (open-air dancing to waltzes, tango, and patriotic songs) at Place de la Bastille and in front of the various town halls. On the 14th, there is a military parade on the Elysées, fireworks on the Champ de Mars, and firefighters' balls in fire stations.

When and How Much: 13 and 14 July. Free.

Paris Quartier d'Eté
Various venues, quartierdete.com

The Lowdown: This quirky arts festival always has something original in store, from dance, world music, and circus arts to installations (in 2004 transparent beehives) and jazz in the Roman arena at Montmartre.

When and How Much: Mid-July to mid-August. Many events are free; others cost up to €15 a ticket.

Cinéma en Plein Air
Parc de La Villette, av. Jean-Jaurès, 19th, 01.40.02.75.75, villette.com

The Lowdown: Thousands gather on the lawns at dusk to watch classic films in a magical starlit setting on Europe's largest inflatable screen. This event captures the laid-back atmosphere of Paris in the summer. Many of the films are in English.

When and How Much: Nightly except Monday, mid-July to end of August. Free. Deck chairs can be rented for a small fee.

Paris Plage
Pont des Arts to Pont de Sully on the right bank, paris.fr

The Lowdown: 2,000 tons of sand, beach umbrellas, palm trees, and ice cream kiosks are imported to bring the beach to Paris by the Seine. A swimming pool, sand-castle competitions, and climbing walls are all part of the fun.

When and How Much: Last week of July to third week of August. Free.

Tour de France
letour.fr

The Lowdown: The national cycling obsession keeps café-sportifs glued to the small screen for weeks before the final stage reaches Paris on the penultimate Sunday in July. Watch them cross the finishing line on the Champs-Elysées followed by a victory parade, or choose an easier-to-see spot on rue de Rivoli to see the final minutes of the race pass in a flash.

When and How Much: First three weeks of July. Free.

August

Cinéma au Clair de Lune
Various locations, forumdesimages.net

The Lowdown: More highbrow than Cinéma en Plein Air, this festival shows films made in Paris in open-air locations close to where they were shot. A chance to discover Paris through the magic of the silver screen. Most films are in French.

When and How Much: Three weeks in August. Free.

Rock en Seine
Domaine National de St-Cloud, 08.92.68.08.92, rockenseine.com

The Lowdown: This two-day rock fest just outside Paris is part of the summer circuit for international names.

When and How Much: Last full weekend in August. Day €39; weekend €65.

September

Maison & Objet
See January

Jazz à La Villette
Cité de la Musique, Grande Halle de La Villette, 01.40.03.75.75, villette.com

The Lowdown: Three venues at La Villette host an exciting festival of contemporary jazz, from renowned improvisors to young talents and master classes.

When and How Much: First two weeks in September. €13-€16 per concert.

Techno Parade
01.42.47.84.76, technopol.net

The Lowdown: Clubbers come out to promote mass euphoria at this high-bpm parade finishing at Bastille. Top DJs come for club nights, and the week-long Rendezvous Electroniques follows with parties and events around town.

When and How Much: Third Saturday in September. The parade is free. Club nights charge €10-€20.

Journées du Patrimoine
journeesdupatrimoine.culture.fr. Full program in *Le Monde* or *Le Parisien*.

The Lowdown: The Ministry of Culture opens the doors of hundreds of historic buildings that are normally closed to the public: ministries, embassies, scientific establishments, architects' houses, and factories. A costumed event, Soirée du Patrimoine, takes place on Saturday night. Private historic buildings let you see inside for one day of the year. Be prepared for long lines.

When and How Much: Third weekend in September. Free.

Festival d'Automne
Various venues, 01.53.45.17.00, festival-automne.com

The Lowdown: The most avant-garde of all the festivals, with an emphasis on contemporary dance (Merce Cunningham has long been involved), theater, and opera, with multimedia and art happenings.

When and How Much: Mid-September to December 25. €10-€30 depending on the event.

October

Fashion Week
See March

Les Puces du Design
See May

Prix de l'Arc de Triomphe
Hippodrome de Longchamp, 16th, 01.49.10.20.30, france-galop.com

The Lowdown: France's richest flat race is a hot date for British and Irish racing fans and hooray Henris who strut about the pelouse at Longchamp. Women in wild hats get in for free. The big race is on Sunday.

When and How Much: First weekend in October. Free on the *pelouse* (lawn); grandstand seats €8.

Nuit Blanche
All over town, 08.20.00.75.75, paris.fr

The Lowdown: Nuit Blanche means staying up all night, and Parisians of all ages wander the streets at all hours. Events throughout Paris have included swimming in colored floodlit Art Deco pools and lights and soundscapes in parks. It's more surreal than fun, turning Paris into a weirdly beautiful theme park.

When and How Much: First Saturday in October. Free.

Foire Internationale d'Art Contemporain
Paris-Expo, Porte de Versailles, 15th, 01.41.90.47.80, fiac-online.com

The Lowdown: Art collectors head to the FIAC where some 200 galleries, about half of them from outside France, show a panorama of modern and contemporary art. The Future Quake section is where you may spot the next big thing.

When and How Much: Five days in mid-October. Entry badges cost €17.

November

Fête du Beaujolais Nouveau
Bars and restaurants around Paris.

The Lowdown: The arrival of the year's crop of Beaujolais Nouveau is an excuse to party as the winter closes in. Some bars add live music to the mix.

When and How Much: Third Thursday in November.

Salon du Chocolat
Paris-Expo, Porte de Versailles, 15th, 01.43.95.37.00, chocoland.com

The Lowdown: Not just a gourmet food fair, the Salon du Chocolat elevates the humble cocoa bean to fashion status: couturiers collaborate with chocolatiers to create fantastic creations that are shown off on the runway.

When and How Much: Penultimate weekend in November. Entry is €12.

December

New Year's Eve
Champs-Elysées, place de la Concorde

The Lowdown: While Christmas is a blink-and-you-miss-it affair, the Réveillon (literally "wake-up call") gets everyone out on the streets honking their horns and letting off firecrackers on the Champs-Elysées, which glisten with white fairy lights all through the winter season. Clubs and restaurants put on extravagant soirées with oysters and Champagne—the plum ticket is for the Hôtel Crillon's banquet with a view of the fireworks on Place de la Concorde.

When and How Much: December 31. Anything from zero to €1000. Tickets to the Crillon banquet cost about €700 for two.

HIT the GROUND RUNNING

In this section, you'll find all the indispensable details to enhance your trip—from tips on what to wear and how to get around to planning resources that will help your vacation come off without a hitch. You'll also find suggestions for making business trips a pleasure, as well as some fun, surprising facts with which to impress the locals.

City Essentials

Getting to Paris: By Air

Roissy–Charles de Gaulle Airport (CDG)
01.48.62.22.80, adp.fr.

Roissy, 18 miles northeast of Paris, is the sole airport for transatlantic flights. In 2003 France spent $900 million on the new, open-plan Terminal 2. In May 2003 it took a tumble with the collapse of part of the terminal, but the government is still set to float Aéroports de Paris on the stock exchange. If you are flying with Air France, Air Canada, American Airlines, Cathay Pacific, or Continental you'll arrive at this swanky new terminal, with its own TGV (high-speed train) and RER (suburban transport) stations and the stunning Sheraton hotel in the center of the complex, and shops and services that have at last brought Roissy into the 21st century. A drugstore, post office, chapel, lost property booth, and car rental are found in the Niveau Espace Services between A, B, C, and D, and first aid is located at the far end of Section A. There are pleasant cafés and restaurants and ATMs throughout. Wi-Fi is available in 2C arrivals and 2E and F departures. Note: It currently has five halls and is being further expanded to an eventual capacity of 50 million a year in 2010. The fact that work is ongoing means you must leave plenty of time to get there, as you may be required to take a shuttle bus once you arrive at 2. Also check your ticket for the exact hall you'll be leaving from.

Flying Times to Paris

From	Time (hr.)
Amsterdam	1
Frankfurt	1
London	1
Los Angeles	11½
Madrid	2
Milan	1½
New York	7
San Francisco	11
Washington, D.C.	8

Terminal 1 (British Airways, United Airlines, Qantas) is undergoing major renovations, ongoing until 2008, which will improve its currently dismal amenities and confusing layout. Give yourself plenty of time to check in on your return journey, and bring snacks—once you get to the departure lounge there is nothing but a plastic cup of espresso and candy bars to sustain you during a delay. Currently first aid and lost property is on Level 2 (departures), tourist information and ATMs on Level 5 (arrivals) and car rental on level 9. A further inconvenience of Terminal 1 is that connec-

tion to the RER is by navette (free minibuses), which you access from Level 5 after reclaiming your baggage. Taxis are also available here. Terminal 3, which you will probably only use if you take an Easyjet flight to another European city, is a simpler affair, accessible on foot from RER stop Aéroport Charles de Gaulle 1.

Airlines Serving Roissy-Charles de Gaulle

Airlines	Website	Phone Number	Terminal
Aer Lingus	aerlingus.com	01.70.20.00.72	1
Air Canada	aircanada.com	0.8.25.88.08.81	2A
Air France	airfrance.fr	08.20.82.08.20	2A, B, C, D, E
Alitalia	alitalia.com	08.25.31.53.15	2F
All Nippon Airways	anaskyweb.com	08.20.80.32.12	1
American Airlines	aa.com	08.10.87.28.72	2A
BMI Baby	bmibaby.com	08.90.71.00.81	1
British Airways	britishairways.com	08.20.82.54.00	1
British Midland	flybmi.com	01.41.91.87.04	1
Cathay Pacific Airways	cathaypacific.com	01.41.43.75.75	2A
Continental Airlines	continental.com	08.10.63.93.36	2A
Easyjet	easyjet.com	08.99.70.00.41	3
El Al	elal.co.il	01.40.20.90.90	1
Emirates	emirates.com	01.53.05.35.35	1
Iberia	iberia.com	08.25.80.09.65	1
Japan Airlines	jal.com	08.10.74.77.00	2F
KLM	klm.com	08.90.71.07.10	1
Lufthansa	ufthansa.com	08.26.10.33.34	1
Northwest Airlines	nwa.com	08.90.71.07.10	1
Qantas Airways	qantas.com	08.20.82.05.00	1
Royal Air Maroc	royalairmaroc.com	08.20.82.18.21	1
SAS	scandinavian.net	08.25.32.53.35	1
Singapore Airlines	singaporeair.com	01.53.65.79.01	1
United Airlines	united.com	08.10.72.72.72	1
US Airways	usairways.com	08.10.63.22.22	1
Varig	varig.com	08.26.10.26.25	1

[Note: Virgin doesn't fly here but has a code share with BMI, change at Heathrow]

Into Town by Taxi: Taxis are quickly found at the airport. A taxi to central Paris can take 30-60 mins depending on traffic (rush hour is 8-10am and 5-7pm) and your destination. Expect to pay €30-€50, plus €1 per piece of luggage. Airportaxis (to/from Paris airports): 01.48.40.17.17, airportaxis.com.

Into Town by Bus: Roissybus buses take about 60 minutes and go directly to rue Scribe, near the Opéra (€8.30). Les Cars Air France buses go direct to Charles de Gaulle–Etoile (Champs-Elysées area) or Montparnasse (€12).

Into Town by Subway: The RER train takes 35 minutes to Gare du Nord, or 45 minutes to Châtelet-Les-Halles. It runs every 15 minutes 5:30am-midnight (€8). You may have to take a bus to reach the RER station within the airport, depending on which terminal you arrive at.

Rental Cars: All of the following major rental car companies have counters inside Roissy.

Agency	Website	Local Number
Avis	avis.com	01.48.62.59.59
Budget	budget.com	01.48.62.70.22
Europcar	europcar.com	08.25.82.54.90
Hertz	hertz.com	08.25.88.97.55

Airport Shuttle Service: Shuttle minibuses operate a door-to-door service on a fixed-price, "the more passengers, the less you pay" system, from €15 to €25 depending on the number of people and the hour. In most cases VIP (minimum €34) rates are enforced from 10pm-5am.

Airport Connection	airport-connection.com	01.43.65.55.55
Paris Airports Service	parisairportservice.com	01.55.98.10.80
Paris Airport Shuttle	paris-airport-shuttle.com	01.42.71.40.31
Parishuttle	parishuttle.com	01.53.39.18.18
Yellow Van Shuttle	yellowvanshuttle.com	01.49.77.01.01

Orly Airport (ORY)
01.49.75.15.15, adp.fr

You may use Orly, 12 miles south of Paris, for an ongoing flight in Europe or further afield (Air France and Easyjet both fly from here). Its two terminals are built to a traditional design and not difficult to navigate. Orly Sud is mainly for international flights and Orly Ouest for domestic flights. Connections to Paris are via the Orlyval rail and RER.

Orly Sud's station is near the baggage reclaim (exit K) and Orly Ouest's on the Departures level (hall 2, exit W). The journey takes 35 minutes.

Beauvais-Tillé Airport (BVA)
08.92.68.20.66, aeroportbeauvais.com

Located 45 miles from Paris and accessible by Ryanair buses (90-120 minutes from Porte Maillot), offers flights by Ryanair (ryanair.com) and other low-cost airlines to Britain, Ireland, Italy, Scandinavia, and Eastern Europe.

Getting to Paris: By Land

By Car: All freeways converging on Paris eventually join the Périphérique ring road that encircles the 20 arrondissements. Enter at the porte that is nearest to your destination. Travel times to the various portes are marked on electronic boards and change according to traffic conditions. Freeways have tollbooths—you can pay by credit card.

By Train: Paris has several stations serving the rest of Europe via the TGV high-speed network. Eurostars from London arrive at the Gare du Nord (2.5 hours); trains from the South of France arrive at the Gare de Lyon (Marseilles 3 hours; Nice 6 hours); trains from Italy and Spain arrive at the Gare d'Austerlitz and Gare de Bercy. Note that this can be more efficient than flying.

Paris: Lay of the Land

Paris has 20 arrondissements. To get your head around the arrondissement system, imagine a snail's shell spiraling in a clockwise direction from the center, the 1st arrondissement, all the way out to the 20th. All Paris addresses have the zip code 750 followed by the number of the arrondissement, and people often refer to an arrondissement simply as "the 7th, the 8th," and so on. In a piece of Napoléonic logic, street numbers always run outward from the Seine, and the numbers increase in the direction of its flow, from east to west.

Getting Around Paris

By Métro: The Paris Métro is one of the most efficient, though not always the sweetest-smelling, underground transport systems in the world. Buy a carnet of 10 tickets (€10.50)—one ticket serves you on any journey and they can also be used on the buses and on the RER within central Paris. Lines are color- and number-coded and marked with their final destination (for instance, Line 5 Bobigny or Place d'Italie). The Métro runs 5:30am-12:40am. Watch your wallet.

By Bus: The bus system is slower, but has the advantage of some great sightseeing routes. Try the 24 (Opéra, Madeleine, Musée d'Orsay, and all along the Left Bank of the Seine to the Latin Quarter), 21 (Opéra, Palais-Royale, the Louvre, Notre-Dame, and the Luxembourg Gardens), or 83 (Champs-Elysées, Invalides, and St-Germain to Montparnasse).

By Car: Only drive in Paris if you get off on the sheer hair-raising thrill of it all. Paris drivers are assertive, to say the least, and don't obey the rules. Parking is hell. Though there are some expensive underground parking lots and some restaurants have a valet service, most of the time you will find yourself driving around in circles and employing the bumper-to-bumper nudging technique to get into an impossibly tight space. You will soon learn the words *Je suis super-mal-garé* (very badly parked) and *Ta gueule!* (no translation). A car is, however, useful for trips out of Paris. Remember that all speed limits are in kilometers per hour.

By Boat: Batobus (batobus.com) runs a river transport system all along the Seine. It's expensive, but a pleasant way to get between sights such as the Eiffel Tower, Musée d'Orsay, and St-Germain-des-Prés.

By Scooter: Do as the Parisians do and get around by scooter. Parking is easy, but the fearful traffic warnings still apply. Scooters can be rented from Holiday bikes near the Etoile of the Champs-Elysées: 01.45.00.06.66.

By Bike: An increasing number of cycle lanes makes cycling in Paris fun, especially along the canal from Bastille to La Villette, and on Sundays when the Right Bank quay of the Seine is a car-free zone. Hire a bike and pick up a map from Maison Roue Libre at Bastille and at nine other points around town: 01.44.54.19.29, rouelibre.fr.

On Foot: The very best way to see Paris. Pick up a Plan de Paris (city map) from any newsstand, or indulge in the Parisian pastime of *flânerie* (walking with no particular aim, just to see what you can see).

By Taxi: 15,000 taxis operate in Paris, day and night, but you'd never believe it when it comes to getting one. First step is to know that a white light signifies that the taxi is free; a yellow light that it is taken. Most taxis will only take three people at a time and not all drivers speak English—have your hotel's business card handy. For short journeys a minimum fee of €5.10 is enforceable. Taxis won't stop on the street if they are near a taxi

CITY ESSENTIALS

Numbers to Know (Hotlines)

Call 18 for the fire brigade *(sapeurs-pompiers)*, 17 for the police, and 15 for an ambulance (SAMU). In a medical emergency such as a road accident, call the sapeurs-pompiers who have trained paramedics and may get there quicker. All emergency services can be reached by dialing 112 from a cell phone.

24-hour emergency rooms

Hôpital Hôtel Dieu 1 pl. du Parvis Notre-Dame, 4th	01.42.34.82.34
Hôpital St-Louis 1 av. Claude Vellefaux, 10th	01.42.49.49.49
Hôpital St-Antoine 184 rue du Fbg. St-Antoine, 12th	01.49.28.20.00
Hôpital de la Pitié-Salpêtrière 47-83 bd. de l'Hôpital, 13th (for emergency dental work too)	01.42.16.00.00
Hôpital Cochin 27 rue du Fbg. St-Jacques, 14th	01.58.41.41.41
Hôpital Européen Georges Pompidou 20 rue Leblanc, 15th	01.56.09.20.00
Urgences Médicales de Paris	01.53.94.94.94
SOS Médecins	01.47.07.77.77
SOS Dentaire	01.43.37.51.00

(Dentists make house calls around the clock for €35 and up per visit; some of their doctors speak English.)

Pharmacies sport a green neon cross. These are open 24/7.

Dérhy/Pharmacie des Champs 84 av. des Champs-Elysées, 8th	01.45.62.02.41
Pharmacie Européenne de la Place de Clichy 6 pl. de Clichy, 9th	01.48.74.65.18
Pharma Presto	01.61.04.04.04

pharma-presto.com, delivers prescription medication 24/7 for a fee.

Hotlines

Poison Hotline	01.40.05.48.48
SOS burns (Hôpital Cochin)	01.58.41.41.41
SOS Help (English-language help line, daily 3-11pm)	01.46.21.46.46

HIT THE GROUND

stand, so try to find one—they are near Métro stations and major road junctions. That said, there may well still be quite a long line, especially at night, and during Fashion Week you haven't a hope in hell. If you call ahead for one, you'll incur the cost of the taxi getting to where you are, but it's nevertheless useful to have a couple of numbers on hand: Alpha: 01.45.85.85.85. G7: 01.47.39.47.39, 01.41.27.66.99 (in English). Taxis Bleus: 08.91.70.10.10, taxis-bleus.com.

Other Practical Information

Money Matters (Currency, Taxes, Tipping, and Service Charges): As is the case in much of Europe, France's currency is the euro (€) and centime (100 to the Euro). For currency rates go to xe.com. Major credit cards are widely accepted, but always check before sitting down to dinner. There are plenty of 24-hour ATMs throughout the city, and most of those are located at major banks. All prices in France are inclusive of service. In restaurants tipping over the obligatory 15% included in the total is entirely at your discretion, but, unless the service is poor, it's normal to leave some change (or notes in the case of haute cuisine restaurants) on the table. In taxis, it is usual to round up the fare to the nearest euro. Tipping hotel staff is usual in luxury hotels only.

Phone Calls: When calling Paris from within France, including from within Paris itself, callers need to dial all ten digits of the phone number. Paris phone numbers begin with 01, cell phone numbers begin with 06, and other areas of France begin with 02 through 05. When dialing from the US, add 011-33 and drop the 0, ie: 011-33-1-eight-digit number. When dialing the US from France, callers should dial 00-1-area code and number. Pay phones do not accept coins, but require that callers purchase a télécarte from a tabac, tourist office, or post office.

> **Tax Refunds**
>
> VAT of 19.5% is already included in all marked prices. If you come from a country outside the European Union and you spend a minimum of €175 in the same store, you can claim back the VAT. Ask for a Tax-free Shopping France invoice when you shop in any major store or "Tax free for tourists" boutique. The amount to be refunded is shown under the heading "montant de la détaxe." You should have your invoices stamped at airport customs on leaving the EU and return the validated pink copies within three months using the stamped addressed envelope given to you when you make your purchases.

Safety: Paris within the Périphérique is an extremely safe city where one can generally walk around at night without fear. The only places you might want to avoid are the mainline stations after they have closed, the 18th and 19th borders, and Les Halles (although a major redevelopment in 2007 will make it more user-friendly). As in all big cities, keep your wallet hidden, as pickpocketing is rife, particularly on the Métro.

Metric Conversion

From	To	Multiply by
Centimeters	Inches	0.39
Meters	Yards	1.1
Kilometers	Miles	0.62
Liters	Gallons	0.26
Kilograms	Pounds	2.2

Gay and Lesbian Travel: With its own gay television channel, Pink TV, and an openly homosexual mayor, they don't call it Gay Paris for nothing. Paris' gay village is the Marais, with a variety of bars, restaurants, and some gay hotels, but same-sex couples checking into a hotel or embracing in public anywhere in Paris will not cause the French to bat an eyelid. The pink propensity for having fun has given rise to some of the hottest club nights in the capital, and when the sun comes out, bronzed bodies line the Seine. The only downside is that French men in general are so well-groomed that it can put your gaydar to the test.

Traveling with Disabilities: Paris is in general poorly equipped for disabled travelers. The only public transport that is wheelchair accessible is Métro line 14, bus lines 20, PC and some 91s, and RER lines A and B in parts. Taxis are obliged by law to take passengers in wheelchairs, and Aihrop (01.41.29.01.29, aihrop.com) can provide transport in adapted vehicles anywhere in Ile-de-France with 48 hours' notice. The best web resource in English is the site of the Paris Convention and Visitors' Bureau, parisinfo.com, in the Practical Information section. It explains the "Tourisme & Handicap" label, by which facilities for visitors with physical, mental, visual, and hearing impairments are signaled on the website and around Paris—part of a countrywide campaign to facilitate tourism for the disabled. It also includes a full list of associations and guides that can help.

Print Media: The foreign press is available at newsstands in tourist areas, and the *International Herald Tribune,* published in Paris, is available everywhere. *Gogo,* a monthly free style and events magazine in English with listings on exhibitions, concerts, theater, film, and clubbing can be picked up from various points around the city, a full list of which is on the mag's website, gogoparis.com. Other free magazines in English include *Paris Voice, Cat's Eyes,* and *Irish Eyes,* with *Fusac* for small ads. The free pocket-sized *Lylo,* in French, lists all the concerts for a given week and is found in many bars as well as in Fnac stores. If you read French, choose between the left-wing, intellectual *Le Monde* and the right-wing *Le Figaro;* both publish a weekly what's-on supplement on Wednesdays. Pocket-sized *Pariscope* and *L'Officiel des Spectacles* have cinema and entertainment listings; *Zurban* is a trendy listings mag with editorial; *Télérama* covers cultural events in depth. *Paris-Match* gives the lowdown on celebrity lives, and *Elle* is the most popular women's magazine with a Paris edition. French television doesn't offer much except minor celebrities in talk shows and "you are the next star" contests, with the exception of Arte, a French-German collaboration showing films, arts programs, and documentaries.

Radio Stations (a selection)

FM Stations

87.8	France Inter	State-run highbrow station with jazz, international news, and discussion slots.
90.4	Nostalgie	French and international oldies.
90.9	Chante France	100 percent French chanson.
92.1	Le Mouv'	New public station aimed at luring the young with pop and rock music.
96.4	BFM	Business and economics.
96.9	Voltage FM	Dance music.
98.2	Radio FG	Beloved of clubbers for its on-the-pulse tips.
99.0	Radio Latina	Latin and salsa music.
100.3	NRJ	"Energy" is a leader with the under-30s.
101.1	Radio Classique	Top-notch, state-run classical music station.
101.5	Radio Nova	Hip-hop, trip-hop, world, jazz.
101.9	Fun Radio	Now embracing techno and Anglo pop hits.
102.3	Ouï FM	Ouï will rock you.
103.9	RFM	Easy listening.
104.3	RTL	The most popular French station nationwide mixes music and talk.
105.1	FIP	An excellent mix of jazz, classical, world, and pop. Its female announcers are famous for having the sexiest voices on French radio.
105.5	France Info	24-hour news, weather, economic updates, and sports bulletins.

In English The BBC World Service is on 648KHz AM, and on 198KHz LW from midnight to 5:30am daily. At other times 198KHz LW carries BBC Radio 4. RFI (738KHz AM) has an English-language program of news and music 7-8am, 2-3pm, and 4:30-5pm daily.

Shopping Hours: Most shops open 10am-7pm Monday through Saturday, though some are closed on Mondays. Small boutiques and banks sometimes close for lunch 12:30-2pm. Thursday nights have late-night shopping till 9 or 10pm at the major department stores, and big stores on the Champs-Elysées are open until midnight every night. Certain areas, such as the Marais, Montmartre, Bercy, and the Canal St-Martin, have Sunday afternoon shopping. *Soldes* (sales) are held in January and June.

Attire: For one of the world's chicest cities, Paris shows little evidence of this on its streets. It's all in the detail: looking "soignée" and dressing appropriately is more important to the French than being the height of fashion. If she wants to look really dressed up, a French woman will go to a hair salon and get a "brushing"—a professional blow-dry—and people generally go home and change before going out in the evening. Many haute cuisine restaurants still require a jacket and tie for men, but the trendier establishments are far more relaxed. What you wear to fit in largely depends on where you are staying: the Left Bank is still the BCBG (preppy) territory of blazers and scarves, the Champs-

Size Conversion

Dress Sizes

US	6	8	10	12	14	16
UK	8	10	12	14	16	18
France	36	38	40	42	44	46
Italy	38	40	42	44	46	48
Europe	34	36	38	40	42	44

Women's Shoes

US	6	6½	7	7½	8	8½
UK	4½	5	5½	6	6½	7
Europe	38	38	39	39	40	41

Men's Suits

US	36	38	40	42	44	46
UK	36	38	40	42	44	46
Europe	46	48	50	52	54	56

Men's Shirts

US	14½	15	15½	16	16½	17
UK	14½	15	15½	16	16½	17
Europe	38	39	40	41	42	43

Men's Shoes

US	8	8½	9½	10½	11½	12
UK	7	7½	8½	9½	10½	11
Europe	41	42	43	44	45	46

Elysées is where you'll want to show off your trendiest, sexiest attire (preferably in black), in the Marais anything goes, and you wouldn't want to be seen dead in the 11th wearing a tie. The posher clubs will turn away people in jeans and sneakers, and getting dressed up in your most glamorous attire can help open the doors to the VIP area. In summer, while women walk around in flimsy little tops, nobody, but nobody, wears shorts in town.

Clubbing: Clubs are divided into those with an entrance charge and relatively reasonably priced drinks, and those with free entry, which are ostensibly "private" clubs and more selective about who they let in. At the latter you will be pressed to order a bottle of Champagne or spirits at a hugely inflated price, but if you call in advance, or mention at the door that you'd like to order a bottle, this can have an "open sesame" effect and you could be ushered straight to a table. Men unaccompanied by women may find the door unfriendly (the most common approach is to chat up women in line and try to enter as a group); girls without men are welcomed with open arms. Wearing something distinctive such as a hat or other high-fashion accessory can also make you look more desirable to the bouncers.

Drinking, Smoking, and Drugs: The legal drinking age is 18, but ID isn't an issue when ordering a drink. You are, however, required by law to carry ID around and the police have a right to ask to see it. The French are heavy smokers and tend to disregard non-smoking signs in cafés and restaurants. A move is afoot to change this, with "100 percent sans tabac" labels in establishments that have opted to ban smoking. The Tourist Office website has a list of such places—not surprisingly, most of them are Starbucks. If you do actually want to buy cigarettes, remember that only tabacs are licensed to sell them, and most close at 8pm; however, some restaurants and bars will sell cigarettes to customers at an inflated price. To request a non-smoking table, ask for *une table non-fumeur*. Some places, such as Drôle d'Endroit pour une Rencontre and Djoon, have started non-smoking brunches or club nights on Sundays. All drugs, from marijuana upward, are illegal, and police have the right to search anyone.

Time Zone: Paris falls within the Central European time zone, Greenwich Mean Time + 1. A note on daylight savings: Clocks are set ahead one hour at 3am on the last Sunday in March and set back one hour at 3am on the last Sunday in October.

Additional Resources for Visitors

Paris Convention & Visitors Bureau Smaller visitors' centers are found at 11 rue Scribe (Opéra), the Eiffel Tower, Gare de Lyon, Gare du Nord, 21 place du Tertre (Montmartre) and in the Carrousel du Louvre. Main Office: 25 rue des Pyramides, 08.92.68.30.00, parisinfo.com.

Foreign Visitors

Passport Requirements: A valid passport is required for all U.S. visitors entering France. You do not need a visa unless you plan to stay more than 90 days. For more information, visit info-france-usa.org/visitingfrance/. If your passport is stolen, visit the U.S. Embassy.

U.S. Embassy in Paris: 2 rue Gabriel, 01.43.12.22.22.

Cell Phones: If you have a triband GSM cellular phone that can use the 900MHz frequency, you can use it in France but will pay high roaming fees for incoming and outgoing calls, even within Paris, as all calls are routed via the U.S. These phones can be rented from phone companies at home, which is normally cheaper than renting them at the airport. But a far more economical system is to get your GSM phone unlocked before you arrive and purchase a French prepaid SIM card from any Bouyges, Orange, or SFR shop, or in advance from California-based company Cellular Abroad: 1-800-287-3020, cellularabroad.com, which can also rent or sell you an unblocked GSM phone. T-Mobile is the only U.S. company that agrees to unlock its customers' phones itself, 90 days after the activation of an account. However, the Travel Insider's "Road Warrior Resources" service (thetravelinsider.com) can unlock most GSM phones for a small fee, depending on the make of phone.

Electrical: Electricity in France runs on 220V. You will need a transformer *(un transformateur)* to use U.S. 110V appliances in France. These are available at BHV and branches of Fnac and Darty.

The Latest-Info Websites

thecatseyes.com	Events guide with ticket booking service.
culture.fr	Current and forthcoming cultural events of all kinds.
expatica.com	Articles and listings of arts, music, and theater events.
fnac.com	Online ticket booking for concerts and other events.
lemonsound.com	Clubbing agenda.
mappy.fr	Maps of Paris and France.
meteo.fr	Weather forecasts/stats from the state meteorology office.
pagesjaunes.fr	Paris yellow pages, with maps, photos of all addresses.
paris.fr	Mairie de Paris website with events and information.
parissi.com	Films, concerts, and a strong calendar of clubbing events.
pidf.com	Official site of the Ile de France tourist board.
ratp.com	Information on buses, Métro, RER, and trams.
pulseguide.com	of course!

Useful Vocabulary

A few key things will help you to slip into the French way of life. When greeting someone (a shopkeeper, taxi driver, maître d'), it is polite to say *Bonjour, Madame* or *Bonjour, Monsieur*; similarly, *Au revoir, Monsieur* or *Bonne journée* (have a nice day) when leaving. There are two forms of you, the amicable *tu* and the formal *vous*, but even French people make mistakes. When in doubt, stick with the more formal form with strangers. When greeting someone they know or are introduced to, Parisians kiss on both cheeks. When you are introduced to someone say *Enchanté*—it sounds quaintly old-fashioned but it's true. When asking for the check, request *l'addition, s'il vous plaît*. Female travelers may be surprised at the audacity of French men, but comments such as *Mademoiselle, vous êtes ravissante* (Miss, you are beautiful) from a complete stranger are meant as a compliment. If he gets persistent, a polite *Laissez-moi tranquille, s'il vous plaît* (Leave me alone please) should suffice.

There are two forms of you:

Vous, the plural form, is also used to show respect and for people you don't know.

Tu or **Toi** is the informal form, used for friends and children. *Toi* is used among young people even when they meet for the first time.

English	French	Pronunciation
Yes	**Oui**	wee
No	**Non**	noh
Hello	**Bonjour**	bonjoor
Hello (informal)	**Salut**	saloo
Hello (on telephone)	**Allo**	allo
Good evening	**Bonsoir**	bonswar
Goodbye (informal)	**Salut**	saloo
Have a nice day	**Bonne journée**	bon jornay
Have a nice evening	**Bonne soirée**	bon swaray
Goodnight	**Bonne nuit**	bon nwee
Sorry/excuse me	**Pardon**	pardon
Excuse me (interrupting)	**Excusez-moi**	Excusay-mwa

In the Restaurant

Non-smoking	**non-fumeur**	non-fumuhr
In the window	**à la fenêtre**	a la fuhnetre
On the terrace	**sur terrasse**	syoor terass

CITY ESSENTIALS

Waiter?	**Monsieur?** (not garçon)	meussieu?
I'd like the ...	**Je prendrai le ...**	Je prondray le ...
Is there a set price menu?	**Est-ce qu'il y a un menu prix-fixe?**	
	Ey seu keelya un meunoo pree-feeks?	
Do you have any wine recommendations?	**Quel est le vin que vous nous conseillez?**	
	Kel ey luh vang kuh voo noo conseyey?	
Where are the restrooms?	**Où est le petit coin, s'il vous plaît?**	
	Oo ey le ptit cwan, seel voo play?	
Could I have the check please?	**L'addition, s'il vous plaît.**	
	L'adiseeon, seel voo play.	

In the Shops

When entering a shop, greet the owner with:	**Bonjour Madame** or **Bonjour Monsieur**	
May I try it on?	**Puis-je l'essayer?**	Pwee juh l'essayay?
I'll take it	**Je le/la prends**	Juh luh/la pron

Making Friends

What's your name (informal)	**Comment t'appelles-tu?**	Comon tapel tyu?
Nice to meet you	**Enchanté**	onchontay
Where are you from?	**Vous venez de quel pays?**	Voo vuhnay de kel pay?
(More common polite way)	(**Vous êtes de quelle origine?**)	
	Voo zet de kel oreegeen?	
I live in the U.S.	**J'habite les Etats-Unis**	Jabite lay zeta zooni
My name is ...	**Je m'appelle ....**	Juh mapel ....
May I introduce my wife	**Je vous présente ma femme**	
	Juh voo praysont ma fam	
my husband	**mon mari**	mon maree
my girlfriend	**ma copine**	ma copeen
my boyfriend	**mon copain**	mon copan
my mistress	**ma maîtresse**	ma maytress
my secretary	**ma secrétaire**	ma sehcreytair
What's the time?	**Vous avez l'heure?**	Voo zavay luhr?
Have you got a light?	**Vous avez du feu?**	Voo zavay doo fuh?
Can I buy you a drink?	**Est-ce que je peux vous offrir un verre?**	
	Eskuh juh puh voo zoffrir un ver?	

HIT THE GROUND

English	French	Pronunciation
Do you know any good bars/nightclubs around here?	**Connaissez-vous un bar/une boîte sympa dans le coin?**	Conessay voo ahn bar/oon bwat sampa don le cwan?
What do you do for a living?	**Qu-est-ce que vous faîtes dans la vie?**	Keskuh voo fet don la vee?
Do you live around here?	**Vous habitez dans le quartier?**	Voo zabitay don le kartiay?
I love this tune, who is it?	**J'adore ce tube, c'est quoi le groupe?**	J'ador se tube, say kwa luh group?
You wouldn't be trying to chat me up?	**Vous ne seriez pas en train de me draguer?**	Voo ne sehriey pa on tran duh muh dragay?
I'd like to see you again	**J'aimerais bien te revoir**	J'emuhray beean tuh revoaar
Here's my number. Give me a call	**Voilà mon numéro. Donne-moi un coup de fil.**	Vwala mon numero. Don-mwa un coo de feel.
Let's get out of this dump!	**C'est nul, on se casse!**	Say nool on suh cass!
(or)	**J'en peux plus, on y va?**	J'on puh ploo on ee va?
Have you got any condoms?	**Tu as des capotes?**	Tyu a day capott?
It's over, man	**C'est fini**	Say fini
It's incredible/awesome	**C'est formidable**	Sey formidabl
It's terrible	**C'est terrible**	Sey terreebl
It's unbelievable! (showing indignation)	**C'est hallucinant!**	Sey alucinon!
What a babe!	**Cette fille, quel bombe!**	Set fee, kel bomb!
What a cute guy!	**Quel mignon!**	Quel minion
A guy	**un type/mec/gar**	un teep/mec/gar
A chick	**une nana/une gonzesse**	oon nana/oon gonzess

The Brushoff

English	French	Pronunciation
I'm married	**Je suis marié**	Je swee mariay
I have a boyfriend/girlfriend	**J'ai un fiancé/une fiancée**	Jay un fionsay/oon fionsay
I am waiting for someone	**J'attends quelqu'un**	J'aton kelkun
Would you mind leaving me in peace?	**Je préférerais que vous me laissiez tranquille**	Je prefereray kuh voo me lessiay tronkeel
Leave me alone, please!	**Laissez-moi tranquille, s'il vous plaît!**	Lessay mwa tronkee, seel voo play!

The Cheat Sheet
(The Very Least You Ought to Know About Paris)

It's always good to know a bit about the place you're going. Here's a countdown of the most essential facts you need to avoid looking like a tourist.

Neighborhoods

Bastille, with its shining monument to the July 1830 revolution, was kick-started into a new era by the building of the new opera house in 1989. In this traditional furniture-making area, the workshops tucked down the narrow, leafy passageways are today coveted as lofts, but efforts have been made to keep craftsmen—now more likely to be fashion or product designers—in situ. There are a good number of buzzy bars and great bistros. (11th and 12th arrondissements)

The Canal St-Martin, the waterway that runs between Bastille and place Stalingrad, is where Amélie Poulain stood on a pretty bridge overarched with chestnut trees in the movie *Amélie,* and it's no less attractive in real life. Cafés and boutiques attract bobos who spend summer afternoons posing, picnicking, and picking each other up by the water. (10th arrondissement)

The Champs-Elysées, the "most beautiful avenue in the world," is more majestic than attractive, as six lanes of traffic snake up to the Arc de Triomphe in a snarl of carbon monoxide. The area, however, has gone from tourist central to the hottest rendezvous in town, with a host of A-list lounges, hotel bars, and clubs to choose from. (8th arrondissement)

The Grands Boulevards, the center of 19th-century high society, have some of the most grandiose Haussmannian architecture, grand hotels, the famous department stores, the Opéra Garnier, and concert hall Olympia. A burgeoning bar and club scene draws party people to the boulevards at night. (2nd and 9th arrondissements)

Invalides, the area surrounding the golden dome where Napoléon is buried, is the ministerial heart of Paris, with Parliament, government departments, and the Military Academy marked by the omnipresence of uniformed guards. Grandiose architecture and formal gardens are the norm—stroll on the Esplanade des Invalides or the tree-lined Champ de Mars in front of the Eiffel Tower. Politicians like fine food, however, and there are plenty of opportunities to eat well around here, as well as a concentration of museums. (7th arrondissement)

The Latin Quarter got its name from the language spoken by medieval students rather than any salsa-and-mojito connotations—though plenty of cheap cocktails are downed around here by today's students. It has the unchanging appeal of a university town, with the romantic Luxembourg Gardens for recreation and the Mosquée de Paris for mint tea. (5th arrondissement)

The Marais, literally "the marsh," is full of aristocratic townhouses built when Henri IV moved his court to the elegant Place des Vosges. After the Revolution it became the Jewish quarter and the mansion houses were used as manufacturing workshops. Private renovations since the '60s have turned this into some of the most desirable real estate in Paris, and the Marais is now filled with trendy boutiques by day and a hopping gay scene by night. The north Marais is currently undergoing a fashionable transformation with the opening of Christian Lacroix's hotel and new restaurants on rue Charlot. (3rd and 4th arrondissements)

Montmartre, home of the Moulin Rouge and the Sacré-Coeur, is a big tourist draw but it also has a trendy side, specifically the lively bar-and-boutique-lined cobbled streets around Abbesses station. Steep steps, or a funicular if you're feeling lazy, run up to the Butte (which means hill) and the Sacré-Coeur. The viewing platform in front of the basilica and place du Tertre are always crowded, but it's easy to escape into villagey streets, squares, and stone staircases that keep their romantic charm. Other happening neighborhoods around the Butte are Lamarck-Caulaincourt on the downward slope to the north and Batignolles to the west. (18th arrondissement)

Montparnasse, the old artists' quarter, has much of its Art Nouveau allure intact despite the monstrosity of the Tour Montparnasse in the center. Two arts foundations are situated here, and this is the place to order a slap-up, multistoried seafood platter in one of its famous brasseries. (14th arrondissement)

St-Germain ain't what it used to be, but who's to say that's a bad thing? Two-cent hotels and dive bars have been replaced by Dior, Armani, and the like, but the legendary cafés once patronized by Sartre and his contemporaries still offer prime terraces for a philosophical drink or two. (6th and 7th arrondissements)

9 Churches

Basilique du Sacré-Coeur The wedding-cake basilica was started in 1877 as an act of penance after the Prussian War. It is filled with neo-Byzantine mosaics and has a heady view of Paris from its dome. 35 rue du Chevalier-de-la-Barre, 18th, 01.53.41.89.00. M° Abbesses.

Cathédrale Notre-Dame de Paris The cathedral and emblem of Paris stands on the Ile de la Cité. A masterpiece of Gothic architecture that took two centuries to build, it was championed by Victor Hugo, who wrote *The Hunchback of Notre-Dame* to save it from neglect. Pl. du Parvis-Notre-Dame, 4th, 01.53.10.07.02. M° Cité.

Eglise de la Madeleine This imposing church flanked by Corinthian columns was commissioned by Napoléon as a "Temple of Glory." You may catch a society wedding or christening. Pl. de la Madeleine, 8th, 01.44.51.69.00. M° Madeleine.

Eglise St-Etienne-du-Mont This elegant, light-filled church next to the Panthéon mixes Gothic and Renaissance styles. It houses the shrine of Geneviève, patron saint of Paris, who saved the city from Attila the Hun. Pl. Ste-Geneviève, 5th, 01.43.54.11.79. M° Cardinal Lemoine.

Eglise St-Julien-le-Pauvre Vying with Eglise St-Germain for the title of oldest church in Paris, St-Julien-le-Pauvre was built in the 12th century as a sanctuary for pilgrims en route to Compostela. It is now a Greek Orthodox church and, approached through a small garden, is an enchanting setting for classical concerts. Rue St-Julien-le-Pauvre, 5th, 01.43.54.52.16. M° Cluny-La Sorbonne.

Eglise St-Roch A magnificent Baroque church built into the facade of the fashionable rue St-Honoré, St-Roch holds the tombs of royal gardener Le Nôtre and writers Corneille and Diderot. Its front is pitted with bullet holes from a 1795 shootout. 296 rue St-Honoré, 1st, 01.42.44.13.20. M° Tuileries.

Eglise St-Séverin This stunning example of Flamboyant Gothic is the parish church of the Latin Quarter. Its jewels include 15th-century stained glass, spiral columns, a carved doorway saved from a church on the Ile de la Cité, and the oldest bell in Paris. 1 rue des Prêtres-St-Séverin, 5th, 01.42.34.93.50. M° Cluny-La Sorbonne.

Eglise St-Sulpice A beautiful Italianate church complete with sunburst altarpiece and murals by Delacroix, St-Sulpice is stunning inside and out. Its square, with an elaborate fountain, is a favorite place to while away a few hours on a café terrace. Don't believe anything written about this church in *The Da Vinci Code*, though. Pl. St-Sulpice, 6th, 01.46.33.21.78. M° St-Sulpice.

La Ste-Chapelle One of the devout acts that got King Louis IX canonized was his building of this church to house a relic thought to be the crown of thorns. Chances are Louis was had, but he left us this symphony of stained glass whose 50-foot-high windows depict Biblical scenes in the minutest detail. 4 bd. du Palais, 1st, 01.53.40.60.80. M° Cité.

Performing Arts Venues

Les Bouffes du Nord Thespians will line up at dawn to get tickets for Brit director Peter Brook's unrenovated venue. Productions in English and French, now with classical music and opera too. 37 bis bd. de la Chapelle, 10th, 01.46.07.33.00, bouffesdunord.com. M° La Chapelle

Châtelet—Théâtre Musical de Paris Big-name pianists and opera stars, symphonic and chamber concerts, with dance performances and regional ballets. 1 pl. du Châtelet, 1st, 01.40.28.28.40, chatelet-theatre.com. M° Châtelet.

L'Olympia Legendary concert venue where all the greats have played hosts everyone from Charles Aznavour to Sting. 28 bd. des Capucins, 9th, 01.55.27.10.00, olympiahall.com. M° Opéra.

Opéra Bastille The new opera house has been panned for its design and acoustics, but still hosts some mighty fine productions by the national company. Pl. de la Bastille, 12th, 01.72.29.35.35, operadeparis.fr. M° Bastille.

Palais Garnier A chance to watch opera and ballet in grand 19th-century style with velvet boxes and a sweeping marble staircase. Pl. de l'Opéra, 9th, 01.72.29.35.35, operadeparis.fr. M° Opéra.

Théâtre National de Chaillot A magnificent setting with an Eiffel Tower view for interval drinks and high-octane performances of tango, flamenco, hip-hop, and ballet interspersed with contemporary French theater. 1 pl. du Trocadéro, 16th, 01.53.65.30.00, theatre-chaillot.fr. M° Trocadéro.

Théâtre de la Ville In its two venues, Théâtre de la Ville programs big names in contemporary dance, hip chamber music, experimental theater, and world music. 2 pl. du Châtelet, 4th, M° Châtelet; 31 rue des Abbesses, 18th, M° Abbesses; 01.42.74.22.77, theatredelaville-paris.com.

Le Zénith Chart-topping bands headline at this major rock venue that holds 2,000 in the Parc de La Villette complex. 211 av. Jean-Jaurès, 19th, 01.42.08.60.00, le-zenith.com. M° Porte de Pantin.

Parks

Bois de Boulogne 2,000 acres of former hunting forest west of Paris containing a lake with its own island restaurant, Jardin de Bagatelle rose garden, Shakespeare in summer, and two racetracks. Bikes and boats can be rented. M° La Muette.

Jardin du Luxembourg Next to an Italianate palace where the French Senate resides, the Luxembourg has it all—avenues of chestnut trees, Renaissance statuary, a lovers' rendezvous at the 1624 Fontaine de Médicis, a pond with quaint toy sailing boats, chic tennis courts, chess, an ice-cream house, an apiary, and an art museum. 6th arrondissement. RER Luxembourg.

Jardin des Tuileries Between the Louvre and Concorde, these formal gardens were laid out by Le Nôtre, who also did Versailles. Gravel avenues and formal parterres are punctuated by dramatic sculptures from classical mythology. The gardens' green metal chairs scattered around its fountain are a classic Paris scene, and a fair sets up here in summer. 1st arrondissement. M° Tuileries or Concorde.

Parc André Citroën This contemporary park by the Seine is a favorite with children in summer, who run in and out of the water jets on a sloping parterre. It also has hothouses, a Japanese garden, and the Eutelsat tethered hot-air balloon. 15th arrondissement. M° Javel.

Parc des Buttes Chaumont An old stone quarry was landscaped in the Haussmann era into this park of grassy hillsides, grottoes, waterfalls, and a lake with a temple. It remains off the beaten track but is well worth a visit as there are few places in Paris where you can lie on the grass and stay until nightfall. 19th arrondissement. M° Buttes Chaumont.

Parc Monceau The quintessential bourgeois park where nannies take children from the neighboring villas, Monceau is landscaped with classical follies. 8th arrondissement. M° Monceau.

Parc de La Villette Open-air concerts and films attract thousands to this futuristic park that also houses the Géode IMAX cinema and science museum. Illuminated walkways and bridges sparkle at night and spooky sounds can be heard at the Garden of Childhood Terrors. 19th arrondissement. M° Porte de La Villette.

CHEAT SHEET

Shopping Districts

Abbesses The cobbled Montmartre streets are the place to hunt for young designers' creations. 18th arrondissement. M° Abbesses.

The Champs-Elysées A-list fashion on glamorous Avenue de Montaigne. Clothing chains, Virgin, and Fnac music megastores and Drugstore Publicis for luxury gifts on the Champs itself are open until midnight and on Sundays. 8th arrondissement. M° George V.

Etienne Marcel Cutting-edge streetwear by French designers in this area near the manufacturing district. 2nd arrondissement. M° Etienne Marcel.

Grands Boulevards Department stores Galeries Lafayette and Printemps with other chains such as Zara and Célio. 9th arrondissement. M° Chaussée d'Antin.

The Marais Bijou boutiques for fashion, homeware, and gifts, many open on Sundays. 3rd and 4th arrondissements. M° St Paul.

St-Germain Top designer names including Dior, Prada, Sonia Rykiel, department store Bon Marché, shoes galore, and gourmet chocolate and pastries. 6th and 7th arrondissements. M° St-Germain-des-Prés or Sèvres Babylone.

World-Class Museums

Musée Guimet Important collection of Asian art, from an Angkor Wat temple entrance to Chinese terra-cotta horses.

Musée du Louvre The biggest museum in the world, containing 300,000 artworks and artifacts in the former palace of the kings of France.

Musée Marmottan Impressionist heaven, with the world's largest Monet collection including his late water lilies and works by Renoir, Manet, and Gauguin.

Musée d'Orsay The former Belle Epoque railway station contains a range of works from the seeds of the Impressionist movement to Klimt.

Centre Pompidou One of the world's greatest modern art collections, housed in Rogers and Piano's radical structure.

Flea Markets

Aligre The oldest and smallest flea market, and the only one within the 20 arrondissements. Secondhand clothes and bric-a-brac join a daily food market. Few bargains but a lot of color. *Tue-Sun 7:30am-1:30pm.* M° Ledru-Rollin.

Montreuil The junkiest and cheapest of the flea markets. Search through acres of old tools, stolen bikes, and TV remote controls to find antique kitchenware at bargain prices. *Sat-Mon 7am-7pm.* M° Porte de Montreuil.

Saint-Ouen (Clignancourt) The mother of all flea markets. Serious antiques dealers specialize in Art Deco, Louis XIV, or crystal chandeliers, and you can also pick up prints, buttons, medals, jewelry, and much more. *Sat-Mon 9am-6pm.* M° Porte de Clignancourt. les-puces.com

Vanves In the south of Paris, Vanves offers rich pickings for anyone looking for old lace, vintage clothes, and silverware. *Sat-Sun 7am-2pm.* M° Porte de Vanves.

Cemeteries

Père Lachaise Jim Morrison's grave is rivaled only by that of murdered French actress Marie Trintignant in terms of cult appeal. With hundreds of other famous names, it's the greatest necropolis in Paris. M° Père Lachaise.

Montmartre Romantic cemetery on the slopes of Montmartre has the graves of Hector Berlioz, Degas, Nijinsky, Adolf Sax, Marie Taglioni, François Truffaut, and can-can star La Gouloue. Egyptian diva and gay icon Dalida gets the prize for the most flowers. M° Blanche.

Montparnasse Celebrities interred here reflect the Rive Gauche's literary and artistic past: Samuel Beckett, Baudelaire, Sartre and de Beauvoir, Man Ray, Serge Gainsbourg, and Jean Seberg are among them. M° Raspail.

Riverbanks

Rive Gauche, the Left Bank, and **Rive Droite**, the Right, traditionally spelled the difference between intellect and commerce. Now the boundaries are blurred, but until the Seine freezes over Parisians will still define themselves by which side they choose to live on.

Singular Sensation

Eiffel Tower The 1,000-foot Iron Lady is the ultimate symbol of the City of Light, now more sparkling than ever with her scintillating illuminations.

Party Conversation—A Few Surprising Facts

- A colony of bees is hived on the roof of the Paris Opéra. You can buy their honey in Fauchon.

- More than 600 people are admitted to the hospital each year after slipping on a *crotte de merde*. The Paris municipality spends nearly 11 million euros a year to keep the city's pavements relatively free of dog dirt, but is fighting a losing battle, despite the ingenious moto-crottes (a kind of motorbike with a super-suction tube).

- Paris' population is shrinking by 3,000 people a year.

- The Louvre contains 12 miles of corridors and 300,000 works of art.

- 100,000 orchids enter the Paris Ritz in a year. Some of them are used to decorate cocktails.

- The expression "City of Light" has nothing to do with illuminations, but refers back to the philosophical Enlightenment of the 18th century.

- Traditional Paris bars are known as "zincs" because of the tin alloy used to make them. It's kind to glasses and kind on the ears and lasts forever.

- Paris' two passions, smoking and striking, went hand in hand in 2004 when tobacconists went on strike to protest the rising price of cigarettes.

- If you can't beat 'em, join 'em. A phalanx of rollerblading police was created as a response to Friday Night Fever's in-line skating rally, and has become a successful crime-fighting element.

- Every building in Paris is within 500 meters of a Métro station.

- Paris has six vineyards, including one on the Butte Montmartre.

- The Eiffel Tower's elevators travel 64,000 miles a year—that's the equivalent of two and a half times round the Earth.

- Bertrand Delanoë is Paris' first openly gay mayor, and the first socialist mayor of Paris since 1867.

- 2,000 tons of sand and 40 palm trees are imported every year to create an artificial beach, Paris Plage, on the banks of the Seine in July and August.

- Baron Haussmann built 85 miles of boulevards in 20 years.

Just for Business and Conventions

Paris' business district is out on a limb, in high-tech La Défense, 10 minutes from the center by RER. The trade fairs are held at the Parc des Expositions by Roissy airport (20 minutes by RER from Gare du Nord) and at the two exhibition centers on the edge of the city at Porte Maillot and Porte de Versailles (both 20 minutes from the center by Métro). High-tech fairs are at CNIT at La Défense. The stock exchange area of Bourse, in the 2nd arrondissement, is where the city suits lunch, but most upscale restaurants, bars, and nightlife are near the Champs-Elysées. Porte de Versailles visitors are near Montparnasse. If you want to be in the center of it all, RER B from the Parc des Expositions passes through the Latin Quarter; the Opéra area links easily to La Défense and Porte de Versailles.

Addresses to Know

Convention Centers
- CNIT
  2 pl. de La Défense (M°/RER Grande Arche de La Défense), La Défense, 01.43.95.37.00, parisexpo.fr
- Palais des Congrès
  2 pl. de la Porte Maillot (M° Porte Maillot), 17th, 01.40.68.22.22, palaisdescongres-paris.com
- Parc des Expositions de Paris-Nord Villepinte (RER Parc des Expositions), Roissy-Charles de Gaulle, 01.48.63.30.30, expoparisnord.com
- Paris-Expo
  Porte de Versailles (M° Porte de Versailles), 15th, 01.43.95.37.00, parisexpo.fr

City Information
- Paris Convention and Visitors Bureau
  25 rue des Pyramides
  (M° Pyramides), 1st, 08.92.68.30.00, parisinfo.com. Daily 9am-7pm
- Paris Chamber of Commerce
  27 av. de Friedland (M° Charles de Gaulle-Etoile), 8th, 01.55.65.55.65, ccip.fr. Mon-Fri 9am-6pm

Convention Hotels

These business hotels are either on the spot or have convenient transport links to the convention centers and have exceptional facilities.

La Défense
Sofitel La Défense Grande Arche This 17-story flatiron is a high point of the skyline. €€ 11 av. de l'Arche, La Défense, 01.47.17.50.00, sofitel.com

Paris
Le Grand InterContinental Grand and high-tech. €€€ 2 rue Scribe, 9th, 01.40.07.30.30, paris-le-grand.intercontinental.com

Hôtel Concorde Lafayette At Porte Maillot, with a panoramic bar on the 33rd floor. €€ 3 pl. du Général Koenig, 17th, 01.40.68.50.68, concorde-lafayette.com

BUSINESS AND CONVENTIONS

Hyatt Regency Paris-Madeleine Fabulous architecture and views and top conferencing facilities. €€€ 24 bd. Malesherbes, 8th, 01.55.27.12.34, hyatt.com

Mercure Terminus Est Stylish business hotel combines contemporary design with stained glass. € 5 rue du 8-mai 1945, 10th, 01.55.26.05.05, mercure.com

Park Hyatt Paris-Vendôme The ultimate in business luxury. (p.60) €€€€ 5 Rue de la Paix, 2nd, 01.58.71.12.34, paris.hyatt.com

Roissy-Charles de Gaulle and Parc des Expositions

Hyatt Regency Paris Spectacular architecture and a good restaurant. €€ Charles de Gaulle, Paris Nord 2, Roissy, 01.48.17.12.34, hyatt.com

Business Entertaining

Need to impress a client or network over drinks? These places will seal the deal.

Bar Panoramique Survey the whole of Paris from luxurious leather seats on the 33rd floor (p.23). Hôtel Concorde Lafayette, 3 pl. du Général Koenig, 17th, 01.40.68.50.68

Bon 2 Philippe Starck restaurant where traders eye stock prices above the bar while sucking oysters. 2 rue du Quatre-Septembre, 2nd, 01.44.55.51.55

Footsie After-work fun for traders at this pub-style bar where the drink prices fluctuate according to sales. 10-12 rue Daunou, 2nd, 01.42.60.07.20

Hiramatsu Perfectly orchestrated French haute cuisine by a Japanese chef. (p.67). 52 rue de Longchamp, 01.56.81.08.80

Also see: **Best Fine Dining** (p.28)
               Best Power Lunches (p.43)

Ducking Out for a Half-Day

All work and no play can't be good for you, so try one of these liberating pursuits.

Bateaux Vedette du Pont Neuf Take in many of the major sights with a boat trip down the Seine. (p.107) €– Square du Vert Galant (Pont Neuf), 01.46.33.98.38

Centre Pompidou Modern art collection rivaled only by MOMA, fab views from the upper floors. (p.79). €– pl. Georges Pompidou, 4th, 01.44.78.12.33

Maison Européenne de la Photographie Enjoy a photo exhibit, then stroll the nearby art galleries. (p.81) €– 5-7 rue de Fourcy (St-Paul), 01.44.78.75.00

Gifts to Bring Home

You are sure to find something suitably Parisian at one of these shops.

Galeries Lafayette Glittering behemoth of a department store (p.110). 40 bd. Haussmann (M° Chaussée d'Antin Lafayette), 01.42.82.34.56

Pierre Marcolini A chocolatier who become the fashionistas' darling. 89 rue de Seine (M° Mabillon), 01.44.07.39.07

Also see: **Best Concept Stores** (p.24)

PARIS REGION

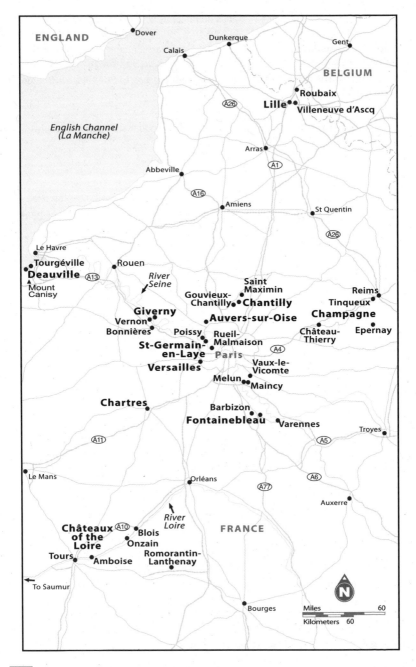

LEAVING PARIS

If you want a break from the Paris scene, a breathtaking variety of excursions are yours for the choosing—from lingering over decadent meals in the French countryside to strolling the grounds of sumptuous old châteaux in the Loire Valley to tasting fabled wines and Champagnes.

95 miles E

Champagne

Hot Tip: Come in June and July for local festivities, or in December for the Christmas market and illuminations.

The Lowdown: Some cities just get all the luck! Not only does Reims (pronounced "rance") have two of the world's man-made wonders, its UNESCO World Heritage–listed Gothic cathedral and St-Rémi Basilica, but nature also endowed it with the perfect conditions for making the world's most glamorous drink. Chalky soil, winter temperatures just above freezing, and a warren of ready-made cellars left behind by the Romans after they quarried for chalk mean that here, and here only, can Champagne be made. Unlike in other wine regions, most of the Champagne houses are in the town itself, with some in neighboring Epernay, so a car is not essential. Some offer paying visits; the more prestigious houses are by appointment only. It is well worth taking a cellar tour and tasting. Afterward, drink your favorite bubbly with a meal in one of the city's gastronomic restaurants. Reims' luck ran out, however, during World War I, when the cathedral and much of the town was badly damaged by fire. Restoration work by local craftspeople has restored the grandeur of the Cathedral while many of its treasures are on display in the neighboring museum. There is also a good fine arts museum.

Best Attractions

Cathédrale de Notre-Dame Awe-inspiring Gothic cathedral where the kings of France were crowned is encrusted with gargoyles and statues. A mystical stained-glass window by Chagall replaces one damaged in World War I. pl. du Cardinal Lucon

Musée des Beaux-Arts French 18th-century painting and a rare set of drawings by Cranach are among the highlights of the fine arts museum. 8 rue de Chancy, 03.26.47.28.44

Palais de Tau The old archepiscopal palace houses massive figures of kings from the cathedral and the 12th-century Charlemagne talisman. Book guided tours of the cathedral here. 2 pl. du Cardinal Lucon, 03.26.47.81.79

St-Rémi Basilica and Museum Older than the cathedral, St-Rémi is also a UNESCO world heritage site. 53 rue Simon, 03.26.85.23.36

Champagne Houses

Information on visits are available from the tourist office. Some of the best are:

Champagne Piper-Heidsieck Piper-Heidsieck's high-tech visit includes touring the dramatically lit cellars in automatic cars with a choice of seven languages. Paying visits. 51 bd. Henry Vasnier, 03.26.84.43.44, piper-heidsieck.com

Champagne Taittinger These cellars are among the most beautiful in the region, incorporating the remains of the 13th-century St-Nicaise Abbey. They take the tasting seriously and it is a good way to learn what to look for in a Champagne. Paying visits. 9 pl. Saint-Nicaise, 03.26.85.45.35, taittinger.com

Champagne Veuve Clicquot It was the widow Clicquot who invented the riddling process that has made modern Champagne what it is. The 15 miles of Gallo-Roman quarries are impressive, and the story of this formidable 19th-century businesswoman is fascinating. Visits by appointment. Ponsardin 1 pl. des Droits de l'Homme, 03 26 89 53 90, veuve-clicquot.com

Best Hotels

Château Les Crayères This Relais & Châteaux hotel has been voted best hotel in the world. The setting is stunning, the food by Michelin-starred Thierry Voisin out of this world. 64 bd. Henry Vasnier, 03.26.82.80.80, gerardboyer.com

Château de la Muire A slightly less opulent stay than Les Crayères, though there is an indoor pool and parkland. Ducasse-trained chef Arnaud Lallemant creates a rich cuisine favoring lobsters and veal at L'Assiette Champenoise. 40 av. Paul Vaillant-Couturier, Tinqueux, 03.26.84.64.64, assiettechampenoise.com.

Best Restaurants

L'Assiette Champenoise (see above).
Le Chardonnay An all-female team headed by Chantal Druart-Lange combines elegant cuisine with a top-class cellar. 184 av. d'Epernay, 03.26.06.08.60
Les Crayères (see above).
Le Millénaire Choose from the dramatic blue dining room, the terrace, or intimate salons upstairs at Laurent and Corinne Laplaige's elegant restaurant, prized for its fish cooking. 4-6 rue Bertin, 03.26.08.26.62

Reims Contacts

Marne Département Tourisme Information on the Route Touristique du Champagne, if you would like to discover the vignoble by car.
03.26.68.37.52, tourisme-en-champagne.com
Tourist Office 03.26.77.45.00, reims-tourisme.com

Getting There: By car take the A4 autoroute, direction Marne-la-Vallée and Metz. For Epernay, exit at Château Thierry and take the N3.
Trains from Gare de l'Est take about 90 minutes for Reims and Epernay.

Châteaux of the Loire

Hot Tip: Allow several days to see this region. Don't expect to see more than two major sites in one day because there's lots to see at each one.

The Lowdown: The Loire valley has it all: fairy-tale castles, rolling countryside, fine restaurants, vineyards, even golf courses. Blois and Tours are the two main cities, each with its own royal château, and the pretty town of Amboise sits right between them on the river. Cars can be rented from either center and once you are on the country roads, driving is a pleasure, allowing you to make your own itinerary as you spot distant spires or are tempted to try a dégustation at a local winery. The castle-rich district from Blois to Saumur extends for 80 miles along the Loire River and the châteaux are rarely more than 10 miles apart. The Loire region is well set up for bicycle touring with some 200 miles of paths and quiet routes.

The Loire châteaux are a true product of the Renaissance—their raison d'être was ostentatious rather than defensive. When the kings decided to take time out here between military campaigns, courtiers followed, each building a more splendid pad to show off his or her culture and ambition. Some are privately owned; others form part of the state heritage. The hotels are beyond your most romantic dreams, and the restaurants among the best.

Best Attractions

Note that some châteaux are closed during the winter.

Château d'Azay-le-Rideau You may weep when you see this moated château rising from an island on the River Indre, it so resembles a childhood fantasy castle. Nocturnal garden visits in summer. 14 miles SW of Tours, 02.47.45.42.04

Château de Brézé This château hides an incredible underground city, including a bakery last used by the Germans in World War II. You can also taste the castle's own Saumur wine. 40 miles W of Tours, 02.41.51.60.15

Château de Chambord This magnificent château built for François I in a forest near Blois looks like Disneyland—amazingly, it's real. 9 miles E of Blois, 08.25.82.60.88

Château de Chenonceau The River Cher flows between the five graceful arches of this Renaissance masterpiece built literally on the river. 20 miles E of Tours, 02.47.23.90.07

Château Royal d'Amboise This is the most Italianate of all the châteaux. The Gothic chapel of St-Hubert holds the tomb of Leonardo da Vinci, who died here in 1519. 14 miles E of Tours, 02.47.57.00.98

Château de Villandry Famed for its Renaissance knot gardens and jardin potager. 9 miles W of Tours, 02.47.50.02.09

Le Clos Lucé In Amboise, the Renaissance manor where Leonardo da Vinci was housed by François I for the last three years of his life. Forty of Leonardo's futuristic machines have been realized by IBM, using materials of the day. 13 miles E of Tours, 02.47.57.00.73

Golf International "Les Bordes" St-Laurent-Nouan This 18-hole course is repeatedly voted number one in Europe by the golfing press. 15 miles NE of Blois, 02.54.87.72.13, lesbordes.com

La Pagode de Chanteloup This strange folly is all that remains of the former Domaine de Chanteloup. A hybrid Chinese pagoda and Tower of Pisa, it has a magnificent view. 13 miles E of Tours, 02.47.57.20.97

Best Hotels and Restaurants

Château de Noizay This enchanting 16th-century pink manor house in the heart of the Vouvray vignoble sits nestled in its own 15 acres of parkland. The restaurant serves exquisite cuisine. 9 miles E of Tours, 02.47.52.11.01, chateaudenoizay.com

Château de Pray Route de Chargé This place feels really authentic with its 18th-century colors and antique-filled rooms. The restaurant has been acclaimed by Alain Ducasse and has its own kitchen garden. Amboise, 13 miles E of Tours, 02.47.57.23.67, praycastel.online.fr

Domaine des Hauts du Loire An old hunting pavilion surrounded by extensive wooded parkland and a lake with swans. Vegetables served at dinner come straight from the garden. Route d'Herbault, Onzain, 9 miles SW of Blois, 02.54.20.72.57, domainehautsloire.com

Grand Hôtel du Lion-d'Or This superb Renaissance manor house in the former king's hunting grounds has been a hotel since the Revolution. Family-run for over two generations, it is filled with books. In January and February winemakers celebrate the patron saint of wine. 69 rue Georges Clemenceau, Romorantin-Lanthenay. 24 miles SE of Blois, 02.54.94.15.15, hotel-liondor.fr

Le Manoir des Minimes The rooms in this 18th-century manor have an elegant sunny décor and plenty of antiques. Best of all are the views of the river and Chateau of Amboise. No meals. 34 quai Charles Guinot, Amboise. 13 miles E of Tours, 02.47.30.40.40, manoirlesminimes.com

Loire Contacts

Les Ailes Tournagelles Offers flights over the châteaux. In the village of Dierre, 25 miles from Amboise, 02.47.57.93.91, lesailestournagelles.com

Blois Tourist Office Excellent website for exploring the area; also has details of themed packages. 02.54.90.41.41, loiredeschateaux.com

Cycle touring Ten itineraries, with info on bike rentals, hotels, and restaurants. chateauxavelo.com

Tours Tourist Office Has web links to all the major châteaux. 02.47.70.37.37, ligeris.com

---

Getting There: By car, take the A10 autoroute to Blois, then follow the Loire along the N152 to Saumur via Amboise and Tours. TGV trains to Blois, Amboise, and Tours leave from Paris Gare d'Austerlitz and take between 1 hour, 40 minutes, and 2 hours, 40 minutes.

Deauville

Hot Tip: Plan to visit in August to be here during the height of the social season. Otherwise, come in September for the Film Festival.

The Lowdown: In 1858 Morny, Napoléon III's half-brother, had the bright idea of creating a tailor-made resort on the Normandy coast, centering around a racecourse and casino. In four years, Deauville was built and aristocratic and bourgeois society followed. Amazingly, this northern seaside has weathered the trend for suntans and is still a glittering holiday town whose population swells from 4,500 to around 75,000 in season. High society flocks here for the Cowes-Deauville regatta in May, the races, the polo and international yearlings sale in August, and the Paris-Deauville vintage motor rally in October. Celebrities descend in September for the American Film Festival, which has now spawned its Asian equivalent in March. With luxury yachts crowding the harbor and its elegant boardwalk, Deauville is the Riviera of the north.

Best Attractions

Algotherm Thalasso-Spa The thalassotherapy spa offers various "vitality cures" based on seawater and algae. 3 rue de Sem, 02.31.87.72.00

Amirauté Golf Club 18-hole championship golf course with the only floodlit course in Europe. CD 278, Tourgéville, 02.31.14.42.00

The Boardwalk Built in 1933, the Boardwalk is where you can spot American film stars' names on the bathing huts, or real stars during the Film Festival.

Casino Barrière de Deauville The glittering halls of this Belle Epoque building offer roulette, boule, stud poker, blackjack, craps, punto baco, and slot machines. Rue Edmond Blanc, 02.31.14.31.14

Mount Canisy Drive to the top of this promontory for spectacular views of the Norman coast.

Pompeian Baths In 1921, the winner of a competition to jazz up the wooden bathing huts created this fantasy pastiche of the ancient world, with atrium, mosaic loggias, and fountains. With a bar and Turkish baths, it's a fashionable place to relax and you can rent a beach hut by the day, week or month.

Villa Strassburger Fantasy Norman villa built by the Rothschilds, open only in August. Av. Strassburger, 02.31.88.20.44

Racecourses

Hippodrome de Deauville-Clairefontaine Racing in July, August, December, and January. Tourgéville, 02.31.14.69.00

Hippodrome de Deauville-La Touques 45 av. Hocquart de Turtot, 02.31.14.20.00

Best Hotels

Normandy Barrière Elegant Anglo-Norman manor evokes the Belle Epoque. 38 rue Jean Mermoz, 02.31.98.66.22, lucienbarriere.com

Royal Barrière A splendid palace where you'll cross paths with film stars, international jet-setters, and racing luminaries depending on the season. Bd. Cornuché, 02.31.98.66.33, lucienbarriere.com

Best Restaurants

Le Ciro's Whole sea bass, oysters, and seafood platters overlooking the beach. 2 rue Edmond Blanc, 02.31.14.31.31

L'Etrier Ducasse disciple Eric Provost just won a Michelin star for his terroir-based haute cuisine. Royal Barrière (see above)

Best Nightlife

The most see-and-be-seen nightlife takes place at the casino, where visitors can either sip a cocktail overlooking the boardwalk at the Bar Soleil or dance the night away at Le Régine's club.

Deauville Contacts

Deauville Yacht Club 02.31.88.38.19
Tourist Office deauville.org

Getting There: By car, take the A13 autoroute all the way to Deauville. Trains take around 2 hours from Gare St-Lazare.

Auvers-sur-Oise

22 miles NE

Hot Tip: Come in high summer to see it as Vincent saw it.

The Lowdown: This is the village where Vincent Van Gogh painted some of his greatest masterpieces, and, in July 1890, shot himself in the chest in the nearby fields. Vincent's cell-like room at the Auberge is strangely moving, and an excellent video and guided tour recounts the story using quotes from his letters to his brother Theo. But Vincent isn't the only reason to visit this pretty village. A signposted walk takes in enchanting lanes and steep streets, leading to the house of Doctor Gachet (Vincent's friend and art collector), the atelier and museum of artist Daubigny, the Château d'Auvers, the Musée de l'Absinthe, which explores the drink that may have contributed to Van Gogh's madness, and the gorgeous little church where Vincent and Theo are buried. Reproductions of paintings around the town let you compare them to their real-life sites, and in the summer, artists living in the village open up their studios. In June Auvers hosts a prestigious classical music festival.

Best Attractions

Auberge Ravoux Vincent Van Gogh's room at this inn can be visited. 52 rue du Général-de-Gaulle, 01.30.36.60.63

Château d'Auvers A 17th-century castle with a display on the Impressionists and elegant gardens. Rue de Léry, 01.34.48.48.45

Maison-Atelier Daubigny Contains a 2,000-square-foot mural painted by Daubigny, Corot, and other artists of their circle. 61 rue Daubigny, 01.34.48.03.03

Musée de l'Absinthe History of the drink with its paraphernalia arranged in a reconstructed literary café. 44 rue Callé, 01.30.36.83.26

Best Restaurants

Auberge Ravoux Though the inn retains all its traditional charm, we guess that the food is a darn sight better than it was in Vincent's day. Feast on hare or lamb served in cast-iron pots. (see above)

Hostellerie du Nord Joël Boilleaut serves a gastronomic menu. 6 rue Général-de-Gaulle, 01.30.36.70.74

Auvers-sur-Oise Contacts

Tourist Office 01.30.36.10.06, auvers-sur-oise.com

Getting There: By car take the A15 out of Paris, leave at exit 7 (St-Ouen-l'Aumône), then follow the N184 toward Amiens-Beauvais. Exit Méry-sur-Oise for Auvers. Or go by train from Gare du Nord, changing at St-Ouen-l'Aumône, but beware of long waits between trains.

Chantilly

22 miles NE

Hot Tip: You'll want to come in June to catch the races.

The Lowdown: Chantilly lace was created here, but it's not the town's only claim to fame. Chantilly hosts the swankiest race meet in France, the Prix de Diane Hermès, on the second Sunday in June. It's definitely a time to get dressed up and hobnob with French high society. If you're not in town for the Prix de Diane, there is racing from April to September, you can visit the horse training center, and the Musée Vivant du Cheval is open year-round with visits to its beautiful stables and dressage shows on the first Sunday of the month from February to November. The Polo Club du Domaine de Chantilly hosts weekend matches and you can take lessons. All this happens against a backdrop of one of France's most stunning châteaux. The park has a classic French garden by Le Nôtre, follies, a maze, a lake, a jardin-potager, and a 17th-century hydraulic system for pumping spring water to the fountains. The countryside and forest are peppered with châteaux, many of which house luxury hotels and restaurants.

Best Attractions

Château de Chantilly Fine museum of historical paintings in grand castle with lavish garden. 03.44.62.62.62
Hippodrome de Chantilly Race calendar: 01.49.10.20.86 Training center: 03.44.67.37.37
Musée Vivant du Cheval Les Grandes Ecuries Chantilly Beautiful stables and dressage shows for fans of all things equestrian. 03.44.57.40.40

Best Restaurants

Chateau de Montvillargenne Hotel and restaurant in a château. The best in the Oise. Al fresco dining in summer. Av. François-Mathet, Gouvieux-Chantilly, 03.44.62.37.37, chateaudemontvillargenne.com
Le Château de la Tour Chemin de la Chaussée A menu featuring many delicacies. Al fresco dining in summer. Gouvieux-Chantilly, 03.44.62.38.38
Le Verbois An old hunting lodge in the forest. Al fresco dining in summer. Route Nationale 16 Chantilly-Creil, Saint Maximin, 03.44.24.06.22

Chantilly Contacts

Polo Club de la Domaine de Chantilly La Ferme d'Apremont, Apremont, 03.44.64.04.30, poloclubchantilly.com
Tourist Office 03.44.67.37.37, chantilly-tourisme.com

Getting There: By car take the A1 out of Paris and exit 7 (to drive through the forest of Chantilly), marked Chantilly, or the N16 or N17 trunk roads. Trains take 27 minutes from Gare du Nord, the RER line D 45 minutes. Taxis from the station to the château cost about €6.

55 miles SW

Chartres

Hot Tip: Come in June for the River Festival or in July and August for organ concerts and illuminations.

The Lowdown: "The Acropolis of the west" according to Rodin, Chartres Cathedral was listed on UNESCO's first World Heritage list. The town acquired its future glory thanks to the gift in 876 of a relic called the "Sacra Camisia," said to be the birthing garment of the Virgin. The present Cathedral was started in 1215 on the site of a former basilica destroyed by a fire. Its mismatched spires rise out of the flat cornfields, dominating the landscape from afar. Close up, it's the spectacular stained glass that takes your breath away, along with the intricately sculpted Royal Portal. Chartres is a town of narrow winding streets and steep lanes and stairways, where you can explore glassmaking workshops and perfume shops. Although dwarfed by the cathedral, other town churches are worth a visit, such as St-Pierre with its 14th-century windows. The International Stained Glass Center holds exhibitions on the history of stained glass and contemporary creation. The Fine Arts Museum includes 18th-century French paintings. Chartres is also famous for Resistance hero Prefect Jean Moulin, who opposed the demands of the occupying forces in 1940 (to find out more, visit the Musée Jean Moulin in Paris, 01.40.64.39.44). The town suffered extensive damage in 1944, before being liberated by the 20th U.S. Corps and local patriots.

Best Attractions

Cathédrale Notre-Dame English-language tours given by the authority on Chartres Cathedral, Malcolm Miller. Place de la Cathédrale, 02.37.21.59.08
Centre International du Vitrail International stained-glass center. 5 rue du Cardinal Pie, 02.37.21.65.72.
Musée des Beaux-Arts Fine arts museum. 29 Cloître Notre-Dame, 02.37.90.45.80

Best Restaurants

Le Buisson Ardent The cuisine combines specialties from different French regions, such as foie gras with apples and Calvados. Lunch menus are a particularly good value. 10 rue au Lait, 02.37.34.04.66
La Vieille Maison Set in a 14th-century building with a 9th-century chiselled-stone ceiling vault. 5 rue au Lait, 02.37.34.10.67

Chartres Contacts

Convention and Visitors' Bureau 02.37.18.26.26, ville-chartres.fr, chartres-tourisme.com, chartres.com (site in English)

Getting There: By car, take the A6 south, then the A10 and A11 direction Nantes. Trains leave from Gare Montparnasse and take 1 hour.

LEAVING PARIS • DAY TRIPS

Fontainebleau and Vaux-le-Vicomte

37 miles SE

Hot Tip: Take your hiking boots for a romp around the forest. Try to schedule your visit to Vaux-le-Vicomte during one of its famed candlelit tours.

The Lowdown: Fontainebleau and Vaux-le-Vicomte are two magnificent châteaux. Unless you are crazy about history, it would be too much to fit them both into one day, so choose one and spend a bucolic afternoon in the forest, by the river, or in the painters' village of Barbizon. The Château de Fontainebleau is smaller than Versailles and rich with Italian influences. It is surrounded by a formal garden and beautiful parkland where you can rent boats and horse-drawn carriages. Vaux-le-Vicomte was built by Louis XIV's Superintendant of Finances, whose tragic mistake was to create a château that was too splendid—Louis XIV flew into a jealous rage when he saw it, condemned the minister to solitary confinement, then promptly commissioned Vaux's architects to build Versailles. In Barbizon, historical and contemporary studios are open to the public. From here, walk into the forest of Fontainebleau. It has footpaths and bikes for rent. Or head out for a picnic on the riverbanks near Fontaine-le-Port and Samois.

Best Attractions

Barbizon Painters' town with two museums along the rue Grande.
Château de Fontainebleau Graceful Renaissance château built by François I. 01.60.71.50.60
Château de Vaux-le-Vicomte The inspiration for Versailles, with spectacular fountain displays and candlelit tours. Maincy, 01.64.14.41.90
Fôret de Fontainebleau Miles of tracks and a rock-climbers' wonderland.

Best Restaurants

Hôtellerie du Bas-Bréau This hotel restaurant serves regional specialties. Don't miss the cheese board. 22 Grande Rue, Barbizon, 01.60.66.40.05
Ile aux Truites A menu of grills and fresh trout by the river—you can even catch your own fish here. 6 chemin Basse Varenne, Vulaines sur Seine, 01.64.23.71.87
La Table des Maréchaux Summer dining on the terrace overlooking a private garden. 9 rue Grande, Fontainebleau, 01.60.39.50.50

Fontainebleau Contacts

Fontainebleau Tourist Office 01.60.74.99.99, fontainebleau-tourisme.com

Getting There: By car, take the A6, then the N7 (75 minutes). Barbizon is en route. Vaux-le-Vicomte is north of here, via the N6. Trains (30 minutes) leave from Gare de Lyon to Fontainebleau and Vaux-le-Vicomte (train to Melun, then a 4-mile taxi). Barbizon is an 8-mile taxi ride from Melun.

Giverny

Hot Tip: Come in August for the water lilies in full bloom. And get here early (it opens at 9:30am) to get the full magic without crowds of other visitors spoiling the view.

The Lowdown: A visit to Giverny is less to do with seeing Monet's paintings—only copies are exhibited here as most of his great works on view in France are in the Musée Marmottan and Musée d'Orsay—than with experiencing his wonderful garden with its Chinese bridge, lily pond, and pergolas of climbing roses bordered with nasturtia. So carefully and lusciously has it been restored that it gives the feeling of being inside one of Monet's paintings. The cottagey house has rooms painted in Monet's trademark blue and yellow, and houses his large collection of Japanese prints. Monetville has another museum too, that of American art. Housing the large collection of printing magnate Daniel J. Terra and affiliated with the Terra Foundation for American Art in Chicago, the museum focuses on the American Impressionists who settled in Giverny and mounts temporary exhibitions covering a wide spectrum of American art. It also has its own beautiful gardens.

Best Attractions

Fondation Claude Monet Monet's house and garden, where he painted the water-lily series. *Closed Nov-Mar.* 84 rue Claude Monet, 02.32.51.28.21

Musée d'Art Américain Museum of American Impressionists, with good temporary exhibitions. 99 rue Claude Monet, 02.32.51.94.65

Best Restaurants

Restaurant Baudy Giverny Because Giverny's appeal is pretty much mass market, good hotels and restaurants are hard to find. This former hotel (it no longer has rooms), however, is a charming spot. Once the hang-out of a group of American artists who had a ball here and paid in canvases, it has a beautiful rose garden and serves inexpensive but delicious French cuisine and salads. Reservations are essential. 81 rue Claude Monet, 02.32.21.10.03

Giverny Contacts

Tourist information from non-profit organization GiVerNet. http://giverny.org

Getting There: By car take the A13 autoroute to Bonnières, then the D201. By train, Gare St-Lazare to Vernon (45 minutes), then a 3-mile taxi ride or bus from the station.

LEAVING PARIS • DAY TRIPS

15 miles W

St-Germain-en-Laye

Hot Tip: Skip the car. It is quickest to get here by RER.

The Lowdown: The "other" St-Germain is an elegant town built around the château where Henri II lived with his wife Catherine de Médicis and mistress Diane de Poitiers. Napoléon converted it into an awe-inspiring archaeological museum. St-Germain-en-Laye also has a museum devoted to the Nabis painters and another to Claude Debussy, which holds evening and afternoon recitals. The home of diplomats and the haute-bourgeoisie, it has some elegant shops and a "Sunday-best feel" as you promenade in front of the château. Nearby are two ancient hunting forests, St-Germain and Marly, and Malmaison, the petite home Napoléon built for Josephine.

Best Attractions

Musée des Antiquités Nationales Antiquities from the Paleolithic age on, with temporary exhibitions. Château, place du Charles de Gaulle, 01.39.10.13.00
Musée Claude Debussy The composer's former home holds recitals. 38 rue au Pain, 01.39.73.02.64
Musée Maurice Denis Houses paintings by Bonnard, Vuillard, Roussel, and Vallotton. "Le Prieuré," 2 bis rue Maurice Denis, 01.39.73.77.87
Petit Malmaison Empress Josephine's dollhouse-like home is a study in Empire style. Av. du Château, Rueil-Malmaison, 01.47.49.48.15
Villa Savoye Modernist masterpiece by Le Corbusier. 82 rue de Villers, Poissy, 01.39.65.01.06

Best Restaurants

Cazaudehore Le Forestière This forest chalet opened as a refreshment stop by a maître d' has become a Relais & Châteaux hotel and restaurant and is still in the same family. Foie gras, sea bream, venison, and lobster are cooked to perfection. av. President Kennedy, Forest of St-Germain-en-Laye, 01.30.61.64.64
Chez Clément In the old Auberge du Coq Hardy painted by Renoir in his *Dance at Bougival*, decent traditional food and a cozy setting with fumoir and library. 15 bis, Quai Rennequin Sualem, Bougival, 01.30.78.20.00

St-Germain-en-Laye Contacts

Tourist Office 01.34.51.05.12, ville-st-germain-en-laye.fr

Getting There: By car, take the A13, then the N186, or take the N13 from La Défense, which passes by Malmaison. By RER, take line A to St-Germain-en-Laye; stop at Rueil-Malmaison for Malmaison.

12.5 miles SW

Versailles

Hot Tip: Visit on summer weekends to see the fountains spout to music.

The Lowdown: In the 1670s, Paris was too dirty for the Sun King, so Louis XIV decided to move his court out to Versailles and rule in splendor from his favorite hunting forest. The palace was designed to be not only his home but a glittering mirror of his greatness and France's superiority in arts and sciences. From here, Louis could work on his myth of quasi-deity, awe foreign visitors, and create an elaborate system of hierarchy. Over-the-top in every way, Versailles was the Graceland of its day, and it's easy to see why the French decided, a century later, that enough was enough. Although always crowded, it's worth a visit just to marvel at the excesses and scale of it. The Petit and Grand Trianon are mini-palaces that Louis XIV built for his children and mistresses. A new attraction is the Ecuries, which have been converted into an equestrian school. The cream of the world's young riders train here. In town, the Quartier Notre-Dame features cobbled streets filled with antiques dealers and a good food market.

Best Attractions

Château and Gardens of Versailles Louis the Sun King's magnificent château and gardens. 01.30.83.78.00, chateauversailles.fr
Grand Trianon/Petit Trianon Two pavilions built for the royal mistresses.
Les Grandes Ecuries Watch the equestrian academy at work on magnificent white horses. 01.39.02.07.14

Best Hotel

Trianon Palace A retreat for the likes of Marlene Dietrich, Queen Elizabeth II, and John Travolta. 1 bd. de la Reine, 01.30.84.50.00

Best Restaurants

Au Chapeau Gris The oldest restaurant in Versailles, the Chapeau Gris has a few secrets in its cellar. 7 rue Hoche, 01.39.50.10.81
Les Manèges Eric Guignon serves prizewinning cuisine at the Sofitel Château de Versailles. 2 bis av. de Paris, 01.39.07.46.05
Les Trois Marches Food fit for a king. Or try the Café Trianon for summer dining. Hôtel Trianon Palace, 1 bd. de la Reine, 01.30.84.52.00

Versailles Contacts

Tourist Office 01.39.24.88.88, versailles-tourisme.com

Getting There: By car, take the A13 and the D182.
By RER, line C, Versailles Rive Gauche.

PARIS BLACK BOOK

You're solo in the city—where's a singles-friendly place to eat? Is there a good lunch spot near the museum? Will the bar be too loud for easy conversation? Get the answers fast in the *Black Book*, a condensed version of every listing in our guide that puts all the essential information at your fingertips.

A quick glance down the page and you'll find the type of food, nightlife, or attractions you are looking for, the phone numbers, and which pages to turn to for more detailed information. How did you ever survive without it?

Paris Black Book By Neighborhood

1st Arrondissement

H	Hôtel Costes		57
	Hôtel Meurice		155
	Hôtel Ritz		92
	Renaissance Paris Vendôme Hôtel		60
R	Angelina		93
	Bioboa		62
	Cabaret		63
	Café Marly	19	95
	Costes*	16	64
	L'Espadon		97
	Le Fumoir	34	66
	Le Grand Véfour		161
	Kong*		67
	Au Pied de Cochon	33	99
	Le Restaurant du Palais Royal		164
	La Table d'Hôte du Palais Royal		100
	Willi's Wine Bar		101
N	Banana Café		134
	Bar Fontainebleau	22	166
	Bar Hemingway	22	102
	Le Cab		74
	Costes*		74
	Le Defender		167
	Kong*	23	75
	Le Paris Paris		139
	Ritz Club		105
	Le Tropic Café		142
	Willi's Wine Bar		106
A	Bateaux Vedette du Pont Neuf		107
	La Bulle Kenzo		79
	Colette	24	79
	La Conciergerie		109
	L'Eclaireur		172
	L'Espace Bien-Etre at the Meurice	46	173
	Jardin des Tuileries	47	80
	Maria Luisa		81
	Musée de la Mode et du Textile	21	82
	Musée du Louvre	47	112
	Palais Royal		175
A	La Ste-Chapelle		114
	Spa Nuxe 32 Montorgueil	46	83
	Surface to Air	24	147

2nd Arrondissement

H	Hôtel Edouard VII		92
	Park Hyatt Paris Vendôme		60
R	A Priori Thé		158
	Bon 2	43	
	Davé	20	65
	Gallopin		161
	Aux Lyonnais		98
	Macéo		162
	Les Orchidées	18	68
	Somo		132
	Le Tambour	33	133
N	Café Noir		136
	Le Pulp		140
	Rex Club	26	140
	Somo		141
	Le Triptyque	26	142
A	Les Bains du Montorgueil		171

3rd Arrondissement

H	Hôtel du Petit Moulin		124
	Murano Urban Resort		59
	Pavillon de la Reine		156
R	Le 404	39	126
	Anahi		126
	Café Baci		63
	Chez Janou		128
	L'Estaminet		129
	Murano	40	68
N	Andy Wahloo		134
	Les Bains Douches		73
	Jokko Bar	35	139
	Murano Bar	48	76
A	Galerie Simone		144
	India & Spa		144
	Marais private galleries		81
	Marché des Enfants-Rouges	37	145
	Musée Carnavalet		111
	Musée Picasso		82

Code: H-Hotels; R-Restaurants; N-Nightlife; A-Attractions. Blue page numbers denote listings in 99 Best; black denotes listings in Experience sections. The Paris Neighborhoods Map is on page 255.

BLACK BOOK BY NEIGHBORHOOD

4th Arrondissement

H	Hôtel Bourg Tibourg		123
R	L'Ambroisie		158
	Chez Marianne		95
	Georges	16	66
	Le Loir dans la Théière		130
	Les Marronniers		68
	Mon Vieil Ami		163
	Les Philosophes*		131
N	L'Amnésia Café	29	73
	La Belle Hortense	34	135
	Chez Richard		136
	L'Etoile Manquante		137
	Open Café	29	139
	La Perle	31	140
	Les Philosophes*		140
	Raidd Bar	29	77
A	Cathédrale Notre Dame de Paris		108
	Centre Pompidou	25	79
	Ile St-Louis		173
	Maison Européenne de la Photographie		81
	Pavillon de l'Arsenal		146

5th Arrondissement

R	La Balle au Bond*		158
	Café Maure de la Mosquée de Paris		159
	L'Equitable		96
	Fogón St Julien		97
	Les Papilles		99
	Le Pré Verre	17	99
	La Tour d'Argent		101
	La Truffière		101
	Le Réminet		164
	Le Ziryab	39	165
N	La Balle au Bond*		166
	Café Delmas		103
	Summer dancing by the Seine		170
A	Marché Mouffetard	37	111
	Musée Nationale du Moyen Age-Thermes et Hôtel de Cluny		112
	Le Panthéon		113
	Shakespeare & Co.		114

6th Arrondissement

H	Esprit Saint Germain		57
	L'Hôtel		155
	Relais Christine		156
R	Allard		93
	La Balle au Bond*		158
	Le Bélier		159
	Les Bouquinistes		63
	Brasserie Lipp		94
	Da Rosa		96
	Les Deux Magots	19	65
	Emporio Armani Caffé	20	65
	Ladurée		161
	Lapérouse		162
	La Méditerranée	44	98
	Le Palanquin		163
	Pères et Filles		99
	Le Rostand		100
	Le Salon d'Hélène		165
	Au Vieux Colombier		165
	Ze Kitchen Galerie		72
N	La Balle au Bond*		166
	Bar du Marché		102
	Le Bilboquet	32	102
	Café de Flore		103
	Café de la Mairie		167
	Chez Castel		103
	La Closerie des Lilas		104
	L'Echelle de Jacob		168
	Les Editeurs	34	104
	Mezzanine de l'Alcazar	36	169
	La Palette		105
	Le Sabot	32	106
	Au Vieux Colombier		170
	Le Wagg		170
A	Jardin du Luxembourg	42	173
	Musée du Luxembourg		174

7th Arrondissement

H	Hôtel Montalembert		58
R	L'Arpège		61
	L'Atelier de Joël Robuchon		62
	Au Bon Accueil	17	94
	Café de l'Esplanade		63
	Le Chamarré		95
	Le Jardin de Varenne		161
	Le Jules Verne		97

7th Arrondissement (cont.)

R	Thiou	72
	Le Voltaire	101
N	Bateau Concorde Atlantique	166
	Café du Marché	103
	Le Tourville	106
A	Eiffel Tower	109
	Les Invalides	111
	Musée d'Orsay	112
	Musée Rodin	47 174

8th Arrondissement

H	Four Seasons George V		91
	Hôtel Le A		123
	Hôtel Le Bristol		91
	Hôtel de Crillon		91
	Hôtel Lancaster		155
	Hôtel Plaza Athénée		58
	Hôtel de Sers		59
R	Alain Ducasse au Plaza Athénée	28	61
	Les Ambassadeurs	18	93
	L'Angle du Faubourg		93
	L'Avenue		62
	Le Bristol		95
	Café Jacquemart-André	18	159
	La Cantine du Faubourg*		64
	Le Chiberta	43	64
	Le Cinq		95
	Flora		160
	Flora Danica		66
	Laurent	41	98
	Maison Blanche	16	67
	Market		68
	Maxim's		162
	Music Hall*	33	68
	Pershing Hall*		69
	Pierre Gagnaire		69
	Pomze		163
	Senderens		70
	Senso		165
	Le Sers		70
	Spoon, Food & Wine		70
	Stella Maris		71
	Le Stresa		71
	La Suite*		71
	Taillevent	28	100

R	Toi		72
	Le Village		72
N	Le Bar at the George V	48	73
	Bar César	22	102
	Le Bar du Plaza	48	73
	Le Baron	31	134
	Le Bound		74
	Buddha Bar		167
	La Cantine du Faubourg*	36	74
	Crazy Horse		104
	Le Jaipur		168
	Man Ray		169
	Mathi's Bar		75
	Le Milliardaire		75
	Music Hall*		76
	Le Néo	45	76
	Pershing Lounge*	38	76
	Pink Paradise		77
	Le Queen		77
	Régine's Club		105
	La Suite*	45	77
	Toi		78
	Le VIP Room	20	78
A	La Collection 1900		172
	Drugstore Publicis		79
	Fauchon		173
	Le Grand Palais		110
	Jeu de Paume		80
	Musée Jacquemart-André		173
	Le Spa at the Four Seasons George V	46	114
	Les Thermes		115

9th Arrondissement

H	Pavillon de Paris	125
	Villa Royale	125
R	Angl'Opera	158
	Les Cakes de Bertrand	160
	Pétrelle	163
N	Café de la Paix	167
	Folies Pigalle	138
	L'Olympia	105
	Opéra National de Paris Palais Garnier	169
	Le Zinzin	142
A	Galeries Lafayette	110
	Printemps	113

BLACK BOOK BY NEIGHBORHOOD

10th Arrondissement
- R Canal 96* — 127
- Chez Prune* — 128
- Julien — 97
- La Madonnina — 130
- La Marine — 130
- Le Martel — 39 130
- Le Sporting — 132
- N Canal 96* — 136
- Chez Prune* — 136
- De la Ville Café — 136
- L'Ile Enchantée — 138
- Le Jemmapes — 138
- New Morning — 32 105
- A Antoine et Lili — 143

11th Arrondissement
- H Le Général — 123
- R Le Bistrot du Peintre — 126
- Café Charbon — 127
- Le Chateaubriand — 128
- Pause Café — 19 131
- Polichinelle Café — 131
- N Café Charbon — 135
- Favela Chic — 138
- A Musée du Fumeur — 145
- O Château — 175

12th Arrondissement
- R Le Baron Rouge — 126
- Chai 33 — 127
- Sardegna a Tavola — 131
- Le Square Trousseau — 17 132
- Swann et Vincent — 133
- Viaduc Café* — 133
- N Chai 33 — 136
- China Club — 36 136
- La Fabrique — 137
- Sanz Sans — 141
- La Scène Bastille — 35 141
- Viaduc Café* — 142
- A Canauxrama — 143
- Cinémathèque Française — 143
- La Maison Rouge (Fondation Antoine de Galbert) — 25 144
- Promenade Plantée — 147

13th Arrondissement
- R L'Avant-Goût — 94
- Djoon — 129
- N Batofar — 26 135
- Djoon — 137
- A Louise Weiss galleries — 144

14th Arrondissement
- H Hôtel Lutetia — 92
- R Apollo — 61
- La Coupole — 44 96
- N Dancing at La Coupole — 104
- Le Rosebud — 106
- A Les Catacombes — 108
- Fondation Cartier — 80
- Fondation Henri Cartier-Bresson — 110
- Friday Night Fever — 144

15th Arrondissement
- R Le Quinzième — 69
- R — 27 164
- A Le Ballon Eutelsat — 171
- Parc André Citroën — 42 175

16th Arrondissement
- H Hôtel Costes K — 57
- Hôtel Sezz — 59
- Trocadéro Dokhan's — 157
- R L'Astrance — 61
- Bon — 40 62
- Café de l'Homme — 27 64
- Le Cristal Room — 40 65
- L'Etoile* — 66
- Hiramatsu — 43 67
- Aux Marches du Palais — 130
- Le Relais du Parc — 41 69
- La Table de Joël Robuchon — 71
- La Table Lauriston — 100
- Tokyo Eat — 27 133
- N Champagne Bar at Le Dokhan's — 167
- L'Etoile* — 45 75
- Jardin Plein Ciel — 23 75
- Tokyo Idem — 142

16th Arrondissement (cont.)

A	Fondation Pierre Bergé-Yves Saint Laurent	21	80
	Musée d'Art Moderne de la Ville de Paris		81
	Musée des Arts Asiatiques-Guimet		82
	Musée Baccarat	21	82
	Musée de la Contrefaçon		82
	Musée Marmottan		174
	Musée de la Vie Romantique		175
	Palais de Tokyo	25	146

17th Arrondissement

R	Le Bistrot d'à Coté Flaubert		94
	Guy Savoy	28	67
	Sora Lena		70
N	Bar Panoramique	23	

18th Arrondissement

H	Kube Rooms		124
R	Café Burq		127
	Chez Toinette		128
	Le Doudingue*		160
	Drôle d'Endroit pour une Rencontre*		129
	La Famille		129
	La Mascotte	44	98
	Le Poulbot Gourmet		99
	Le Sancerre*		131
	Le Square		132
N	Botak Café		166
	Divan du Monde		168
	Le Doudingue*		168

N	Drôle d'Endroit pour une Rencontre*	38	137
	Elysée Montmartre	35	137
	Kube Lounge and Ice Kube		139
	Moulin Rouge		104
	Le Progrès	38	140
	Le Sancerre*		141
	Au Soleil de la Butte		141
A	Basilique du Sacré-Coeur		107
	Musée de l'Erotisme		145
	Musée de Montmartre		112
	Spree	24	147

19th Arrondissement

N	Bar Ourcq		134
	Café Chéri(e)	31	135
A	Parc des Buttes Chaumont	42	146
	La Villette		147

20th Arrondissement

A	Cimetière de Père Lachaise		108

Bois de Boulogne (BB)

R	Le Chalet des Iles	41	160
	Le Pré Catelan		164
A	Bois de Boulogne		171

St-Ouen (SO)

R	Chez Louisette		128
	Le Soleil		132
A	Marché aux Puces de St-Ouen (Clignancourt)	37	145

Notes

Paris Black Book

Hotels

NAME TYPE (ROOMS)	ADDRESS (METRO) WEBSITE	AREA	PHONE (01) PRICE	EXPERIENCE	PAGE
Esprit Saint-Germain Trendy (31)	22 rue St-Sulpice (Mabillon) espritsaintgermain.com	6th	53.10.55.55 €€	Hot & Cool	57
Four Seasons George V Grand (245)	31 av. George V (Alma-Marceau) fourseasons.com	8th	49.52.70.00 €€€€	Classic	91
Le Général Trendy (47)	5-7 rue Rampon (Oberkampf) legeneralhotel.com	11th	47.00.41.57 €	Bobo	123
L'Hôtel Trendy (20)	13 rue des Beaux-Arts (St-Germain-des-Prés) l-hotel.com	6th	44.41.99.00 €€	Romantic	155
Hôtel Le A Trendy (25)	4 rue d'Artois (St-Philippe-du-Roule) paris-hotel-a.com	8th	42.56.99.99 €€	Bobo	123
Hôtel Bourg Tibourg Trendy (31)	19 rue du Bourg-Tibourg (St-Paul) hotelbourgtibourg.com	4th	42.78.47.39 €€	Bobo	123
Hôtel Le Bristol Grand (175)	112 rue du Fbg. St-Honoré (Miromesnil) hotel-bristol.com	8th	53.43.43.00 €€€€	Classic	91
Hôtel Costes Trendy (82)	239 rue St-Honoré (Tuileries) hotelcostes.com	1st	42.44.50.00 €€€€	Hot & Cool	57
Hôtel Costes K Trendy (83)	81 av. Kléber (Trocadéro)	16th	44.05.75.75 €€€	Hot & Cool	57
Hôtel de Crillon Grand (127)	10 pl. de la Concorde (Concorde) crillon.com	8th	44.71.15.00 €€€€	Classic	91
Hôtel Edouard VII Modern (69)	39 av. de l'Opéra (Opéra) edouard7hotel.com	2nd	42.61.56.90 €€€	Classic	92
Hôtel Lancaster Trendy (60)	7 rue de Berri (George V) hotel-lancaster.fr	8th	40.76.40.76 €€€€	Romantic	155
Hôtel Lutetia Grand (259)	45 bd. Raspail (Rue du Bac) lutetia-paris.com	14th	49.54.46.46 €€€€	Classic	92
Hôtel Meurice Grand (125)	228 rue de Rivoli (Concorde) meuricehotel.com	1st	44.58.10.10 €€€€	Romantic	155
Hôtel Montalembert Trendy (56)	3 rue de Montalembert (Rue du Bac) montalembert.com	7th	45.49.68.68 €€€	Hot & Cool	58
Hôtel du Petit Moulin Trendy (17)	29-31 rue de Poitou (Filles du Calvaire) hoteldupetitmoulin.com	3rd	42.74.10.10 €€	Bobo	124
Hôtel Plaza Athénée Grand (188)	25 av. Montaigne (Alma-Marceau) plaza-athenee-paris.com	8th	53.67.66.65 €€€€	Hot & Cool	58
Hôtel Ritz Grand (175)	15 pl. Vendôme (Tuileries) ritzparis.com	1st	43.16.30.70 €€€€	Classic	92

Neighborhood (Area) Key

Numbers refer to arrondissement; **BB** = Bois de Boulogne; **SD** = St-Denis; **SO** = St-Ouen; **VA** = Various

Use the prefix 01 when calling from anywhere within France, including Paris. Use the prefix 06 or 08 (instead of 01) where indicated next to the number. For international calls dial the country code 33 and omit the "0."

Hotels (cont.)

NAME TYPE (ROOMS)	ADDRESS (METRO) WEBSITE	AREA PRICE	PHONE (01)	EXPERIENCE	PAGE
Hôtel de Sers Trendy (52)	41 av. de Pierre 1er de Serbie (George V) hotel-de-sers.com	8th €€€	53.23.75.75	Hot & Cool	59
Hôtel Sezz Trendy (27)	6 av. Frémiet (Passy) hotelsezz.com	16th €€	56.75.26.26	Hot & Cool	59
Kube Rooms Trendy (40)	1-5 passage Ruelle (La Chapelle) kubehotel.com	18th €€	42.05.20.00	Bobo	124
Murano Urban Resort Trendy (52)	13 bd. du Temple (Filles du Calvaire) muranoresort.com	3rd €€€	42.71.20.00	Hot & Cool	59
Park Hyatt Paris Vendôme Modern (177)	5 rue de la Paix (Opéra) paris.hyatt.com	2nd €€€€	58.71.12.34	Hot & Cool	60
Pavillon de Paris Trendy (30)	7 rue de Parme (Place-de-Clichy) pavillondeparis.com	9th €€	55.31.60.00	Bobo	125
Pavillon de la Reine Timeless (56)	28 pl. des Vosges (Chemin Vert) pavillon-de-la-reine.com	3rd €€€	40.29.19.19	Romantic	156
Relais Christine Timeless (51)	3 rue Christine (Odéon) relais-christine.com	6th €€€	40.51.60.80	Romantic	156
Renaissance Paris Vendôme Trendy (97)	4 rue du Mont Thabor (Tuileries) plazaparisvendome.com	1st €€€€	40.20.20.00	Hot & Cool	60
Trocadéro Dokhan's Timeless (59)	117 rue Lauriston (Boissière) dokhans.com	16th €€	53.65.66.99	Romantic	157
Villa Royale Trendy (31)	2 rue Duperré (Pigalle) leshotelsdeparis.com	9th €€	55.31.78.78	Bobo	125

Restaurants

NAME TYPE	ADDRESS (METRO) WEBSITE	AREA PRICE	PHONE (01) SINGLES/NOISE	EXPERIENCE 99 BEST	PAGE PAGE
Le 404 North African	69 rue des Gravilliers (Arts-et-Métiers)	3rd €€	42.74.57.81 - ≡	Bobo North African	*117*, 126 39
A Priori Thé Tearoom	35-37 galerie Vivienne (Bourse)	2nd € -	42.97.48.75 - ≡	Romantic	158
Alain Ducasse au Plaza Athénée Gastronomic	25 av. Montaigne (Alma-Marceau) alain-ducasse.com	8th €€€€ -	53.67.65.00 ⊑	Hot & Cool Fine Dining	*53*, 61 28
Allard Traditional	41 rue St-André-des-Arts (Odéon)	6th €	43.26.48.23 - ≡	Classic	93

Restaurant and Nightlife Symbols

Restaurants
Singles Friendly (eat and/or meet)
- ▯ = Communal table
- ▯ = Bar scene
- B = Limited bar menu
- F = Full menu served at bar

Nightlife
Price Warning
- C = Cover or ticket charge
  Food served at bar or club
- B = Limited bar menu
- F = Full menu served at bar

Restaurant + Nightlife
Prime time noise levels
- ⊑ = Quiet
- ≡ = A buzz, but still conversational
- ≡ = Loud

Note regarding page numbers: Italic = itinerary listing; Roman = description in Experience section listing.

NAME / TYPE	ADDRESS (METRO) / WEBSITE	AREA / PRICE	PHONE (01) / SINGLES/NOISE	EXPERIENCE / 99 BEST	PAGE / PAGE
Les Ambassadeurs / Gastronomic	10 pl. de la Concorde (Concorde) / crillon.com	8th / €€€€	44.71.16.16 / -	Classic / Brunches	88, 93 / 18
L'Ambroisie / Gastronomic	9 pl. des Vosges (Bastille)	4th / €€€€	42.78.51.45 / -	Romantic	152, 158
Anahi / Argentinian	49 rue Volta (Arts-et-Métiers)	3rd / €€	48.87.88.24	Bobo	117, 126
Angelina / Tearoom	226 rue de Rivoli (Tuileries)	1st / €	42.60.82.00 / -	Classic	85, 93
Angl'Opera / Contemporary	39 av. de l'Opéra (Opéra) / edouard7hotel.com	9th / €	42.61.86.25 / -	Romantic	150, 158
L'Angle du Faubourg / Contemporary	195 rue du Fbg. St-Honoré (Charles de Gaulle-Etoile) / taillevent.com	8th / €€	40.74.20.20 / -	Classic	93
Apollo / Trendy	3 pl. Denfert-Rochereau (Denfert-Rochereau)	14th / €€	45.38.76.77	Hot & Cool	61
L'Arpège / Gastronomic	84 rue de Varenne (Sèvres-Babylone) / alain-passard.com	7th / €€€€	47.05.09.06	Hot & Cool	61
L'Astrance / Gastronomic	4 rue Beethoven (Passy)	16th / €€€	40.50.84.40 / -	Hot & Cool	61
L'Atelier de Joël Robuchon / Contemporary	5 rue de Montalembert (Rue du Bac) / robuchon.com	7th / €€	42.22.56.56	Hot & Cool	53, 62
L'Avant-Goût / Bistro	26 rue Bobillot (Place d'Italie)	13th / €	53.80.24.00 / -	Classic	94
L'Avenue / Trendy	41 av. Montaigne (Alma-Marceau)	8th / €€	40.70.14.91	Hot & Cool	62
La Balle au Bond* / Restaurant/Jazz Club	55 quai de la Tournelle (Maubert Mutualité) / laballeaubond.fr	5th/6th / € -	40.46.85.12	Romantic	158
Le Baron Rouge / Wine Bar	1 rue Théophile-Roussel (Ledru-Rollin)	12th / € -	43.43.14.32	Bobo	126
Le Bélier / Trendy	13 rue des Beaux-Arts (St-Germain-des-Prés) / l-hotel.com	6th / €€	44.41.99.01	Romantic	151, 159
Bioboa / Trendy	3 rue Danielle Casanova (Pyramides)	1st / € -	42.61.17.67 / -	Hot & Cool	62
Le Bistrot d'à Coté Flaubert / Bistro	10 rue Gustave-Flaubert (Ternes) / michelrostang.com	17th / €€	42.67.05.81 / -	Classic	94
Le Bistrot du Peintre / Bistro	116 av. Ledru-Rollin (Bastille)	11th / €	47.00.34.39	Bobo	126
Bon / Trendy	25 rue de la Pompe (La Muette)	16th / €€	40.72.70.00	Hot & Cool / Of-the-Moment	53, 62 / 40
Bon 2 / Business	2 rue du Quatre-Septembre (Bourse) / bon.fr	2nd / €€	44.55.51.55	Power Lunches	43
Au Bon Accueil / Bistro	14 rue Monttessuy (Alma-Marceau)	7th / €	47.05.46.11 / -	Classic / Bistros	86, 94 / 17
Les Bouquinistes / Contemporary	53 quai Grands-Augustins (St-Michel) / lesbouquinistes.com	6th / €€	43.25.45.94	Hot & Cool	63
Brasserie Lipp / Brasserie	151 bd. St-Germain (Rue du Bac) / brasserie-lipp.fr	6th / €€	45.48.53.91 / -	Classic	87, 94

Restaurants (cont.)

NAME / TYPE	ADDRESS (METRO) / WEBSITE	AREA / PRICE	PHONE (01) / SINGLES/NOISE	EXPERIENCE / 99 BEST	PAGE / PAGE
Le Bristol / Gastronomic	112 rue du Fbg. St-Honoré (Miromesnil) / lebristolparis.com	8th / €€€€	53.43.43.00	Classic	95
Cabaret / Trendy	2 pl. du Palais-Royal (Palais Royal-Musée de Louvre) / cabaret.fr	1st / €€	58.62.56.25	Hot & Cool	63
Café Baci / Trendy	36 rue de Turenne (St-Sébastien-Froissart)	3rd / €	42.71.36.70	Hot & Cool	51, 63
Café Burq / Bistro	6 rue Burq (Abbesses)	18th / €	42.52.81.27	Bobo	119, 127
Café Charbon / Café/Bar	109 rue Oberkampf (Parmentier)	11th / €	43.57.55.13	Bobo	127
Café de l' Esplanade / Trendy	52 rue Fabert (La Tour-Maubourg)	7th / €€	47.05.38.80	Hot & Cool	54, 63
Café de l'Homme / Trendy	17 pl. du Trocadéro (Trocadéro) / cafedelhomme.com	16th / €€	44.05.30.15	Hot & Cool / Eiffel Tower Views	54, 64 / 27
Café Jacquemart-André / Tearoom	158 bd. Haussmann (St-Philippe-du-Roule) / musee-jacquemart-andre.com	8th / €	45.62.11.59	Romantic / Brunches	152, 159 / 18
Café Marly / Trendy	93 rue de Rivoli (Palais Royal-Musée de Louvre)	1st / €	49.26.06.60	Classic / Café Terraces	85, 95 / 19
Café Maure de la Mosquée de Paris / Tearoom	39 rue Geoffroy St-Hilaire (Place Monge)	5th / €	43.31.38.20	Romantic	159
Les Cakes de Bertrand / Tearoom	7 rue Bourdaloue (Notre-Dame-de-Lorette) / lescakesdebertrand.com	9th / € -	40.16.16.28	Romantic	150, 160
Canal 96* / Café	96 quai de Jemmapes (Jacques Bonsergent)	10th / €	42.02.87.95	Bobo	127
La Cantine du Faubourg* / Trendy	105 rue du Fbg. St-Honoré (St-Philippe-du-Roule)	8th / €€	42.56.22.22	Hot & Cool	64
Chai 33 / Trendy	33 cour St-Emilion (Cour St-Emilion) / chai33.org	12th / €€	53.44.01.01	Bobo	127
Le Chalet des Iles / Traditional	Carrefour des Cascades (La Muette) / lechaletdesiles.net	BB / €€	42.88.04.69	Romantic / Outdoor Dining	152, 160 / 41
Le Chamarré / Contemporary	13 bd. de la Tour-Maubourg (La Tour-Maubourg)	7th / €€€€	47.05.50.18	Classic	86, 95
Le Chateaubriand / Bistro	129 av. Parmentier (Goncourt)	11th / €	43.57.45.95	Bobo	128
Chez Janou / Bistro	2 rue Roger-Verlomme (Chemin Vert)	3rd / €	42.72.28.41	Bobo	117, 128
Chez Louisette / Brasserie	130 av. Michelet, St-Ouen (Porte de Clignancourt)	SO / €	40.12.10.14	Bobo	119, 128
Chez Marianne / Jewish	2 rue des Hospitalières-St-Gervais (St-Paul)	4th / € -	42.72.18.86	Classic	95
Chez Prune* / Café	71 quai de Valmy (République)	10th / €	42.41.30.47	Bobo	128
Chez Toinette / Bistro	20 rue Germain-Pilon (Abbesses) / chez-toinette.com	18th / €	42.54.44.36	Bobo	119, 128
Le Chiberta / Contemporary	3 rue Arsène-Houssaye (Charles de Gaulle -Etoile) / lechiberta.com	8th / €€€€	53.53.42.00	Hot & Cool / Power Lunches	64 / 43

236

PARIS BLACK BOOK

NAME / TYPE	ADDRESS (METRO) / WEBSITE	AREA / PRICE	PHONE (01) / SINGLES/NOISE	EXPERIENCE / 99 BEST	PAGE / PAGE
Le Cinq / Gastronomic	31 av. George V (Alma-Marceau) / fourseasons.com	8th / €€€€	49.52.70.00	Classic	95
Costes* / Hotel Bar	239 rue St-Honoré (Tuileries)	1st / €€	42.44.50.25	Hot & Cool / Always-Trendy	52, 64 / 16
La Coupole / Brasserie	102 bd. du Montparnasse (Duroc) / coupoleparis.com	14th / €€	43.20.14.20	Classic / Seafood Feasts	87, 96 / 44
Le Cristal Room / Trendy	11 pl. des Etats-Unis (Boissière)	16th / €€€	40.22.11.10	Hot & Cool / Of-the-Moment	54, 65 / 40
Da Rosa / Café	62 rue de Seine (Mabillon) / darosa.fr	6th / €	40.51.00.09	Classic	96
Davé / Trendy	12 rue de Richelieu (Palais Royal-Musée du Louvre)	2nd / €€	42.61.49.48	Hot & Cool / Celebrity Spotting	65 / 20
Les Deux Magots / Café	6 pl. St-Germain-des-Prés (St-Germain-des-Prés) / lesdeuxmagots.com	6th / €€	45.48.55.25	Hot & Cool / Café Terraces	52, 65 / 19
Djoon / Restaurant/Club	22-24 bd. Vincent-Auriol (Quai de la Gare) / djoon.fr	13th / €€	45.70.83.49	Bobo	129
Le Doudingue* / Bar/Restaurant	24 rue Durantin (Abbesses)	18th / €	42.54.88.08	Romantic	150, 160
Drôle d'Endroit pour une Rencontre* / Bar/Rest.	46 rue Caulaincourt (Lamarck Caulaincourt)	18th / €	42.55.14.25	Bobo	129
Emporio Armani Caffé / Trendy	149 bd. St-Germain (St-Germain-des-Prés)	6th / €€	45.48.62.15	Hot & Cool / Celebrity Spotting	53, 65 / 20
L'Equitable / Bistro	1 rue des Fossés-St-Marcel (Censier-Daubenton)	5th / €	43.31.69.20	Classic	96
L'Espadon / Gastronomic	15 pl. Vendôme (Tuileries) / ritz.com	1st / €€€€	43.16.30.80	Classic	97
L'Estaminet / Wine Bar	39 rue de Bretagne (Temple) / aromes-et-cepages.com	3rd / €	42.72.34.85	Bobo	120, 129
L'Etoile* / Gastronomic	12 rue de Presbourg (Charles de Gaulle-Etoile) / letoileparis.com	16th / €€€€	45.00.78.70	Hot & Cool	53, 66
La Famille / Bistro	41 rue des Trois-Frères (Abbesses)	18th / €	42.52.11.12	Bobo	119, 129
Flora / Contemporary	36 av. George V (George V)	8th / €€	40.70.10.49	Romantic	160
Flora Danica / Contemporary	142 av. des Champs-Elysées (Charles de Gaulle-Etoile) / maisondudanemark.dk	8th / €€	44.13.86.26	Hot & Cool	66
Fogón St Julien / Spanish	10 rue St Julien-le-Pauvre (Maubert-Mutualité)	5th / €	43.54.31.33	Classic	97
Le Fumoir / Trendy	6 rue de l'Amiral-de-Coligny (Louvre-Rivoli) / lefumoir.com	1st / €€	42.92.00.24	Hot & Cool / Literary Bars	66 / 34
Gallopin / Brasserie	40 rue Notre-Dame-des-Victoires (Bourse) / brasseriegallopin.com	2nd / €€	42.36.45.38	Romantic	150, 161
Georges / Trendy	6th floor, Centre Pompidou (Rambuteau)	4th / €€	44.78.47.99	Hot & Cool / Always-Trendy	52, 66 / 16
Le Grand Véfour / Gastronomic	17 rue de Beaujolais (Palais Royal-Musée du Louvre) / relaischateaux.com	1st / €€€€	42.96.56.27	Romantic	149, 161

237

Restaurants (cont.)

NAME TYPE	ADDRESS (METRO) WEBSITE	AREA PRICE	PHONE (01) SINGLES/NOISE	EXPERIENCE 99 BEST	PAGE PAGE
Guy Savoy Gastronomic	18 rue Troyon (Charles de Gaulle-Etoile) guysavoy.com	17th €€€€	43.80.40.61 -	Hot & Cool Fine Dining	67 28
Hiramatsu Gastronomic	52 rue de Longchamp (Trocadéro)	16th €€€€	56.81.08.80 -	Hot & Cool Power Lunches	67 43
Le Jardin de Varenne Café	77 rue de Varenne (Varenne)	7th €	44.18.61.10 -	Romantic	150, 161
Le Jules Verne Gastronomic	Eiffel Tower, Champ de Mars (Bir-Hakeim) tour-eiffel.fr	7th €€€€	45.55.61.44 -	Classic	86, 97
Julien Brasserie	16 rue du Fbg. St-Denis (Strasbourg- St-Denis) julienparis.com	10th €€	47.70.12.06 -	Classic	88, 97
Kong* Trendy	1 rue du Pont Neuf (Pont Neuf) kong.fr	1st €€	40.39.09.00	Hot & Cool	67
Ladurée Tearoom	21 rue Bonaparte (Mabillon) laduree.fr	6th €	44.07.64.87 -	Romantic	161
Lapérouse Gastronomic	41 quai des Grands Augustins (Cité)	6th €€€€	43.26.68.04 -	Romantic	152, 162
Laurent Gastronomic	41 av. Gabriel (Champs-Elysées- Clémenceau) le-laurent.com	8th €€€€	42.25.00.39 -	Classic Outdoor Dining	98 41
Le Loir dans la Théière Tearoom	3 rue des Rosiers (St-Paul)	4th €	42.72.90.61 -	Bobo	120, 130
Aux Lyonnais Traditional	32 rue St-Marc (Bourse)	2nd €€	42.96.65.04 -	Classic	88, 98
Macéo Contemporary	15 rue des Petits Champs (Pyramides) maceorestaurant.com	2nd €€	42.97.53.85 -	Romantic	162
La Madonnina Italian	10 rue Marie-et-Louise (Goncourt)	10th €	42.01.25.26 -	Bobo	130
Maison Blanche Trendy	15 av. Montaigne (Alma-Marceau) maison-blanche.fr	8th €€€€	47.23.55.99 -	Hot & Cool Always-Trendy	54, 67 16
Aux Marches du Palais Bistro	5 rue de la Manutention (Alma-Marceau)	16th €	47.23.52.80 -	Bobo	130
La Marine Bistro	55 bis quai de Valmy (République)	10th €	42.39.69.81 -	Bobo	130
Market Contemporary	15 av. Matignon (Champs-Elysées- Clémenceau) jean-georges.com	8th €€	56.43.40.90 -	Hot & Cool	68
Les Marronniers Café	18 rue des Archives (Hôtel de Ville)	4th €	40.27.87.72 -	Hot & Cool	51, 68
Le Martel North African	3 rue Martel (Château d'Eau)	10th €	47.70.67.56	Bobo North African	130 39
La Mascotte Brasserie	52 rue des Abbesses (Abbesses)	18th €	46.06.28.15 -	Classic Seafood Feasts	88, 98 44
Maxim's Traditional	3 rue Royale (Concorde) maxims-de-paris.com	8th €€€€	42.65.27.94 -	Romantic	152, 162
La Méditerranée Gastronomic	2 pl. de l'Odéon (Odéon) la-mediterranee.com	6th €€	43.26.02.30 -	Classic Seafood Feasts	87, 98 44
Mon Vieil Ami Contemporary	69 rue St-Louis-en-l'Ile (Pont Marie)	4th €€	40.46.01.35 -	Romantic	163

PARIS BLACK BOOK

NAME / TYPE	ADDRESS (METRO) / WEBSITE	AREA / PRICE	PHONE (01) / SINGLES/NOISE	EXPERIENCE / 99 BEST	PAGE / PAGE
Murano / Trendy	13 bd. du Temple (Filles du Calvaire) / muranoresort.com	3rd / €€€	42.71.20.00	Hot & Cool / Of-the-Moment	*52*, 68 / 40
Music Hall* / Trendy	63 av. Franklin D. Roosevelt (Franklin D. Roosevelt)	8th / €	45.61.03.63	Hot & Cool / Late-Night Eats	*54*, 68 / 33
Les Orchidées / Contemporary	3-5 rue de la Paix (Opéra) / paris.vendome.hyatt.fr	2nd / €€	58.71.12.34	Hot & Cool / Brunches	*54*, 68 / 18
Le Palanquin / Vietnamese	12 rue Princesse (Mabillon) / lepalanquin.com	6th / €	43.29.77.66	Romantic	*151*, 163
Les Papilles / Wine Bar	30 rue Gay-Lussac (RER Luxembourg) / lespapilles.fr	5th / €	43.25.20.79	Classic	*87*, 99
Pause Café / Café	41 rue de Charonne (Ledru-Rollin)	11th / €	48.06.08.33	Bobo / Café Terraces	*118*, 131 / 19
Pères et Filles / Café	81 rue de Seine (Mabillon)	6th / €	43.25.00.28	Classic	99
Pershing Hall / Trendy	49 rue Pierre Charron (Charles de Gaulle -Etoile) / pershinghall.com	8th / €€	58.36.58.00	Hot & Cool	69
Pétrelle / Contemporary	34 rue Pétrelle (Anvers)	9th / €€	42.82.11.02	Romantic	163
Les Philosophes* / Café	28 rue Vieille-du-Temple (St-Paul) / cafeine.com	4th / €	48.87.49.64	Bobo	131
Au Pied de Cochon / Brasserie	6 rue Coquillière (Les Halles) / pieddecochon.com	1st / €	40.13.77.00	Classic / Late-Night Eats	*88*, 99 / 33
Pierre Gagnaire / Gastronomic	6 rue Balzac (George V) / pierre-gagnaire.com	8th / €€€€	58.36.12.50	Hot & Cool	69
Polichinelle Café / Bistro	64-66 rue de Charonne (Ledru-Rollin)	11th / €	58.30.63.52	Bobo	131
Pomze / Contemporary	109 bd. Haussmann (Miromesnil) / pomze.com	8th / €€	42.65.65.83	Romantic	163
Le Poulbot Gourmet / Bistro	39 rue Lamarck (Lamarck Caulaincourt)	18th / €	46.06.86.00	Classic	*88*, 99
Le Pré Catelan / Gastronomic	Route de Suresnes, Bois de Boulogne (Porte Maillot, taxi) / lenotre.fr	BB / €€€€	44.14.41.14	Romantic	*152*, 164
Le Pré Verre / Bistro	8 rue Thenard (Maubert-Mutualité)	5th / €	43.54.59.47	Classic / Bistros	*87*, 99 / 17
Le Quinzième / Trendy	14 rue Cauchy (Javel)	15th / €€€	45.54.43.43	Hot & Cool	69
R / Contemporary	8 rue de la Cavalerie, 8th fl. (La Motte-Picquet-Grenelle) / le-r.com	15th / €€	45.67.06.85	Romantic / Eiffel Tower Views	*151*, 164 / 27
Le Relais du Parc / Gastronomic	51 av. Raymond-Poincaré (Boissière) / sofitel.com	16th / €€€	44.05.66.10	Hot & Cool / Outdoor Dining	69 / 41
Le Réminet / Bistro	3 rue des Grands-Degrés (Maubert-Mutualité)	5th / €	44.07.04.24	Romantic	*151*, 164
Le Restaurant du Palais Royal / Contemporary	110 galerie Valois (Bourse)	1st / €€	40.20.00.27	Romantic	*149*, 164
Le Rostand / Café	6 pl. Edmond Rostand (RER Luxembourg)	6th / €	43.54.61.58		*86*, 100

239

Restaurants (cont.)

NAME TYPE	ADDRESS (METRO) WEBSITE	AREA PRICE	PHONE (01) SINGLES/NOISE	EXPERIENCE 99 BEST	PAGE PAGE
Le Salon d'Hélène Contemporary	4 rue d'Assas (Sèvres-Babylone)	6th €€	42.22.00.11	Romantic	*150*, 165
Le Sancerre* Café/Bar	35 rue des Abbesses (Abbesses)	18th €	42.58.08.20	Bobo	131
Sardegna a Tavola Italian	1 rue de Cotte (Ledru-Rollin)	12th €	44.75.03.28	Bobo	*118*, 131
Senderens Trendy	9 pl. de la Madeleine (Madeleine) lucascarton.com	8th €€€	42.65.22.90	Hot & Cool	70
Senso Contemporary	16 rue de la Trémoille (Franklin D. Roosevelt) hotel-tremoille.com	8th €€	56.52.14.14	Romantic	165
Le Sers Trendy	41 av. Pierre 1er de Serbie (George V) hotel-de-sers.com	8th €	53.23.75.75	Hot & Cool	70
Le Soleil Bistro	109 av. Michelet (Porte de Clignancourt)	SO €€	40.10.08.08	Bobo	*119*, 132
Somo Lounge Bar	168 rue Montmartre (Sentier) hip-bars.com/somo	2nd €	40.13.08.80	Bobo	132
Sora Lena Trendy	18 rue Bayen (Ternes)	17th €€	45.74.73.73	Hot & Cool	70
Spoon, Food & Wine Trendy	14 rue de Marignan (Franklin D. Roosevelt) spoon.tm.fr	8th €€€	40.76.34.44	Hot & Cool	*54*, 70
Le Sporting Café	3 rue des Récollets (Gare de L'Est)	10th €	46.07.02.00	Bobo	132
Le Square Bistro	227 bis rue Marcadet (Guy Moquet)	18th €	53.11.08.41	Bobo	132
Le Square Trousseau Bistro	1 rue Antoine-Vollon (Ledru-Rollin)	12th €€	43.43.06.00	Bobo Bistros	*118*, 132 17
Stella Maris Gastronomic	4 rue Arsène-Houssaye (Charles de Gaulle-Etoile)	8th €€€€	42.89.16.22	Hot & Cool	71
Le Stresa Italian	7 rue Chambiges (Alma-Marceau)	8th €€€	47.23.51.62	Hot & Cool	71
La Suite* Trendy	40 av. George V (George V) lasuite.fr	8th €€	53.57.49.49	Hot & Cool	71
Swann et Vincent Italian	7 rue St-Nicolas (Ledru-Rollin)	12th €	43.43.49.40	Bobo	*120*, 133
La Table d'Hôte du Palais Royal Bistro	8 rue du Beaujolais (Bourse) carollsinclair.com	1st €	42.61.25.30	Classic	*86*, 100
La Table de Joël Robuchon Contemporary	16 av. Bugeaud (Victor Hugo)	16th €€€€	56.28.16.16	Hot & Cool	71
La Table Lauriston Bistro	129 rue de Lauriston (Trocadéro)	16th €€	47.27.00.07	Classic	100
Taillevent Gastronomic	15 rue Lamennais (Charles de Gaulle-Etoile) taillevent.com	8th €€€€	44.95.15.01	Classic Fine Dining	100 28
Le Tambour All-Night Café	41 rue Montmartre (Sentier)	2nd €	42.33.06.90	Bobo Late-Night Eats	*119*, 133 33
Thiou Trendy	49 quai d'Orsay (Invalides)	7th €€	40.62.96.50	Hot & Cool	72

PARIS BLACK BOOK

NAME / TYPE	ADDRESS (METRO) / WEBSITE	AREA / PRICE	PHONE (01) / SINGLES/NOISE	EXPERIENCE / 99 BEST	PAGE / PAGE
Toi / Trendy	27 rue du Colisée (Franklin D. Roosevelt) / restaurant-toi.com	8th / €	42.56.56.58 / ♀♂ ≡	Hot & Cool	72
Tokyo Eat / Trendy	13 av. du Président Wilson (Alma-Marceau)	16th / €	47.20.00.29 / - ≡	Bobo / Eiffel Tower Views	*120*, 133 / 27
La Tour d'Argent / Gastronomic	15-17 quai de la Tournelle (Pont Marie) / tourdargent.com	5th / €€€€	43.54.23.31 / - ▭	Classic	101
La Truffière / Traditional	4 rue Blainville (Place Monge) / latruffiere.com	5th / €€€	46.33.29.82 / - ≡	Classic	*88*, 101
Viaduc Café* / Café	43 av. Daumesnil (Ledru-Rollin)	12th / €	44.74.70.70 / - ≡	Bobo	*118*, 133
Au Vieux Colombier / Café	65 rue de Rennes (St-Sulpice)	6th / €	45.48.53.81 / - ▭	Romantic	*149*, 165
Le Village / Trendy	25 rue Royale (Madeleine)	8th / €€	40.17.02.19 / - ≡	Hot & Cool	*53*, 72
Le Voltaire / Traditional	27 quai Voltaire (Rue du Bac)	7th / €€€	42.61.17.49 / - ≡	Classic	101
Willi's Wine Bar / Bistro	13 rue des Petits-Champs (Pyramides) / williswinebar.com	1st / €	42.61.05.09 / ♀♂ ▭	Classic	101
Ze Kitchen Galerie / Contemporary	4 rue des Grands-Augustins (St-Michel)	6th / €€	44.32.00.32 / - ≡	Hot & Cool	72
Le Ziryab / North African	1 rue des Fossés St-Bernard (Jussieu) / imarabe.org	5th / €€	53.10.10.16 / - ▭	Romantic / North African	165 / 39

Nightlife

NAME / TYPE	ADDRESS (METRO) / WEBSITE	AREA / COVER	PHONE (01) / FOOD/NOISE	EXPERIENCE / 99 BEST	PAGE / PAGE
L'Amnésia Café / Gay Bar	42 rue Vieille-du-Temple (Hôtel de Ville) / amnesia-cafe.com	4th / -	42.72.16.94 / - ≡	Hot & Cool / Gay Bars	73 / 29
Andy Wahloo / Bar	69 rue des Gravilliers (Arts-et-Métiers)	3rd / -	42.71.20.38 / B ≡	Bobo	*118*, 134
Les Bains Douches / Dance Club	7 rue du Bourg-l'Abbé (Etienne-Marcel) / lesbainsdouches.net	3rd / -	48.87.01.80 / - -	Hot & Cool	*54*, 73
La Balle au Bond / Restaurant/Jazz Club	55 quai de la Tournelle (Maubert-Mutualité) / laballeaubond.fr	5th/6th / C	40.46.85.12 / - ≡	Romantic	*150*, 166
Banana Café / Gay Bar	13 rue de la Ferronnerie (Châtelet) / bananacafeparis.com	1st / -	42.33.35.31 / - ≡	Bobo	*118*, 134
Le Bar at the George V / Hotel Bar	31 av. George V (Alma-Marceau) / fourseasons.com	8th / -	49.52.70.00 / - ▭	Hot & Cool / Vodka Cocktails	*54*, 73 / 48
Bar César / Hotel Bar	10 pl. de la Concorde (Concorde) / crillon.com	8th / -	44.71.15.39 / - ▭	Classic / Classic Hotel Bars	*88*, 102 / 22
Bar Fontainebleau / Hotel Bar	228 rue de Rivoli (Concorde) / meuricehotel.com	1st / -	44.58.10.10 / - ▭	Romantic / Classic Hotel Bars	*152*, 166 / 22
Bar Hemingway / Hotel Bar	15 pl. Vendôme (Tuileries) / ritzparis.com	1st / -	43.16.33.65 / - ≡	Classic / Classic Hotel Bars	*88*, 102 / 22

Nightlife (cont.)

NAME TYPE	ADDRESS (METRO) WEBSITE	AREA	PHONE (01) COVER FOOD/NOISE	EXPERIENCE 99 BEST	PAGE PAGE
Bar du Marché Bar	75 rue de Seine (Mabillon)	6th	43.26.55.15 - B =	Classic	86, 102
Bar Ourcq DJ Bar	68 quai de la Loire (Laumière)	19th	42.40.12.26 - B ≡	Bobo	120, 134
Bar Panoramique DJ Bar	3 pl. du Général Koenig (Porte Maillot)	17th	40.68.50.68 - B ⊟	Cocktails with View	23
Le Bar du Plaza Hotel Bar	25 av. Montaigne (Alma-Marceau) plaza-athenee-paris.com	8th	53.67.66.00 - B ≡	Hot & Cool Vodka Cocktails	53, 73 48
Le Baron Private Club	6 av. Marceau (Alma-Marceau) clublebaron.com	8th	47.20.04.01 - - ≡	Bobo Hipster Hangouts	120, 134 31
Bateau Concorde Atlantique Dance Club	By 25 quai Anatole France (Assemblée Nationale) concorde-atlantique.com	7th C	47.05.71.03 - - ≡	Romantic	152, 166
Batofar Dance Club	Facing 11 quai François Mauriac (Quai de la Gare) batofar.org	13th C	53.60.17.30 B ≡	Bobo Dance Clubs	120, 135 26
La Belle Hortense Wine-Bar	31 rue Vieille-du-Temple (St-Paul)	4th	48.04.71.60 - - ⊟	Bobo Literary Bars	117, 135 34
Le Bilboquet Jazz Club	13 rue St-Benoît (St-Germain-des-Prés)	6th C	45.48.81.84 - - ≡	Classic Jazz Clubs	86, 102 32
Botak Café Café	1 rue Paul Albert (Anvers) botak-cafe.com	18th	46.06.98.30 - - ≡	Romantic	150, 166
Le Bound Cocktail Bar	49 av. George V (George V) buddhabar.com	8th	53.67.84.60 - B -	Hot & Cool	74
Buddha Bar Lounge Bar/ Restaurant	8 bis rue Boissy d'Anglas (Concorde) buddhabar.com	8th	53.05.90.00 - - ≡	Romantic	152, 167
Le Cab Lounge/Club	2 pl. du Palais-Royal (Palais Royal-Musée du Louvre) cabaret.fr	1st C	58.62.56.25 - - ≡	Hot & Cool	52, 74
Café Charbon Café/Bar	109 rue Oberkampf (Parmentier)	11th	43.57.55.13 - - ≡	Bobo	135
Café Chéri(e) DJ Bar	44 bd. la Villette (Belleville)	19th	42.02.07.87 - B ≡	Bobo Hipster Hangouts	119, 135 31
Café Delmas Café	2-4 pl. de la Contrescarpe (Place Monge)	5th	43.26.51.26 - - ≡	Classic	103
Café de Flore Café	172 bd. St-Germain (St-Germain-des-Prés) cafe-de-flore.com	6th	45.48.55.26 - - -	Classic	87, 103
Café de la Mairie Café	8 pl. St-Sulpice (St-Sulpice)	6th	43.26.67.82 - - -	Romantic	151, 167
Café du Marché Café	38 rue Cler (Ecole-Militaire)	7th	47.05.51.27 - - ≡	Classic	86, 103
Café Noir Café/Bar	65 rue Montmartre (Sentier)	2nd	40.39.07.36 - F ≡	Bobo	136
Café de la Paix Café	12 bd. des Capucines (Opéra) paris-le-grand.intercontinental.com	9th	40.07.30.20 - - ≡	Romantic	150, 167
Canal 96* Café	96 quai de Jemmapes (Jacques Bonsergent)	10th	42.02.87.95 - - ⊟	Bobo	120, 136
La Cantine du Faubourg* Lounge Bar	105 rue du Fbg. St-Honoré (St-Philippe- du-Roule)	8th C	42.56.22.22 B ≡	Hot & Cool Lounge Bars	52, 74 36

PARIS BLACK BOOK

NAME / TYPE	ADDRESS (METRO) / WEBSITE	AREA	PHONE (01) COVER / FOOD / NOISE	EXPERIENCE / 99 BEST	PAGE / PAGE
Chai 33 / Wine Bar	33 cour St-Emilion (Cour St-Emilion) / chai33.com	12th	53.44.01.01 / - / B / ≡	Bobo	136
Champagne Bar at Le Dokhan's / Hotel Bar	117 rue Lauriston (Boissière) / dokhans.com	16th	53.65.66.99 / - / - / ≡	Romantic	152, 167
Chez Castel / Private Club	15 rue Princesse (Mabillon)	6th	40.51.52.80 / - / - / ≡	Classic	87, 103
Chez Prune* / Café	71 quai de Valmy (République)	10th	42.41.30.47 / - / F / ≡	Bobo	120, 136
Chez Richard / Bar	37 rue Vieille-du-Temple (St-Paul)	4th	42.74.31.65 / - / B / ≡	Bobo	118, 136
China Club / Lounge Bar	50 rue de Charenton (Bastille)	12th	43.43.82.02 / C / B / ≡	Bobo / Lounge Bars	120, 136 / 36
La Closerie des Lilas / Bar/Brasserie	171 bd. du Montparnasse (Vavin)	6th	40.51.34.50 / - / - / ≡	Classic	87, 104
Costes* / Hotel Bar	239 rue St-Honoré (Tuileries)	1st	42.44.50.25 / - / F / ≡	Hot & Cool	52, 74
La Coupole / Brasserie	102 bd. du Montparnasse (Duroc) / coupoleparis.com	14th	43.20.14.20 / - / - / ≡	Classic	87, 96
Crazy Horse / Cabaret	12 av. George V (George V) / crazyhorse.fr	8th	47.23.32.32 / C / - / ≡	Classic	104
Dancing at La Coupole / Brasserie	104 bd. du Montparnasse (Vavin) / flobrasseries.com/coupoleparis	14th	43.27.56.00 / C / - / ≡	Classic	104
De la Ville Café / DJ Bar	34 bd. Bonne-Nouvelle (Bonne Nouvelle)	10th	48.24.48.09 / - / B / ≡	Bobo	136
Le Defender / Hotel Bar	pl. André Malraux (Palais Royal-Musée du Louvre) / hoteldulouvre.com	1st	44.58.37.89 / - / - / ▢	Romantic	152, 167
Le Divan du Monde / Dance Club	75 rue des Martyrs (Pigalle) / divandumonde.com	18th	40.05.06.99 / - / - / ≡	Romantic	150, 168
Djoon / Restaurant/Club	22 bd. Vincent-Auriol (Quai de la Gare) / djoon.fr	13th	45.70.83.49 / - / - / ≡	Bobo	137
Le Doudingue* / Bar/Restaurant	24 rue Durantin (Abbesses)	18th	42.54.88.08 / - / B / ≡	Romantic	150, 168
Drôle d'Endroit pour une Rencontre* / Bar/Rest.	46 rue Caulaincourt (Lamarck-Caulaincourt)	18th	42.55.14.25 / - / B / ≡	Bobo / Meet Markets	119, 137 / 38
L'Echelle de Jacob / Lounge Bar	12 rue Jacob (Mabillon)	6th	46.34.00.29 / - / - / ≡	Romantic	151, 168
Les Editeurs / Café	4 carrefour de l'Odéon (Odéon) / leseditieurs.fr	6th	43.26.67.76 / - / F / ▢	Classic / Literary Bars	87, 104 / 34
Elysée Montmartre / Concert Hall/Dance Club	72 bd. Rochechouart (Anvers) / elyseemontmartre.com	18th	41.57.32.33 / C / - / ≡	Bobo / Live Music	119, 137 / 35
L'Etoile* / Private Club	12 rue de Presbourg (Charles de Gaulle-Etoile) / letoileparis.com	16th	45.00.78.70 / - / F / ≡	Hot & Cool / See-and-Be-Seen	53, 75 / 45
L'Etoile Manquante / Café/Bar	34 rue Vieille-du-Temple (St-Paul)	4th	42.72.48.34 / - / B / ≡	Bobo	118, 137
La Fabrique / DJ Bar	53 rue du Fbg. St-Antoine (Ledru-Rollin) / fabrique.fr	12th	43.07.67.07 / - / - / ≡	Bobo	137

Nightlife (cont.)

NAME	ADDRESS (METRO)	AREA	PHONE (01)	EXPERIENCE	PAGE
TYPE	WEBSITE		COVER FOOD/NOISE	99 BEST	PAGE
Favela Chic	18 rue du Fbg-du-Temple (République)	11th	40.21.38.14	Bobo	119, 138
Restaurant/Club	favelachic.com		- B ≡		
Folies Pigalle	11 pl. Pigalle (Pigalle)	9th	48.78.55.25	Bobo	119, 138
Dance Club	folies-pigalle.com		- - ≡		
L'Ile Enchantée	65 bd. de la Villette (Colonel Fabien)	10th	42.01.67.99	Bobo	119, 138
DJ Bar			- B ≡		
Le Jaipur	25 rue Vernet (George V)	8th	44.31.98.06	Romantic	152, 168
Hotel Bar	hotelvernet.com		- - —		
Jardin Plein Ciel	17 av. Kléber (Kléber)	16th	53.64.32.00	Hot & Cool	53, 75
Hotel Bar	raphael-hotel.com		- - —	Cocktails with View	23
Le Jemmapes	82 quai de Jemmapes (Jacques Bonsergent)	10th	40.40.02.35	Bobo	120, 138
Café			- B ≡		
Jokko Bar	5 rue Elzévir (St-Sébastien-Froissart)	3rd	42.74.35.96	Bobo	118, 139
Music Bar	jokko.net		- B ≡	Live Music	35
Kong*	1 rue du Pont Neuf (Pont Neuf)	1st	40.39.09.00	Hot & Cool	52, 75
Bar/Restaurant	kong.fr		- - ≡	Cocktails with View	23
Kube Lounge and Ice Kube	1-5 passage Ruelle (La Chapelle)	18th	42.05.20.00	Bobo	139
Lounge Bar	kubehotel.com		- - ≡		
Man Ray	34 rue Marbeuf (Franklin D. Roosevelt)	8th	56.88.36.36	Romantic	152, 169
Restaurant/Club	manray.fr		C B ≡		
Mathi's Bar	3 rue de Ponthieu (Franklin D. Roosevelt)	8th	53.76.01.62	Hot & Cool	54, 75
Hotel Bar			- - —		
Mezzanine de l'Alcazar	62 rue Mazarine (Odéon)	6th	53.10.19.99	Romantic	151, 169
Lounge	alcazar.com		- B ≡	Lounge Bars	36
Le Milliardaire	68 rue Pierre Charron (Franklin D. Roosevelt)	8th	42.89.44.14	Hot & Cool	75
Private Club	lemilliardaire.com		C - ≡		
Moulin Rouge	82 bd. de Clichy (Blanche)	18th	53.09.82.82	Classic	104
Cabaret	moulin-rouge.com		C - ≡		
Murano Bar	13 bd. du Temple (Filles du Calvaire)	3rd	42.71.20.00	Hot & Cool	52, 76
Hotel Bar	muranoresort.com		- B ≡	Vodka Cocktails	48
Music Hall*	63 av. Franklin D. Roosevelt (Franklin D. Roosevelt)	8th	45.61.03.63	Hot & Cool	54, 76
Late-Night Restaurant	music-hallparis.com		- B ≡		
Le Néo	23 rue de Ponthieu (Franklin D. Roosevelt)	8th	42.25.57.14	Hot & Cool	54, 76
Private Club			- - -	See-and-Be-Seen	45
New Morning	7-9 rue des Petites-Ecuries (Château d'Eau)	10th	45.23.51.41	Classic	88, 105
Jazz Club	newmorning.com		C - ≡	Jazz Clubs	32
L'Olympia	28 bd. des Capucines (Opéra)	9th	55.27.10.00	Classic	88, 105
Concert Hall	olympiahall.com		C - ≡		
Open Café	17 rue des Archives (Hôtel de Ville)	4th	42.72.26.18	Bobo	118, 139
Gay Bar			- B ≡	Gay Bars	29
Opéra National de Paris	pl de l'Opéra (Opéra)	9th	36.69.78.68 [08]	Romantic	150, 169
Palais Garnier Opera Hse	opera-de-paris.fr		C - ≡		
La Palette	43 rue de Seine (Mabillon)	6th	43.26.68.15	Classic	105
Café			- - ≡		
Le Paris Paris	5 av. de l'Opéra (Pyramides)	1st		Bobo	120, 139
Dance Club	leparisparis.com		- - ≡		

PARIS BLACK BOOK

NAME TYPE	ADDRESS (METRO) WEBSITE	AREA	PHONE (01) COVER FOOD/NOISE	EXPERIENCE 99 BEST	PAGE PAGE
La Perle Café/Bar	78 rue Vieille-du-Temple (St-Sébastien -Froissart)	4th	42.72.69.93 - B ≡	Bobo Hipster Hangouts	118, 140 31
Pershing Lounge* Hotel Bar	49 rue Pierre Charron (Charles de Gaulle -Etoile) pershinghall.com	8th	58.36.58.36 - B ≡	Hot & Cool Meet Markets	53, 76 38
Les Philosophes* Café	28 rue Vieille-du-Temple (St-Paul)	4th	48.87.49.64 - ≡	Bobo	117, 140
Pink Paradise Strip Club	49 rue de Ponthieu (George V) pinkparadise.fr	8th	58.36.19.20 C ≡	Hot & Cool	77
Le Progrès Café/Bar	7 rue des Trois-Frères (Abbesses)	18th	42.64.07.37 - B ≡	Bobo Meet Markets	119, 140 38
Le Pulp Dance Club	25 bd. Poissonnière (Grands Boulevards) pulp-paris.com	2nd	40.26.01.93 C	Bobo	140
Le Queen Dance Club	102 av. des Champs-Elysées (George V) queen.fr	8th	92.70.73.30 06 - ≡	Hot & Cool	53, 77
Raidd Bar Gay Bar	23 rue du Temple (Hôtel de Ville) raiddbar.com	4th	48.87.80.25 - ≡	Hot & Cool Gay Bars	77 29
Régine's Club Private Club	49-51 rue de Ponthieu (George V) regine-paris.com	8th	43.59.21.13 ≡	Classic	88, 105
Rex Club Dance Club	5 bd. Poissonnière (Bonne Nouvelle) rexclub.com	2nd	42.36.10.96 C - ≡	Bobo Dance Clubs	140 26
Ritz Club Private Club	38 rue Cambon (Madeleine) ritz.com	1st	43.16.30.90 C -	Classic	88, 105
Le Rosebud Cocktail Bar	11 bis rue Delambre (Vavin)	14th	43.20.44.13 - ≡	Classic	87, 106
Le Sabot Jazz Club	6 rue du Sabot (St-Germain-des-Prés)	6th	42.22.21.56 - - ≡	Classic Jazz Clubs	86, 106 32
Le Sancerre* Café/Bar	35 rue des Abbesses (Abbesses)	18th	42.58.08.20 F ≡	Bobo	119, 141
Sanz Sans DJ Bar	49 rue du Fbg. St-Antoine (Ledru-Rollin) sanzsans.com	12th	44.75.78.78 - ≡	Bobo	120, 141
La Scène Bastille Concert Hall/Dance Club	2 bis rue des Taillandiers (Ledru-Rollin) la-scene.com	12th	48.06.50.70 C - ≡	Bobo Live Music	120, 141 35
Au Soleil de la Butte DJ Bar	32 rue Muller (Château Rouge)	18th	46.06.18.24 - ≡	Bobo	119, 141
Somo Lounge Bar	168 rue Montmartre (Sentier) hip-bars.com/somo	2nd	40.13.08.80 C B ≡	Bobo	141
La Suite* Bar/Club	40 av. George V (George V) lasuite.fr	8th	53.57.49.49 -	Hot & Cool See-and-Be-Seen	54, 77 45
Summer dancing by the Seine Dance Scene	Jardins Tino-Rossi, quai St-Bernard (Jussieu)	5th	- - ≡	Romantic	151, 170
Toi Lounge	27 rue du Colisée (Franklin D. Roosevelt) restaurant-toi.com	8th	42.56.56.58 F ≡	Hot & Cool	78
Tokyo Idem Café	13 av. du Président Wilson (Alma-Marceau)	16th	47.20.00.29 - ≡	Bobo	120, 142
Le Tourville Café/Bar	43 av. de la Motte Picquet (Ecole Militaire)	7th	44.18.05.08 B ≡	Classic	86, 106

245

BLACK BOOK

Nightlife (cont.)

NAME	ADDRESS (METRO)	AREA	PHONE (01)	EXPERIENCE	PAGE
TYPE	WEBSITE	COVER	FOOD/NOISE	99 BEST	PAGE
Le Triptyque Dance Club	142 rue Montmartre (Grands Boulevards) letriptyque.com	2nd C	40.28.05.55 -	Bobo Dance Clubs	120, 142 26
Le Tropic Café Gay Bar	66 rue des Lombards (Châtelet)	1st -	40.13.92.62 B	Bobo	118, 142
Viaduc Café* Café	43 av. Daumesnil (Ledru-Rollin)	12th -	44.74.70.70 -	Bobo	142
Au Vieux Colombier Café	64 rue de Rennes (St-Sulpice)	6th -	45.48.53.81 -	Romantic	170
Le VIP Room Private Club	76 av. des Champs-Elysées (George V) viproom.fr	8th -	56.69.16.66 B	Hot & Cool Celebrity Spotting	53, 78 20
Le Wagg Dance Club	62 rue Mazarine (Odéon) wagg.fr	6th C	55.42.22.01 -	Romantic	151, 170
Willi's Wine Bar Wine Bar	13 rue des Petits-Champs (Pyramides) williswinebar.com	1st -	42.61.05.09 F	Classic	106
Le Zinzin Dance Club	8 bd. de la Madeleine (Madeleine) lezinzin.com	9th -	- -	Bobo	142

Attractions

NAME	ADDRESS (CROSS STREET)	AREA	PHONE (01)	EXPERIENCE	PAGE
TYPE	WEBSITE	PRICE		99 BEST	PAGE
4 Roues Sous 1 Parapluie Guided Tours	various (various) 4roues-sous-1parapluie.com	VA €€€€	67.32.26.68 [06]	Romantic Guided Tours	151, 171 30
Antoine et Lili Store	95 quai de Valmy (Jacques Bonsergent) altribu.com	10th -	40.37.41.55	Bobo	143
Les Bains du Montorgueil Spa	55 rue Montorgueil (Etienne-Marcel)	2nd €€€€	44.88.01.78	Romantic	152, 171
Le Ballon Eutelsat Activity	Parc André-Citroën (Balard) aeroparis.com	15th € -	44.26.20.00	Romantic	151, 171
Basilique du Sacré-Coeur Monument	35 rue du Chevalier-de-la-Barre (Abbesses) sacre-coeur-montmartre.com	18th -	53.41.89.00	Classic	88, 107
Basilique St-Denis Monument	1 rue de la Légion d'Honneur (Basilique de St-Denis) monum.fr	SD € -	48.09.83.54	Classic	107
Bateaux Vedette du Pont Neuf Boat Trip	Square du Vert Galant (Pont Neuf) vedettesdupontneuf.com	1st € -	46.33.98.38	Classic	86, 107
Batobus Boat Trip	various stops along Seine batobus.fr	VA € -	25.05.01.01 [08]	Classic	86, 108
Bois de Boulogne Park	(La Muette)	BB -		Romantic	151, 171
La Bulle Kenzo Spa	1 rue du Pont Neuf (Châtelet) labullekenzo.com	1st €€€€	73.04.20.04	Hot & Cool	52, 79
Canauxrama Boat Trip	Depart Port de l'Arsenal, opp. 50 bd. de la Bastille (Bastille) canauxrama.com	12th € -	42.39.15.00	Bobo	120, 143
Les Catacombes Sight	1 pl. Denfert Rochereau (Denfert-Rochereau) 	14th € -	43.22.47.63	Classic	108

PARIS BLACK BOOK

NAME / TYPE	ADDRESS (METRO) / WEBSITE	AREA / PRICE	PHONE (01)	EXPERIENCE / 99 BEST	PAGE / PAGE
Cathédrale Notre Dame de Paris Monument	Pl. du Parvis Notre-Dame (Cité) cathedraledeparis.com	4th -	42.34.56.10	Classic	88, 108
Centre Pompidou Art Museum	Pl. Georges Pompidou (Rambuteau) centrepompidou.fr	4th € -	44.78.12.33	Hot & Cool Contemporary Art	52, 79 25
Cimetière de Père Lachaise Cemetery	Bd. de Ménilmontant (Père-Lachaise)	20th	55.25.82.10	Classic	88, 108
Cinémathèque Française Museum/Movie Theater	51 rue de Bercy (Bercy) cinemathequefrancaise.com	12th € -	71.19.33.33	Bobo	143
Colette Store	213 rue St-Honoré (Tuileries) colette.fr	1st -	55.35.33.90	Hot & Cool Concept Stores	53, 79 24
La Collection 1900 Museum	Maxim's, 3 rue Royale (Concorde) maxims-musee.artnouveau.com	8th € -	42.65.30.47	Romantic	152, 172
La Conciergerie Monument	2-4 bd. du Palais (Cité) monum.fr/m_conciergerie	1st € -	53.40.60.93	Classic	88, 109
Covered passages Walk	various parisinconnu.com/passages	VA -		Romantic	149, 172
Drugstore Publicis Store	133 av. des Champs-Elysées (Charles de Gaulle-Etoile) publicisdrugstore.com	8th -	44.43.79.00	Hot & Cool	79
L'Eclaireur Store	131 galerie de Valois (Palais Royal- Musée du Louvre) leclaireur.com	1st -	40.20.42.52	Romantic	172
Edible Paris Guided Tour	various edible-paris.com	VA €€€€		Classic	109
Eiffel Tower Monument	Champ de Mars (Bir-Hakeim) tour-eiffel.fr	7th €	44.11.23.23	Classic	86, 109
L'Espace Bien-Etre at the Meurice Spa	228 rue de Rivoli (Concorde) meuricehotel.com	1st €€€€	44.58.10.77	Romantic Spas	173 46
Fauchon Store	26-30 pl. de la Madeleine (Madeleine) fauchon.com	8th -	47.42.60.11	Romantic	173
Fondation Cartier Photography Gallery	261 bd. Raspail (Raspail) fondation.cartier.fr	14th € -	42.18.56.72	Hot & Cool	52, 80
Fondation Henri Cartier-Bresson Photo Gallery	2 impasse Lebouis (Gaîté) henricartierbresson.org	14th € -	56.80.27.00	Classic	110
Fondation Pierre Bergé-YSL Fashion Museum	1 rue Léonce-Reynaud (Alma-Marceau) ysl-hautecouture.com	16th € -	44.31.64.00	Hot & Cool Chic Museums	54, 80 21
Friday Night Fever Activity	Starts pl. Raoul Dautry (Montparnasse-Bienvenüe) pari-roller.com	14th -	43.36.89.81	Bobo	144
Galerie Simone Store	124 rue Vieille-du-Temple (St-Sébastien-Froissart)	3rd	42.74.21.28	Bobo	144
Galeries Lafayette Store	40 bd. Haussmann (Chaussée d'Antin-Lafayette) galerieslafayette.com	9th	42.82.34.56	Classic	110
Le Grand Palais Art Museum	3 av. du Général Eisenhower (Clemenceau) rmn.fr/galeriesnationalesdugrandpalais	8th € -	44.13.17.30	Classic	110
Ile de la Cité Island	(Cité)	1st/4th -		Classic	110
Ile St-Louis Island	Island on Seine (Pont Marie)	4th -		Romantic	173

247

Attractions (cont.)

NAME / TYPE	ADDRESS (METRO) / WEBSITE	AREA / PRICE	PHONE (01)	EXPERIENCE / 99 BEST	PAGE / PAGE
India & Spa / Spa	76 rue Charlot (Filles du Calvaire)	3rd / €€€€	42.77.82.10	Bobo	119, 144
Les Invalides / Monument/Museum	Esplanade des Invalides (Invalides) / invalides.org	7th / € -	44.42.38.77	Classic	86, 111
Jardin des Tuileries / Park	Rue de Rivoli (Tuileries)	1st / -		Hot & Cool / Statuary	54, 80 / 47
Jardins du Luxembourg / Park	Rue de Vaugirard, pl. Edmond Rostand (Odéon)	6th / -		Romantic / Parks	149, 173 / 42
Jeu de Paume / Photography Gallery	1 pl. de la Concorde (Concorde) / jeudepaume.org	8th / € -	47.03.12.50	Hot & Cool	80
Louise Weiss galleries / Art Galleries	Rue Louise Weiss (Chevaleret) / louise13.fr	13th / -	48.51.33.21	Bobo	144
La Maison Rouge / Art Gallery	10 bd. de la Bastille (Bastille) / lamaisonrouge.org	12th / € -	40.01.08.81	Bobo / Contemporary Art	118, 144 / 25
Maison Européenne de la Photographie Art Gallery	5-7 rue de Fourcy (St-Paul) / mep-fr.org	4th / € -	44.78.75.00	Hot & Cool	51, 81
Marais private galleries / Art Galleries	various (Hôtel de Ville/St-Paul)	3rd / -		Hot & Cool	81
Marché des Enfants-Rouges / Food Market	39 rue de Bretagne (Temple)	3rd / -		Bobo / Markets	120, 145 / 37
Marché Mouffetard / Food Market	Rue Mouffetard (Censier-Daubenton)	5th / -		Classic / Markets	111 / 37
Marché aux Puces de St-Ouen Flea Market	Rue des Rosiers (Porte de Clignancourt) / les-puces.com	SO / -		Bobo / Markets	119, 145 / 37
Maria Luisa / Store	2 rue Cambon (Concorde)	1st / -	47.03.48.08	Hot & Cool	81
Musée d'Art Moderne de la Ville de Paris Art Museum	11 av. du Président-Wilson (Iéna) / mam.paris.fr	16th / € -	53.67.40.00	Hot & Cool	81
Musée des Arts Asiatiques-Guimet Art Museum	6 pl. d'Iéna (Iéna) / museeguimet.fr	16th / € -	56.52.53.00	Hot & Cool	54, 82
Musée Baccarat / Design Museum	11 pl. des Etats-Unis (Boissière) / baccarat.fr	16th / € -	40.22.11.00	Hot & Cool / Chic Museums	54, 82 / 21
Musée Carnavalet / Museum	23 rue de Sévigné (St-Paul) / carnavalet.paris.fr	3rd / -	44.59.58.58	Classic	111
Musée de l'Erotisme / Museum	72 bd. de Clichy (Blanche)	18th / € -	42.58.28.73	Bobo	119, 145
Musée de la Contrefaçon / Museum	16 rue de la Faisanderie (Porte Dauphine)	16th / € -	56.26.14.00	Hot & Cool	82
Musée de la Mode et du Textile Fashion	107 rue de Rivoli (Palais Royal-Musée du Louvre) ucad.fr	1st / € -	44.55.57.50	Hot & Cool / Chic Museums	54, 82 / 21
Musée du Fumeur / Museum	7 rue Pache (Voltaire) / museedufumeur.net	11th / € -	46.59.05.51	Bobo	118, 145
Musée Jacquemart-André / Museum	158 bd. Haussmann (St-Philippe-du-Roule) / musee-jacquemart-andre.com	8th / € -	45.62.11.59	Romantic	152, 173
Musée du Louvre / Art Museum	Rue de Rivoli (Palais Royal-Musée du Louvre) / louvre.fr	1st / € -	40.20.50.50	Classic / Statuary	85, 112 / 47

PARIS BLACK BOOK

NAME TYPE	ADDRESS (METRO) WEBSITE	AREA PRICE	PHONE (01)	EXPERIENCE 99 BEST	PAGE PAGE
Musée du Luxembourg Art Museum	19 rue de Vaugirard (Odéon) museeduluxembourg.fr	6th € -	42.34.25.95	Romantic	149, 174
Musée Marmottan Art Museum	2 rue Louis-Boilly (La Muette) marmottan.com	16th € -	44.96.50.33	Romantic	151, 174
Musée de Montmartre Museum	12 rue Cortot (Abbesses) museedemontmartre.com	18th € -	46.06.61.11	Classic	88, 112
Musée Nationale du Moyen Age-Thermes Museum	6 place Paul-Painlevé (Cluny-La Sorbonne) musee-moyenage.fr	5th € -	53.73.78.00	Classic	86, 112
Musée d'Orsay Art Museum	1 rue de la Légion d'Honneur (RER Musée d'Orsay/M°Solférino) musee-orsay.fr	7th € -	40.49.49.78	Classic	87, 112
Musée Picasso Art Museum	Hôtel Salé, 5 rue de Thorigny (St-Sébastien- Froissart) musee-picasso.fr	3rd € -	42.71.25.21	Hot & Cool	51, 82
Musée Rodin Art Museum	77 rue de Varenne (Varenne) musee-rodin.fr	7th € -	44.18.61.10	Romantic Statuary	150, 174 47
Musée de la Vie Romantique Museum	16 rue Chaptal (Blanche) vieromantique.paris.fr	9th -	55.31.95.67	Romantic	150, 175
O Château Wine Tasting	100 rue de la Folie Méricourt (Oberkampf) o-chateau.com	11th €€€€	44.73.97.80	Romantic	152, 175
Palais de Tokyo Art Gallery	13 av. du Président Wilson (Alma-Marceau) palaisdetokyo.com	16th € -	47.23.54.01	Bobo Contemporary Art	120, 146 25
Palais Royal Monument	Pl. du Palais-Royal (Palais Royal-Musée du Louvre)	1st -		Romantic	149, 175
Le Panthéon Monument	Pl. du Panthéon (Cardinal Lemoine)	5th € -	44.32.18.00	Classic	87, 113
Parc André Citroën Park	Rue St-Charles (Balard)	15th -	44.26.20.00	Romantic Parks	151, 175 42
Parc des Buttes Chaumont Park	Rue Botzaris (Botzaris)	19th -		Bobo Parks	120, 146 42
Paris Muse Guided Tour	various parismuse.com	VA €€€€	73.77.33.52 [06]	Classic Guided Tours	85, 113 30
Paris Walks Guided Tour	various paris-walks.com	VA € -	48.09.21.40	Classic Guided Tours	113 30
Pavillon de l'Arsenal Museum	21 bd. Morland (Sully-Morland) pavillon-arsenal.com	4th -	42.76.33.97	Bobo	118, 146
Printemps Store	64 bd. Haussmann (Havre-Caumartin) printemps.com	9th -	42.82.57.87	Classic	113
Promenade Plantée Planted Walkway	Follows av. Daumesnil (Bastille) viaduc-des-arts.com	12th -		Bobo	118, 147
La Ste-Chapelle Monument	4 bd. du Palais (Cité)	1st € -	53.40.60.80	Classic	88, 114
Shakespeare & Co. Store	37 rue de la Bûcherie (Maubert-Mutualité) -	5th	43.25.40.93	Classic	114
Le Spa at the Four Seasons George V Spa	31 av. George V (Alma-Marceau) fourseasons.com	8th €€€€	49.52.72.00	Classic Spas	88, 114 46
Spa Nuxe 32 Montorgueil Spa	32 rue Montorgueil (Les Halles) nuxe.com	1st €€€€	55.80.71.40	Hot & Cool Spas	53, 83 46

249

Attractions (cont.)

NAME TYPE	ADDRESS (METRO) WEBSITE	AREA PRICE	PHONE (01)	EXPERIENCE 99 BEST	PAGE PAGE
Spree Store	16 rue de la Vieuville (Abbesses)	18th -	42.23.41.40	Bobo Concept Stores	147 24
Surface to Air Store	46 rue de l'Arbre Sec (Pont Neuf) surface2air.com	1st -	49.27.04.54	Bobo Concept Stores	147 24
Les Thermes Spa	13 av. Hoche (Charles de Gaulle-Etoile) royalmonceau.com	8th €€€€	42.99.88.00	Classic	115
La Villette Park/Museum/Concert Venue	211 av. Jean-Jaurés (Porte de Pantin) villette.com	19th -	40.03.75.75	Bobo	147

Notes

Notes

Paris Unique Shopping Index

NAME	PHONE	PRODUCTS	PAGE
A la Mère de Famille	01.47.70.83.69	Traditional food shop	90
A-Poc	01.44.54.07.05	Cutting-edge women's apparel	56
AB33	01 42 71 02 82	Women's apparel	122
Abbey Bookshop	01.46.33.16.24	English-language books	90
Anna Joliet	01.49.27.98.60	Music boxes	154
Antoine et Lili	01.40.37.41.55	Funky apparel and accessories	122, 143
Artazart	01.40.40.24.00	Design books	122
Barbara Bui	01.44.59.94.06	Women's apparel	56
Base One	01.53.28.04.52	Concept shop	122
Boucheron	01.42.61.58.16	Jewelry	154
Chanel Joaillerie	01.55.35.50.05	Jewelry	154
Code 3	01.32.71.41.90	Home furnishings, lighting, and art	122
Coin Canal	01.42.38.00.30	Retro home furnishings, lighting, art	122
Colette	01.55.35.33.90	Concept shop	24, 56, 79
Détaille	01.48.78.68.50	Perfumes	90
Didier Ludot	01.42.96.06.56	Vintage haute-couture	154
Drugstore Publicis	01.44.43.79.00	Food, wine, cosmetics, newspapers	79
L'Eclaireur	01.40.20.42.52	Home accessories	154, 172
Emilio Robba	01.42.61.71.43	Artificial flowers	154
Fauchon	01.47.42.60.11	Gourmet food	154, 173
Fifi Chachnil	01.42.61.21.83	Lingerie	56
Les Filles à l'Anis	01.42.64.40.54	Funky women's apparel	122
Galerie Simone	01.42.74.21.28	Cutting-edge women's apparel	122, 144
Galeries Lafayette	01.42.82.34.56	Department store	90, 110
Ginger Lyly	01.42.06.07.73	Funky women's apparel and accessories	122
Iris	01.42.22.89.81	Women's apparel	56
Jacenko	01.42.71.80.38	Men's apparel	122
Lili Perpink	01.42.52.37.24	Cutting-edge women's apparel	122
La Maison des Trois Thés	01.43.36.93.84	Tea Shop	90
Maria Luisa	01.47.03.48.08	Cutting-edge women's apparel	56, 81
Martin Grant	01.42.71.39.49	Women's apparel	56
Oscar Carvallo	01.40.20.12.13	Cutting-edge women's apparel	56
Papeterie Laffitte	01.47.70.38.83	Stationery and gifts	90
Patricia Louisor	01.42.62.10.42	Women's apparel	122

PARIS UNIQUE SHOPPING INDEX

NAME	PHONE	PRODUCTS	PAGE
Pierre Marcolini	01.44.07.39.07	Chocolates	56
Pressing Shop	01.40.29.16.96	Men's apparel	56
Printemps	01.42.82.57.87	Department store	90, 113
Quidam de Revel	06.15.95.74.83	Vintage apparel	122
Résonances	01.44.51.63.70	Home accessories	154
Salons du Palais-Royal	01.49.27.09.09	Perfumes	154
San Francisco Book Co.	01.43.25.40.93	English-language books	90
Shakespeare & Co.	01.43.25.40.93	English-language books	90, 114
Spree	01.42.23.41.40	Concept shop	24, 122, 147
Surface to Air	01.49.27.04.54	Concept shop	24, 147
Vanessa Bruno	01.43.54.41.04	Sequined bags and apparel	56
Vannina Vesperini	01.42.84.37.62	Lingerie	56
Village Voice	01.46.33.36.47	English-language books	90
Viveka Bergström	01.40.03.04.92	Jewelry	122

Notes

PARIS ACTION CENTRAL MAP

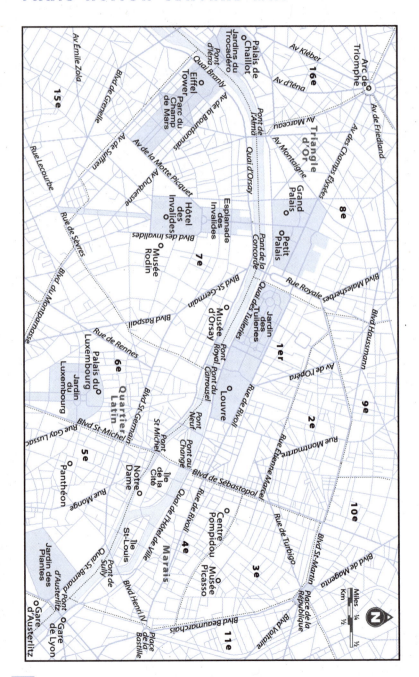

PARIS NEIGHBORHOODS MAP

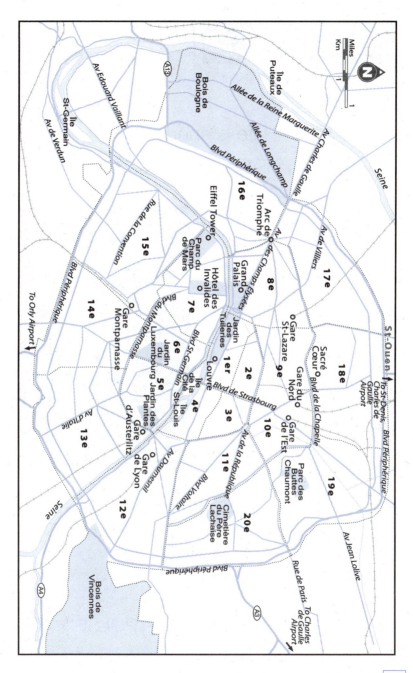

NIGHT+DAY
The *Cool Cities* Series

Life is short...
But the list of Cool Cities isn't.

2006 Night + Day Guides

Amsterdam
Athens
Chicago
D. C.
Las Vegas
Los Angeles
London
Miami
New York
Paris
San Francisco
Sydney

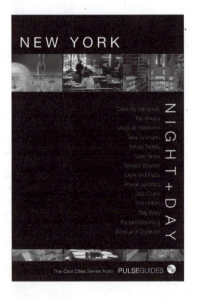

Buy books, contact us, get info, have fun, and more ... at pulseguides.com

PULSEGUIDES